RADICAL VISIONS

RADICAL VISIONS
POETRY BY VIETNAM VETERANS
VINCE GOTERA :: :: :: :: :: ::

THE UNIVERSITY OF GEORGIA PRESS   ATHENS AND LONDON

© 1994 by the University of Georgia Press
Athens, Georgia 30602
All rights reserved

Designed by Sandra Strother Hudson
Set in 10 on 13 Times Roman by Tseng Information Systems, Inc.
Printed and bound by Maple-Vail
The paper in this book meets the guidelines
for permanence and durability of the Committee on
Production Guidelines for Book Longevity
of the Council on Library Resources.

Printed in the United States of America
98 97 96 95 94 C 5 4 3 2 1

Library of Congress Cataloging in Publication Data

Gotera, Vicente F.
Radical visions : poetry by Vietnam Veterans / Vince Gotera.
        p.   cm.
Includes bibliographical references and index.
ISBN 0-8203-1510-9 (alk. paper)
1. American poetry—20th century—History and criticism.
2. Vietnamese Conflict, 1961–1975—Literature and the conflict.
3. Veterans' writings, American—History and criticism.
4. War poetry, American—History and criticism.
5. Radicalism in literature.   I. Title.
PS310.V54G67   1994   92-27595
        811'.5409358—dc20   CIP

British Library Cataloging in Publication Data available

In memory of my father

MARTIN A. GOTERA
1921–1989

a Soldier Poet
and
a Veteran Activist
in his own right

CONTENTS

List of Abbreviations and Terminology   *ix*

Preface   *xi*

Acknowledgments   *xv*

Introduction   *3*

PART ONE. THE 'NAM

One. The Wild West Revisited   *33*

Two. Machine in the Jungle   *60*

Three. A New Babel   *93*

Four. New Generation, No Generation   *130*

PART TWO. THE WORLD

Five. When Adam Comes Marching Home—
What About Eve?   *195*

Six. Warriors Against War   *246*

Seven. Bruce Weigl: "Useful to the Wind"   *283*

Eight. Yusef Komunyakaa: "Depending on the Light"   *302*

Conclusion. Radical Visions Extended   *317*

Notes   *321*

Works Cited   *337*

Index   *355*

ABBREVIATIONS
AND TERMINOLOGY

I am using the following abbreviated titles for poetry anthologies:

Winning   Larry Rottmann, Jan Barry, and Basil T. Paquet, eds. *Winning Hearts and Minds: War Poems by Vietnam Veterans*

Demilitarized   Jan Barry and W. D. Ehrhart, eds. *Demilitarized Zones: Veterans After Vietnam*

Peace   Jan Barry, ed. *Peace Is Our Profession: Poems and Passages of War Protest*

Darkness   W. D. Ehrhart, ed. *Carrying the Darkness: American Indochina—The Poetry of the Vietnam War*

Mercy   W. D. Ehrhart, ed. *Unaccustomed Mercy: Soldier-Poets of the Vietnam War*

Visions   Lynda Van Devanter and Joan A. Furey, eds. *Visions of War, Dreams of Peace: Writings of Women in the Vietnam War*

I use the words *Vietnam* and *Vietnamese* instead of *Viet Nam* and *Viet* (the terms preferred in Vietnam) in order to coincide with American usage during the war and its aftermath; I am also using *Vietcong,* again to reflect American usage, instead of *National Liberation Front* (even though the term *Vietcong* was a pejorative label imposed by the Diêm government). One departure I have made from typical American usage, however, is to avoid the term *Vietnam* as synecdoche, as shorthand, for *the Vietnam war.*

PREFACE

My phrase *radical visions* is a play on three ideas: (1) a new and unprecedented way of seeing, (2) a basic "root" perspective, derived from the Latin noun *radix,* and (3) the viewpoint of countercultural politicization. This linguistic play is also based on the metaphor of *poetry as vision* and of myth as a kind of lens, a way of seeing; "the very principle of myth," as Roland Barthes suggests, is that "it transforms history into nature" (129), or as Northrop Frye argues, "the function of the epic, in its origin, seems to be primarily to teach the nation, or whatever we call the social unit which the poet is addressing, its own traditions [which] are chiefly concerned with the national religion and the national history" (*Symmetry* 316). I submit that Frye's word "epic" here is equivalent with "poem" (even in the contemporary sense of the short lyric) and also, by extension, with mythic structures as a whole.

My general thesis is that poetry by Vietnam veterans—as a part of all innovative writing about the Vietnam war and its aftermath—shows how the uniqueness of that war affected our basic ways of seeing and interpreting the world through the lens of myth and resulted in reconfiguration of myth. Perhaps "uniqueness" may not be quite the proper word, because such diction implies that the Vietnam war was somehow an aberration; instead, it was *different* from other American wars in (1) the extremeness of the cultural and geographical differences of Vietnam from America; (2) the overwhelming hegemony of "technowar"; (3) the unprecedented range of tautological official language; (4) the extraordinary neglect that the Vietnam veteran faced on returning to America; and (5) the widespread resistance to the war by American soldiers and veterans. These differences are rooted deep within the national psyche and can be related to traditional American myths; we can discern this correlation by charting the failure of these myths to make sense of the Vietnam war and what followed—a failure visible in poetry written by Vietnam veterans. The *radical vision* is in/through the eye of the Vietnam-veteran poet, and others can learn to see in a similar way. To rephrase Frye, this body of poetry can teach the nation (and each individual reader) a great deal about our "national religion and national history," especially when we consider how coincident this "religion" is with the body politic.

Literary critics such as John Felstiner and Jeffrey Walsh have argued that "lyric poetry of a traditional kind has proved inappropriate to communicate the character of the Vietnam war, its remoteness, its jargonised recapitulations, its seeming imperviousness to aesthetics" (Walsh 203–4). Yet there has been an unprecedented outpouring of poetry from the Vietnam war: from civilian war resisters as well as from veterans. In the context of the war, poetry became a cogent political instrument to awaken the American people to horrors occurring in the name of American credibility and solipsism. After American troops vacated Vietnam and after the war itself ended in 1975, the civilian antiwar protest poem faded nearly from view, but the poetry of Vietnam veterans has continued unabated. As poet/critic Robert Peters has noted, "Vietnam unleashed poetic energies as no war had before for American poets. Even the Civil War, which smeared such nightmarish cicatrices over American psyches, didn't come close" (342). My basic question is: why has there been such a preponderance of poetry, if in fact literary critics are correct in pointing out that "lyric poetry" is unable to convey "the character of the Vietnam war"? (It is important here to add as well that the usual literary-critical standards may not apply to many poems by Vietnam veterans; one must put away literary snobbishness because these poets, speaking as they so often do from beyond the pale of peacetime America, frequently bypass questions of literariness.)

Radical Visions investigates Vietnam-veteran poetry to determine what it tells us about the Vietnam war and about America. Lorrie Smith has suggested that this poetry "dismantles the popular myth that we have regained our national innocence [by confessing] that U.S. involvement in Vietnam was a mistake" ("Sense-Making" 14). Much of this poetry is concerned with myth and its incompetence in helping Americans comprehend the Vietnam-war experience. In *Radical Visions,* I focus on the myths of the "Wild West" (as a violent extension of the macho myth of the "virgin land"); the "machine in the garden"; the "city on the hill" (represented as a new Babel); "regeneration through violence"; the "American Adam"; and a newly reconfigured oxymoronic myth—"the warrior against war." What is revealed is the inability of the Wild West mentality to apprehend Vietnam as land and culture; the inappropriateness of "technowar" in Vietnam; the tautological distortions of government language; the guilt rather than regeneration resulting from military violence; the uselessness of Adamic ahistorical innocence in veterans' readjustment to America, particularly for female veterans; and the resulting radicalization of many of those veterans, which ensues in a restructuring of the most basic of myths—Joseph Campbell's monomythic "hero of a thousand faces"—into the beginnings of a developing mythology: "the new soldier" or "the warrior against war." (These are closely related to the five characteristics I outlined above to differentiate the Vietnam war from other American wars.)

In addition, poetry by Vietnam veterans uncovers a struggle between traditional lyric poetry and a Vietnam-war "brand" of antipoetry. As John Clark Pratt writes in his preface to the anthology *Unaccustomed Mercy,* "the poems in this collection are essentially non-'literary'; that is, they require little explication; they come from no recognizable tradition; they usually invent their own forms; and their only context is that of the rice paddy, the landing zone, or the jungle" (viii). Although Pratt's statement is arguable, the particular circumstances surrounding Vietnam-veteran poetry result in three basic modes: antipoetic, aesthetic, and cathartic. The differences between and among these modes of prosody problematize the representation of Vietnam and the Vietnam war in poetry by veterans, and I suggest that the poems of Bruce Weigl and Yusef Komunyakaa solve and transcend these problematics by balancing personal catharsis and poetic aesthetics without compromising the realities of the Vietnam war.

The Gulf war in 1991 revived "the popular myth that we have regained our national innocence," to use Lorrie Smith's phrase, *without* a confession "that U.S. involvement in Vietnam [or in Panama or in Kuwait] was a mistake." At the 1991 annual meeting of the Popular Culture Association, a discussion ensued in the final panel sponsored by the Vietnam Area: scholars of various disciplines—history, literary studies, American studies, popular culture—speculated on how the Gulf war affected the future of Vietnam-war studies. Although the discussion was vigorously argumentative, there was consensus on certain points: (1) that important cultural lessons offered by the Vietnam war had not yet been learned; (2) that the federal government, by using the rhetoric of WWII in the Gulf war, attempted to *erase* the Vietnam war (note George Bush's notorious claim to have "exorcised the specter of the Vietnam syndrome"); and (3) that open-eyed study of the Vietnam war must proceed with enhanced vigor to balance the heady resurgence of militarism.

Study of Vietnam-war poetry in particular is made even more urgent by the example of the Gulf war. Journalism in that war—as we saw countless times on CNN and other television networks—was co-opted by government to the extent that governance was virtually exercised *through* the media. The only discourse that can effectively counter such a hegemonic situation is literature; poetry in particular is an energetic way for people "to get the news," William Carlos Williams notwithstanding. Vietnam-war poetry clearly demonstrates this view: not only have more poets than ever been driven personally to confront war, but their body of poetry serves on a national level as both remedy and jeremiad. Despite the euphoric whirlwind of militarism in the Gulf war (or perhaps because of that euphoria), it is imperative that Americans, as a nation, note and heed the warnings contained in poetry of the Vietnam war, particularly through the witness of Vietnam veterans.

Because of this imperative, I have envisioned an audience wider than the American literary critical community; this study strives to connect with the general public as well. My approach therefore has been to meld sociohistorical commentary with close readings of poems—particularly from my personal perspective as a practicing poet familiar with process and exigency in the writing of poetry. With the exception of my treatment of Language Poetry in chapter 3, I have also avoided, as much as may be possible nowadays, the language of poststructuralist and postmodern critical discourse in my desire to include nonacademic readers. I am aware, nevertheless, that the most interested readers of this book will be poets and literary critics; to provide a theoretical base, therefore, I have applied the methodology of myth criticism. Although myth criticism has not lately been in the mainstream of literary theory, I propose that it is a widely accessible method (even if for many people mythic thinking is an untutored, even subconscious, process), a knowledge which we inevitably absorb as Americans through the media, through the myths reinscribed by popular culture into the cultural ideologies that unavoidably encode our identities, condition our selves.

ACKNOWLEDGMENTS

For me, this acknowledgments page is at the same time the most joyful as well as the most important element of this book, for without the gracious help of the following people and institutions, this book would still be in its infancy, perhaps might never have emerged into the light. My gratitude to Mary Ann Blue Gotera is inexpressible—for love, for faith, for support—and for all the dinners she prepared and sinkloads of dishes she washed when it was my turn, so that I could write. My thanks as well to Marty, Amanda, and Amelia for their loving patience while this book claimed their father's attention and energies for such a long time.

For their advice on this project and for their friendship, I am grateful to Jim Justus, Yusef Komunyakaa, John McCluskey, and Roger Mitchell—all at Indiana University where this project first took shape as my dissertation. My thanks to poets Bill Ehrhart and Basil Paquet for their assistance, to David Willson at Green River Community College for his help in procuring obscure texts, and especially to Lorrie Smith at St. Michael's College: her comments on various portions of this book were indeed helpful in helping me shape and refine my subject. A special debt of gratitude is due to Nancy Grayson Holmes and to Kelly Caudle at the University of Georgia Press for their untiring support of this project—no matter how many times the manuscript was delayed by the exigencies of university teaching and family life. The final revision of the book was enabled by released time granted to me for faculty development. My thanks to Humboldt State University for this support.

I also am grateful to the editors of the following publications in which portions of this work have appeared: *Search and Clear: Critical Responses to Selected Literature and Films of the Vietnam War*, edited by William J. Searle; *America Rediscovered: Critical Essays on Literature and Film of the Vietnam War*, edited by Owen J. Gilman, Jr., and Lorrie Smith; and the journals *Callaloo*, *Viet Nam Generation*, and the *Journal of American Culture*.

Grateful acknowledgment is made to the following authors and publishers for permission to quote from poems held in copyright:

Adams, Lily Lee. "Being a Vet Is Like Losing a Baby" from *Visions of War, Dreams of Peace: Writings of Women in the Vietnam War,* edited by Lynda Van Devanter and Joan A. Furey. Warner Books, 1991. Copyright 1990 by Lily Lee Adams. Reprinted by permission of the author.

Barry, Jan. "Floating Petals" from *Winning Hearts and Minds: War Poems by Vietnam Veterans,* edited by Larry Rottmann, Jan Barry, and Basil T. Paquet. Copyright 1972 by 1st Casualty Press. Reprinted by permission of the author.

Barth, R. L. "Nightpiece" from *Forced-Marching to the Styx: Vietnam War Poems* by R. L. Barth. Perivale Press, 1983. Copyright 1983 by R. L. Barth. Reprinted by permission of the author. "Fieldcraft," "Forest of the Suicides," "Letter to the Dead," "Nightpiece," "Office of the Dead," "Reading the *Iliad,*" and "Two for Any Memorial Day" from *A Soldier's Time: Vietnam War Poems.* John Daniel, 1987. Copyright 1987 by R. L. Barth. Reprinted by permission of the author.

Berry, D. C. "An airplane jets," "The dark mountains rise," "Lightning reaching out with electric," "A poem ought to be a salt lick," "The sun goes," and "The way popcorn pops is" from *saigon cemetery* by D. C. Berry. Copyright 1972 by the University of Georgia Press. Reprinted by permission of the author.

Brown, D. F. "Bluto Addresses the Real," "Illumination," and "When I Am 19 I Was a Medic" from *Returning Fire* by D. F. Brown. Copyright 1984 by Associated Students of San Francisco State University. Reprinted by permission of the author.

Coleman, Horace. "OK Corral East / Brothers in the Nam" from *Unaccustomed Mercy,* edited by W. D. Ehrhart. Texas Tech University Press, 1989. Originally published in *Between a Rock and a Hard Place.* BkMk Press, 1977. Copyright 1977 by Horace Coleman. Reprinted by permission of the author. "I Drive the Valiant" from *Peace Is Our Profession: Poems and Passages of War Protest,* edited by Jan Barry. East River Anthology, 1981. Copyright 1981 by Horace Coleman. Reprinted by permission of the author.

Ehrhart, W. D. "Coming Home," "Invasion of Grenada," "Letter," "The Next Step," and "Sniper's Mark" from *To Those Who Have Gone Home Tired: New and Selected Poems* by W. D. Ehrhart. Thunder's Mouth Press, 1984. Copyright 1984 by W. D. Ehrhart. Reprinted by permission of the author.

Griffiths, Norma J. "Keep Mum" from *Visions of War, Dreams of Peace: Writings of Women in the Vietnam War,* edited by Lynda Van Devanter and Joan A. Furey. Warner Books, 1991. Copyright 1991 by Norma J. Griffiths. Reprinted by permission of the author.

Huddle, David. "Cousin," "Nerves," "Them," "Vermont," "Work," and "Words" from *Stopping by Home* by David Huddle. Peregrine Smith Books, 1988. Copyright 1988 by David Huddle. Reprinted by permission of Gibbs Smith, Publisher.

Jarrell, Randall. "The Death of the Ball Turret Gunner" from the *Complete Poems* by Randall Jarrell. Copyright 1945 and 1972 by Mrs. Randall Jarrell. Reprinted by permission of Farrar, Straus and Giroux, Inc. and Faber and Faber Ltd.

Komunyakaa, Yusef. "Death Threat" from *Lost in the Bonewheel Factory* by Yusef Komunyakaa. Lynx House Press, 1979. Copyright 1978 by Yusef Komunyakaa. Reprinted by permission of the author. "Facing It," "2527th Birthday of the Buddha," and "You and I Are Disappearing" from *Dien Cai Dau* by Yusef Komunyakaa. Wesleyan University Press, 1988. Copyright 1988 by Yusef Komunyakaa. Reprinted by permission of the author.

McCarthy, Gerald. "Ambuscade" and "I'll Bring You a Frozen Chocolate Pie" from *War Story: Vietnam War Poems* by Gerald McCarthy. Crossing Press, 1977. Copyright 1977 by Gerald McCarthy. Reprinted by permission of the author.

McDonald, Walter. "Veteran" from *Burning the Fence* by Walter McDonald. Copyright 1981 by Texas Tech University Press. Reprinted by permission of the publisher.

Miller, Stephen P. "Catch a Falling Star" from *An Act of God* by Stephen P. Miller. Miller Press, 1982; Northcoast View Press, 1987. Copyright 1982, 1987 by Stephen P. Miller. Reprinted by permission of the author.

Oldham, Perry. "Evening Pastimes" from *Vinh Long* by Perry Oldham. Copyright 1976 by Northwoods Press. Reprinted by permission of the author.

Paquet, Basil T. "Basket Case," "Christmas '67," "Easter '68," "Graves Registration," "Morning—A Death," "Night Dust-Off," and "They Do Not Go

Gentle" from *Winning Hearts and Minds: War Poems by Vietnam Veterans,* edited by Larry Rottmann, Jan Barry, and Basil T. Paquet. Copyright 1972 by 1st Casualty Press. Reprinted by permission of the author.

Quintana, Leroy V. "Jump School—Detail" from *Interrogations* by Leroy V. Quintana. Viet Nam Generation and Burning Cities Press, 1992. Copyright 1990 by Leroy V. Quintana. Reprinted by permission of the author.

Rawlings, Doug. "Jen," "Mainline Quatrains," and "A Soldier's Lament" from *Demilitarized Zones: Veterans After Vietnam,* edited by Jan Barry and W. D. Ehrhart. Copyright 1976 by East River Anthology. Reprinted by permission of the author.

Receveur, Don. "Cobra Pilot," "Doper's Dream," and "night fear" from *Winning Hearts and Minds: War Poems by Vietnam Veterans,* edited by Larry Rottmann, Jan Barry, and Basil T. Paquet. Copyright 1972 by 1st Casualty Press. Reprinted by permission of the author.

Richman, Elliot. "Jungle Ambush in Monument Valley" from *A Bucket of Nails: Poems from the Second Indochina War* by Elliot Richman. Samisdat, 1990. Copyright 1990 by Elliot Richman. Reprinted by permission of the author.

Rottmann, Larry. "Man of God," "S. O. P.," and "The Weather of Vietnam" from *Winning Hearts and Minds: War Poems by Vietnam Veterans,* edited by Larry Rottmann, Jan Barry, and Basil T. Paquet. Copyright 1972 by 1st Casualty Press. Reprinted by permission of the author.

Shields, Bill. "A Daughter" and "Saving Grace" from *Nam: Selected Poems* by Bill Shields. P. O. Press, 1989. Copyright 1989 by Bill Shields. Reprinted by permission of the author.

Weigl, Bruce. "Anna Grasa" from *A Romance* by Bruce Weigl. University of Pittsburgh Press, 1979. Copyright 1979 by Bruce Weigl. Reprinted by permission of the author. "Amnesia" from *The Monkey Wars* by Bruce Weigl. University of Georgia Press, 1985. Copyright 1985 by Bruce Weigl. Reprinted by permission of the author. "Elegy," "The Kiss," and "LZ Nowhere" from *Song of Napalm* by Bruce Weigl. Atlantic Monthly Press, 1988. Copyright 1988 by Bruce Weigl. Reprinted by permission of the author.

RADICAL VISIONS

INTRODUCTION

There have been poetic respondents to war—raconteurs, jeremiahs, mytho-poetic glorifiers—at least since the age of Homer in European-based civiliza-tion, and certainly in other times and cultures. The role of the soldier-poet is therefore a familiar one: not merely a witness to battle, but also an initiate, and hence a voice of authority. Because war has become such a ubiquitous shaper of experience in the twentieth century, literature has come to deal with it more and more. The "apprehension of war constitutes a distinctive and central ele-ment in the modern literary American consciousness," writes Jeffrey Walsh. "Military terrain and situations have become familiar, often assuming mythic connotations" (1). Literature—particularly poetry—offers a unique view of war. Maurice Bowra, referring to the flood of poems from WWI, points out that war poetry

> provides no facts which we cannot learn better from elsewhere; it does not
> begin to compete . . . with history or the realistic novel. But it does what
> nothing else can do. It not only gives a coherent form to moods which
> at the time were almost indiscernible in the general welter of emotions,
> but . . . provides a criticism of them . . . through the character of its
> approach and [its] power or insight. (3)

Thus, a society that fails to heed its war poets will wallow in the redundant quagmire of history.[1] Vietnam-veteran poets quite soberly envision themselves in precisely this jeremiad role; their model is the best-known WWI poet, Wilfred Owen, who wrote, "All a poet can do to-day is warn" (40–41), shortly before his death by machine gun. For the most part, however, Vietnam-veteran poets, while they may acknowledge Owen and his peers as *predecessors,* do not consider themselves Owen's *literary descendants.* My fourfold purpose in this introduction is to sketch in a landscape: (1) the documentary impulse that drives Vietnam-war literature, (2) the significance of myth in the context of the war, (3) an introduction to poetry in English by veterans in twentieth-century wars before the war in Vietnam, and (4) a brief explanation of the elemental modes of Vietnam-veteran poetry. This survey of antecedent war poets will provide a historical background for Vietnam-veteran poetry, but always with the caveat that a wide gap of poetic philosophy may yawn between the soldier-poets of WWI and WWII and those of Vietnam[2]—a gap that underlines why Vietnam-veteran poets write three basic types of poems: antipoetic, cathartic, and aesthetic.

The Vietnam War and Contemporary Memory: "Telling It"

In *Dispatches,* a technodelic, autotelic memoir of being a journalist in Vietnam, Michael Herr reports how infantry soldiers, who called themselves *grunts,* "would ask you with an emotion whose intensity would shock you to please *tell it* because they really did have the feeling . . . that they were going through all of this and that somehow no one back in the World knew about it" (206, emphasis mine). And this need to "tell it" to the World—the term the soldiers themselves used for America—becomes a heavy obsession. Herr continues:

> There was a Marine in Hue who had . . . been locked in that horror for nearly two weeks while I'd shuttled in and out for two or three days at a time. . . . His face was all but blank with exhaustion, but he had enough feeling left to say, "Okay, man, you go on, you go on out of here you cocksucker, but I mean it, you tell it! You tell it, man." (207)

To "tell it" is one of the dominant impulses informing Vietnam-war literature: the documentary urge, the drive to make the horrors, the senselessness of war, and the incredibility of Vietnam concrete to Americans back home. One way of "telling it" is the *memoir* or *personal narrative*—now a common staple of literature on Vietnam because of the inherent "truth-telling" implied by the stance of witness, what Philip Beidler has called the "profound experiential authority" through which these writers "in the inscription out of memory into art . . . become in the fullest sense the creators of cultural myth for new times" (*Re-Writing* 2).

The three most critically acclaimed soldier's memoirs are Tim O'Brien's *If I Die in a Combat Zone,* Ron Kovic's *Born on the Fourth of July,* and Philip Caputo's *A Rumor of War.* There exists in each of these three memoirs (as in many other personal narratives on Vietnam[3]) a common pattern of development, a concern with two settings: (1) the 'Nam (the twelve-month period *in-country,* or thirteen months for Marines) and (2) the World (sometimes subdivided into "before" and "after" service in Vietnam). Kovic, for example, jump-cuts back and forth to emphasize how paralysis differentiates his post-Vietnam days from his life before the Vietnam war. The memoirist's shuttling between these two realms of existence postulates a dilemma, the double horns of which are "the 'Nam" and "the World," an obsessive dialectic of truth and memory: how does one make sense and order out of such diametrical opposition?

The inevitable juggling and balancing of these two polarities—really two mind-sets—arises as an obsession in poetry by Vietnam veterans as well, so that in poem after poem the major mode of presentation is the juxtaposition of widely divergent phenomena and the significations they carry, often creating bitter ironies. Such irony is indicative of the poet's own disillusionment, fueled by the discrepancy between the realities of the 'Nam and the myths of the World. And the poet's crucible, it would seem, is whether each poem is able to convey what the war was like, "tell it like it was": the smells and sounds, the tint of sky, "the rotten human carrion" [4]—the surreal mix of commonplace and absurd. The documentary impulse is transformed into obsession, journalistic but also more than journalistic.

Myth as Lens: Focusing and Refracting the Real

Another commonplace of Vietnam-war literary studies is the preponderance of myth-based analyses. The classic example is John Hellmann's *American Myth and the Legacy of Vietnam,* which maps out the collision of the archetypal Frontier and the Frontier Hero (imaged by "the Green Beret as a rebirth of America's central mythic hero" [46]) with the demythologizing effect of the Vietnam war. Philip Beidler, in *American Literature and the Experience of Vietnam,* has a similar project. Beidler claims that the surreal, absurdist literary images we associate with the war "seem to move the literature of Vietnam toward some compelling new architecture of vision uniquely its own" at the same time that they paradoxically "recall that sense of grand and enduring mythical centrality often associated with so much of our classic tradition" (25). In *Walking Point,* Thomas Myers argues that "the war novel makes the leviathan of the national cultural paradigm sound and surface. . . . and it is a lasting cultural document [that] responds to the rending and reconstituting of national mythos" (10)—imaged here as a Moby-Dick continually inscribed, revised, and reinscribed. In the introduction to his collection of essays, *Fourteen Landing Zones,* Philip K. Jason observes that "the more provocative stories [of] the literature of the Vietnam war are not simply or finally stories of armed conflict in a distant land. . . . They are understandings, and sometimes underminings, of American myths" so that criticism of this literature must be "alert to the ways in which the literature confronts the myths of American innocence, American invulnerability, and American righteousness" (xiii). Apparently even the Vietnam-war experience in certain non-American literatures also revolves around myth. For example, Peter Pierce notes that, in Australian literature on the war, Vietnam is figured as " 'the funny place' . . . a site of various, though not essentially contesting Australian myths [such as] the myth of a hostile homefront, the myth of incompetent allies [and] the myth of 'the legend of Anzac upheld' " (100). The Vietnam war was of course a real war— that is, a war with all the attendant realities of genocide and destruction—but evidently it was simultaneously a *war of myth.* [5]

The Gulf war mirrors this point of view. In his *Newsweek* review of Bob Woodward's account of that war, *The Commanders,* Evan Thomas culls an interesting quotation from the book. In the days before Operation Desert Shield metastasized into Desert Storm, General Colin Powell's reactions are monitored: "To Powell," writes Woodward, "it was almost as if the President had six-shooters in both hands and he was blazing away" (18). The multilayering here is significant. Not only has a seasoned writer (Woodward) used the Wild West mythos as a kind of shorthand, but another journalist (Thomas) has picked that very sentence to demonstrate the flavor of the book. Colin Powell is represented as an acolyte of myth (and this is crucial since, as chair of the Joint Chiefs of Staff, he is at the apex of all U.S. military echelons). Most important, however, is the political use of the Wild West—a broad hint that such myths are being gerrymandered and jury-rigged by George Bush to shore up Washington's foreign policy.

Bush's rhetoric before and during the war is liberally laced with myths. His recurrent phrase "the rape of Kuwait" is reminiscent of the "regeneration through violence" myth. Richard Slotkin has shown how government rhetoric in the Vietnam war was rooted in such language: "LBJ and Robert McNamara invoke the image of the family. . . . 'South Vietnam, a member of the free world family, is striving to preserve its independence from Communist attack.' . . . 'And it is a war of unparalleled brutality. . . . Women and children are strangled in the night. . . . And helpless villages are ravaged.' " Slotkin connects this to the Indian captivity narrative—Mary Rowlandson, author of the first captivity narrative, had "prefigured Lyndon Baines Johnson by 300 years: '. . . the Infidels haling Mothers one way, and Children another' " ("Dreams" 52). Bush's "rape" metaphor is part and parcel of this sort of mythmaking language. As Slotkin notes, the myth of "regeneration through violence" is based on "an intimate conflict between male avatars of wilderness and civilization for *possession* of the white female captive" (*Regeneration* 179, emphasis mine). Saddam Hussein is thus imaged as a rapist, an "avatar of wilderness," and as we heard again and again, a "Hitler" (capitalizing on "good war" myths from WWII).

Roland Barthes has argued that *"myth is a type of speech. . . . it is a system of communication. . . . it is a message"* (109). Henry Nash Smith has called myth "an intellectual construction that fuses concept and emotion into an image [which has] the further characteristic of being collective representations rather than the work of a single mind" (xi). Slotkin defines myths as "stories, drawn from history, that have acquired through usage over many generations a symbolizing function that is central to the cultural functioning of the society that produces them"; they are "a set of powerfully evocative and resonant 'icons' " (*Fatal* 16). As a collective expression and vehicle of cultural value, myth should help the individual make sense of social environment and historical time—under ideal conditions. According to Mircea Eliade, "the foremost function of myth is to reveal the exemplary models for all human rites and for all significant human activities" (8). Slotkin's version of this process is predicated on "the powerful force of tradition and habits of feeling and thought. It is this aspect of myth [that posits an] implicit demand that we make of the story a guide to perception and behavior" (*Fatal* 19). There are, therefore, intimate connections between history and myth, between reality and narrative; the real world provides the stuff of narrative, and the narrative encoded as myth offers a way to interpret that world, a lens through which to view reality. "What the world supplies to myth is an historical reality," Barthes asserts, "defined . . . by the way in which men have produced it or used it; and what myth gives in return is a *natural* image of this reality" (142). It is just such a naturalization of experience that the writer on the Vietnam war seeks, and that finally seems inevitably out of reach.

In his study of WWI literature, Bernard Bergonzi discovered a similar dialectic:

> The dominant movement in the literature of the Great War was . . . *from a myth-dominated world to a demythologized world.* Violent action could be regarded as meaningful . . . when it was sanctified by the traditional canons of heroic behaviour; when these canons came to seem no longer acceptable, then killing or being killed in war appeared meaningless and horrible. (198, emphasis mine)

Bergonzi's focus here is British literature and culture. I propose that such a movement is ultimately to be found in literature on the Vietnam war, and that it is most obvious in the poetry. In *Radical Vision*'s two sections—"The 'Nam" and "The World"—I delineate how these two sites become "demythologized worlds." To use Barthes's term, conventional American cultural myths simply could not "naturalize" the veterans' experience of the actuality of Vietnam and of their subsequent experience back in America, and poetry written by Vietnam veterans reveals the precise ways in which those myths were inadequate to the task and how these poets began to revamp mythic structures.

At this point, the skeptic may ask, when have myths *ever* effectively naturalized anyone's experience in American history and culture? I suggest that this objection may be somewhat beside the point; the important notion is that people continually *attempt* to use myth as a naturalizing force, as a lens through which to view experience. As the "six-shooter" Bush example demonstrates, myths and mythmaking are ineffably connected with ideology and with political praxis, and various representations of myths and mythic figures have always been used by those in power to preserve their perch (recall LBJ's characterization of South Vietnam as a "member of the free world family" and Bush's phrase "the rape of Kuwait"). A particularly revelatory example is Bush's declaration that the Gulf war "exorcised the specter of the Vietnam syndrome"; here, gnostic distinctions of light and dark, of heavenly and chthonic, are manipulated in arrogant chiaroscuro to cast the Gulf war as an en*light*ened action in contrast with the be*night*ed, obscurant memory of horror and defeat in the Vietnam war. This cynical representation of the two events implies a too-hurried impulse toward closure, hinting that dis-ease still festers under the so-called "healing" of the Gulf war. For the poet, the relationship of language to myth—and by extension, literature to myth—is a complex and even conflicted interaction, because the poet (or any artist) is involved in mythmaking and myth-revision in exactly the same way as the politician. "Art is finally a public activity," Stephen Behrendt asserts, "and artists must accept the responsibility for what they set in motion. . . . Like the making of art, of which process it is a culturally significant portion, the mythologization of history is a seductive process whose workings are never far removed from propaganda" (30).

One final point about myth-criticism: the conventional view is that it is dated, that as a basically structuralist project it has not weathered the assault of post-structuralism, and of deconstruction in particular. Yet Northrop Frye, whose *Anatomy of Criticism* has been a handbook for the archetypal critic, published in 1990 his book of selected essays, *Myth and Metaphor*, in which "Derrida turns out to be the most frequently cited contemporary critic," according to editor Robert Denham, although it should be no surprise that Frye's "relation to the central tenets of deconstruction is opposition" (xv–xvi). Frye's approach to contemporary critical theory may be tangential, but the important point is that he is considering their views while continuing to uphold myth-criticism.

In the burgeoning revolt against contemporary critical theory, there have been proponents for the recuperation of myth-criticism. Colin Falck's *Myth, Truth, and Literature,* for example, argues in favor of "a 'paradigm-shift' which will enable us to restore the concepts of truth or of vision to our discussions of literature" (xii). Falck advocates "a true post-modernist literature [that] goes on from the 'fictionality-awareness' of modernism to the actual finding of revelatory fictions" (162); he complains that in current postmodern criticism "the concern for truth or reality" has been "dismissed as a pre-Saussurian delusion" (162–63). Falck thus recommends "abandonment of some of the less relevant . . . myths or stories of the traditional religions and their replacement by other myths or stories which lie culturally nearer to hand" (144)—in other words, poetry. Following Matthew Arnold and Wallace Stevens, Falck argues that the "authentic religion of the future can only be: authentic living. Its scriptures can only be: poetry" (170).

In the larger culture beyond literary critical circles, similar recuperations of myth are also occurring. Psychologist Rollo May in *The Cry for Myth* connects "the very birth and proliferation of psychotherapy in our contemporary age [to] the disintegration of our myths" (15) and then relates selected myths—Oedipus, the American Frontier, the fairy tale of Briar Rose (or Sleeping Beauty), Faust, Moby-Dick and Ahab, etc.—to the patients' narratives he encounters in his psychotherapy practice in order to argue that myth is necessary to our planetary survival, to foster "a new world community [of] sisters and brothers, at last in the same family" (302). Starhawk's *Spiral Dance: A Rebirth of the Ancient Religion of the Ancient Goddess* and Robert Bly's *Iron John,* books which harbinger the uses of myth in feminist cultural revision and the fledgling men's movement, are also reflections of this popular "cry for myth."

Whether or not such restorations of traditional myth (irrespective of ideological usage) would appeal to Vietnam veterans is not clear, but the intimate relationship Colin Falck projects between "authentic living" and "poetry" is probably a position which the majority of Vietnam-veteran poets would applaud, and the British WWI poets would undoubtedly have been in concert with them—a choosing of life and the scripture of poetry in place of death and war's senselessness.

Twentieth-Century War Poetry by Veterans

The poet Edmund Blunden, introducing a collection of WWI poetry, asserted that England "was not after all a nation of shopkeepers but of poets" (Gardner vii). This statement may be hyperbolic, but it can be supported by statistics. As the war was winding down, *For Remembrance* (an anthology edited by A. St. John Adcock) featured *forty-four* "fallen" soldier-poets, and this is clearly an incomplete listing—both Owen and Isaac Rosenberg are not included. And then, of course, there are the many soldier-poets who had not "fallen": Blunden himself, Robert Graves, David Jones, Herbert Read, Siegfried Sassoon, and others less notable. Contrasted with the American WWI poets, England's roster is indeed impressive. Among American writers, Alan Seeger and Joyce Kilmer are overshadowed by e. e. cummings, who did not serve as a soldier but had "first-hand knowledge of death in war as an ambulance driver" (Walsh 25).

The most renowned of the British WWI poets is Wilfred Owen. Jon Silkin catalogs "the constituents of his poetry" as "the detailed description of war's effects; the outrage and indignation; the Biblical references; and the pity" (*Battle* 202). These aspects are all present—with biblical allusions replaced by church associations—in Owen's sonnet, "Anthem for Doomed Youth." In this poem, Owen mourns the pitiful waste of soldiers with such diction as "these who die as cattle," "monstrous," and "pallor." We can discern Owen's predilection for trenchant irony as words customarily found in religious contexts ("passing-bells," "orisons," "prayers," "choirs") are twisted into new significations in the collocations of war: "the stuttering rifles' rapid rattle / [as] hasty orisons" or the "shrill, demented choirs of wailing shells." What comes through most clearly is what one critic has termed Owen's "lyric sensibility vainly attempting to find order and significance on a level of experience where these values could not exist—where, in fact, they had been destroyed" (Johnston 207). At the end of the sonnet, Owen tries to rescue the "doomed youth," if only imagistically; instead of candles, there are only "the holy glimmers of goodbyes" in the eyes of survivors.

> The pallor of girls' brows shall be their pall;
> Their flowers the tenderness of patient minds,
> And each slow dusk a drawing down of blinds.   (80)

The close of the poem, on the literal level, evokes the domestic vision of these soldiers' loved ones preparing for sleep, while on a deeper metaphorical plane, the "slow dusk" on the battlefield is lovingly paralleled with the simple and familiar action of "drawing down [the] blinds," so that, somehow, these soon-to-be corpses are afforded some measure of solace: they can at least imagine home. At the last moment, however, Owen's diction underlines the futility of war. The word "blinds" refers literally and figuratively to oncoming death—

the sightless cadaver as well as the empty eye sockets of the mythic Grim Reaper.

In "Anthem," Owen holds up the folks back home as a potential source of comfort for the soldier mired in the trenches. Siegfried Sassoon held the diametrically opposite view; a critic suggests, "Had one only the record of Sassoon's verse, one might conclude that the war was fought between soldiers and civilians" (Crawford 125). His sonnet entitled "Glory of Women" illustrates Sassoon's contempt for the (female) civilian: "You love us when we're heroes" begins the poem, "[but] can't believe that British troops "retire" / When hell's last horror breaks them, and they run"—lines spoken in severe sarcasm. Sassoon's vision of opposed realms of existence is highlighted by his pairs of rhymed words: *leave/believe, place/disgrace, delight/fight, thrilled/killed, retire/fire, run/son,* and *blood/mud.* The tension between home and trench is the unresolvable conflict between "chivalry" and "hell's last horror," so that when we reach the closing lines—"O German mother dreaming by the fire, / While you are knitting socks to send your son / His face is trodden deeper in the mud" (100)—we can read the nightmarish rhyme yoking "run" with "son" (that is, the chivalric hope of the parents reduced to blind flight), followed by "blood" and "mud," as an expression of how the sanguine esprit, the essence of life itself, is "trodden" into primeval "mud." That this poem is found in a book entitled *Counter-Attack* is entirely fitting; as John Johnston notes, the book's "ironically ambiguous title" shows that Sassoon "was at war not so much with the enemy as with war itself and the people who were for one reason or another insensible to its terrible import. In pursuing these intentions he produced. . . . the first real attempt to present the truth of war" (107). What surfaces in Sassoon's poetry is his anger, and this is manifested in the stark, relentless reality of his war scenes—"Trampling the terrible corpses—blind with blood"—carefully orchestrated to shock and dislocate his civilian reader, particularly (as the title hints) women. Among many Vietnam-veteran poets, this conflict between battlefield and homefront also becomes a central issue; oblivious in general to the example of Sassoon, they would need to reinvent ways to deal with the question poetically.

Vera Brittain served as a nurse during WWI with the Voluntary Aid Detachment in Malta and France; she subsequently published two collections of war poetry, *Verses of a V.A.D.* (1918) and *Poems of the War and After* (1934). Nosheen Khan argues that Brittain's life was "affected by her wartime experiences; she changed from an ordinary patriotic woman into a convinced pacifist" (134), although the antiwar content of her work was continually "undercut

by her nostalgia for the intensities of wartime and by her loyalty to the memory
of her dead lover, brother, and friends" (Hanley 137). The closing stanza from
her 1917 poem "To Them"—an elegy for her brother and lover, both dead in
WWI—illustrates her nostalgic tendencies as well as her poetic skills.

> The flowers are gay in gardens that you knew,
>   The woods you loved are sweet with summer rain,
> The fields you trod are empty now, but you
>   Will never come again.   (*Verses* 35)

In each stanza of this poem, the finely crafted iambic pentameter lines, couched
in pastoral imagery, are truncated by the matter-of-fact trimeter of the fourth
line; the stanza thus replays over and over the speaker's ambivalence—a deeply
felt desire for the elegiac consolations of the pastoral undercut continually by
the realities of war.

Brittain's retrospective 1932 poem "We Shall Come No More" opens by
describing the arrival of V.A.D. nurses in Malta: "we came to the Island, /
Lissom and young, with the radiant sun in our faces" eager for "the magic adventure" among "shimmering . . . fields of asphodel." A pacifist note is struck
by the poem's center.

> *O Captain of our Voyage,*
> *What of the Dead?*
> *Dead days, dead hopes, dead loves, dead dreams, dead sorrows—*
> *O Captain of our Voyage,*
> *Do the Dead walk again?*

There is an interesting hint here, in the word "Captain," of a feminist voice
blaming war on patriarchy (God, the military, or the captain of the ship trans-
porting the nurses), but the poem relinquishes this perspective and ends on a
nostalgic note. The lines "On the ocean bed the shattered ships lie crumbling /
Where lost men's bones gleam white in the shrouded silence" hardly constitute
the antiwar comment expected of an outspoken pacifist, and the final image is a
wistful *ubi sunt* admission that the "fields of asphodel" are now surrounded by
"twilight," no longer "shimmering." (*Testament* 290). Brittain is best known
as a feminist and pacifist writer: a journalist, autobiographer, biographer, nov-
elist, historian, travel writer, and poet; she published twenty-nine books within
her lifetime, and more texts are being edited and published by scholars.[6]

Isaac Rosenberg would prove the most innovative of the British WWI poets.

In his foreword to Rosenberg's *Collected Poems,* Sassoon praised the way "he *modelled* words with fierce energy and aspiration, finding ecstasy in form, dreaming in grandeurs of superb light and deep shadow" (vii). In perhaps the finest of WWI poems, "Break of Day in the Trenches," Rosenberg contrasts the drab man-made trench world ("the darkness crumbles away") with the only "live thing" traversing the dawn: "A queer sardonic rat" who has "touched this English hand / [and] will do the same to a German." In other words, the rat is a symbol of Nature, with its "Strong eyes, fine limbs," thriving amid the "torn fields of France." As he wonders what the rat (and hence Nature itself) conceives of the war's "shrieking iron and flame," Rosenberg implicates himself in the bellicose destruction—"I pull the parapet's poppy / To stick behind my ear"—and seems presciently to forecast his own death in the poem's closing lines:

> Poppies whose roots are in man's veins
> Drop, and are ever dropping;
> But mine in my ear is safe,
> Just a little white with the dust.   (73)

Silkin points out that, for these poets, the "principal poetic patrimony was a pre-lapsarian pastoralism" (*Battle* 155), and clearly, Rosenberg is reaching in these lines toward the pastoral. The poppy should become the transcendent antidote to the rat's emblematization of a debased natural world, but it cannot. It is much too late for that. The poppies are now rooted in, drawing their sustenance from, "man's veins" (the *blood/mud* rhymic equivalence set up in Sassoon's sonnet "Glory of Women"), and, corrupted, they "are ever dropping." Even the poppy which the speaker means to save "is in roughly the place where the bullet would enter if he should stick his head up above the parapet, where the rat has scampered safely" (Fussell 252). So the poppy, "Just a little white with the dust," is already dying, preternaturally aged. And of course "dust" recalls the biblical memento mori: "Dust thou art." The speaker, in this very act of symbolic creation—*rescuing* the poppy from "dropping," inserting some beauty into his own life (the flower "behind my ear")—strips his action of all salvific grace: he has added to the devolution which surrounds him by killing the flower. It will soon be completely white with dust, and this dust is metaphorically contagious.

What is starkly surprising about Rosenberg's work is the way he prophesies the Modernist aesthetic and subject, though he is ultimately Romantic. Note, for example, the uncanny echo with the opening lines of Eliot's *Waste Land*—

"April is the cruellest month, breeding / Lilacs out of the dead land . . ." (37). As Paul Fussell reminds us (253), Keith Douglas in his poem "Desert Flowers" writes, "the body can fill / the hungry flowers . . . / But that is not new," and Douglas admits, "Rosenberg I only repeat what you were saying" (102). In "Break of Day," Rosenberg is wholly *imagist,* in the sense that the Modernists used that word, making a conceit out of that single poppy and extending the image into synecdoche to encompass Nature, the War, and Death—all in the magnificent crescendo of the poem's last four lines.

   In America, e. e. cummings was as innovative and influential as Rosenberg (and perhaps more so) and certainly had a much more significant reputation— though of course he *did* survive the war. His experimentation with lineation, orthography, visual/concrete poetry, and his distortions of syntax and mean- ing—"what Pound termed logopoeia, language used out of its familiar con- texts" (Walsh 26)—spawned new prosodies in ways unparalleled except by Dickinson and Whitman the century before. Sassoon would have appreciated cummings's poem "next to of course god america i" as it parodies and satirizes both the politician and the everyday civilian. Here are the opening lines:

> "next to of course god america i
> love you land of the pilgrims' and so forth oh
> say can you see by the dawn's early my
> country 'tis of centuries come and go . . ."

Walsh notes that "Cummings's war poetry seems designed as a counterblast to the self-styled 'voices of liberty' the paid creators of verbal stereotypes such as public relations experts or politicians who were, he believed, undermining the quality of American life by their pyrotechnic blurb" (26). In this sonnet, more than the quality of life is at stake. The speaker, perhaps an orator at a Fourth of July gathering, strings patriotic buzzwords and jingoistic catch- words in a tautological litany to gloss over the deaths of "thy sons" in war, allegedly to "acclaim [the] glorious name" of "god" and "america." The sons are therefore "heroic happy dead [who] did not stop to think"; the payoff, the punchline, given the sacrifice of these "beaut- / iful" children, is delivered by the line "shall the voice of liberty be mute?" In other words, how can we afford *not* to be patriotic? Well, of course, liberty *shall* be mute—gagged and choked by the speaker's force-feeding of patriotic pabulum, chalky and insipid, to his audience, to us. Even the speaker must himself pause to drink "rapidly a glass of water" (268).

   In terms of innovativeness, cummings here is appropriately stellar and full of fireworks, given the poem's occasion. Line break and enjambment, for example, subtly underpin the robust surface ironies. Splitting the phrase "i love you" before "love" leaves the three words "god america i" at the important terminal position in the first line, emphasizing the speaker's personal emphasis. The hyphenated break in the middle of "beautiful" calls attention to the speaker's mendacity, functioning as an embarrassingly timed stutter might in a conversational setting. The lack of punctuation in the speaker's oration forces the reader to rush breathlessly through the poem, and the experience of reading mimetically approximates that of the speaker as he rushes through his speech in order to "pull the wool" quickly over the audience's eyes (or ears). Perhaps the most startling feature to note is the rhyme scheme: this poem is a tightly crafted sonnet. What cummings has forged is an antisonnet, twisting the love lyric into a self-condemning political device—a multiplex structure wherein cummings himself, naughty grin and all, poises himself in the interstices of the poem ("between the lines") to deliver his sledgehammer blow in the sudden silence at the end of the poem, sans period.

Keith Douglas, born after WWI had ended, was fated to become one of the major poetic voices of WWII. When he joined the army in 1939, very soon after war was declared, he was already an experienced and published poet; fully three years before, he had assembled his first collection of poems (Douglas xiii). As his apostrophe to Rosenberg in "Desert Flowers" indicates, he had read widely in the WWI poets and was meticulously aware of what he must do to transcend their accomplishments. Douglas's poem "Landscape with Figures I" accurately represents the warfare of his time. The poem begins with an aerial perspective that, in its cinematic drama, doubtless owes much to 1930s Hollywood cinematography. The poem opens with a director's establishing shot ("Perched on a great fall of air / a pilot or angel looking down"), and then the camera/poem tilts down, zooming in ever closer, noting first the "sand vehicles / squashed . . . like beetles," and then closer, "legs, heads," dismembered on the sandy ground, until we come to the ultimate close-up, our zoom lens like "fingers in the wounds," focusing with "monument[al]" finality on "metal posies": the bullets deep in the violated body ("each disordered tomb"), the bullets' "steel . . . torn like fronds." There is an almost clinical perspective here—everything is metal or distant, except for "you who like Thomas come / to poke fingers in the wounds" (103)—that is, the morbidly fascinated and unbloodied civilian, the disbeliever. The soldier is numbed, unmoved by the scattered body parts, because this war's technology allows him to kill from a great distance, both vertical and horizontal—an anesthetizing distance. The metaphorical bridges to living nature are ineradicably abortive; the

"beetles" are dead, fragmented, mere "scattered wingcases"; the only flowers
(cf. Rosenberg's dying poppy) had never been alive—they are only metallic
counterfeits, shrapnel posing as petal, murderous. Douglas "is re-creating, not
only the thing as it was, but the sense of unreality that the soldier . . . experienced amidst such carnage and desolation, the protective film that came
between the watching eye and the things observed" (Scannell 51).

Sarah Churchill served "in the Women's Royal Air Force first as an aircraft-
woman and subsequently as a commissioned officer from 1941 until 1945"
(Reilly, *Chaos* 132). Her poem "The Bombers" showcases her intimate familiarity with military aircraft and hardware.

> I feel the mass of metal and guns
> Delicate instruments, deadweight tons
> Awkward, slow, bomb racks full
> Straining away from the downward pull
> Straining away from home and base

Churchill's meter and diction in this passage dramatize the ponderous, lumbering flight of bombers pregnant with destruction; her alliteration (the d's in
"delicate," "deadweight," and "downward," for example) and her full mono-
syllabic rhymes aptly figure the plodding regimen of military life. As may befit
the daughter of Winston Churchill, however, the poem's closure borders on
appropriate conventionality: "And steel my heart to say, / 'Thy will be done.' "
The speaker metaphorically grits her teeth in sacrifice *pro patria,* despite her
earlier misgivings about the youth of the bomber pilot: "a *boy* who's just left
school" but is already responsible for "the lives of the *men* in his crew" (em-
phases mine). Sarah Churchill relinquishes any admission of war as finally a
masculine construct, and her feminine response is only the maternal duty to
"care and pray for every one" (Reilly, *Chaos* 24).

Olivia FitzRoy was stationed in Ceylon as a flight direction officer with
the Women's Royal Naval Service during WWII. Her poem "Toast" captures
another side of war—utter ennui. The poem opens with a convincingly detailed
description of setting.

> All the way back from the air field
> Along the jolting road,
> Past the paddy fields
> And the mud-covered water-buffalo,
> I have been pretending to myself
> That I am not thinking about letters.

But today she has no letter and must rely on "the thought of toast for tea, /
Hot toast and lots of butter, / Even jam." At the mess, she again encounters
disappointment: "There is no jam but meat-paste." The speaker must subsequently avoid listening to her fellow soldiers discuss the news in their letters.
The poem's close is an anticlimactic insight.

> I am a little afraid, for when the toast is finished
> There will be nothing to look forward to,
> And so it was yesterday
> And so it will be tomorrow. (Reilly, *Chaos* 45–46)

"Toast" documents precisely a moment of existential despair, a moment made
more painful by endless repetition.[7]

Although John Ciardi's war was vastly different from that of Douglas and
Churchill, his experience was probably similar to FitzRoy's because of Ciardi's
setting: the Pacific, specifically the island of Saipan. Walsh sees him as representative: "The most typical Second World War poet wrote like John Ciardi,
in an ironic and slightly self-mocking tone. . . . from a common standpoint
of subversive irony" (154). The classic example is "Elegy Just in Case,"
which opens:

> Here lie Ciardi's pearly bones
> In their ripe organic mess.
> Jungle blown, his chromosomes
> Breed to a new address. (103)

This quatrain is meant, in its prosody, to reverberate with literary allusion. The
word "pearly" immediately resurrects Shakespeare's lyric "Full Fathom Five"
—"Of his bones are coral made; / Those are pearls that were his eyes"—sung
(aptly for Ciardi's tongue-in-cheek stance) by an airy spirit on a magic island
(*Tempest* I.ii.398–99). Read Ciardi as Saipan's Ariel. The rhyme scheme and
meter point to Emily Dickinson (especially her poems in which the dead speak
from beyond the grave) and beyond her to a church-based ambience—after
all, this brand of quatrain is labeled a "hymnal stanza." Of course, the diction
also points away from the past (both Amherst and Stratford) to the technocratic future, poised on the heels of the WWII present, via such vocabulary
as "organic" and "chromosomes." And there is a certain American flavor
here, a flippant, slangy quality conveyed by the phrase "Jungle blown." And
of course, the scatological puns of "blown," "chromosomes," and "breed"
charmingly add to Ciardi's wide-eyed "oh gosh!" American posture.

Ciardi, like Douglas and their ancestors in the WWI trenches, also subscribes
to the pastoral, but he invests it with irony, undercutting the beauty of nature
with the cutting edge of technology. Unlike Douglas, however, Ciardi seems to
find a sort of comfort in his work; note the second quatrain of "V-J Day":

> Halfway past Iwo we jettisoned to sea
> Our gift of bombs like tears and tears like bombs
> To spring a frolic fountain daintily
> Out of the blue metallic seas of doom.   (105)

Unlike Douglas's barren "metal posies" or Rosenberg's dying poppy, Ciardi
is able to create a transcendent object by fusing destructive, sterile technology
with the equally destructive ocean, lifting up a "frolic fountain." But the feeling of transcendence for today's reader quickly fades as the "fountain" begins
to slip on the guise of the "atomic mushroom cloud." We are reminded by
the name "Iwo" of the capture of the island of Iwo Jima (an event now lifted
into hagiographic American myth), a victory that would later be horrifically
mirrored by the bombing of Hiroshima (a name which is almost a rhythmic
and rhymic reflection/refraction of Iwo Jima, the punch line delivered by the
congruences of sound and intonation).

A similar tension of beauty and danger is achieved by Richard Wilbur in
his poem "On the Eyes of an SS Officer," which compares the SS officer
to the explorer Amundsen, "amorist of violent virgin snows" and to a blind
"Bombay saint asquat in the market place." Walsh suggests that Wilbur "frequently contrasts the grace and elegance found in the setting of war against
its true mechanised horror" (174). Reminiscent of Frost's epigrammatic "Fire
and Ice"—in which the world ultimately ends, whether by burning or freez-
ing (220)—Wilbur's lyric finally focuses into a curse, whether the officer is an
"Amundsen" or a "Bombay saint."

> But this one's iced or ashen eyes devise,
> Foul purities, in flesh their wildness,
> Their fire; I ask my makeshift God of this
> My opulent bric-a-brac earth to damn his eyes.   (348)

The point is that the officer is a fanatic, a devotee of death, and even though
the world is reduced to "bric-a-brac"—ersatz interchangeable figurines, meter
counters or placeholders, no matter how "opulent"—and God is only "make-
shift," created from despair and expediency, the officer *must* be damned.

Wilbur's forte in this poem is the nonchalance of the poem's motion, an ease disguising innards as meticulously machined as jeweled Swiss watch movements. The exacting rhymes, often with variance in spelling (e.g., *plateaus/snows* or *wilderness/God of this*) are contrapuntally offset by the lively music, the meter embroidered with atypical feet: anapests, spondees, dactyls. All of these factors combine to underline the poem's structural form and argument, a tripartite skeleton on which the poem's syllogism is hung. First, ice: "Amundsen" and his cold obsessions. Second, fire: the "Bombay saint" and his love affair with the "acetylene" sun resulting in his own acetylene "eye, / . . . in a blind face." Third, the SS officer and his truth, the evil for which he must be damned. The operative phrase in the final stanza is "damn his eyes"—the old cliché fleshed out into new significance. The important point is Wilbur's easygoing yet sharply barbed witty stance, a cosmopolitan urbanity which lends a certain flavor of authority.

Like Ciardi and Wilbur, Richard Eberhart is torn between appreciating and eschewing the aesthetics of war, resulting in an internalized tug-of-war, a tension that fuels and peoples his work. Eberhart has in fact written a meditative poem discussing this problem, "Aesthetic after War." William Brown points to a sequence in the poem:

> Was the Italian airman crazy
> When he saw aesthetic purity
> In bombs flowering like roses a mile below?
> He could not see nor feel the pain of man.
> Our own men testify to awe,
> If not to aesthetic charm,
> On seeing man's total malice over Hiroshima,
> That gigantic, surrealistic, picture-mushroom
> And objectification of megalomania.   (123–24)

Clearly, Eberhart is drawn, along with his "Italian airman," to love the beauty of "bombs flowering like roses," as illustrated by the fanciful description of the A-bomb as a "gigantic, surrealistic, picture-mushroom." The flat, uninteresting phrases "man's total malice" and "objectification of megalomania"—which are here perhaps because the speaker feels that, morally, they ought to be here—cannot stand up *mano a mano* to that brutally beautiful "picture-mushroom." As Brown points out:

> The speaker's guilty fascination with the modern war machine seems to be the mainspring of the poem. . . . with its mechanical beauty and its ability to kill elegantly. . . . the instruments of war: the electric gun sight,

radar, and military aircraft. These appliances of war fascinate the poet, but he wonders whether their beauty and mystery are characteristic of the objects themselves or of man their creator. (23)

The question points toward a Conradian "heart-of-darkness" motif. Eberhart can only resolve the debate by looking outside the human being to "Christ [who] contemplated the ultimate origin, / But originated the ultimate rules of action" (128). As we move closer to the Vietnam war, the particular issues that characterize that war begin to emerge. Technological sophistication and its aesthetic distancing are questions that Vietnam-veteran poets would certainly have to face.

Mitsuye Yamada's *Camp Notes* also presents an experience cognate to the Vietnam veteran's. "Japanese-American women . . . experienced the war very much at 'firsthand,' " Susan Schweik observes. "The texts they produced in response to internment challenge assumptions about both gender and warfare that have informed the aesthetics of the prevailing canon of war poetry" ("Needle" 226). Schweik also suggests that Yamada's poems, in particular, "develop a specifically *feminine* poetic narrative which strongly resembles, and equally strongly revises, the masculine plot of conventional modern ironic war literature" (*Gulf* 201). Yamada's poems are poignant meditations on the internment experience and on the subsequent thirty years of psychological repression. Her poem "Cincinnati," set after her release from camp, portrays the speaker attempting to recommence her life in a distant midwestern city, but only distant in terms of space from the western setting of her internment, it turns out. In the poem, the speaker declares that "no one knew" her in Cincinnati.

> No one except one
> hissing voice that said
> dirty jap
> warm spittle on my right cheek.

In shame, the speaker turns away, tears mixing with the spit on her face. In a moment of sudden and profound alienation, the speaker sees the city, the people (and by extension, the United States) as machinelike, impassive, indifferent.

> In Government Square
> people criss-crossed
> the street

> like the spokes of
> a giant wheel.

And she is merely a cog within this machine which is surely intertwined with WWII, the war effort. Wiping off the tears and spit with her handkerchief, the speaker

> . . . edged toward the curb
> loosened my fisthold
> and the bleached laced
> mother-ironed hankie blossomed in
> the gutter atop teeth marked
> gum wads and heeled candy wrappers.[8]
>
> > (*Camp Notes* 42–43)

Such treatment of a victim of war and her resulting sense of anomie is strongly reminiscent of the difficult readjustment many Vietnam veterans would go through, particularly women vets who were "double-whammied," excluded by their fellow (male) vets as they were simultaneously excluded by their mother country, much as the "bleached laced / mother-ironed hankie" does not finally protect the speaker but must be shed along with the negative reactions of others and, more significantly, by the speaker herself.

Perhaps the most accomplished of the WWII poets is Randall Jarrell, who "has emerged as the most permanently interesting of those American poets who wrote extensively of the Second World War" (Walsh 157). "The Death of the Ball Turret Gunner," perhaps the most renowned of American WWII poems, explores issues of innocence and guilt.

> From my mother's sleep I fell into the State,
> And I hunched in its belly till my wet fur froze.
> Six miles from earth, loosed from its dream of life,
> I woke to black flak and the nightmare fighters.
> When I died they washed me out of the turret with a hose.
>
> > (144)

"Jarrell sees war as totally destructive and pointless," writes Vernon Scannell, "the circumstances wholly degrading, robbing the individual of all that separates him from the predatory beasts" (190). In this short narrative poem, the gunner is a victim who has been conscripted, still as innocent as a suckling child, trading one cocoon—the family—for the "State" cocoon of the Air Corps, and ending up finally in the cold metallic "belly" of the bomber, the womb/symbol/instrument of the government at war. To use Scannell's phrase, these "wholly degrading" surroundings make the gunner into a "beast"—but nevertheless an innocent one, still unborn, "my wet fur froze[n]." The gunner, in the space of a few collapsed minutes, is catapulted from innocence into experience in the air battle, and then just as quickly launched into oblivion. In the course of the fourth line, therefore, an adult life is lived albeit telescoped into a few explosive moments. The closing line returns us to Sassoon's image of "blood" and "mud," as the callousness of "wash[ing the gunner] out . . . with a hose" recalls Sassoon's obsession with inhumanity toward the combatant by the people on his side. Walsh notes that

> Jarrell's poetic impulse towards concretisation, his fusion of intellect and directed passion, resists stereotyping, and the suggestion of mystification . . . accruing from a voice speaking out in death, [is] flatly dismantled by the precision of his concluding line. (158)

The speaker is not speaking from beyond the grave therefore to share some revelation from the "other side" as do some of Dickinson's and Thomas Hardy's personae; instead, the speaker is merely warning us about his horrific initiation into experience using the deadpan innocent language which is the only way he knows to speak: as a child, mature beyond his years, but with only a child's skills. The poem hence becomes a metonym for the universal and repugnant condition of war, an utterance which is both allegorical as well as coldly realistic.

Peter Bowman's 1945 novel, *Beach Red,* is a forgotten yet fascinating poetic experiment: an antiwar verse novel written in second person. During the heyday of the Vietnam war in 1967, a Hollywood movie based on *Beach Red* was produced; this film is a Vietnam-war allegory disguised as a WWII movie. The plot of Bowman's 122-page epic involves an American expeditionary force landing on a Japanese-held island in the South Pacific, the effects of the invasion upon young soldiers green to combat (especially the character "you"), and then the events of a reconnaissance patrol which "you" end up leading. Peppered throughout the story are short meditations on jungle fighting and its discomforts, the Japanese national character and the Japanese soldier, and dying under fire.

Bowman's style is recurrently Whitmanesque, and his tone oscillates between the witty and the sardonic, and from time to time he delivers a startling image. The book begins as the troop transport is anchored off the island.

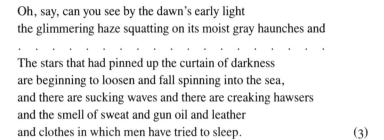

> Oh, say, can you see by the dawn's early light
> the glimmering haze squatting on its moist gray haunches and
>
> . . . .
>
> The stars that had pinned up the curtain of darkness
> are beginning to loosen and fall spinning into the sea,
> and there are sucking waves and there are creaking hawsers
> and the smell of sweat and gun oil and leather
> and clothes in which men have tried to sleep.   (3)

Bowman continually resists the temptation to glorify the war, concentrating instead on the camaraderie among the men, and on unselfish, silent heroism: "Gallantry isn't written of or talked about. It is done" (24). Bowman does not romanticize the actual fighting.

> The air is sticky with smoke and flame and wreckage,
> and the earth feasts on a macabre pot of flesh.
> Here is a victory garden of ripe corpses, grinning heads
> like rounded cabbage and arms and legs in natural disorder
> stained with the bright juice of tomatoes, plump and petulant.
>
>   (20)

The ironic reference to a "victory garden" and "tomatoes" is calculated both to shock the noncombatant and to exploit the surreality of the setting, so that the mind, in attempting to apprehend the horror, can only make analogies to what is familiar and mundane.

In the action of the novel, the "you" character is volunteered by an officer for a jungle patrol, where "you" must subsequently take charge after "your" sergeant is wounded. Eventually outnumbered, "you" are the only survivor of a firefight, and as "you" lie on the ground,

> Blood from the wound in your side still seeps through
> your clothing and dampens the earth . . .
>
> . . . .
>
> Darkness seems to be crawling all around you and little
> gusts of heat tumble over the ground and the trees

> are jibbering with flecked mouths of green and space is
> split with trembling. . . .   (III)

Bowman reels "you" through "your" life and memories: "an ordinary house
with an ordinary tree in an ordinary / back yard. A broken toy and the bright
penny in / the tight fist for the square of chocolate" (113), friends and schools,
waiting for "your" wife "like an / empty glass for the bright bubbly champagne
of her coming" (115), a dream of going home where "starched shirts come
out of a paper / package and you can sit on a toilet seat in / privacy" (117).
There are disjointed discussions with "yourself" about the nature of society
and fellowship, about "how to die. Your father did it and his father / did it and
so did his and his. There must / be something inside of you that will tell you"
(120). Eventually "you" begin to hallucinate: "the hill is floating up to em-
brace you and / the trees are hoisting their shimmering green banners of hope"
(122). When "you" are found by "your" fellow Americans, "You do not hear
Lieutenant Nixon come forward to the / group and ask Whitney whether or not
you're still alive. // 'Lieutenant,' he replies, 'there is nothing moving but his
watch'" (122). At the end of the novel, "you"—an introspective young man
given to flights of poetic fancy—become finally what the Army has been trying
to make of "you": a clockwork man.

Beach Red has obvious failings, despite Bowman's courage as an experimental writer (Random House obviously had faith in him and his project). The best
parts of the narrative are those which are grounded in fact—the authenticity
of the terrain, the believability of character motivation, the intimate details of
soldiering in tropical jungle—all of which testify that Bowman had probably
been a jungle fighter, with intimate knowledge of the sensations, thoughts, and
feelings experienced in such an environment. Where Bowman fails is in his use
of language: he assumes that the reader is a kindred spirit who experiences the
world in terms of highfalutin metaphorical language. In fact, it is too much of a
strain for Bowman to maintain that level of expression through 122 pages, and
the exigencies of fictional narration force him into a more quotidian language,
thus calling attention to the more poeticized passages, to the detriment of the
epic as a whole. In addition, the didactic content, Bowman's polemic intent,
leads him away from the factually realistic, and he launches "you" into dis-
quisitions on society and the intrinsic worth of the individual. Bowman's hope
is that the reader will mourn for the death of "you" because of "your" inward-
ness and honest self-searching at the point of death. In the final analysis, the
use of second person as a protagonist only serves to distance the reader, rather

than inviting the reader to identify with the character, as the use of "you" was supposed to accomplish.

Beach Red is, however, a significant comparison text as a prototype for the sort of poetry which would surface out of the Vietnam War: avowedly political and based on the jungle experience (a parallel at least for Vietnam-veteran poets who were infantry soldiers in the jungle). The great majority of the Vietnam-veteran poets, especially those who were members of the organization Vietnam Veterans Against the War, would find themselves wrestling with many of the same aesthetic and prosodic considerations with which Bowman struggled before *Beach Red* was published. There are indications in Bowman's novel that he was undergoing similar adjustment problems to those which have become cultural commonplaces in the readjustment of the Vietnam veteran to American society: reference to "a peacetime war that will go on and on and / on and on and you will never really get it / out of you. . . . And so there will / be a little block of strangeness that will have to / be chipped and sculpted" (117–18). In fact, it is quite probable that *Beach Red* was written as a cathartic act, almost as a procedure of self-psychoanalysis. The problem of how to accommodate and combine the warring impulses of political activism, faithfulness to the violent (even savage) truths of the Vietnam experience, the expunging of guilt, and reentry into American society within poetic texts is at the heart of the Vietnam-veteran poet's quest. Bowman had already been there.

It is literally impossible to draw some megaconclusion about these poets of the two world wars. In the context of Vietnam-war poetry, however, the crucial thing to notice is the obvious devotion of these earlier writers to poetry and the enterprise of poetry. Their unquestioned assumption is that poetry is *the* proper response to war, whether the poem feeds the official line or else protests against war and war policies. These artists pay devout attention to poetics (often to rhyme, meter, and inherited forms) in an attempt to extend the poetic corpus. In other words, they are cognizant and deliberate in writing fine *literature*. Vietnam-veteran poets would call these assumptions into question.

Three Modes: Antipoetic, Aesthetic, Cathartic

What the antipoetic, aesthetic, and cathartic modes have in common is their base in the documentary motivation that underpins Vietnam-war literature; Deborah Holdstein has labeled the body of poems by Vietnam veterans as "docupoetry" (60). The proponents of all three methods would agree that their

primary objective is to re-create the Vietnam-war experience in all its weirdness. Such a commitment means that "documentation" signifies getting not
only the physical "facts" right but also the mental and spiritual: horror, ennui,
comradeship, recurring nightmare. The distinctions between and among the
practitioners of the three modes center on how to convey this second realm: the
internal condition rather than external mundanity.

The poets who subscribe to the antipoetic stance convey this internal landscape through ordinary, nonliterary language, and occasionally through shock
tactics. They feel that attention to prosody, to sonic devices, to linguistic flair,
somehow betrays the realities of the Vietnam war; they may also feel that
traditional aesthetics and sentiment shore up myth-based preconceptions that
war can be glorious and regenerative. Even Wilfred Owen had felt this connection and attempted to explode it. Stephen Spender observes that "Owen's
irony consisted of turning Romanticism on its head while retaining the idiom
of Keats" (3). Yet, in his introduction to Michael Casey's *Obscenities,* Stanley
Kunitz suggests:

> We can no longer respond to rhetorical flourishes and sentiments bor-
> rowed from the poets who fought—and too often died—in the earlier
> wars of the century. Casey begins as a poet with an act of rejection [by
> writing] a kind of anti-poetry that befits a kind of war empty of any kind
> of glory. (vii)

Often the antipoetic poets write in a laconic, terse, deadpan style. Leroy V.
Quintana is a good example. Quintana's untitled poem that begins with the
temporal setting "Eight years after Viet Nam" describes the speaker's "M-16
mind / on recon patrol" continuously, seeing "everybody / even my family /
[with] slant eyes"; what results is the speaker's commitment to writing, despite
free-floating anxiety and alienation.

> Nine years after Viet Nam
> where friendly woodchoppers by day
> would be Viet Cong by night
> I'm still on recon patrol.
> Everybody has slant eyes.
> It's an M-16 world.
>
> Teacher by day, tonight
> I'm at the trigger

of an electric typewriter.
This paper has yellow skin.
This poem has slant eyes.   (*Sangre* 56)

This poem celebrates the poet's explosion into poetry out of the exigencies of postwar distress. Interestingly, Quintana has revised this poem for *Interrogations* (his book of Vietnam-war poems) and this time titled it "The Years After," beginning the poem with the line "Twenty years after Viet Nam" (97). Evidently the process of recovery from the war can be ongoing, perhaps unending.

Along with Quintana, I would class Bill Shields, Michael Casey, Lamont Steptoe, Jon Forrest Glade, Don Receveur, Dick Shea, McAvoy Layne, Stephen Miller, and Geoffrey Stamm, among others, as antipoets. It is important to be absolutely clear here. I do *not* argue that they are *bad* poets or *not* poets; instead, I propose that these writers make an active political choice to forgo some or all of the traditional accouterments of verse—rhyme, meter, poetic diction, sonic device, metaphor, image, lyricism, euphony—in order to oppose war. Their theoretical patron might be Bertolt Brecht, who argued for an "alienation effect" in literature and art, urging artists to *think crudely,* to shatter complacency. As Raman Selden writes of Brecht's drama, the "situation, emotions and dilemmas of the characters must be understood from the outside and presented as strange and problematic" in order that "a process of critical assessment can be set in motion" (32). Antipoetry by Vietnam veterans targets a "critical (re)assessment" of themselves, of the readers' own consciences, and of national ideology, myth, and policy.

To some extent, the contrast between the aesthetic and the antipoetic modes is congruent with distinctions between form and content; one might argue that the antipoetic stance focuses more on content and the aesthetic on form. On the back cover of R. L. Barth's *A Soldier's Time,* blurbs connect Barth with "Lucretius and Martial" as well as "Owen, Blunden, and Sassoon." The important thing to note is that these blurb writers situate Barth within poetic tradition. John Clark Pratt classifies Vietnam-veteran poets into two groups: "Some of these men are too consciously writing 'poetry'; others seem trying only to tell it the way they think it was by means of short lines" (Preface ix). The ones who are "consciously writing 'poetry' " with a capital P are the aestheticists. For an example, let us consider the closing lines of Basil Paquet's sonnet "Christmas '67"; the setting describes a firebase under attack, with soldiers under cover and

> . . . waiting for the promise
> Of thudding hosannas, like a gathering of devout
> Moths, aching for the flames, but frozen by the hiss
> And whistle of mortars and rockets sliding
> Down their air pews in a choiring of dying.   (*Winning* 36)

Paquet's elevated diction and rhyme point to his aestheticist leanings. In particular, his use of high-poetic devices links him to Wilfred Owen; Paquet is updating Owen in much the same way that Owen had updated Keats to create a poetic that could encompass the brutality of WWI. Paquet's slant rhyme *sliding/dying* is also a formalistic connection with Owen; Fred Crawford labels Owen "something of an innovator in his development of pararhyme," particularly his characteristic "sustained terminal pararhyme" (187–88). Among Vietnam veterans, I would group Barth and Paquet with D. C. Berry, Walter McDonald, Horace Coleman, Dana Shuster, David Huddle, and D. F. Brown, among others, as poets who focus on aesthetics; at the risk of overgeneralizing, I will suggest that these writers share a common faith that beauty and vision in poetry are finally salvational.

The cathartic mode in Vietnam-veteran poetry stands midway between the two modes of antipoetic and aesthetic. Like the antipoetic, this mode is closely tied to the documentary impulse. Through a stance of witness, the poet makes the war's incredibility somehow credible to the reader, but the more significant agenda is "confessing" (almost in the sacramental sense), attempting to purge guilt and memory (through a virtual, self-referential psychoanalysis). The critical assertion that aesthetical poetic modes are "inappropriate to communicate the character of the Vietnam war" (Walsh 204) is, in the context of catharsis, beside the point. Through a re-creation of the Vietnam-war experience, the poet addresses two goals: self-purgation and "telling it" (recall Herr's charge in *Dispatches*). Norma J. Griffiths's poem "The Statue" is an able demonstration of these objectives. The speaker envisions a memorial statue, "a young woman, standing by the side of a green canvas litter." Supine on the litter, a "badly wounded" soldier is holding hands with the standing woman. Griffiths is driven to "tell it," to document the nurse's experience—"I recall our hands were too busy to do that"—but she also realizes intimately the gulf between such journalistic reality and her dream.

> I guess when heroes dream of statues,
> they dream of men with guns.

> I dream of a woman
> with only her heart, hands, and mind
> her "weapons"
> to deal with the world of carnage.　　　　(*Visions* 196)

The catharsis in Griffiths's poem is manifold: a meditation on the nurturant role of nurses in the Vietnam war, on the horrible memories of a "world of carnage," and a comment on the present reality of the statue installed next to the Vietnam Veterans Memorial, a statue of "men with guns." In the "telling" of the poem, there is release and cleansing, a poignant reminder of the *public* nature of the nurses' contribution. Along with Griffiths, the cathartic Vietnam-veteran poets include Steve Mason, W. D. Ehrhart, Marilyn McMahon, Lynda Van Devanter Buckley, and Jan Barry. These poets attempt, through a mediation between the aesthetic and antipoetic, between hard journalistic reality and psychological terror, to achieve sanity and balance, even if only momentarily, in the poem's fleeting moment.

It must be admitted, of course, that categories of this sort can never be hard-edged and exclusive. Each of the poets I have classified inevitably crosses over the boundaries I delineate. Gerald McCarthy, for example, whom I have not categorized, uses each of the three modes in his book *War Story*. The modes themselves cross over and cross-pollinate. Aesthetic and antipoetic are only the terminal nodes of a continuum of poetic approaches; in fact, technically speaking, catharsis is not analogous to the other two terms, since it is a reader-response (as well as a writer-centered) effect, whereas aesthetics and antipoetics are formalistic concerns. My purpose in proffering the three modes is to provide a framework for discussing the poetry and to foreground three basic directions which Vietnam veterans have taken in writing war poems. The culmination of *Radical Visions* is a focus on Bruce Weigl and Yusef Komunyakaa, two poets who ultimately transcend these categories. Each in his own way, Komunyakaa and Weigl juggle and balance the psychological needs which underlie the three modes: the need for *truth* coded as journalistic documentation, the need for *beauty* as potentially upheld by poetic innovation, and the need for *sanity* (in the root sense of the Latin *sanitas,* health), not only of the mind, but of the full person, through ritual purification. Weigl's and Komunyakaa's achievement of their own radical visions holds out as individual and national promise the liminal possibility of a saner American mythos.

PART ONE. THE 'NAM

What does a man do? A man stands alone against impossible odds, meets the Apache chief in single combat to protect the manifest destiny of the wagon train, plays guitar and gets the girl, leaps tall buildings in a single bound, plants the flag on Iwo Jima, falls on a grenade to save his foxhole buddies and then takes a bow to thundering applause.

MARK BAKER, Nam, p. 23.

Cobra Pilot

Plastic blue eyes
and hair
the color of toggle switches.
He flies his cobra-shark
with the precision
of a god
or a gunfighter.
(Hickok
with a 38 in his armpit)
His nebraska smile
is a mini-gun
and his bowels
are full of rockets.
He hunts
the Indian-gooks
in the Wild West
of his mind

DON RECEVEUR,
Winning Hearts and Minds, p. 49.

ONE. THE WILD WEST REVISITED

'Come on,' the captain said, 'we'll take you out to play Cowboys and Indians' " (Herr 61). The metaphor was rampant; everyone used it. "Out there . . . you're in Indian Country," remarked one vet upon returning home (Baker 263). According to Loren Baritz:

> Everyone in Vietnam called dangerous areas Indian country. Paraphrasing a bit of Americana, some GIs painted on their flak jackets THE ONLY GOOD GOOK IS A DEAD ONE. They called their Vietnamese scouts who defected from the Communists Kit Carsons. (51–52)

These connections inevitably arise from Hollywood and TV clichés. One veteran recalled that FNGs (*fucking new guys*) were always told this story:

> "Two second lieutenants, brand new in-country, were playing poker one night and got drunk. They decided they would have a *Gunsmoke* shootout. They stood in the middle of the company street with their .45s and had a fast draw contest and killed each other." (Baker 55–56)

Clearly, Americans were using the shorthand of western-movie myth to express the combination of strangeness and danger in Vietnam.

The nefarious underside of this myth is that these mythic gestures are based on historical imperialism during the westering movement, and the killing of Native Americans was promulgated as part of the myth of the "virgin land"— that is, land or resources untouched as well as ready for the taking (note the macho assumptions inherent in the myth). Henry Nash Smith points out that "the picturesque Wild West" had behind it "the domesticated West. . . . [where pioneers] plowed the virgin land and put in crops . . . and transformed it into a garden: for the imagination, the Garden of the World" (123). By extension, Vietnam as the target of a publicly unacknowledged imperialism could be envisioned as such a "virgin land" and potential "garden."

Philip Caputo recalls his 1965 arrival with the first Marine unit in Vietnam.

To him, the landscape "did not look like a war torn country. . . . Groves of bamboo and coconut palm rose out of rice paddies like islands from a jade-colored sea" (54). Caputo's language resembles a travel advertisement:

> VIETNAM. Discover the Pacific. Friendly, hospitable people, a cosmopolitan blend of Orient and occident, beautiful scenery, delightful mountain retreats, unrivalled beaches, the charm of ancient imperial cities, and the thrills of big game hunting.[1] (Helmer 153)

Annette Kolodny has documented the use of this kind of language to advertise the New World as a virginal woman.

> a particular mode of English response, articulated most explicitly by Raleigh himself in 1595 [describing] "a country that hath yet her maydenhead, never sackt, turned, nor wrought." It was an invitation utilized by Robert Johnson in his "Nova Britannia" (1609), when he described not only Virginia's "Valleyes and plaines streaming with sweete Springs, like veynes in a naturall bodie," but also that territory's "hills and mountaines making a sensible proffer of hidden treasure, neuer yet searched"; and again by John Smith, in 1616, when he praised even the rough New England seacoast as a kind of virginal garden, "her treasures hauing yet neuer beene opened, nor her originalls wasted, consumed, nor abused."[2] (*Lay* 11–12)

Sexual assumptions in this excerpt point to the objectification and commodification of women as treasures to be plundered; note the gendered diction of "maydenhead" and the rape-oriented terminology: "sackt," "neuer yet searched," treasures [never] opened," "her originalls [not yet] wasted . . . nor abused." Kolodny points, however, to the "inevitable paradox" of this metaphor: "the success of settlement depended on the ability to master the land, transforming the virgin territories into something else . . . finally, an urban nation"—a realization that "despoliation of the land appeared more and more an inevitable consequence" (*Lay* 7). For Kolodny, this paradox and realization becomes the basis for a feminist stance.

Thinking in high levels of American government during the war apparently mirrored this macho rhetoric isolated by Kolodny, along with its "paradox of despoliation," not merely in the sense of "protecting" Vietnamese resources from the communists, but more specifically in the unavoidable destructive results, both in Vietnam and in the United States. Lyndon Johnson spoke in this sort of macho lingo and ironically prophesied the defeat of the United States as well as the defoliation of Vietnam. "If I left the woman I really loved—the Great Society—in order to get involved with that bitch of a war on the other side of the world, then I would lose everything at home" (Kearns 251). In fact, Vietnam was no Eden for Americans, but rather a truly alien landscape, as reflected by grunts who referred to the war or to Vietnam as "this motherfucker," an indication of where the rhetorical machismo of land-as-woman really ends up: misogyny.

The first index of this alien landscape encountered by arriving Americans was the tropical heat: "when we first landed . . . the only thing that got us was the heat. When we came off the plane it must have been a hundred and change. There's no air or nothing" (Baker 71). In narrative after narrative, in various oral histories, veterans attest to this ubiquitous first impression. Larry Rottmann's poem "The Weather of Vietnam" highlights the effect of the heat on the climatocentric American.

> There are two kinds of weather in Vietnam
> Hot and dry and
> Hot and wet
>
> During the hot and dry
> The dust is as fine as talcum powder
> And hangs like a gritty mist in the air
>
> During the hot and wet
> The monsoon wind blows so hard
> That it rains sideways   (*Winning* 8)

The key word, of course, is "hot." What surfaces from beneath the heat, however, is the sense of estrangement the weather causes—the feeling that one is indeed in a very alien and hostile place—fueled by the overlapping connotations of "hangs" and "sideways," an ambience of danger as well as suspense.

Even the fertile greenness Caputo remarked on his arrival turns insidious: "the unremitting heat . . . and the long days of staring at that alien landscape; a lovely landscape, yes, but after a while all that jungle green became as monotonous as the beige of the desert or the white of the Arctic" (68–69). Jan Barry's poem "Green Hell, Green Death" reflects this insipid yet threatening monotony.

> Green hell of the jungle:
>   green fire, green death,

> green ghosts,
>   green
> grim bodies
>
> Green jungle all around: hot,
>   full of death
>   fox-fire,
>   floating ghosts,
> ghosts of the quick and the dead . . .

There floats in this poem a sense of dread, the engulfing lethargy of the color *green,* and the form of the stanza emphasizes this feeling; orthographically, the opening line and the closing line in each stanza seem to constrict the three lines in between. The result is a structural representation of the speaker's state of mind surrounded by the oppressiveness of jungle so that all are ghosts—both "the quick and the dead." Barry orchestrates the emotions of this poem to increase the feeling of anomie; in the following stanza, the soldiers trapped in the jungle are doomed by the very color of their uniforms and equipment, camouflage turned awry. The enemy soldiers, however, are not imprisoned by the jungle; their "green bodies" and "quick green limbs" in the fourth stanza reside in the opening and closing lines which enclose. The Vietcong are portrayed *in control* of the greenness of the jungle, turning it to their advantage. As Caputo puts it, "It is as if the sun and the land itself were in league with the Viet Cong, wearing us down, driving us mad, killing us" (106). In the final crescendo of "green," Barry's speaker verges on insanity: "green fire: from green fingers / on green guns— / green jungle: green hellfire: green death" (*Winning* 65). By the end of the poem, the phrase "green death" has acquired a symbolic weight which condemns self-reflexively. The speaker, as he fires "green guns," is partaking in "green hellfire: green death," so that he is subsumed, digested, and corrupted by "green jungle."

For those grunts who are fighting in the jungle—no wide-open American "spacious skies" or "waves of grain," no rolling prairie or "fruited plain"—the lack of visibility becomes tantamount to a lack of reference points, especially moral ones. R. L. Barth alludes to this in the first stanza of his poem "Letter from the Bush":

> The triple canopy—
> Huge trees, bamboo, and vines—
> Constricts the vision. . . .
>
>   .   .   .   .

> . . . we never sight
> Objects that, distant enough,
> Permit an azimuth reading.   (*Soldier's Time* 37)

The impossibility of an "azimuth reading" refers here not only to the literal condition of being lost in the wilderness, but to being lost spiritually. In Caputo's phrase, "It was the dawn of creation in the Indochina bush, an ethical as well as a geographical wilderness" (xviii).

The feeling of estrangement does not arise only from landscape and weather. One was fully estranged from everything Vietnamese: the people, their customs, their language, their beliefs. Historian Ralph Smith proposes "that culturally Viet-Nam is quite beyond the normal range of occidental comprehension." An example is the self-immolation of the Buddhist monk Quang Duc and other fire-suicides in 1963; "eventually many American observers came to conclude," Smith writes, "that fire-suicides have no significance at all." Nothing could be further from the truth. In the context of Asian Buddhism and Vietnamese politics, such a suicide, Smith claims, is "a way of proving superior virtue in face of a powerful but unvirtuous enemy [thus becoming] a weapon of considerable force" (4–5). With the benefit of hindsight, it is obvious that these self-immolations in fact catalyzed the eventual coup against President Ngô Dinh Diêm and his assassination.

Jan Barry's poem "A Nun in Ninh Hoa" dramatizes the extreme mental dislocation of one American, Jimmy Sharpe, as he witnesses a fire-suicide: "It was quite a sight for a boy from Tennessee." That Jimmy is present at this moment because he is " 'just along for the ride' " indicates his spiritual disposition; he is an observer, an epitome of American innocence. The persuasive undercutting of the suicide's horror is very effective here; the nun is merely "dressed in fire," the "smoke plume" only a "costume." The point is that, for the "solemn silent crowd," this action is understood, valued (the nun is "mocking the flames"), heroic. The tragedy (repeated time and again by Americans in Vietnam) is that Jimmy retreats to American isolationism.

> Safe back at the base, Jimmy's chatter
> circled the nightmare he could still taste.
> He grinned—shivered—then softly swore:
> "Jesus! How'd we get in this crazy place?"   (*War Baby* 8)

His final words rationalize the nun's action as an oddity attributable to "this crazy place" and the phrase "How'd we get in" implies that "we can get out."

The stereotyped soldiers' responses to the Vietnamese people include the "babies with grenades" rumor, the "slant-eyed" prostitute, the stoic farmer, the betel-nut-chewing old woman—all images now conventionalized into cliché by the movies and TV—but the actual responses within Vietnam-veteran poetry are considerably more complex. Kathleen Trew's "Mamasan" begins with a conventional image: "Mamasan / Squats at her basin / [with] blackened teeth." Then Trew shifts gears to present a poeticized image—"Orange clouds of dust / Chase black silk pajamas"—almost as if the speaker will give way to an urge to romanticize. But the poem closes with a frank admission of the mutually exclusive territories of the American and the Vietnamese: "our world" and "hers" are separated by "a simple gate" (*Visions* 23). Although the "gate" may be "simple" or commonplace (an index of the possibility of sisterhood between the American nurse and this "Mamasan"), the gate nevertheless also underlines—almost in paradox—the alienness of the "Mamasan" to the speaker who is finally unable to enter the other's realm.

Jon Forrest Glade's "City Kid" describes two diametrically opposed reactions to what is perceived as the strangeness of Vietnam. The speaker and "New York"—the "city kid" of the title—witness a "mama-san kill[ing] a chicken":

> She did it in the time-honored way;
> simply put her foot on its head
> and jerked its body upwards
> by the legs.

"New York" is horrified as the "headless chicken" runs around in galvanic frenzy, its "blood jetting" all over him. "Mama-san just laughed, / picked up the corpse, and went to fix lunch." "New York, . . . spooked," calls the Vietnamese a "barbarous race," but the speaker remembers that "outside Ft. Laramie, / . . . I had watched my own mother / kill beaucoup chickens" (15). Glade's perceived equivalency between his mother and the "mama-san" implies a continuum of response ranging from contempt and rejection to identification with and acceptance of the Vietnamese. Despite its currency as slang, the word "mama-san" is revelatory.

Frances FitzGerald, in her Pulitzer Prize-winning book *Fire in the Lake,* points to American cultural misunderstandings of and in Vietnam. According to the American "national myth . . . of creativity and progress, of a steady climbing upward into power and prosperity," she writes,

Americans see history as a straight line and themselves standing at the cutting edge of it. . . . In their sense of time and space, the Vietnamese and Americans stand in the relationship of a reversed mirror image, for the very notion of competition, invention, and change is an extremely new one for most Vietnamese. . . . For traditional Vietnamese the sense of limitation and enclosure was as much a part of individual life as of the life of the nation. (8)

This gulf of understanding is illustrated by the South Vietnamese election of 1966. "Brought up in a tradition that prescribes free elections as the proper solution for most political conflicts," FitzGerald notes, "the Americans had come to look upon them as the moral foundations of a state" (329). The Vietnamese, however, did not understand what seems self-evident and basic to Americans; they

saw no reason why the government should ask their advice. . . . The idea that their vote might actually help change the government was an almost impermissible one, for it implied that there was no authority above them. And if there was no authority, then there was nothing but chaos and "confusion." To be given a choice by means of a vote was therefore to be handed an instrument of terror—an unthinkable one. (330)

Michael Casey's poem "Hoa Binh" (Vietnamese for *peace*) relates how his female Vietnamese coworker "Stanley" (so named by Casey and his confreres) responded to an election in 1969.

> Stanley was all excited
> She just made eighteen
> And got to vote
> For the first time

Unlike the two-party system in the United States (called *Hoa Kỳ* in Vietnamese), this election has sixteen parties and each "slate / Wanted Hoa Binh." After voting, Stanley returns to the office, exhilarated:

> Casee
> I vote for Hoa Binh
> That's nice, Stanley

> I did   too
> Back in Hoa Ky
> I hope your vote counts   (67)

What is immediately obvious is Stanley's misapprehension of election hype, but underneath that misunderstanding is the more basic fact that, for the Vietnamese, it is not the various parties or particular issues at stake but rather the grim polarities of war and peace. From the response of "Casee," it also becomes clear that this young American's faith in the electoral process—even in Hoa Kỳ, the United States—has been demolished, and in this poem Casey's laconic style makes this alienation bitterly clear in its terseness.

Dick Shea: The Antipoetic Stance

The question of how the alien character of Vietnam—the land, the people, their beliefs and customs—affected Americans is taken up by the first book of poetry published by a Vietnam veteran, Dick Shea's *vietnam simply* (1967). This book is monumental in terms of quantity: a verse novel containing 158 untitled sections in 193 unnumbered pages. The book chronicles Shea's tour of duty in Vietnam: his "education" from his arrival in-country to his first days back in the World. The vignettes have the feel of being unmediated impressions, almost as if they have been lifted from a diary, because Shea uses no punctuation except parentheses, quotation marks, and apostrophes. The only modulation of meaning telegraphed by the structure of language is accomplished therefore through line break.

Shea (or more properly the speaker whom I will call "Shea") is wholly flabbergasted by Vietnam's exotica, and the volume of his work indicates his total perplexity. Shea starts at the conventional beginning—"35 thousand feet over vietnam / in a military iron bird"—and his characteristic first impressions are the same ones that would eventually coalesce into cliché: "a green land / peacefully there beneath flowing white clouds" followed by a "blast of hot air hits me" [1]. The incredibility of the countryside and its inhabitants hits Shea when he enters Saigon.

> next to a busy street
> and in the midst of a crowd of people
> two boy kids squatting on top a railroad tie fence
> five feet off the ground

no pants
defecating in unison [4]

Shea's introduction to local cuisine is apparently innocuous but transforms into
an encounter as dislocating as the sight of "two boy kids squatting" had been.

squashed fried squid
yellow cakes filled with ground goat meat
hard toasted garlic bread
little mushy hunks of meat
delicious peanuts
and garlic

The result of this meal is a night spent "in wild painful ecstasy / on white
porcelain plumbing / with stomach throbbing" [9–10]. Shea learns pidgin—
"everything good is 'number one' / everything bad is 'number ten' " [11]—the
bipolar, antipodal thinking that seems endemic to the Vietnam war and everything associated with it. He rides in the Vietnamese mixture of bicycle and rick-
shaw: "cyclos are unsightly / a hunk of dirty manually powered metal" [13].

Shea finds the people equally incredible, discovering the image of the country mama-san, again an image that would become a cliché in Vietnam-war
literature.

i see an old wrinkled brown woman
used up
barefoot in dirty black silk
a sloping straw hat
carrying
two baskets of wood
hanging on each end of a pole
balanced in a groove
worn into her shoulder
her eyes are spiritless
and distant
and her mouth is dripping red
juice of a narcotic betel nut [18]

What impresses Shea is the apparent purposelessness of this old woman's life:
"she walks forever / in the same directions / and is replaced in time / by

another"—an eternal round which makes the Vietnamese appear to Shea (and by extension, to other Americans) dispensable, insignificant, replaceable.

That Vietnamese male behavior differs from American ways leads Shea to the inevitable macho, homophobic conclusion.

> male vietnamese warriors
> walk down the roads
> hand in hand
>
> on bicycles
> when two bicycles are involved
> they ride side by side
> hand in hand
> when riding double
> on one bicycle
> the male in back
> often holds the crotch
> of the male in front
>
> some call it custom
> or a sign of friendship
> or a way of life   [26]

Shea's phrase "way of life" is revelatory here, not only of a homophobia which is of course not Shea's alone, but also a widely held American sentiment that undermined the morale of some American soldiers in Vietnam: if the ARVNs or South Vietnamese soldiers were homosexual, why should Americans be fighting their war for them?

Throughout *vietnam simply,* Shea keeps a wide-eyed fascination, an innocence akin to that of Barry's "boy from Tennessee"; the writing therefore craftily displays a double perspective: the guileless observer on the scene and the judgmental cynic writing at his desk back in the World. For example:

> there was a buddhist viet cong led demonstration today
> they marched past american buildings
> and stoned them
> i love a parade   [35]

This poem displays the speaker's innocence (or more properly, ignorance) of the political situation: that "buddhist" and "viet cong" are discrete categories. The clever touch here, however, is the closing line; "i love a parade" can be read simultaneously as an utterance by the kid-on-Main-Street aspect of Shea's persona as well as the postwar poet's incisive irony.

Shea the poet fluidly orchestrates Shea the speaker's incremental loss of innocence and awakening of political savvy. In a section that begins "caltex gas station," Shea contrasts the station on one side of a street ("flattened tin beer can roof / empty steel barrels . . . for walls") with its "usual gang" of "hot car jockeys" to another "across the street / a shell station / modern everything." Shea's revelation is that the "hot car jockeys" on the Shell side have the identical "long hair / and dirt" as those on the Caltex side: "they are the same on both sides of the street." Shea's closing couplet displays an epiphanic insight— "you can't change a culture / by building a better gas station"—a damning perception for the entire tenor of the American mission in Indochina [53].

Shea begins to cultivate an understanding of the Vietnamese on a personal level: "our vietnamese cook / makes the best pie crust / i have ever tasted" even though "he is ancient / and dirty / and smiles toothlessly / and can't speak english" [61]. He begins to emerge from a sense of American superiority and criticizes the typical American response to the Third World.

> orient is strange
> different perspective
> but their life is livable
> and everything in their atmosphere meshes
> except for one clog
> the american
> he can not understand
> life other than his own
> he tries to convert other peoples
> to his way
> and he does not do it subtly
> in fact   he does not do it at all   [76]

Shea's realization of this lack of subtlety in the American way of "convert[ing] other peoples" leads him to make friends with the Vietnamese: he shows a film to orphans in a Catholic orphanage ("they respond with laughter / in the wrong places / and mixed emotion / when someone hits someone" [81]); for fixing his shoes, he pays an old cobbler woman twenty piastres instead of the ten she charges him; he befriends two street urchins at the Saigon zoo; he siphons gas from his jeep for a stranded Vietnamese dump-truck driver; he offers an aged "papa-san" a ride.

an old man was there
ancient
with long white beard and walking stick
asked him if he wanted a ride
his eyes lit up
and he got in jeep with walking stick
he did not know how to sit exactly
or how to act
his first time i guessed riding in anything
i wound her up to 20 miles per hour
and his face was large and bright   [142]

These are small acts of kindness, but, in the context of what the war would become after the military-advisor period in which Shea went to Vietnam, these are significant acts. They illustrate a humane side of the American presence and dramatize Shea's maturation. Even public defecation begins to have ameliorating character.

she squatted
her baggy body
and dropped her
black pajama bottoms
to fertilize the roadside

perhaps a tree will grow there   [153]

By the end of his tour, only one prejudice against the Vietnamese remains: "seeing the men in the military / sleeping very close to each other / makes me wonder what the women do / to have babies" [178]. Interestingly, however, the penultimate section set in Vietnam stands a full 180° about-face from Shea's initial impressions.

vietnam
land of people
simple people
happy people
not wanting communism
not wanting democracy
not wanting war

                    not wanting change
                    wanting to live and die
                    peacefully
                    simply   [180]

Of course, this is heavily romanticized—Shea does not mention the most important motivating attitude in both North and South Vietnam, *nationalism*—
but nevertheless an amazing statement. The final section set in Vietnam has
only one eloquent line: "i like the vietnamese" [181].

The sections which relate Shea's homecoming uncover many of the situations and conditions that later Vietnam veterans (those who were "grunts" and
not "advisors") would experience. Shea feels isolated in the World, a stranger
in a strange land.

                    i feel nothing on being back
                    just the feeling of wanting to be somewhere else
                    not back there
                    or here

                    just somewhere else   [186]

This sense of rootlessness, of anomie, of some sort of existential despair,
would become a clichéd situation for the returning veteran. What is interesting,
therefore, about Shea's book is its prophetic nature: the way it predicts how
other young American soldiers would feel in and about Vietnam as the war
escalates, and, perhaps more important, how it was possible even during the
war's early phases for a compassionate person to realize insights that, from the
perspective of hindsight, are precise and appropriate—that the war would not
be won by brute force and that the Vietnamese are a valuable people.

There are parallels between Peter Bowman's *Beach Red* and Shea's *vietnam
simply*. Both of them verse novels, they are also ultimately works of philosophy which employ characterization to dramatize their assertions. Both are
bildungsromans chronicling the education of an innocent American in the face
of foreignness and violence. They are political novels, but with different purposes. Bowman's epic carries an antiwar message, whereas Shea upholds the
importance of Vietnam in changing America. The closing section of Shea's
book demonstrates this attitude:

                    this is actually a good war for the americans
                    it gives them experience

in something they know little about

war

and something they are not concerned with

other people   [193]

Shea wants the nation to have the same experience as he has had; it is the logic of *e pluribus unum,* the American fantasy which equates the country with its people in patriotic metonymy. If I was bettered by Vietnam (Shea would have us believe), wouldn't America also be? It is an overly romantic and optimistic viewpoint, of course, and one which predates the *credibility gap* that would arise as government press conferences and fact continued to diverge. Shea retains a certain brand of innocence, despite his experiences in Vietnam.

A crucial difference between Bowman and Shea is that Bowman is very clearly striving for a highly poetic document (hoping that *Beach Red* would become the *Iliad* of WWII), whereas Shea is continually undermining the potential aestheticism of his work. That he does not capitalize, that he uses no periods or commas, that his language is pedestrian—all these are not merely nods toward poetic fashion but are meant to keep his poetry from becoming poetry. And such an antipoetic stance seems somehow apt to his subject. Vietnam, in its apparent squalor and poverty, must have seemed hardly a poetic subject to Shea. It is important to add that this stance does not indicate a lack of poetic talent; Shea *has* written artful descriptions in *vietnam simply:*

vietnamese
highly trained jungle fighter
over polished boots
form fitting camouflage uniform
neatly pressed and pretty
appropriate medals and decorations
long nails
pastel green undershirt
green beret tilted picturesquely
over laquered swept back long hair
a slight well cared for face
with a touch of a moustache
a voice that speaks with candy words
and all covered with a strong sickening scent   [114]

As characterization, this proceeds in a highly craftsmanlike way. The details are carefully placed: "pastel green" juxtaposed to "green beret" and then followed by "over laquered [*sic*] swept back long hair" show us a puffed-up martinet while revealing at the same time Shea's homophobia. Lineation here is well-appointed and graduated, so that the catalog of details, confined to lines of varied lengths, do not acquire a litanylike monotone. Shea's nerve fails here only at the end with the use of "candy" and "sickening," almost as if he had not trusted the subtlety of his portrait to give his reader the appropriate cues; "candy" and "sickening" are simply too ironic and too direct, unlike the well-placed "appropriate" to describe the soldier's typicality.

Shea certainly has the knack of using a well-chosen image to display irony through contrast and juxtaposition, without didactic comment on the poet's part.

> in war zone
> on river of ancient junks
> and basket boats
> maneuvered by ill clad ill fed vietnamese
> flashes by a shiny special services speed boat
> towing an american warrior on water skis
> he is white and pudgy
> with water wings   [168]

Here, Shea uses a symmetrical line pattern to hammer the comparison home: four lines devoted to the Vietnamese term of this syllogism, the lines growing longer; and four lines for the American term, with the lines growing shorter. This visual effect calls attention to the opening and closing—"in war zone" and "with water wings"—to show the ultimate frivolity and impropriety of this American presence. The look of the vignette is likewise a visual echo of the shape of the boat, with its bow pointing toward the right edge of the page, as well as an evocation of the wake behind the boat; this visualness thus creates a metaphor for American motion and American technology, hence progress. What is left, as the unsaid third term of the syllogism, is an aftershock like the violent ripples and waves left by the boat's wake—an aftershock in the reader's mind akin to the "junks / and basket boats" bobbing long after the speedboat has passed.

Shea also delivers one vignette in *vietnam simply* in (almost) traditional rhyme and form.

> i sit together
> in a space of darkness and light
> with limbs twined around me
> shaking away the night
>
> teeth faintly chattering
> stillness prevails
> wind gushes from trees
> like a child's wails
>
> legs tremble slightly
> then more and more
> knob turns slowly
> death is at the door
>
> eyes bugged and tearing
> waiting for death
> door opens slowly
> damn it man
> you scared the shit out of me   [95]

Using quatrains rhymed *abcb* in a very loose trimeter with an occasional lapse into dimeter, Shea opens with a reversal of the slang "together" (to mean *organized, integral,* and hence *effective*) to describe what this vignette is about; it dramatizes the horrors of living in Vietnam, the feeling that death can strike at any moment. Shea therefore borrows from the gothic tradition, fed through Alfred Hitchcock and the slasher film. The speaker's phantasmagoric illusions convince him that perhaps a Vietcong sapper has penetrated to his hooch. Of course, as in the early moments of a slasher film, this fear turns out to be merely sentimental and unfounded. Nevertheless, the audience knows that there *is* a slasher, and this is precisely the effect that Shea wants: to convey the feeling that, despite any macho posturing at the end of the poem, death is potential and sudden in Vietnam. As Michael Herr describes this existential terror:

> You could be in the most protected space in Vietnam and still know that your safety was provisional, that early death, blindness, loss of legs, arms or balls, major and lasting disfigurement—the whole rotten deal— could come in on the freakyfluky as easily as in the so-called expected ways. (14)

Shea's speaker has his "shit" "together" at the end, but he could lose it at any moment.

At the close of this section, Shea abandons the quatrain and returns to his characteristic free-verse mode, although the metrically unmatched rhyme *slowly / out of me* remains. What is perhaps even more important to notice here is the movement into the colloquial: "damn it man / you scared the shit out of me" is a gesture away from high poetics. Although Shea does not explicitly allude to myths of the American West, this use of language reflects a certain kind of westernness, in the sense of cultured easterners and roughshod westerners: slangy, easygoing, brutally innocent.

Richard Currey: Surrealism as a Path to Catharsis

The cathartic poem sometimes relies on violent imagery coupled with the alienness of Vietnam as witnessed through the eyes of youthful Americans—the poem as confession of one's complicity with evil. Don Receveur's "night fear" is a typical example.

> i heard my meatless bones
> clunk together
> saw the ants drink
> from my eyes
> like red ponies
> at brown pools of water
> and the worms in my belly
> moved sluggishly
> delighted. (*Winning* 15)

This poem teeters on the verge of triteness and overstatement, but what rescues it is the projection in the reader's mind of an *actual* experience that certainly lies behind the poem, prompted by Receveur's insistent concreteness—a vision of a dead body rotting in open air, and the speaker's fantasy of entering that dead person's mind. The absurdity and unbelievability of Vietnam is both inside *and* outside the mind. The horrors of firefights and Bouncing Betty mines metastasize into the poet's brain, producing a surrealism which extends not only within the mindscape but also outward into the landscape. Jeffrey Walsh has noted that in Receveur's work "the war seem[s] actualized, made urgent through its particularity" (204). And this urgency implodes into cathartic release for both reader and poet.

This entry of the surrealism of Vietnam into the mind forecasts its arrival in America, carried like shrapnel in flesh. Steven Ford Brown's "After the Vietnam War" dramatizes this state of mind: a fantasy that on calm, moonlit nights, "like a tv set in a dark room / the vietnam dead rise." Brown's allusion to the "tv set" is an indictment of all Americans who watched the war in their living rooms. The point is that they are also implicated, and the apparitions come for them as well: "bodyless heads arms & legs / skitter down pock marked roads." This poem's setting is a landscape of guilt, personal guilt at having participated in the dismembering of these "bodyless" parts of human beings and also the TV viewers' guilt as they vicariously watch while "in the villages / small dark women kneel" to pray or to die. In the closing image, the women cut off their hair and smear ashes on their faces in mourning: "their cries are almost human" (*Demilitarized* 120). The referent for "their" is not merely the mourning "small dark women" and "the vietnam dead" but also by extension the readers—all of whom have been dehumanized—especially when we recall how the U.S. government had claimed that the Vietnamese did not feel sorrow and joy as Americans do. The word "cries" here alludes to all human communication, to poetry, so that writing the poem (as a cathartic act) becomes finally an attempt to recover one's humanity.

Surrealism and fantasy also become an escape from Vietnam, as in Tim O'Brien's novel *Going After Cacciato,* in which the protagonist, during the course of a night of guard duty, fantasizes pursuing a deserter walking from Vietnam to Paris, rationalizing it through a dogged imagining of the realistic requirements at each locale encountered in such a picaresque adventure.

Richard Currey's prose-poetry collection *Crossing Over* is first of all a cathartic document, but interestingly it capitalizes often on the salvific possibilities in surrealism. First comes the admission of beauty in the terrain of Vietnam—lyrical approaching surreal—as in Currey's canto "fourteen":

There is a recurring notion of violin music in the dark, I can't trace it: a thread of what's recalled or forgotten. Looking at everything I can see: sun rising out of the Pacific, all transcendental magenta and scarlet, rain forest rowing north, into a settled haze and mountain, mythological, azure and green. Me at the open port dreaming the view of more than one river at once. ([16], unpaginated)

Currey's persona is here suspended in a helicopter, with all the realistic evocations of such an aerial perspective. In dreams, this surrealism also surfaces as an index of the strangeness of Vietnam—"I dream about two Vietnamese monks. . . . [and] they become trees, the shapes of their bodies the shapes of trees, their feet taking root, their arms and heads branching and leafing and flowering endlessly" ["nineteen" 21]—telegraphing the speaker's romanticized identification of the Vietnamese with a fecund and omnipresent Nature. When, however, the speaker is "humping the boonies" (as the grunts referred to patrolling in the countryside), Currey lifts into the surreal as the only way to express the alienness of what he sees: "Everything about the forest is glazed and bizarre: trees hanging upside down with dark birds floating in the stark roots like fish." The speaker's feet are "huge and foreign, shapeless black oblongs that are connected to me but I cannot feel." And he feels his head "drifting weightless above the feet and legs and chest like a helium balloon towed in a parade" ("thirty-nine" [43]). Even when Currey is back in the rear, in a temporary haven, he finds himself in bed, trapped in a hypnagogic state: "Pearl in my ear. Continual trees, the fabric of my moving hands. Scars still complaining after being told to leave well enough alone" ("twenty-one" [23]).

Currey's poems are memories, reevocations of isolation and extreme anomie, of schism between mind and body: the head "drifting" and dragged along by the rest of the body, the dismemberment of feet as "shapeless black oblongs" to mirror, within the mind's eye, witnessed dismemberment: "A captain is decapitated and his head has rolled to the front of the van where it sticks, looking at me" ("eight" [9]), or "Maldonado in the ditch bottom whispering in Spanish, . . . hands fluting the air . . . His leg gone at the thigh" ("one" [1]). Currey's title *Crossing Over* hence signifies a complex of cultural connotations: Currey as ferryman over the Styx, the duplicate movements of crossing to the 'Nam and then crossing to the World (all crossings over water), the symbology of the *cross* and its connections with sacrifice and salvation, and (perhaps more important) the "crossing over" from mind to body and back— the act of *re*membering as an opposite for *dis*membering. Hence, writing becomes a potential antidote to the violent parceling of bodies in the Vietnam experience.

The problem, however, is that back in the World the speaker *still* feels fragmented, as in the final section of *Crossing Over:*

My hands in front of me on a bus. I never hope for anything. I cannot tell a story, drill sergeants and bus riding erased me, a thousand push ups

for losing my weapon, my piece, my friend. And the long dead rides into
forest. Swamp air lunging at the windshield. The engines of history and
loss above me. ("forty-six" [51])

Writing as antidote is thus a conflicted activity. At the end of *Crossing Over*,
catharsis is still only a possibility and not yet achieved. The act of writing, for
Currey, must continue and does, as the only source for any kind of release,
cleansing, catharsis.

D. C. Berry: e. e. cummings (Re)Aestheticized

D. C. Berry's *saigon cemetery* is a book-length attempt to engage the horror, the tragedy, the absurdity of Vietnam through the surreal as well as the
poetic. As such, Berry operates under a completely opposite assumption from
Shea: that poetry with its entire panoply of imagery, texture of language, and
orchestration of sound is appropriate to render Vietnam—in all of its unreal
magnificence—and ultimately to develop a new poetic aesthetic to encompass
that terrible subject. According to Philip Beidler, Berry feels "the need both to
preserve and fix the experiential memory of Vietnam in all its terrible immediacy and at the same time to suggest its new possibilities of meaning within
some larger, imaginative context of vision common to us all" (*American* 122–
23). *saigon cemetery*'s opening poem takes on a subject similar to that of *Beach
Red*'s closing cantos: what happens in the mind as the thinker lies dying in the
jungle from wounds?

> The sun   gocs
>   down
> a different way when
>
>   you
> are lungshot in a rice
> paddy and you
> are taking a drink of
> your own unhomeostatic
> globules each
>
> Time
>
> you swallow a pail
> of air   pumping like you
> were

bailing out the whole
world   throw
  ing it in your leak
  ing   collapsible lung
that won't hold even
a good quart   and on
top of that   the sun
goes down

    Bang

ing the lung completely
flat.   (3)

This poem is about the betrayal of Nature, the universe suddenly revealing another face, a death's head. The sun, rather than being the giver of life, becomes instead its taker, and the sun's "Bang" at the end is the universe's echo or replication of the rifle's earlier "Bang." The betrayal is complete; air turns into water (from the viewpoint, both cerebral and physical, of the dying man), a distortion of the classical elements. The body itself is complicit in the betrayal, its own "homeostatic / globules" now "un," so that the body's equilibrium is liquidating. Death appropriately comes in darkness, focused on the sole period at the end of the poem.

Berry's poetic ancestor, obviously, is e. e. cummings. It is not only the unusual placement of words on the page, the bizarre lineation, the atypical typography; Berry's characterization of the universe here also reflects cummings's use of natural imagery, for example in a poem like "in Just- / spring" wherein "the world . . . puddle-wonderful" takes on the importance of a personage seemingly ready to cavort with "eddieandbill" and "bettyandisbel" and the "balloonMan" (24).

In "The sun   goes," Berry emulates cummings-style wordplay and letter-play. The poem pivots on the word "Time" so obviously emphasized at the middle of the poem. Since time is what the "you" character here has very little of, it is appropriate that the world (and the poem) begin to revolve around it. But the sun, as the world's clock, is now "different" and so time also has been altered. Essentially, being itself is affected, and Berry signals this by breaking gerunds at "ing"; the effect of this is that the nounlike "throwing" is wrenched violently into its verb form "throw," calling attention to the terrible despair of the dying man as he fights for breath. And *breath* is also important prosodically here, in Charles Olson's projective sense; the heaving lung ("collapsible") can

muster only enough breath to launch one syllable ("throw" or "leak") before
having to draw another breath to project the next syllable ("ing"). By the end
of the poem, this dynamic becomes the instrument of death as "Banging"
becomes "Bang"—the ultimate piledriver.

The Vietnamese landscape becomes inextricably tied to the people in Berry's
poems, and surreal imagery becomes a currency applicable to all. Note this
evocation of night:

> The dark mountains   rise
>   (mystery
> in the skies ten
> miles high
> in Orient ink
> black as a
> Vietdame's harlot
>   bought hair
> hung down to her thumbed
>   navel
>
> black as a
> Vietdame's harlot
>   bought hair
> hung down to her thumbed
>   navel
>
>   but
> not black as her mystery
> sold for retail!)
> black as the Vietdame
> Virgin who waits like
>   a mustard seed
>   for them to be crushed
> by her
> glacier of Hope   (35)

The word "black" here becomes equated to "mystery." For the grunt, after
all, dark is the realm of the Vietcong, and the night is shrouded in danger and
furious enigma. As Herr put it: "one place or another it was always going on,
rock around the clock, we had the days and he had the nights" (14). Berry's
speaker tries here to domesticate the night by equating it to a "Vietdame's . . .
hair"—after all, it's only a "harlot['s] bought" wig, right? The analogy is re-

peated in the poem, almost as if the speaker is repeating "Right? Right?" in a flurry of desperate rationalization. But nevertheless the "mystery" refuses to be demystified, even though it is "sold for retail!"

The crucial typographical device to notice here is Berry's parentheses, which enclose the section in which the speaker is attempting to rationalize and de-mystify the night. In fact, there is a larger truth, beyond any American ratio-nality: the "mountains," Nature itself, are mystically associated with a "Viet-dame / Virgin." And this Virgin is the *land,* which "waits . . . for [Americans] to be crushed"; the "glacier of Hope" is the hope of the Vietnamese magnified by the mythical lens of the land herself. The "mustard seed" and the "Virgin" of course are biblical allusions, which underline the ways in which the seem-ingly insignificant have the potential to *engender* terrible power. This poem is therefore a mythic paean to Vietnam as a vessel of victory and to the folly of contesting Nature.

Berry reminds us in poem after poem that in Vietnam there was an unavoid-able mixture of popular myth, and these intrusions into the traditional fabric of Vietnam were incongruous, lending to the absurdity and surreality. "If I'm zapped   bury me / with a / comicbook," writes Berry, "let // Tennyson keep his / buried William Shakespeare." Elite culture is displaced by popular cul-ture. The speaker then fantasizes the life after being zapped: "in my new life I'll be // Clark Kent // instead / of // Superman" (38). The point is that death in this context is belittled by slang, and hence domesticated; given a second chance, the speaker would choose to be human rather than superhuman—in the World instead of in the 'Nam. Not to be superhuman involves avoiding life-and-death choices, a retreat into a "comicbook" world.

The transfusion of American popular culture is of course intended to make Vietnam seem somehow more like home, but the obvious distortions which accrue become dislocating. There are rockets "bursting / rudely // in spasms / of James Brown // Soul" shooting out of "Armed Forces Radio" (44); the supreme irony in this, Berry notes, is that the American radio network is effec-tively "the VC's / Forward Artillery Observer" announcing "between bursts of / rock and roll and soul / music" where Vietcong ordnance is striking. It is almost as if the radio (a technological intrusion) is in collusion with the Viet-cong as the land itself seems to be, and at the close of the poem the "spasms of James Brown Soul" can almost be read "the spasms of James Brown's Soul"— that is, the death of Americans and Americanism.

There are references to nineteenth-century American popular myth. "At Dak To Casey Jones / was killed in a gunship" rather than in a train, but here this Casey Jones does not die a romantically heroic death. He only makes a mistake: "he let [the helicopter] whirr / hot-throttle into Hill 919" (45). In other words, the human being does not transcend the curse of technology; he is merely swallowed up by it.

There are allusions to literary culture. A poem apostrophizes "Miss Flannery O'Connor" who is in "Saigon cemetery . . . casual about death. / your tongue gone / black chalk" (49). Even O'Connor's grotesques, steeped as they are in southern gothic, are unable to withstand the alienness of Vietnam, and even chalk, the teacher's writing instrument, is reversed, made negative. Another poem begins "Go catch a falling burningstar / and give it to the Vietnamese Piers / Plowman peasant," alluding in several quick breaths to the whole of English literature, from the medieval Langland through John Donne to the present whose contribution is an *illumination flare;* the tension here is between realms of knowledge, between technology and the organic "mandrake-root" wisdom of the peasant. The speaker advises what to do with the "burningstar": "tell [the peasant] it is rice given / from heaven," that is, fabricate lies like "body counts," and "pacification," and "light at the end of the tunnel," and the peasant will not be fooled, "knowing rain / can't / rainup" (19).

What remains most memorable about *saigon cemetery,* finally, is Berry's aestheticism: a Modernist poetic based on haunting visual imagery and cummings-style orthography. Such lines as "Tangerines and white / marshmallows pop before the / soldier's eyesbriefly   with the pop / of the AK-47" (24) or "a 20mm red-tailed tracer / tearing like a comet into his face" (46) are burned into memory as they attempt to bring the unknowable into our ken through analogy with what we might know: "marshmallows," "a comet." Sometimes, Berry is successful in marrying this visual quality to his orchestration of the poem on the page:

> An airplane   jets
> cross sky that
> carries it
> with its
> bellyload of dumbbombs til
> the airplane   jets   in
> to a pock of
> flak   flak flak   flak   that
> flaks it
>
> jetswatter

splat

the

jetplane

fumble/tumbles

down

like

a common house

fly.   (9)

The poem *becomes* its own image, dramatizing in the placement of the words on the page the narrative itself. When the bomber's crash occurs at the end of the poem, we find an elaborate extended pun: the bomber is turned into a "common house // fly" and the unheard crash itself is an ironic overturning of the verb "fly." W. D. Ehrhart suggests, "In many of Berry's poems, lines, pieces of lines, and words are scattered across the page like dismembered body parts, mimicking that all-too-frequent reality of the war" ("Soldier-Poets" 249). To illustrate Ehrhart's point, consider the following sequence which refers to Time:

> . . . when
> you don't watch
>
>   it it
>
> 's
>
> running pummeling pell
> mell   hell
>
> ter
>   skel
>
> ter
>
>   like a thing   (17)

This technique most resembles Ehrhart's suggestion when actual words are broken, uncovering words like "hell" and "terror," uncompleted as "ter."

Clearly, Berry's poetry is a heroic attempt to come to grips with an experi-

ence that seems beyond any ability to be reproduced, and Berry is attempting architectonically to create a poetry with the flexibility to accomplish that.
Where Berry is weakest is when he sacrifices his vision to puns that are too easy.
For example, tanks portrayed with "hard   feeted / tracks" later find themselves in "de feet" as their "several // patellas   pop" (13); it is difficult enough
to seriously connect "patellas" with "tanks," but "de feet" simply makes it
ludicrous. Or the verbal tic of a soldier's "spinal chord" knocked "completely
out of tune" (48), a pun that relies too heavily on our orthographic recognition
that a letter "h" has been inserted into the word "cord."

As Beidler points out, however, Berry's book "ends on a note of possibility . . . that serviceable meaning can be made, the memory of things at least
at times assimilated into common imaginative terms that consciousness can
bear" (*American* 129). In the final poem, Berry admits his faith in poetry:

> A poem ought to be a salt lick
> rather than sugar candy.
> A preservative.
> Something to make a tongue
> tough enough to taste
> the full flavor
> of beauty and grief.

Whether or not Berry feels he has accomplished poetry "to make a tongue /
tough enough," he nevertheless registers his faith that it can be so. The poem
and the book address the reader directly:

> Already my tongue bleeds from
> the yellow slash of Forsythia
> that must be blooming
> where you are.   (50)

Berry seems to suggest that the poet can reach out of the 'Nam and into the
World to reestablish connections, come home. And for Berry this is best done
through a commitment to highly aestheticized poetics.

Coda: The Wild West as Failed Myth

These poems—by Shea, Currey, Berry, or a host of others—reveal the inadequacy of mythic conceptions of a Wild West or a virgin land to apprehend

Vietnam. The country, the land, the people are completely and utterly beyond the grasp of this myth. As a result, when Vietnam veterans literally use the myth of the American West in poems on Vietnam, they are forced to admit the solipsism of such mythopoeia. When Don Receveur, for example, creates a gunship pilot who operates "in the Wild West / of his mind" (*Winning* 49), his language is careful to point out that this "Wild West" exists only in the western-movie mentality of the pilot. It is significant that John F. Kennedy created the metaphor of the New Frontier; as Caputo put it, "we believed in all the myths created by that most articulate and elegant mythmaker, John Kennedy. If he was the King of Camelot, then we were his knights and Vietnam our crusade" (69–70). Effectively, Kennedy had welded chivalry and the West, galvanizing the country with his famous inaugural imperative: "Ask not what your country can do for you. . . ." But in November 1963 his New Frontier was assassinated with him. "It all seemed wild and crazy like some Texas shoot-out," remembers Ron Kovic (59)—and LBJ, the true heir of the West, seemed to have betrayed the sacred western myths as American credibility grew thinner and more rarefied. JFK "had celebrated the American mythic landscape in a poetic image . . . bound up in America's past geographical drive West into a many-leveled pursuit of national adventure and mission," argues John Hellmann, "but a decade after his death Vietnam seemed to have cut Americans off from both their past and future frontiers" (95).

TWO. MACHINE IN THE JUNGLE

The year following the fall of Diêm in Saigon (an event that accelerated the escalation of American intervention in Vietnam), Leo Marx coined the phrase "Machine in the Garden" as a "cultural symbol" to emblematize the "powerful metaphor of contradiction" (4) that epitomizes the hybridization of technology with the pastoral ideal in American culture, imaged as the train's penetration into the American interior. Note the inherent machismo contained in the ideological encoding of this myth. If Vietnam was seen as an expansion of the Wild West territory, a virgin land with the potential to be a garden, then it is inevitable, given American presence, that the machine would intrude. This machine, however, was not Marx's symbolic "train" but rather the entire machinery of the American military-industrial complex and the technologically oriented set of mind. Forty years before American involvement in Vietnam, D. H. Lawrence had already prophesied the hegemony of technology in the Vietnam war: "the most idealist nations invent most machines. America simply teems with mechanical inventions, because nobody in America ever wants to *do* anything. They are idealists. Let a machine do the doing" (32). In the Vietnam war, this would be altered into "let a machine do the killing."

The grunts—true Lawrentian Americans—were keenly aware of their tools:

> The only technology you have is death: M-16s—black plastic rifles—grenades, pocket bombs, Claymores, M-79s, M-60s, mortars, jungle utilities, flak jackets, jungle boots, C4, radios and jet planes to drop the napalm. That was the only technology happening. (Baker 102)

This veteran's catalog defines only the M-16, falling back on the jargony shorthand of the military. The M-79 is a grenade launcher, the M-60 a "general purpose" machine gun, and C4 a plastic explosive. The account leaves out the flamethrower (and its little brother, the Zippo lighter, a ubiquitous piece of grunt equipment) as well as the LAW (or light antitank weapon, a miniature, plastic, *disposable* bazooka) and yet other hand-held weapons.

There were mines. These were not merely explosive devices buried underground, but highly specialized weapons designed to inflict particular kinds of injuries and deaths. For example, there was the "Bouncing Betty," which first jumps a yard into the air before exploding; its purpose was to cut a person in half. Claymores were directional mines, crescent-shaped and planted above ground; when set off, they would explode buckshot from the convex side, serving as an explosive barrier to protect the soldier on the concave side. William Westmoreland describes a mine of which he seems particularly proud. "Little gravel mines, which took their name from their appearance, were sufficient to incapacitate a man who stepped on one, yet friendly troops could enter the area later because the mines self-sterilized in a few weeks" (281). And there were other horribly sophisticated armaments. " 'Beehive' artillery rounds," according to Westmoreland, "released thousands of little pellets," actually fléchettes (281). A whole array of artillery pieces fired rounds like the "beehive" and conventional shells. All sorts of "track" vehicles: armored personnel carriers (or APCs), tanks. Perhaps the most horrific and best-known bit of technology was napalm, a jellied gasoline that stuck to human skin and was extremely difficult to remove as it burned.

Effectively, Vietnam became a laboratory for the technowar[1] brokers and weapons addicts of the Pentagon. Westmoreland, writing of weaponry, registers an almost religious faith in technology:

> Some of the electronic developments were impressive. By magnifying light from the stars, the "Starlight Scope" enabled men . . . to see at night. "People Sniffers" could detect human presence, primarily from the odor of urine. The Mark 36 destructor was a mine dropped from planes [which] once it was in position detonated if moved or if movement occurred near it. (281)

Westmoreland had been the number-one technocrat and prophet of technowar. In 1969 he revealed his creed[2] that "we are on the threshold of an entirely new battlefield concept." This concept was the "automated battlefield" on which "enemy forces will be located, tracked, and targeted almost instantaneously through the use of data links, computer assisted intelligence evaluation, and automated fire control." The presence of "24 hour real or near real time surveillance" would mean "we can destroy anything we can locate through instant communications and the almost instantaneous application of highly lethal firepower." This strategy would involve a complex combination of "hundreds of surveillance, target acquisition, night observation and information processing systems either in being, in development, or in engineering" (Dickson 218–22). And this kind of thinking[3] is still rampant in the United States, as evidenced by the Strategic Defense Initiative (SDI)—the proposed network of "defense" machinery orbiting in space. "Let a machine do the doing," said Lawrence.

Inevitably, poems by Vietnam veterans reflect this war-machine environment. For Stanley Brownstein, the "Sounds of War" were intrinsically bound up with this technology: such sounds as the "tympanic boom" of bomb-strikes, the "lightning crash" of fighter planes overhead, the "whizzing slash" of shrapnel in air, "the thud of napalm as it hits the ground, / And the click of your weapon as you chamber a round." Interestingly, Brownstein uses rhyme and meter here to achieve a mechanistic drone, nicely complementing his subject matter. When human sounds are heard, their voicings are occasioned by technological power: "screams," "whispered prayers," and "silence of the dead" (*Winning* 10). At the close, Brownstein abandons the rhyme scheme in order to dissociate people from machines, and as the final stanza unfolds, there is an incremental hushing of noise.

An often-used poetic strategy is juxtaposing technology with nature for effect—a concretization of Leo Marx's metaphoric "machine in the garden"— as in "One Night on Guard Duty" by W. D. Ehrhart, where the speaker, startled by "the first salvo" of artillery fire, is abruptly seized by the conceit that the seemingly illimitable power of the American war machine is wrinkling the very fabric of the universe, expressed in a strikingly apt image, aural as well as visual: "The shells arc up, / tearing through the air like some invisible hand / crinkling giant sheets of cellophane among the stars." The speaker, "breathless," projects his own breathlessness onto the night, the chaos of darkness and wilderness beyond civilization's perimeter "till the far horizon erupts in brilliant / pulsing silence" (*Tired* 7). In fact, however, the night in its magnitude merely *absorbs* the concussion, a "brilliant / pulsing" but nevertheless a "silence." On the literal level, it is distance from the target which keeps us from hearing the explosion of the shell as we see it; but on the level of symbol, the night has here reestablished its dominion, belying the tenuous authority of "the guns." Hence, Ehrhart's poem is an imaginative critique of the American strategy of "harassment and interdiction" artillery fire in which uncountable rounds were fired during the night on unseen targets chosen at random (almost by lottery of grid coordinates) in the hope that this would somehow hamper the Vietcong's readiness and will to fight.

Occasionally, poems would turn to the lighter side of military technology, but at the same time the comedy of technological snafus is shown as being personally dangerous. Balancing the title of Larry Rottman's poem, "Rifle, 5.56MM, XM16E1," against its epigraph, "The M-16 rifle you are armed with is the best weapon there is for use here in Vietnam," uncovers its laconic irony:

> The M-16 sure is a marvelous gun.
> In a god-awful war
> it provides some keen fun.

Rottmann's cutting sarcasm in this poem is accomplished by pitting the first line of each stanza with the shorter second and third lines; in fact, the closing lines are really half-lines which, if put together, would make the stanza a rhymed iambic pentameter couplet. What Rottmann has done is to disassemble the *heroic couplet* and, by making it unheroic, to call attention to the irony of the message. Rottmann alludes here to the tendency of the M-16 to jam in the heat of a firefight, so that "keen fun" turns out to be a serious, life-threatening matter.

> Listen to Ichord and forget that stuck bolt.
> You aren't as important
> as a kickback from Colt.   (*Winning* 11)

A marine who had fought in Khe Sanh in 1967 wrote an angry complaint to Congress: "Do you know what killed most of us? Our own rifles. Practically every one of our dead was found with his rifle torn down next to him where he was trying to fix it" (Doleman 39). Rottmann's phrase "a kickback from Colt" is of course a condemnation of general officers (who would presumably receive the "kickback") and American corporations. In point of fact, though, there were mechanical problems with the M-16, resulting from government ineptitude, and Congressman Ichord's inquiry resulted in some improvements, but the M-16 never achieved its mechanical potential.[4] The Catch-22 aspects of this situation are succinctly encapsulated by Rottmann's lines, "Just pray you won't need [your M16] / While you're in Vietnam."

Rottmann's style and language are interesting because he uses the language of everyday speech, shaped into rhyming units, that qualify it essentially as doggerel. In fact, this is quite appropriate both for Rottmann's subject—the day-by-day existence of the soldier—as well as his audience—veterans and soldiers who, as part of their military training, have learned marching songs, cadences that are also doggerel. For example:

I Wanna Go To Viet-Nam
I Wanna Kill A Viet-Cong

With A Knife Or With A Gun
Either Way Will Be Good Fun

Stomp 'Em, Beat 'Em, Kick 'Em In The Ass
Hide Their Bodies In The Grass

Airborne, Ranger, C.I.B.
Nobody's Gonna Fuck With Me

But If I Die In The Combat Zone
Box Me Up And Ship Me Home

Fold My Arms Across My Chest
Tell My Folks I Done My Best

Place A Bible In My Hand
For My Trip To The Promised Land   (*Winning* 1)

This cadence is, in fact, one used in a training setting, but this sort of verse
appears in many other military contexts. Helicopter pilot Robert Mason, in his
memoir *Chickenhawk,* recalled one company song, *"The Fuckee's Hymn"*:

He stood on the steeple
And pissed on the people
But the people couldn't
Piss on him.
Amen   (158)

On the day Mason arrived at another unit, he discovered a group at the officers'
club composing a ditty:

Army Aviators sing this song,
It won't be long for the Vietcong.
The sky troopers sail through the air,
To set our traps like catchin' bears.   (385)

Interestingly, these men are composing the poem for a contest: " 'We get a
decent song, we get invited to Saigon for two days in the sing-off. . . . You
wanna have two days to fuck off in Saigon, don'cha?' " (387).

But such doggerel is not always so humorous or lighthearted. One sample "Composed by GIs of the 1st Air Cavalry Div[ision]" (a unit in which Mason served in Vietnam) highlights in its refrain a particularly grisly conjunction of military technology and civilians:

> We shoot the sick, the young, the lame,
> We do our best to kill and maim,
> Because the kills count all the same,
> Napalm sticks to kids.

Moral distancing from the consequences of killing—the hallmark of such technology—is apparent in this stanza:

> Blues out on a road recon,
> See some children with their mom,
> What the hell, let's drop the bomb,
> Napalm sticks to kids.   (*Peace* 22)

Whether or not the "GIs" who composed this verse were necessarily aware of the horrible ironies voiced by these stanzas, what *is* unavoidable is that *napalm* and its effects have constituted and continue to constitute an unavoidable (and unforgettable) image of the Vietnam war.

In *The Great War and Modern Memory,* Paul Fussell proposes that the characteristic image of WWI was the *trench,* a word and phenomenon so ubiquitous it governed the life and thinking of the combatants (37). In fact, military terminology used in Vietnam (and still currently in use) were holdovers from trench warfare, including *sapper, stand-to,* and *stand-down.* The term sapper is the noun form of the verb *to sap,* which refers to extending one's trench to intersect the enemy trench as a surprise attack. The other two terms refer to a ledge or step built up on the side of a trench; stand-to meant to prepare for action by standing up on the ledge, rifle in hand, to face the enemy also standing-to on his ledge; stand-down, therefore, meant "rest," by literally stepping off the ledge so that one's head would drop below the line of fire. In current military usage, these terms still mean "to be prepared, be on alert" and "to relax," generally applied to entire units.

To match the WWI trench, the central image of the Vietnam war is the *helicopter,* appropriated and now assimilated by American media. A clear example of this assimilation is the television program *China Beach:* the trademark auditory logo of the show, played before and after commercials, is two or three

seconds of helicopter rotor wash. The sonic image alone is sufficient to semaphore "Vietnam" to anyone born before 1960 and perhaps even later. The
grunt-oriented TV show *Tour of Duty* opens with Huey helicopters in flight—
"slicks" or troop carriers—with the Rolling Stones' "Paint It Black" accompanying the wind rushing through the open cabins in which fully armed soldiers
tensely slouch. These visual images have acquired a currency in popular culture; witness the raw power and gung ho excitement of the scene in the film
Apocalypse Now where gunships attack a village, tracers strafing the entire
landscape. Michael Herr captures the gestalt of choppers:

> In the months after I got back the hundreds of helicopters I'd flown in
> began to draw together until they'd formed a collective meta-chopper,
> and in my mind it was the sexiest thing going; saver-destroyer, provider-
> waster, right hand–left hand, nimble, fluent, canny and human; hot steel,
> grease, jungle-saturated canvas webbing, sweat cooling and warming up
> again, cassette rock and roll in one ear and door-gun fire in the other, fuel,
> heat, vitality and death, death itself, hardly an intruder. (9)

"Airmobility" was the military name for it, a doctrine predicated on the helicopter's vaunted flexibility to subsume so many functions—troop carrier, gunship, scout aircraft, ambulance, matériel transport—as well as its speed and
its ability to take off and land vertically in relatively small spaces (compared
to fixed-wing aircraft). Washington considered it the ultimate "counterinsur-
gency" weapon.[5]

The deadliest helicopter was the slim Huey Cobra, used solely as a gunship.
It carried only two persons, the gunner and the pilot, and was very heavily
armed, typically with grenade launchers, rocket pods, and miniguns (a misleading term—this weapon could fire "6,000 rounds per minute, and up to
56 manually-dispensed flares" [Francillon 71]). It is of course inevitable that
such a macho multiplex of weapons would become an object of awe as well
as guts-and-glory romance. Don Receveur's poem "Cobra Pilot" opens with
a description of the pilot's "Plastic blue eyes / and hair / the color of toggle
switches" and continues, "His Nebraska smile / is a mini-gun / and his bowels /
are full of rockets." The pilot and his Cobra mythically merge into a cyborg—a
cybernetic organism, the ultimate merger of machine and human.[6] As the pilot
begins to take on the characteristics of a manufactured object—"plastic blue"
and "the color of toggle switches"—the helicopter appropriates qualities of a
living animal; it becomes a "cobra-shark" which the pilot "flies . . . with the
precision / of a god / or a gunfighter." The "precision" offered by technology

is equated to "god[hood]," and the mythic realm is revealed by the parallel of "god" and "gunfighter."[7] The significant lines of Receveur's poem are found in the closing: the ubiquitous mythic/historic equation of "Indians" and "gooks," yes, but more important, "the Wild West / *of his mind*" (*Winning* 49, emphasis mine). Receveur's critique is plain. This collusion of technology and the Wild West myth results in the self-deception of the "gunfighter" persona, given the actuality of Vietnam.

Such delusions were tragically lethal for Vietnamese. Mark Baker interviewed a helicopter door gunner who recalled the aftermath of a ground-air firefight:

> There were literally hundreds and hundreds of Vietnamese fleeing the area, any way they could. Panic. . . . Time to get the hell out of Dodge. . . . They were leaving in boats, slogging on foot, anything. I don't know if they ran out of ammunition or what, but we were taking very little fire at that point and we were just killing everybody.
> It turned into a turkey shoot. They were defenseless. There were three or four light fire teams working the area. Hundreds of people were being mowed down. Bodies were floating in the water. Insane. . . . I remember thinking this insane thought, that I'm God and retribution is here, now, in the form of my machine gun and the Miniguns that I take care of and the rockets that we are firing. (Baker 154)

Again, we find the helicopter at the nexus of conflation: the Wild West and technology. Certain phrases are revelatory: "get the hell out of Dodge," "turkey shoot," and "God and retribution." The clichéd confrontation in western movies between the good guy and the bad guy is here realized; the soldier has appropriated the Marshal Dillon role, and the Vietnamese are being figuratively evicted from town by sundown (though of course the reality is inexpressibly worse). That the phrase "get the hell out of Dodge" was a common expression in the military and later throughout much of American culture only reveals how epidemic is the "Wild West" myth. "Turkey shoot," of course, refers to a western contest of marksmanship in which the reward is a prize turkey; in the door gunner's context, the unavoidable equation is between the Vietnamese and the turkey, an ugly and stupid bird. Of course, the phrase "turkey shoot" is now such a dead metaphor that it becomes difficult for us to recapture its original signification, but its vernacular currency is even more widespread than "get the hell out of Dodge."

That the fact of being *in* the air and having a "godly" perspective alongside

the cliché of the western good guy cleaning up Main Street would combine
into "God and retribution" becomes patently obvious—a disastrous side effect
of airmobility. Jack Strahan's poem "God Is My Helicopter" deals with this
same oxymoron, troping on the phrase "God is my co-pilot"; the poem is an
apostrophe to the helicopter: "I am awed in your fearful beauty, / sculptured
steel-green metal slick." Strahan pushes the conceit to the ultimate: "Alive,
alive, we drank your sweet, clean wine / . . . your pilot-priest, gunner-acolyte,
flying, / machine guns sighing holy rage / . . . dropping / napalm-psalms and
one-point-two-inch rocket mana." The speaker, undercut by the poet's strident
ironic tone, virtually worships the helicopter and its terrible proximity by radio:
"We knelt in honest fervor . . . for your sacred airborne blessing. / What God
has ever stood so fast in answered prayer" (Topham, *Vietnam Literature Anthology* 24). Strahan perhaps pushes the poem too far into the didactic, losing
the point through redundancy, but it is interesting to note how Strahan uses
Old Testament language—"shadow of your power," "David's modern sling,"
"borne again" (a delightful pun on *born again,* referring here, however, to
chopper rescue). Strahan underlines the ways in which technowar becomes a
kind of religion sufficient unto itself.

The heart of the matter is that airmobility was not the "godsend" which
technowar bureaucrats assumed it would be. Even as helicopter strategy was
being developed and refined in Vietnam, military expertise lobbied against
the helicopter's use. "Opponents of helicopters feel . . . they are too easy to
shoot down or trap. . . . But a subtle argument against helicopters is that they
tend to create a reliance on the part of Vietnamese troops and commanders on
gadgetry" (Browne, *New Face* 55). A U.S. Army advisor in Vietnam admitted:

> "After all . . . the Viet Cong have no helicopters or airplanes. They didn't
> have any during the Indochina War either, but they still won. Helicopters
> are a partial substitute for infantry discipline, dedication and energy. They
> are useful in emergencies. But they are no substitute for first-class in-
> fantrymen willing to fight.
>
> "After all, when you come to think of it, the use of helicopters is a
> tacit admission that we don't control the ground. And in the long run,
> it's control of the ground that wins or loses wars." (Browne, *New Face*
> 55–56)

Herr, whose experience in Vietnam was during the heyday of airmobility,
points up the issue of ground vs. air:

The ground was always in play, always being swept. Under the ground was his, above it was ours. We had the air, we could get up in it but not disappear in *to* it, we could run but we couldn't hide, and he could do each so well that sometimes it looked like he was doing them both at once, while our finder just went limp. (14)

In fact, the airmobile concept carried its weaknesses intrinsically. James Gibson has observed that "the noises of war machines—planes, helicopters, and armored vehicles—and the highly routinized pattern of most search-and-destroy missions meant that the Vietnamese knew where American forces were" (104). In fact, since LZs (or landing zones) were first reconnoitered by aircraft, marked with a "smoke round," "prepared" by artillery bombarding the surrounding area, and so on, the element of surprise which airmobility could offer is easily lost.[8]

Besides the tactical disadvantages of airmobility, there were other costs. Gabriel Kolko notes that "the early UH-1s could carry only eight to ten combat soldiers, and therefore the army required them in ever-growing numbers" (192). Gloria Emerson points to the price tags: "the little fat UH-1 Huey, called a slick or bird, which cost $300,000, . . . the daintier OH-6 for observation which cost $100,000. . . . the Cobra gunship—cost, $500,000; the CH-47 Chinook . . . which cost $1,500,000 . . . and the Flying Crane, the $2,000,000 CH-54" (263). Development, purchase, and replacement costs, especially for damaged and lost machines, were not all, however. Kolko emphasizes the "routine cost [that] was even more of a burden. Each hour in the air required ten hours of maintenance, and the choppers' fuel consumption was enormous" (192).

One humanistic use of the helicopter was "medevac" or "dust-off," that is, airlifting wounded troops out of the combat zone to a hospital. One result is that, although of course grunts at the time considered the helicopter as a kind of saving angel, the experience of the dust-off could become the stuff of nightmare for the veteran back in the World. Basil Paquet's "Night Dust-Off" illustrates this.

> A sound like hundreds of barbers
> stropping furiously, increases;
> suddenly the night lights,
> flashing blades thin bodies
> into red strips

> hunched against the wind
> of a settling slickship.
>
> Litters clatter open,
> hands reaching
> into the dark belly of the ship
> touch toward moans,
> they are thrust into a privy,
> feeling into wounds,
> the dark belly all wound,
> all wet screams riven limbs
> moving in the beaten night.   (*Winning* 18)

Paquet, a medic in Vietnam, alludes in the poem's opening lines to the historical fact that medieval barbers were surgeons, and he connects thereby both technowar and the technology of modern medicine to a "less civilized" era. The "barber" image also puns on the helicopter's rotors as razors, so that the wounded waiting to be evacuated are "thin bodies" metaphorically sliced "into red strips." Paquet's syntax hurtles intently here from fully formed sentences into nightmarish fragments, the language appropriating the condition of "riven limbs," as the medic immersed in horror struggles to save life, "feeling into wounds." The rescue helicopter itself becomes inseparable from the rapacious war machine, whose representation here is both rough beast—"the dark belly of the ship"—and fecal repository—"a privy."

Michael Herr's impressionistic evaluation of the helicopter in Vietnam is finally, perhaps, the most eloquent.

> Airmobility, dig it, you weren't going anywhere. It made you feel safe, it made you feel Omni, but it was only a stunt, technology. Mobility was just mobility, it saved lives or took them all the time . . . what you really needed was a flexibility far greater than anything the technology could provide." (13)

Ron Kovic occasionally wondered if the helicopter really was beneficial. "He was a half-dead corpse. . . . brought back with all their new helicopters and wonderful new ways of killing people, all that incredible advancement in technology. He would never have come back from any other war" (151).

The helicopter was not the only aerial technology used in Vietnam. One of the most diabolical debacles of the war was the spraying of the herbicide Agent Orange, which contains *dioxin*—" 'the most toxic small molecule known to man' " (Matthew Meleson quoted by Wilcox xv). This action was an utter negation of the mythic potentiality of Vietnam as garden, in diametrical opposition to America's advertised "greening" in preserving the environment. This reversal was linguistically emphasized by the defoliators' motto, "Only You Can Prevent Forests" (Westmoreland 304). It was a similar irony that the name of the defoliation program was "Operation Ranch Hand" (note the Wild West connection), especially when defoliants were used to destroy Vietnamese *crops*.[9]

This devastating intrusion of the machine into the garden was intended to deny the Vietcong ground cover, but it was hardly an effective strategy, and in fact there was a tremendous backfire vis-à-vis the safety of the grunts.[10] R. L. Barth's "The Last Patrol; or, The Dangers of Agent Orange" narrates "Smitty's last patrol" as "typical" until "their cover ended. / Neither briefing nor map amended / Defoliated jungle green." The soldiers cross the "strange clearing":

> Half across,
> Ambushed, they lay like broken joss-
> Sticks on the dust. Though cover denied
> Charlie in theory, all eight died.
> And oddly, it seemed somehow right,
> When only rifles have fore-sight.   (*Soldier's Time* 58)

Despite the glib pun in the closing couplet, this poem eloquently dramatizes a lack of imagination in American policy, a shortsightedness in not realizing that, although jungle gave cover to the Vietcong, it also provided cover for Americans.

Of course, defoliation had other effects on American combatants, effects with deadly ramifications in the World. As one Vietnam veteran admitted on TV, " 'I died in Vietnam, but I didn't even know it' " (Wilcox ix). The U.S. Army distributed leaflets marked " 'Set your mind at ease, because these chemicals do not harm your health or lives' " (Robert Chandler quoted by Gibson 289). But this reassurance has since been proved false, even mendacious, as veterans and their children have suffered "skin rashes, weakness of limbs, nervous disorders, liver disease, heart murmurs, cancer, loss of libido" (Wilcox 13), "chloracne, a severe skin rash similar to teenage acne . . . and multiple birth defects" (Wilcox xi). Wilcox also records that the U.S. Food and Drug Administration has called dioxin " '100,000 times more potent than thalidomide as a cause of birth defects in some species' " (Jacqueline Verrett quoted by Wilcox xi). The continuing tragedy is that the Veterans Administration has offered little help in this epidemic situation.[11]

Agent Orange in America has been surfacing more and more as a theme in the work of Vietnam-veteran poets. Steve Mason refers to it in a portion of a long poem entitled "The Casualty."

> The combat veteran of Vietnam
> lived in a world
> where medals occasionally pinned themselves
> on donkeys
> and the green disappeared from the trees—
> attacked by the one word in his language
> which refused to rhyme;
> Orange.
>
> Years later,
> It would bleach the rainbows
> from his children's eyes
> and then, nothing rhymed.
> (not even God)
> and least of all, DOW.
>
> The combat trooper searched to destroy.
> In the end,
> as a veteran,
> he searched only to understand.   (*Johnny's Song* 77–78)

In these prosaic lines, Mason's point is patently obvious: even in the Vietnam war, irrational as it was, Agent Orange was even more irrational ("refused to rhyme"), and its spillover into the World was an even greater irrationality ("nothing rhymed"). All the veteran wants now is somehow to rationalize the craziness, *naturalize* it (in Barthes's term), if "only to understand."

Somewhat more personal and immediate is John P. McAfee's "A War Story," which begins "Son, I'll not tell you war stories / For you are one," and then describes the four-year-old son in a hospital bed recovering from surgery to correct Agent Orange deformities: "surgeon's shrapnel scars / From your penis to your belly." The interesting turn of the screw here is a reference to myth—something the father and son share as American males—they have both been "Fed on John Wayne and Agent 007." Of course, "Agent 007" is licensed to kill (a macho desire), but the other "Agent" is realistically a killer. The losses are dynastic—Agent Orange "killed our future bloodlines"—but more immediately they are deeply personal and devastating (Topham, *Vietnam Heroes II* 5).

As more and more cases of Agent Orange poisoning arise, the ongoing poetry of Vietnam veterans has turned increasingly toward this important topic. In the poetry of Bill Shields, particularly, the history of a family's deep tragedy and sorrow can be traced. "A Daughter" speaks of the juxtapositional ironies of legacy.

> My Navy Cross under her bed
> these fourteen years
> framed with my honorable discharge
> & her own genetic flak jacket
> I also brought
> home   (*Nam* 33)

In "My Daughter," Shields begins with the lines "I lie awake nights thinking of you dying / that small blond head dwarfed by adult pillows / your screams of pain," and he ends with a father's double-edged wish for the daughter's peace: "waiting / for the Agent Orange / to finish the job" (*Drinking* [22], unpaginated). Shields's "how the hell can" tries to awaken the reader, to "make the pain . . . sit next to you in your livingroom." The speaker can see no purpose in "describ[ing] Agent Orange in shades / of vivid cancers & sad birth defects," and he points the reader instead toward "the grave of my 6 year old daughter" (73). The recurrent trope (in poems by Shields and others) is that the child afflicted with Agent Orange maladies is fully a Vietnam veteran—again, the intrusion of the "machine" (either the U.S. war machine or the engineered dioxin molecule) into the "garden" of home.

Poetry by "friends of veterans" (as J. Topham calls nonveteran contributors to his series of anthologies) also deals with the subject; for example, J. Hollis's "Defoliation—Agent Orange": ". . . Evil made of evil seed. // Out of evil what will grow? / Earth above and earth below" (*Vietnam Heroes II* 28). This poem provides no insight—poetically or in general—about Agent Orange, but it does call attention to the virulent violation not only of veterans and Vietnamese but also of the earth itself; all that "will grow" is death and deaths, the condition of being surrounded, with terrible finality, by earth.

The most technologically sophisticated complex of machines used in Vietnam was the airplane—jet fighters, B-52 bombers, and fixed-wing gunships, such as "Puff the Magic Dragon" and "Spooky," which were armed with Gatling-style machine guns that fired three hundred bullets per second: "a

round in every square inch of a football field in less than a minute" (Herr 133).
R. L. Barth calls attention to the lethal beauty of "Puff" in "Nightpiece."

> No moon, no stars, only the leech-black sky
> Until Puff renders the darkness, spewing out
> His thin red flames, and then the quick reply
> Of blue-green tracers climbing all about.
> In night such lovely ways to kill, to die.
>
> (*Forced-Marching* 4)

This poem is actually a conversation with Fulke Greville, whose lines form an epigraph: "*In night when colors all to black are cast, / Distinction lost, or gone down with the light.*" The poem begins by agreeing with Greville's version of "night," but the next three lines highlight what turns out to be a new organism, "Puff" (referred to as a *he*). The point is that there is something loose in the universe which Greville could not have predicted, something which "writes" on the night, "renders." And the new rendition is a novel aesthetic of war: "such lovely ways." In an earlier version of this poem (*Looking For Peace*, 1981) Barth had used "rends," diction which is perhaps too one-dimensional; "renders" is a marvelous revision because it already implies "rends" but carries its own arresting ambiguity. Unfortunately, in the latest (and presumably final) version of the poem (*A Soldier's Time*, published in 1987), Barth has revised it back to "rends" and removed the Greville epigraph. Although Barth admitted in a letter that these changes arise from a "typo," it is clear that Barth is himself ambivalent about this terrible beauty—he finds it simultaneously repulsive and attractive. This is demonstrated by his personification of "Puff" into a dragon of romance, its tracers rendered as "thin red flames."

Larry Rottmann's "Frolicking in the Autumn Mist" (whose title is a line from the folk song "Puff the Magic Dragon") treats the image in a similar way, describing the gunship "Lumbering across the sky in huge, awkward circles / like some sated bird of prey" firing a "crimson waterfall" (*Winning* 73). This dialectic of natural and technological melding into a new, terrible hybrid—as imaged already in Receveur's "Cobra Pilot"—is a version of the "machine in the garden" which appears again and again in poetry about Vietnam techno-war.

The bombing conducted by the U.S. Air Force in Indochina was and is a continuing controversy. This air war was undoubtedly the largest ever conducted. "From 1965 through 1973, the United States dropped *at minimum* over eight million tons of munitions from aircraft onto Southeast Asia. . . . the equivalent in explosive force to 640 atomic bombs of the size used at Hiroshima"—compared to the "over two million tons of bombs and other munitions [dropped] from aircraft" in all of WWII (Gibson 319). The significant twist here is that this air war was conducted as a *semiotic phenomenon.* "Bombing was conceptualized as a *way of communicating* to the North Vietnamese" (Gibson 319). The communiqué was an unimaginative offer: "give up or die"; the point was to demoralize, to inhibit North Vietnam's waging of war (for example, to sever the Ho Chi Minh trail), and to force peace negotiations.[12] The oxymoronic phrase here "to force peace" telegraphs the end result. As Baritz summarized it, "North Vietnam finally . . . was willing to accept more death than we considered rational. That is why the bombing campaigns failed" (325).

There was also wide bombing in *South* Vietnam. One objective of the bombing was "to generate refugees" as military argot termed it. The Air Force's goal " 'was to separate the VC from the people by forcing refugee movements into GVN controlled areas' " (1967 U.S. Air Force study quoted by Gibson, 230). According to one U.S. field commander, " 'If the people are to the guerrillas as oceans are to the fish . . . we are going to dry up that ocean' " (Merton 108). In fact, as might be expected, this procedure, along with other "refugee-generating" operations such as the defoliation of crops and the forcible emptying of villages by troops, undoubtedly produced more "fish" for the Vietcong rather than "drying up the ocean."

Vietnam-veteran poetry about the bombing has been almost exclusively from the perspective of the soldier on the ground rather than from the vantage point of the bomber pilot. Grunts saw a connection between the bombing in the North and their own condition in the "boonies." According to an Army rifleman, "we knew that whenever they would stop the bombing, it meant more American deaths" (Santoli, *Everything* 150). Bob Sanders admitted, "I couldn't understand why [LBJ] halted the bombing in 1968 and left us in the field. . . . At that time, enemy activity stepped up. We lost more dead and wounded. We believed that the bombing slowed down infiltration, and that it protected us" (Goff and Sanders 142). The poetry, however, reveals the realization by some grunts that the bombing seemed at odds with their notion of American character (in other words, merely another betrayal by the war machine). Jan Barry's poem "Christmas in Hanoi" is typical: "Great black iron birds of prey, / the bombers flew on Christmas eve, / . . . like Roman legions traveling in phalanx" (*Demilitarized* 117). In the Christian myth of the Nativity (and throughout the New Testament), the SS troops are the Roman legionnaires, much as the Redcoats were the bogeymen of the American Revolution. In this poem, therefore, Barry is turning on its head the hawkish attribution of evil to the North Viet-

namese (cf. Ronald Reagan's "evil empire" label for the Soviet Union early
in his presidency). In Barry's reversal, the "bright star in the east" (traditionally a symbol for the birth of Christ) is instead the central star in the flag of
North Vietnam. Barry's revisionist strategy does not rely only on Christian
symbology but on American cultural symbols as well; the North Vietnamese
"red flag / still raised in the red sky / made by the bombers" are lines which
clearly echo the American national anthem. Barry writes out the year ("one
thousand, nine hundred / and seventy-two"), paradoxically recouping its force
as a number, rather than the wordlike "1972," in order to underline the mega-
importance of numbers and counting in this war. The poem's final irony—the
bomber crews "whooping 'Bomb Hanoi' while singing / 'peace on earth, good
will to men' " (*Demilitarized* 117)—completes Barry's critique of American
policy through a scathing juxtaposition of warlike and pacifist mottoes.

   Many "bomber" poems are set in the World, perhaps explaining their dovish
leanings, especially since many of these poets became involved in antiwar activity. Often, these poems engage the intrusion of air war into the World. For
example, Frank A. Cross, Jr.'s "B-52s Over Home" opens by recalling the
colors of bombers in Vietnam, ranging from black through camouflaged to silver; the attendant irony is that the lightest-colored bomber is the deadliest one,
underlining the irony of the question "For H-bombs / To keep us free?" Cross
compares the bombers to terrible birds of prey: "necks outstretched, / Tails
pouring with dysentery: / Rolls of black smoke," with landing gear "Like ready
talons." Cross imagines the invisible pilots as they rush "for cocktail hour /
At the officers' club . . . / Bomb doors locked and shut"; they are blind to the
lethality of their weapons, to the resemblance of their craft (and by extension
themselves) to killer birds and lovers of carrion. It is all just part of a routine.

> My fields are smooth,
> My ditches run straight,
> My house still stands,
> —But under the terrible
> Swept-back, swift shadows:
>   I shudder.   (*Peace* 165)

The farm is described here as if seen from high above, and although the "bomb
doors [are] locked and shut," Cross is intimately aware of the realities of the
air war in Vietnam, where

> There was no good bureaucratic reason for the pilots actually to reach
> their target because they would get credit for a sortie even if, as many did,

they dropped their bombs on fish in the sea, or on places already destroyed by bombs, or on places where there was nothing to bomb, except *perhaps the rice paddies which fed the people*. (Baritz 257, emphasis mine)

That is, farms. Cross's persona shudders because it is indefatigably clear (and we know this from the second stanza, especially the "officers' club" lines which indicate a self-serving laissez-faire) that the U.S. Air Force has not learned its lesson from the Vietnam war, and noncombatants will die again.

Michael Herr has recorded the intimate connection between sex and aircraft in Vietnam. He refers to the tiny observation helicopters affectionately called "Loaches":

It was incredible, those little ships were the most beautiful things flying in Vietnam (you had to stop once in a while and admire the machinery), they just hung there above those bunkers like wasps outside a nest. "That's sex," the captain said. "That's pure sex." (160)

But the "sexiest" (and hence most romanticized) aerial technology in Vietnam was the jet fighter.[13] One soldier remembered taking a break from "humping the boonies" by swimming in the South China Sea:

I was jumping around in the waves one time, and I saw a speck way off shore. All of a sudden I was eye to eye with a Phantom jet pilot. He gave me a nod and I'm looking at tail pipes, a black speck and he's gone. Came and went in the wink of an eye, about five feet over the water.

I said, "Wow, that guy must be coming in his pants. What a fucking rush that's got to be." (Baker 118)

Notwithstanding such observations by nonflyers—whether civilian or military—the pilots often had similar views about flying jet fighters: "Step out to that airplane, and you might as well be getting into bed with Denise Nicholas or Pam Grier. Because you just go *Oooooo*. You just gotta get it off now. You are in the preorgasmic mindset of the military person." Inevitably, the climax turns out to be associated not with the airplane itself but with its weaponry. "And when you're in the airplane, and you fire a rocket, and you hear that whoosh leave your wing, then all of a sudden it hits. POW. It's like an orgasm" (Horne 174).

There are few fighter-pilot poets (in the same way that there is a paucity of poems by bomber pilots).[14] There are, however, poems *about* fighter planes, again from the perspective of the person on the ground. D. C. Berry has writ-

ten a poem contrasting violent natural forces with the power of the jet fighter.
"Lightning reaching out with electric / wrinkles etches / insanely against the /
negronight" is juxtaposed against "The GI flys his phantom, craft / ing in / air
the map's frenzy / of / earth reaching . . . for / the unbroken bridge." There is
a one-to-one congruency set up here. "Lightning" = "GI"; both are "reaching"; "negronight" = "unbroken bridge." As we have seen again and again,
the mechanistic (here the GI rather than the plane) becomes the lightning, appropriating its raw voltaic energy. The denouement, however, dissipates this
sense of infinite power:

> The bridge and night gone;
> the lightning committed
> to the Transmission Wire Asylum
> and the Phantom
> asleep on safe
> rubber wheels.   (20)

In fact, the lightning's power has been tamed, even though the "night" is
"gone." The inference we might draw is that the disappearance of the "bridge"
is like that of the "night"—only a part of some cycle. So the "Phantom" will
itself succumb in some future turn of that cycle, and this defeat is already hinted
at by the "safe / rubber wheels," the airplane now insulated from anything
energetic.

A somewhat less enigmatic poem is Ehrhart's "The Hawk and Two Suns."
This poem begins as a gung ho technowar wet dream. The "silver hawk" with
"cross-haired eyes" (the old cyborg standby once more), incorporating "grid-
coordinate" technics as well as "silver-talon" organics, launches its horrible
weapon (a "sun / that spreads a brilliant orange sun-storm"—napalm); here
is a pseudonatural phenomenon that has the power of violently taking life and
distorting nature ("leav[ing] behind burnt black bodies" and "lungs / burst
outward"). This is all patent. Where the poem catapults into significance is at
the end when Ehrhart introduces the "greater sun."

> The hawk shrieks his predatory victory cry,
> and wheels away to join the greater sun
> he drains with every raid.   (*Tired* 14)

The "greater sun" is endowed with a wonderful ambiguity. On the most super-
ficial level, this image refers to the sun itself, and "drains with every raid"

refers to some sort of devolution of the universe as a result of napalm attack. On a deeper sociopolitical level, the "greater sun" suggests America and its military mission—devalued by escalating financial costs, by fading credibility, and, most important, by a continuing diminution of spiritual fiber. On an even deeper mythical and moral level, however, the "greater sun" is what might have been called in an earlier age the God of War, Mars—that is, the mystique and allure of war, of bellicose and warlike sentiments. Ehrhart assures us in this poem that, because of the Vietnam war, such romanticization of war will pass away, made impossible by the bloody realities of Vietnam.

In his memoir about being a Marine fighter pilot, *Phantom Over Vietnam,* John Trotti evinces a romanticized passion for flying combat missions which should not be surprising. Near the end of the book, his radar officer tells him, " 'I'm not looking to get wasted over here because you want to play your loony games with the guns.' " And Trotti realizes, "Somewhere I'd crossed a line I'd suspected was there but hadn't seen. There is something in war that drives so deeply into you that death ceases to be the enemy, merely another participant in a game you don't wish to end" (216). He ends his narrative, then, on a war-as-adventure note, despite the memory of a fellow pilot's crash: "So while I could look at a flight like Todd's and know that it was worthless and probably worse, there was always the promise that tomorrow held the great mission—the one that was always just behind the next row of clouds" (216).

Poetry by two fighter pilots who served in Vietnam exhibits some of this sort of romanticism—more to be expected from earlier wars. John Clark Pratt is maudlin about WWI fighters in an elegy, "Words for Don Morris"; the poem refers to the persistent images of "Spads and Fokkers [which] dueled" and of "Men with tiny airplanes, shined boots, / smiles and scarves." After the statement "Now, technology intrudes," however, the poem continues in an *ubi sunt* mode, a lament for the lost days of "Bombs rigged with lading wire" when, one would suppose, pilots were *men* who "could care less about refueling tracks or radar plots." The poem ends on a sentimental note. "It is good to know that some men / Still fly with scarves and laughter / As real pilots always have / and always will" (Kiley and Dater 65). This poem is a disappointing piece of writing from the author of the marvelous novel *The Laotian Fragments;* undoubtedly, there is honest feeling here, but Pratt is capable of much more.

Tony Dater's poem "Thunderbirds" seems to exhibit an ambivalence about the technology of fighter planes. He describes jet fighters at an air show: ". . . Four warplanes / Resplendent in bright ceremonial dress, / Streaming bold white smoke pennants, / Turbines calling throaty cadence." The climax of the

opening stanza occurs as the four airplanes reach the high point of their exhibi-
tion: "Color poised balanced inverted / A moment against bright sky." Set up as
a foil for this scene, the second stanza is a Vietnam-war memory of "Yank[ing]
six or seven G's in a / Jolting Thunderbird in dull war paint"; preoccupied with
his "craning neck and sweat stung eyes," the pilot "apprehend[s]":

> A solumn procession of
> Bright
> Red
> Fireballs
> Marching up
> To some imagined apex.   (Kiley and Dater 86)

The second stanza is more compelling than the first in its immediacy, its projection of what it is like to operate in high gravity. The question ascendant here
is how to interpret the "solumn [*sic*] procession of / Bright / Red / Fireballs."
Are we to mourn the fact of people being incinerated by these fireballs? Or
are we to appreciate their aesthetic beauty? Or are we to be proud of a job
well done? The speaker's action of "apprehend[ing]" is neutral and does not
give enough of a clue. The choice of the closing words "some imagined apex"
implies through its Latinate vocabulary that we are meant to be admiring. The
romantic description of the stunt planes in "bright ceremonial dress" and the
bellicose appreciation of "dull war paint" in the second stanza also supports
this view. Clearly, the speaker loves the jet fighter—a completely opposite view
from Pratt's—but the meaning of the "Fireballs / Marching up" is up for grabs.
At best, I sense an ambivalence that casts doubt finally on the applicability of
"the machine in the jungle."

Walter McDonald: After the (Machine) Noise of Saigon

Walter McDonald was a U.S. Air Force pilot from 1957 to 1971. He has published several books of poetry, including *Caliban in Blue and Other Poems*
(1976), *Burning the Fence* (1981), *The Flying Dutchman* (1987), *After the Noise
of Saigon* (1988), and *Night Landings* (1989). *The Flying Dutchman* won the
1987 George Elliston Poetry Prize, and *After the Noise of Saigon* garnered
the 1987 Juniper Prize, both prestigious awards. Since McDonald served in
Vietnam during 1969–70, it is inevitable that his poems would reflect that experience. He leans more toward the aesthetic than the antipoetic, with catharsis
always an impulse important to his work.

McDonald's poem "Caliban in Blue" (the title poem of his first book) presents a novel view of being a fighter pilot—a fascinating meld of literary allusion and machine sex.

> Off again,
> thrusting up at scald
> of copper in orient west
> I climb into such blue skies.
> Skies even here
> belong to Setobos:
> calls it air power.

The allusion here is to Shakespeare's play *The Tempest*, an interesting choice [15] in our context because Leo Marx in *Machine in the Garden* called this play "Shakespeare's American Fable" in its confrontation between Prospero's magic and the natural terrain and aborigines of an inhospitable island (34–72). According to Marx, "The topography of *The Tempest* anticipates the moral geography of the American imagination" (72). McDonald uses *The Tempest* to invest his poem with a sense of moral and national decay, inwardly unacknowledged by the pilot and his nation. Caliban is a slave, a Neanderthal of sorts. "What have we here? a man or a fish? dead or alive?" a clown asks upon encountering Caliban, suggesting that he is unclassifiable but nevertheless a monster (*Tempest* II.ii.24–25). McDonald's "Setobos" alludes to Caliban's "dam's god, Setobos" (I.ii.373). Since Caliban's dam is "the foul witch Sycorax" (I.ii.258) whose "charms [are] toads, beetles, bats" (I.ii.339–40), we might infer that Setobos is a devil, a witch's familiar. Certainly the magic arts of Caliban's master, Prospero, are stronger than those of Setobos. Caliban admits, "His art is of such pow'r / It would control . . . Setobos, and make a vassal of him" (I.ii.372–74); Setobos may then be a relatively minor devil.

In McDonald's allegory, the fighter pilot is imaged as Caliban to imply that he is enslaved and yet relatively masterless, since Setobos and not Prospero is in control. For Setobos, read Uncle Sam, who rules "blue skies . . . Skies even here" in Vietnam. Based as this hegemony is on "air power" (i.e., technology propagandized as "peace power"), it must be a relatively minor dominion, set as it is against the lyric force of nature: "scald / of copper in orient west." According to *Brewer's Dictionary of Phrase and Fable,* Setobos is a "devil worshipped by the Patagonians [of South America, whose cult] was first known in Europe through Magellan's voyage around the world." The connection of McDonald's Setobos with America is therefore valid, especially given the context of Magellanic, imperialistic exploration. McDonald is essentially saying that the United States, complacent in its imperialistic catechism, is in actuality the weaker force in Vietnam because of its reliance on military power rather than on nature, air rather than earth.

> For this, I trained to salivate
> and tingle, target-diving,
> hand enfolding hard throttle
> in solitary masculine delight. . . .

The inevitable moment of attack is imaged as

> pulsing orgasm,
> savage release;
> pull out
> and off we go again
> thrusting deep
> into the martial lascivious blue
> of uncle's sky.   (*Caliban* 11)

The portrayal of the fighter-pilot mystique and experience as macho mastur-bation ("hand enfolding hard throttle") implies that the "pulsing orgasm, / savage release" of aerial attack, lethal as it may be, is futile, purposeless, un-generative. The pilot, however, on some barely unconscious level conceives of the attack—in parodic echo of LBJ's bombing metaphor (Gibson 329)—as *rape* ("pull out / and off we go again / thrusting deep") or *seduction* ("into the martial lascivious blue," the word "lascivious" implying some sort of co-operation). But this is self-deception after all, because the sky is ultimately "uncle's sky"—not Uncle Sam, with a capital U, but a smaller "uncle," un-doubtedly Uncle Ho. The "blue" that Caliban is *in* is not at all his territory, as he thought, but rather a "blue" that is *hostilely* "martial" and inevitably victo-rious. The poem's allegory hence severely criticizes America's fatal innocence in Vietnam.[16]

McDonald's poems about the nitty-gritty war portray not flying missions but rather ground action. "Rocket Attack" has an epigraph taken from a news story, "Damage was reported light. Four Americans were wounded, and three Vietnamese civilians were killed"; in the middle of a rocket barrage and fear of death ("concussion sharp as wood on wood / slamming shut my coffin"), the

speaker has an epiphany about who these "three Vietnamese civilians" are—
he recalls a memory of "Little mouths / little hands I saw / in the Vietnamese
airmen's / shacks." In a flash of sympathy, the war is brought "home" to the
speaker, who prays:

> Daughter, oh God, my daughter
> may she never
> safe at home
> Never hear the horrible
> sucking sound a rocket makes when it   (*Caliban* 17–18)

The ending is a bit melodramatic, but it is also startling. We have been eaves-
dropping on the final thoughts of an American about to be killed by a rocket.
The poem is a linguistic, humanistic antidote to the dispassionate language
of the Associated Press, reminding us that each of these statistics is (was) a
breathing, thinking human being.

In his second collection, McDonald's poem "Taking Aim" provides a sense
of community and initiation. The persona speaking describes how one should
hold an M-16:

> muzzle down,
> sniffing
> like a hundred-dollar dog.

This voice is clearly speaking in dialect (although not indicated through the
usual orthographics) as the simile "like a hundred-dollar dog" hints. The persona is a seasoned grunt—a squad leader, say—imparting crucial information
to FNGs, literally to save their lives.

> Keep it on automatic.
> Anything moves in the bushes,
> you open fire . . .

McDonald's terse delivery here craftily evokes the scene. The FNGs are gath-
ered around the squad leader, who is pantomiming his advice. McDonald's line
breaks reflect actual pauses in the lesson, the pauses where the squad leader
demonstrates how to grip the rifle, how to point it ("Kind of pull it sideways"
and "just a touch / on the trigger"):

> If you're holding it
> like this
> it'll get him.   (*Burning* 28)

This is knowledge not received in basic training or infantry training; only the exigency of actually setting foot in the boonies can command this sort of attention. The FNGs will understand this wisdom kinesthetically only after some experience in the field, but at least they will have more of a chance, and the squad leader has now begun to mold his men into an entity, a community.

McDonald's award-winning third collection, *The Flying Dutchman*, contains a mere handful of poems dealing directly with Vietnam. Instead, we find technology pitted *against* nature. "Praying a Stall Won't Spin Us," the pilot "Letting down through thunderstorms" tries to "keep the needle centered, / boots toe-dancing the rudders." Two fields of diction dramatize this elemental confrontation: "thunderstorms," "gusts," "volcano blasts," and "lightning" are juxtaposed against "canopy," "needle," "rudders," "wings," "geiger counter," and "nosecone." Certain technological words immediately semaphore late twentieth-century technology, especially "geiger counter" and "nosecone," both of which have collocations with atomic vocabulary: radiation and missiles. What makes the difference here is the skill and faith of the pilot: "toe-dancing" as well as "praying." The speaker recalls that, in the face of death, certain universal truths become lucid and accessible, but they are dimly expressible only in metaphors.

> In unstable air
> we find what dreams are made of,
> why some birds hunt in water,
> why eagles scorn the wide flat world.   (*Dutchman* 47)

Interestingly, this poem is quite possibly an allegory for the national experience of "balancing" such an undertaking as the Vietnam war; what matters is the leadership ability and moral integrity of the nation's leaders, and perhaps the Vietnamese Confucian concept of "divine mandate." In the case of the Vietnam war, "a stall did spin America," and the nation never apprehended "why eagles scorn the wide flat world."

The more important poems in *The Flying Dutchman* concern themselves with the hardscrabble desert country of Texas where McDonald grew up and lives. "Getting It Done" honors this land as well as McDonald's wife in lyrical terms: amazement at the "same burnt sienna land we live on begin[ning] to glow / under her brush. . . . Weaving a delicate balance." In this portrait of an artist, McDonald evokes the importance of art: to take something and make it one's own, emphasize its beauty. It is significant that the artist "gathers and blesses," converting the desert into a "garden of stones and cactus" (*Dutchman* 69)—a mythic consummation of the virgin land, although without macho rhetoric.

In McDonald's book *After the Noise of Saigon,* the poems concerned with Vietnam either recall a lyric moment or concentrate on the process of recovery from the war. In "The Food Pickers of Saigon," McDonald describes a hellish scene, like a modern-day *Inferno.*

> Rubbish like compost heaps burned every hour
> of my days and nights at Tan Son Nhut.
> Ragpickers scoured the edges of our junk,
> risking the flames. . . .

The poet's mind cannot evade metaphor. The garbage dump is compared to "a coal mine fire burning / out of control, or Moses' holy bush / which was not consumed." Rather than describe them to his wife in the letter he is writing, the speaker instead recalls "bears in Yellowstone / our first good summer in a tent. . . . how they waddled to the road and begged." The contrast of cultures is striking: the Vietnamese "ragpickers" reduced to the level of the "bears," the sense of danger (merely imagined) on the part of the speaker— "No campers / had died in that Disneyland national park / for years." The poem's closing emphasizes how Vietnam continues to haunt McDonald. When his children "leave / good broccoli or green beans / on their plates," the speaker chastises them, recalling the "two beautiful children // I found staring at me one night / through the screen of my window, / at Tan Son Nhut, bone-faced." The strategy of this poem resembles that of "Rocket Attack," drawing the inescapable connections between the children of Vietnam and their counterparts in America. The speaker insists on feeding his children in America because in Vietnam "when I crawled out of my stifling monsoon / dream to feed them, they were gone" (*After* 5–6); the speaker knows that very little separates both groups of children, and the plight of the Vietnamese child could very easily happen to the American. McDonald attempts to pierce through the veneer of security which makes the workaday American complacent, reveal this veneer in all its pasteboard flimsiness, awaken Americans in some way as lasting as "Moses' holy bush / which was not consumed."

A poem of lyric epiphany, "New Guy," portrays an encounter with Vietnamese culture in all of its alienness.

> I saw girls squatting against the wall,
> and backed out, surely the men's shower,
> and it was, the sign said it was mine,
> my first day under mortars and rockets . . .

This poem illustrates how far from technowar McDonald has moved. The only technology which appears here are "mortars and rockets," and they appear only offstage. The center of the action is a primitive shower stall in which not only grime is washed away, but also American hang-ups about nudity in the face of the Vietnamese women's offhand and guileless nonchalance ("They never glanced at me, three girls // and a wrinkled woman"). The only awkward moment of the poem is the blatant echo of Frost ("With miles of maps / to go over before I slept")—a passage that suffers from being somewhat less gracefully rhythmic than Frost's famous line. The closing moment, however, is lovely.

> I stripped, shivered and soaped in the cold
> water of Saigon, my eyes closed,
> listening underwater to alien voices
> like angels speaking in tongues.   (*After* 53)

These lines emphasize not only the estrangement of the American in Vietnam, but also the beauty of the people and the land, without a trace of condescension or ridicule and without leaning to the other extreme of sentimentalism.

There *are* poems which feature technology in *After the Noise of Saigon,* but they remain for the most part lyrical and refrain from heavy-handed political or social criticism. The exception is "How the World Ends," a poem that mirrors Frank Cross's "B-52's Over Home." The poem opens with the speaker riding on a "saddled stallion," watching a sunset against "the plains horizon," when "Behind me, out of the east" flies

> a jet, overhead by the time
> I heard the roar,
> the contrail like a comet,
> the bomber burning white . . .

This poem's opening is so reminiscent of a western-movie sunset (especially with "the saddled stallion") that one is almost not surprised by the appearance of the bomber in furious negation of the lyric beauty of the scene. And yet the plane is also outlined in a natural simile—"the contrail like a comet"—a line whose loveliness resides also in its subtle alliteration. McDonald is walking a tightrope here, skirting both sledgehammer polemics and overbeautification. McDonald's solution to have the bomber "chasing the sun, / and gaining" (*After* 46) is reminiscent of Ehrhart's jet fighter, the "greater sun / drain[ed]," but here McDonald's sun resists interpretation as anything *but* the sun, lending the bomber "gaining" a genuinely apocalyptic force.

The overall ambience of the book, however, is one of quiet resignation and acceptance. "Crosswind Landings" describes the sensations of landing a "rented Cessna whining / like a scared fair-weather friend" in bad winds—now in America and not in the Vietnam of memory. The poem celebrates skill and coolheadedness. "Let the black-streaked runway, / your only world, bend steep and savage, / keep your fists loose . . . / and at the last second before a stall, / kick the nose cone perfect / and the tires will touch" (*After* 47). There are also poems about flying before the war. "We Called It Entering Heaven" describes "Heaven's gate, two rocks the size of towers, / straight up from the desert floor." The action is a macho initiation—a dive in a jet fighter.

> From twenty thousand feet, split-S,
> and level out at five, and glide
> head on toward those twin devil's towers
>
> . . . .
>
> face to face with two levels
> of stone, trying to dive
> through the eye of a needle.   (*After* 52)

Again, the technology invoked in the poem is an excuse to prove oneself, a motif running through McDonald's work: the human self pitted against an indifferent yet lyrically beautiful nature, but *not* the male warrior fired in the crucible of war. Here, the "eye of the needle" refers on one level to Christ's parable emblematizing the difficulty which the rich will encounter in trying to enter heaven. In this poem, however, again given the unavoidable context of Vietnam (introduced actually by the very title of the book, *After the Noise of Saigon*), the "eye of the needle" actually becomes a metaphor for the war itself. To pass through it is metaphorically to reenter the World—the grunt's heaven.

The game therefore is a practice run for inevitable survival (and not merely from the pragmatic view that it hones one's flying skills to survive the war). More important, the recovery within the poem of the epiphanic moment in the past before the war is the poet's own passport, his own flight "through the eye" to *stay* in the World, not to be engulfed by nightly souvenirs of the 'Nam.

Such nightmares are never easy to conquer, and the book's title poem delineates the opposite experience as well: "here I am, alone with a cougar I've stalked for hours" with the uneasy knowledge that "my aim with a bow / is no better at twenty yards / than forty." The speaker calls this hunt "the strangest nightmare of all," stranger than "dreams I've floundered in / for years." The poet's retreat is to the woods and away from cities, armed only with primitive technology, where, ironically, "These blue trees have nothing / and all to do with what I'm here for / after the noise of Saigon." The point is that McDonald's sincerest hope is that there, in the wilderness, where he confronts the rankling "heart of darkness" within his own soul, hunting a cougar with a bow, there may be some regeneration to be found, some cleansing, some purging of "the simple bitter sap that rises in me / like bad blood." Only there can he pierce the technocratic mask and come to grips with his own guilt and release—become something other than some "damned / madman stumbling for his life" (*After* 64–65).

Night Landings continues in much the same vein as the previous books. The technologically oriented poems often have to do not necessarily with technowar in Vietnam but with training, and the titles of poems convey this existential territory: "Night Landings," "Flying a Perfect Loop," "Ejecting from Jets," and "First Solo in Thunderstorms." Interestingly, the poems which deal directly with Vietnam do not highlight technology. "The Wild Swans of Da Lat" dramatizes nature's quietly insistent victory over technowar. The significant contrast in the poem is between *fliers:* the machine with its dangerous "propellers / *whop-whopping* like ground fire" and the "wild swans / graceful on bomb craters," noble as "marble mounted on pylons." Where the machine is "exposed" and hence vulnerable, the swans are "somehow able / to find their way down / under tiered trees to breed" within the protection of the jungle that now also encompasses the "bomb craters" into its beauty (*Night* 20).

The cognate poem to "The Wild Swans of Da Lat" is "Bluejays in Summer." In this poem, the bluejays are described as "blue flames / up ladders of air," as "angels, div[ing] down," their blue heads / like helmets." (This diction and imagery are reminiscent of the "martial lascivious blue" of "Caliban in Blue.") The bluejays swarming after pecans are portrayed as "swirling like crepe paper tossed / in a whirlwind" (*Night* 46)—an image that sarcastically refers to the confetti-storm parades which Vietnam veterans did *not* get. But the image also evokes McDonald's narrative for the end of war in "The Last Still Days in a Bunker," where an intelligence officer feeds "another sealed order / into the whirring shredder, wondering / how many tons of bombs we'd abandon, / how many battles we might stop" (*Night* 21). However, the image of the whirlwind in "Bluejays in Summer" belies any end, because the birds are still "swirling" in battle; the bluejays are representative either of the American war machine in Vietnam or of all warring powers. McDonald emphasizes, however, that the common person is nevertheless able to survive, to cope with war: the jays drop "the meat / in cracked shells for sparrows / hopping on the grass" (*Night* 46). In McDonald's memories, these sparrows resemble "The Children of Saigon" who are "crawling the last flare of the sun // spangled on garbage," a motley group made up of "children and old men // ragged and golden"; they accept the speaker's guilt-ridden gifts from "nights // . . . without supper, / . . . leftovers I begged / . . . passing it all to children / who grabbed it and backed away" (*Night* 22–23).

For McDonald, the important lesson is *coping,* regardless of the odds. This may involve "Learning to Live with Nightmares," accepting nightmares finally as ephemeral. "At night, / I dream my life ends / at Saigon," but during the day, "no rockets, I've stopped reaching to check for wounds." What is important is "reaching to lace my shoes, / my own shoes" (*Night* 28); the importance of the words "my own" has to do with the acceptance of self, including one's own guilt. In "After the Rains of Saigon," coping also involves understanding that "Nothing / about this flat dry land is like Vietnam / but my own damned eyes and ears" (*Night* 29). This is going beyond the acceptance of self—that Vietnam is carried within—but also an acceptance of the land as it is, the honorable hardscrabble landscape. Finally, these acceptances involve a responsibility for the landscape. In "After a Year in Korea," the speaker's uncle, embittered by his own war, is always complaining "about a country where they'd done something // awful to the weather, maybe pesticides, / the bomb, good summers short, / the winters hard, more bitter every year" (*Night* 58). The important discovery of this poem is human complicity in the environment's deterioration, a phenomenon related to technology, whether military or not. The fight to end such complicity is part of *living on hardscrabble*—for McDonald, an ennobling struggle and experience.

It is patently unfair to McDonald to brand him as *only* a Vietnam-veteran poet. In *Night Landings,* for example, only five of forty-two poems expressly mention Vietnam. In *After the Noise of Saigon,* only seven of forty-nine poems are even remotely about Vietnam. In *The Flying Dutchman,* only two of forty-five poems touch on Vietnam in some direct way; these two are found, however, in a section entitled "Whoever Loses a War"—the implication being that these poems are, on some level deep below the literal surface, glosses on the Vietnam war. In fact, here may be the way to approach McDonald's poetry. The phrase "after the noise of Saigon," which appears in two separate poems in the book with that title, implies that the life between the covers of that book is ineffably affected by Vietnam. In some respects, Vietnam becomes the determiner, the event by which everything else is dated. Therefore, McDonald's search for mythic resurrection in the wilderness of hardscrabble country—an amalgam of Wild West myths, the virgin land, and some sort of regeneration through physical activity (hunting, say, or rafting) and the beauty of the open plains (camping, the cowboy life)—is couched in poems which are hardly ever antipoetic but relentlessly aesthetic, and which continually reach for catharsis without finally achieving it. This search and these poems are a quest dictated, enjoined by McDonald's experience in the Vietnam war. Walter McDonald is the marvelous poet he is both because of and despite Vietnam.

Coda: Machines (Rusting) in the Jungle

The application of overwhelming military technology in Vietnam is evidently a fallacy, a completely inappropriate strategy, given the situation. As early as 1963, John Paul Vann, a field-grade officer who eventually became a civilian supervisor of military advisors in Vietnam, admitted:

> "This is a political war and it calls for discrimination in killing. The best weapon for killing would be a knife, but I'm afraid we can't do it that way. The worst is an airplane. The next worst is artillery. Barring a knife, the best is a rifle—you know who you're killing." (Halberstam 84)

Shades of Lawrence, again. It has been proposed that American technology, in fact, irresistibly led to American defeat. "Sir Robert Thompson, the British plenipotentiary in Malaysia during the Communist insurgency in the 1950s," suggested that the helicopter

> "exaggerated the two great weaknesses of the American character—impatience and aggressiveness. . . . It is probable that without the helicopter 'search and destroy' would not have been possible and in this sense the helicopter was one of the major contributions to the failure of strategy." (Gibson 105)

In postmortem, Tran Van Don, an influential South Vietnamese general who helped plan the decisive coup against Diêm, admitted:

> In Vietnam, the reliance on air power included the ever-present heli-copters, marvelous devices which, to a rich and technically proficient nation like the United States, became an integral part of transport and fire-power. Following the American lead, when we Vietnamese were sent into an operation, we frequently were transported there by helicopter carrier while helicopter gunships flew ahead to cover the objective, except that after a period of time we became unduly dependent on them for every-thing. It was really too rich for our blood, in a land where one usually walks from one place to another, carrying one's goods by backpack. (160)

Vann had already prophesied this when he proposed that " 'By giving [the South Vietnamese] too much gear—airplanes and helicopters—we may be helping them to pick up bad habits instead of teaching them to spend more time in the swamps than the enemy' " (Halberstam 84). The Vietcong, on the other hand, did not pick up such "bad habits" despite the matériel they re-ceived from communist allies. Instead, they used their familiarity with the land, based on the long history of Vietnam as an agrarian country. Captain Nguyen Thanh Linh, the commander of the famous Vietcong tunnel complex at Cu Chi, describes the tunnels as " 'something very Vietnamese . . . and one must understand what the relationship is between the Vietnamese peasant and the earth, *his* earth. Without that then everything here [i.e., the tunnel complex] is without real meaning' " (Mangold and Penycate 66–67). One Army medic recalled his amazement at what tunnels could contain: "you'd go down a little rathole and find a surgical operating theater with enamel walls and mercury-vapor lamps and the newest equipment from France as good as anything we had, all just down a little rathole covered over with a cooking pot" (Santoli, *Everything* 46).

Linh's description of the type of war they fought in the Cu Chi tunnels during a major American operation in early 1966 is similarly revealing:

> "We were in our spider-hole firing positions—the Americans never saw us at all. I ordered my men to fire, one GI fell down, the others just stood around looking at him. They were so bewildered, they did not hide or take defensive positions. They did not even know where the bullets had come from. We kept on shooting. . . . [When] they called for artillery. . . . we simply went into the communication tunnels and went on to another

place. The Americans continued advancing, but we'd gone. That was the pattern; there was nothing special." (Mangold and Penycate 50)

Interestingly, the Vietcong successes at Cu Chi were based on the proverbial wisdom, "Less is more." Linh actually

argued against being given command of too many men to defend the tunnels. "The more men I had, the more casualties I would receive. . . . Fighting from the tunnels was an advantage if I did not have too many men. Often one or two riflemen would be enough, five or six rifles would be sufficient. In this kind of war one should attack numerous enemy troops with only a few men." (Mangold and Penycate 46)

This is of course early in the involvement of American troops as opposed to advisors, and warfare differed considerably from place to place, from one type of terrain to another—but the vastly different *assumptions* of Linh and his men from those of the Americans contribute much to an evaluation of American technowar involvement in Vietnam, especially against the backdrop of all the American hardware left to rust in the Vietnamese jungle.

"[T]here is a certain hubris built into technological thinking," Thomas Merton suggests, "that encloses it within itself and its own suppositions and makes it fatally ignore decisive realities that do not fit those suppositions" (115). The fateful question now is whether Americans have learned this lesson from Vietnam: the self-reflexive tyranny of the "machine" whether in the "American garden" or transposed to some "jungle." The apparent answer to this question, given the technowar focus of Operation Desert Storm in the 1991 Gulf war, is *no*.

THREE. A NEW BABEL

Language is an inescapably important element in the transmission and preservation of myth. A useful example is the 1630 sermon that John Winthrop, the governor of the Massachusetts Bay colony, gave to his fellow Puritans on the ship *Arbella* as they neared New England. Perhaps the most quoted portion of Winthrop's exhortation is the "city upon a hill" section:

> the Lord will be our God and delight to dwell among us, as his owne people, and will commaund a blessing upon us in all our wayes, soe that wee shall see much more of His wisdome, power, goodnes, and truthe then formerly wee have beene acquainted with, wee shall finde that the God of Israell is among us, when tenn of us shall be able to resist a thousand of our enemies, when hee shall make us a prayse and glory, that men shall say of succeeding plantacions: the lord make it like that of New England: for wee must Consider that wee shall be as a Citty upon a Hill, the eyes of all people are uppon us. (198)

Winthrop's immediate source for the metaphor is the Gospel of Matthew: "Ye are the light of the world. A city that is set on an hill cannot be hid" (5:14). But the *image* of the raised city is an ancient one, used in the first book of the Bible, the story of the Tower of Babel:

> And the whole earth was of one language, and of one speech. And it came to pass, as they journeyed from the east, that they found a plain in the land of Shinär; and they dwelt there. And they said to one another, Go to, let us make brick, and burn them thoroughly. And they had brick for stone, and slime had they for mortar. And they said, Go to, let us build us a city and a tower, whose top *may reach* unto heaven; and let us make us a name, lest we be scattered abroad upon the face of the whole earth. And the Lord came down to see the city and the tower, which the children of men builded. And the Lord said, Behold, the people *is* one, and they have all one language; and this they begin to do: and now nothing will be

restrained from them, which they have imagined to do. Go to, let us go down, and there confound their language, that they may not understand one another's speech. So the Lord scattered them abroad from thence upon the face of all the earth: and they left off to build the city. Therefore is the name of it called Babel. . . . (Gen. 11:1–9)

There are more connections between these two texts: both peoples assume that the Lord "will commaund a blessing upon us"; both are concerned with "mak[ing] a name"; both have emigrated to a place where prosperity is either expected or has been achieved. The dissimilarities are also significant: the people of Babel are punished for their pride, whereas the Massachusetts Bay colony thrives despite the colonists' ostentatious pride.

I have quoted both of these passages at length to emphasize the way language has been used for mythic purposes. A sentence such as Winthrop's "the Lord will be our God and delight to dwell among us" is stylistically equivalent to the syntax and cadences of the King James Bible; the difference here is one of emphasis—Winthrop is using religious language to further political and social ends. Winthrop asserts, for example, that if "the God of Israell is among us, [then] tenn of us shall be able to resist a thousand of our enemies." Of course, this is metaphor, but it can be *understood* as fact (as contemporary fundamentalist Christianity may demonstrate). The mythic image of the city on an hill as a linguistic construction is really meant to be fostered and sustained through language (e.g., the reputation of the colony with other "plantacions"), and so the continuance of the myth through our day has also been a direct result of language. Ronald Reagan used this language again and again in political speeches: "We will become that shining city on a hill." [1] In this chapter, I am not as concerned with the myth of the city on a hill per se but rather with the topic of language and its ideological use in the Vietnam war, especially in terms of tautology and the preservation of myth.

Language and Ideology: The Jargon Stream

In the Vietnam war, distortion of language was widespread. Philip Caputo refers to the opacity of military language. "To be in battle was to be 'in a combat situation'; a helicopter assault was a 'vertical envelopment'; an M-14 rifle a 'hand-held, gas-operated, magazine-fed, semiautomatic shoulder weapon.'" But this language is lucidly clear compared to battle orders which "made the Rosetta Stone look like a Dick-and-Jane reader."

"*Enemy sit.* Aggressor forces in div strength holding MLR Hill 820 complex gc AT 940713-951716 w/fwd elements est. bn strength junction at gc AT 948715 (See Annex A, COMPHIBPAC intell. summary period ending 25 June) . . . *Mission:* BLT 1/7 seize, hold and defend obj. A gc 948715 . . . *Execution:* BLT 1/7 land LZ X-RAY AT 946710 at H-Hour 310600 . . . A co. GSF estab. LZ security LZ X-RAY H minus 10 . . . B co. advance axis BLUE H plus 5 estab. blocking pos. vic gs AT 948710 . . . A, C, D cos. maneuver element commence advance axis BROWN H plus 10 . . . Bn tacnet freq 52.9 . . . shackle code HAZTRCEGBD . . . div. tacair dir. air spt callsign PLAYBOY . . . Mark friendly pos w/air panels or green smoke. Mark tgt. w/WP." (14–15)

There are adequate reasons, certainly, for such jargon, including hindering the enemy from understanding captured documents or decoding radio chatter. What inevitably happens, however, is that military personnel become habituated to this sort of language, and all speech and writing are riddled by formulaic and opaque expression. The direct result, then, is the use of vague language toward the public, not necessarily because of duplicity (although as the war dragged on, such duplicity became increasingly difficult to rule out), but perhaps merely from a habit of mind.

The duplicitous use of vagueness and euphemism in war by governments to their people has become a fact of the twentieth century—always defended as a "protection" of the people on the homefront. In the Vietnam war, this type of language increased to such a degree that the language itself became one basis of the credibility gap.

Michael Herr coined a neologism for these deceptive euphemisms—the "jargon stream"—pointing to such terminology as "*Frontier sealing, census grievance, black operations . . . revolutionary development, armed propaganda*" (52). Caputo records that casualty "reports had to be written in that clinical, euphemistic language the military prefers to simple English. . . . Shrapnel wounds were called 'multiple fragment lacerations,' and the phrase for dismemberment, . . . was 'traumatic amputation.' " (166). Echoing Caputo, Herr cites the especially understated term " 'response-to-impact' [for] bodies wrenched too fast and violently into unbelievable contortion" (18). Herr also observes that there was even "a small language for our fire: 'discreet burst,' 'probe,' 'prime selection,' 'constructive load' " (62). Jeffrey Walsh points out the bottom line: how the jargon stream's "incongruity can hide the reality of moral outrage" (206).

Two decades before the Vietnam war, George Orwell had augured this linguistic status quo: how language, subordinated to politics, and perhaps most specifically during wartime, is debased and used "largely [in] defence of the indefensible" ("Politics" 136). This debasement is traceable in writing to "a lifeless, imitative style" consisting of "gumming together long strips of words which have already been set in order by someone else, and making the results presentable by sheer humbug" ("Politics" 134–35). The situation becomes even worse when this debased language is used mendaciously for political purposes. "All issues are political issues, and politics itself is a mass of lies, evasions, folly, hatred and schizophrenia. When the general atmosphere is bad, language must suffer" ("Politics" 137). And the phraseology of such a language "has to consist largely of euphemism, question-begging and sheer cloudy vagueness" ("Politics" 136). Orwell, in fact, mentions as an example a term used in 1946 which perfectly foreshadows its use in the Vietnam war: "Defenceless villages are bombarded from the air, the inhabitants driven out into the countryside, the cattle machine-gunned, the huts set on fire with incendiary bullets: this is called *pacification*" ("Politics" 136). This term was used in the Vietnam war for exactly the same actions. Orwell's closing salvo accurately describes the language of the American government during the war: "designed to make lies sound truthful and murder respectable, and to give an appearance of solidity to pure wind" ("Politics" 139).

Thomas Merton's essay "War and the Crisis of Language" applies some of Orwell's arguments specifically to the Vietnam situation. "Official statements made in Washington, about the Vietnam War . . . are symptoms of a national— indeed worldwide—illness. . . . the gap between words and actions that is characteristic of modern war, [and] also characteristic of political life in general" (100). Merton's classic example is an American major's account of his shelling of Ben Tre in South Vietnam: " 'regardless of civilian casualties. . . . to rout the Vietcong. . . . It became necessary to destroy the town in order to save it.' Here we see, again, an insatiable appetite for the tautological, the definitive, the *final*"; Merton compares it with Hitler's "language and logic . . . for his notorious 'final solution' " (105). And this brand of tautology was not, of course, limited to the battlefield, with its "kill ratios" and "free fire zones." Merton points an accusing finger as well at the "war mandarins in government offices and military think-tanks. . . . playing out 'scenarios' and considering 'acceptable levels' in megadeaths" via language that is "scientifically antiseptic, businesslike, uncontaminated with sentimental concern for life—other than their own" (108). Merton demonstrates how the jargon stream, in Vietnam as well as in Washington, fed a war "*fought to vindicate the assumptions*

upon which it [was] being fought" (114–15). And the most basic of these assumptions, Merton argues, is that America "has decided to rule the world
without paying serious attention to anybody else's view of what the world is all
about. . . . [a] solipsistic, . . . basically isolationist and sometimes even para-
noid, attitude" (116). The language of the Vietnam war, therefore, consisting
of "double-talk, tautology, ambiguous cliché, self-righteous and doctrinaire
pomposity, and pseudoscientific jargon that mask a total callousness and moral
insensitivity, indeed a basic contempt for man" (117), Merton fears, may be a
universal phenomenon; if so, the only language to oppose it is a revolutionary
idiom—"racy, insolent, direct, profane, iconoclastic, and earthy"—which is
nevertheless also a "language of power . . . [and] self-enclosed finality" (118).
Merton posits a grim situation indeed.

Lorrie Smith has traced the roots and history of the American brand of this
tautology.

> The genocide of a native population and the theft of their land are still
> conceived as an "errand into the wilderness" or, more secularly, as "ex-
> pansion" and "manifest destiny"; revolution and self-determination in
> the New World colonies are noble and enlightened, in the Third World
> evil and benighted; dropping atomic bombs on Hiroshima and Naga-
> saki makes the world "safe for democracy"; the invasion of Cambodia
> is an "incursion"; the suppression of self-determination in Nicaragua is
> a "freedom fight" using the techniques of "post-Vietnam low-intensity
> conflict." ("Disarming" 87)

Parallel to all these instances of language distortion, "Washington's need"
in Vietnam, according to John Felstiner, "was to sanitize reality and quarantine the fact from the word—precisely what much poetry avoids" ("American
Poetry" 10). Frank A. Cross, Jr., tries to break through that quarantine of fact
and word in his poem "Gliding Baskets."

> "Eight Six Foxtrot—Eight Six Foxtrot.
> This is One One Zulu. Over."
>   The woman in blue
>   Carried the weight swiftly, with grace.

This poem dramatizes a conversation between a forward artillery observer and
a gunner, juxtaposed by what (who) they are talking about: a "woman in blue."
Through the perspective of the speaker of the poem, we eavesdrop on the tar-

geting of the "Fire Mission" and we also see, quite vividly, the woman—"Her face . . . hidden by her / Conical rice straw hat." These alternating scenes are presented in two different languages, reflecting Felstiner's categories of "fact" and "word." Here, the "words" of the forward observer and the gunner refuse to acknowledge the "fact" of the woman's humanity, using militarese as well as derogatory slang.

> . . . I have Fire Mission.
> Dink in the open, Grid: Bravo Sierra,
> Five Six Niner, Four Six Five, Range:
> Three thousand, Proximity: Eight Hundred.

The language used to portray the woman, however, is lyrical and expressive, so that we cannot help but see the "woman in blue" as a person, even if her "face [is] hidden." We see her "grace," the "blue" of her dress; we delight in the "gliding" of her baskets. We imagine the weight of her "two heavy baskets," surmise how the "Chogi stick" might feel on our shoulders. That the weight of the baskets brings them "close to the hard path," that the path in fact is hard, forces us to feel *with* her the hardships of her life, perhaps the ache in her back or her feet. On the other hand, we are unable to enter the psyches of the gunner and the forward observer; they are masked by the antiseptic language they use. Even "Dink in the open" is said dispassionately, without any avowal, on a conscious level, of its derogatory quality—the language merely a fact of life. The observer in fact distances himself even further from the woman by converting her into grid coordinates, her speed and direction, depersonalizing her into a target, merely a job to be done.

The contrasting languages are focused ultimately on widely varying technologies: a sophisticated technology devoted to death and the simple device of the Chogi stick, a technology devoted to life, to making a living. It is fitting therefore that in the final stanza, the technologies confront each other first before the woman's death is acknowledged—"the shrapnel catch[ing] the gliding baskets / And they crumple with the woman in blue" (Karlin et al., *Free Fire Zone* ix). Margaret Stewart is absolutely right when she points out that the presence of "these differing perspectives" predicates a focus "not just on the killing but on the attitudes that support the act" so that "stopping the killing is . . . a matter of illuminating and changing habits of mind that dehumanize other people in imagination before they are deprived of life in fact" ("Death and Growth" 2–3), and these "habits of mind" are inextricably bound up with language.

Other linguistic dehumanizations occurred in Vietnam via the pidgin which

Americans and South Vietnamese spoke to one another. The clichéd situation is the conversation between the whore and the soldier. One veteran remembered an encounter with a prostitute.

> Her entire vocabulary was fuck and suck and yes and no. We talked for the entire evening, believe it or not. We were totally able to converse.
> She would go, "Me no suck-suck. Me fuck-fuck."
> I replied, "Me no want you to fuck-fuck. Me want you to suck-suck. You bien?"
> "No-no-no-no-no, me no suck-suck. Me fuck-fuck."
> "Listen, I want you to suck-suck first, then we fuck-fuck later. Okay?"
> "No-no-no-no-no, me no suck-suck, me fuck-fuck." That's how we passed the whole evening and I had a marvelous time. I swear to God. (Baker 207)

This language arises partly from expediency and partly from Americans feeling that these women are only sexual receptacles, an opinion which parallels an assumption that all Vietnamese are somehow less than human, fit only to fulfill one's own gratification—from sex to rape, murder, whatever.[2] In turn, however, the pidgin eventually functions to convince the American of Vietnamese inferiority. John Clark Pratt's poem "Words and *Thoughts*"—from his novel *The Laotian Fragments*—engages this issue (the woman is Thai rather than Vietnamese, but the pidgin is similar; the speaker is a fighter pilot based in Thailand who flies sorties over Laos).

> Hey, you, *you slant-eyed, luscious brown-skinned broad,*
> Why you no smile tonight? What you no hab?
> Where your zoomie tealoch-man who keep you,
> Pay you, love you? He butterfly around again?

Pratt's device of presenting the speaker's words in roman type and *his thoughts in italics* seems clumsy at first glance, but it works. The dialectic between the two levels of discourse, external and internal, is fascinating as the speaker moves from macho womanizer to sensitive human being. He begins by teasing his friend's live-in Thai girlfriend ("tealoch"), eventually tormenting her with the revelation that his friend is married in America—a Madame Butterfly context. At the same time, his thoughts revolve hungrily around the woman's physical attributes; there is not much divergence between words and *thoughts:* "You not nit-noy ['small']. You super-Thai" is perhaps less linguistically precise but not different in content from "*long legs, great calves, soft, rounded*

thighs," especially given the interesting end rhyme. That the speaker is crass
becomes clear as he offers to replace his friend who is "short-time" or soon to
return to America ("You be my tealoch, I extend a year. / I make love good—
always use balloon"). Tears are her reaction, and he fumblingly tries to assuage
her sorrow.

> *Don't cry, please. I'm sorry.* I no try
> To hurt you. I just make damn silly joke.
> *I'm just a pilot, very far from home,*
> *Who plays the game.* I dumb GI.

When he discovers that his friend has crashed, he realizes his horrible impropriety—he has underestimated the depth of feeling in this woman. In the last
stanza, he is willing to grant her humanity, especially since they now share a
grief, and he asks her forgiveness not only for himself, but for all Americans,
in light of all their lies.

> *I didn't know. Flew last night. Slept all day.*
>
> *You loved that part of him he let you love, I know.*
> *But so did we.*
> *Please stop your crying and forgive us all,*
> *As well as me.*   (192–93)

What makes this poem poignant at the end is that the last five lines are all in
the speaker's thoughts; the pidgin Thai they have been speaking is not adequate
to express his grief, his sorrow, his contrition. The language they share is only
sufficient to describe that he can "make love good—always use balloon," not
that he can truly love her. Any offer of romantic or platonic love, no matter
how sincere and heartfelt, can only be received in the limited sense of sex as
commodity.

D. C. Berry capitalizes on the uniqueness of military language in Vietnam—
its jargonized flavor but especially its sonic qualities. Berry's poetry is an active
act against linguistic conditioning. In the following poem, he demonstrates the
sterility and futility of the jargon stream in the face of death.

> The way popcorn   pops   is
> the way punji sticks snap
> into your skin and stab
>
> pricking urine
> into   cardiovascular

systems and apparatus
apparently
unorganizing then demonstrating
it.

      then you die
either from the spike,
the   p,
or the

sun gone to grain
expanding

in your eye.   (41)

Berry uses sound adroitly in this poem: the labial explosion of the plosive consonant "p" and the onomatopoeic "pop." The "p" sounds are not only initial or terminal (as in "snap"), but also medial ("apparatus," "spike," and "expanding"). In fact, Berry is even more clever when he uses the letter "p" separated from the rest of the line by white space to indicate "urine" rather than the slang "pee," which a more prosaic poet might have used. Note as well the jargon-stream diction: "cardiovascular / systems and apparatus / apparently / unorganizing." This allegedly articulate language, a species of labeling, is unable to counteract the approach of death, and the dying man seems to experience at the end of this poem some sort of epiphany, as the sun begins "expanding // in your eye." It is almost as if, at the moment of death, "you" become part of some pantheistic nature; the "sun gone to grain" alludes to the "popcorn" at the opening, or, more exactly, "corn" itself as a symbol of continuing life in the cyclical round of the seasons. The poem seems to take a bow toward the classical elegy, replacing the traditional flower imagery with "sun" and "corn"; in either case, the transcendence of death occurs in the fructification of nature.

Cross, Pratt, and Berry are wrestling in these poems not only with Felstiner's "quarantine of fact and word" but with the constrictions of human feeling and attitude which result from such limitations of language. In a larger sense, however, the poems are attempts to transcend these constrictions, to reveal the limitations through juxtapositional irony. Four other poets—Michael Casey, David Huddle, Basil T. Paquet, and D. F. Brown—concern themselves with language and its possibilities as they unfold their own Vietnam-war experiences. Walsh proposes that "the best American combatant poets, such as Michael Casey or Basil T. Paquet, offer to the reader precise renderings of small incidents in the war, personal anecdotes or insights calling upon technical knowledge which make the fighting accessible" (203), and this is characteristic as well of David Huddle and D. F. Brown. The general success of these four poets may be found in the *quality* of that precision in rendering—a precision that resides, finally, in attention to language (particularly vis-à-vis Brown's allegiance to Language Poetry) and, for Huddle, in the use of poetic form. In such precision of truth-telling, all four attempt to rise above the quandaries of language that riddle the Vietnam-war experience.

Michael Casey: Antipoetic Obscenities

In 1972, Michael Casey won the Yale Younger Poets Prize with *Obscenities*. Stanley Kunitz's foreword to this collection calls it "the first significant book of poems written by an American to spring from the war in Vietnam" (vii). Comparing Casey to Wilfred Owen, who "wanted above all to depict the senseless horrors and inhumanity of war [but whose] compassion and elevation of his style inevitably exalted his agonists-in-khaki" (vii), or to Keith Douglas, whose war poetry "appears rather stilted and formalistic now" (viii), or to Randall Jarrell, "more vital and clever" but whose "irony . . . begins to wear a bit thin in places" (ix), Kunitz found Casey new and, if not exactly refreshing, vividly different. Casey owed no indebtedness to the "rhetorical flourishes and sentiments [of] the poets who fought . . . in the earlier wars of the century" (vii). Kunitz's dilemma is how one is to confront the ambiguity, the absurdity, the mendacity of the Vietnam war in the poetic medium. And he finds one solution in these poems: Casey, through "an act of rejection. . . . has had the original insight and the controls to produce a kind of anti-poetry that befits a kind of war empty of any kind of glory" (vii). Perhaps the most praised of Casey's poems is "The LZ Gator Body Collector." The speaker, a young American soldier with the grisly duty of clearing a landing zone of dead bodies, ingenuously begins to narrate what he sees.

> See
> Her back is arched
> Like something's under it
> That's why I thought
> It was booby trapped . . .   (56)

Kunitz notes that "the language is so simple and open, so plausible, that one scarcely notices the artfulness of the compression, the understatement" (xii). The speaker cannot tell the gender of the body until he accidentally touches

"Down there," but then he reassures the reader that he "had gloves on then"; Felstiner observes that, by "merely reassuring us that his death encounter was sanitary, Casey lets the war's full insanity come in on us with everything he does not say" ("American Poetry" 11).

In prosodic terms, what is most interesting about this poem is that it is essentially a love lyric turned inside out. Eros and thanatos combined in an uneasy tension. The language is a parody of romance and pornography: "Her back is arched," "stiffened," "I grabbed / Down there"; the neologism "corpus morta" not only replaces "rigor mortis" but also emphasizes the connotations of "body" here. That the speaker says everything is okay because "I had gloves on then" (56) is hence fitting (and psychologically appropriate for a properly brought-up American)—not to mention appropriately scatological.

"The LZ Gator Body Collector" demonstrates Casey's general poetic strategy in *Obscenities*. The speaker is a spare, cut-down version of Casey himself: a figure "Sort of big / Sort of doofus looking" (61). Kunitz proposes that "*Obscenities* is conceived as a book, not as a random collection of poems" (x), and in the course of this skeletal novel Casey's stick-man self slowly puts on flesh, growing incrementally into his maturity. "I recommend reading this book straight through," Kunitz advises, "from first to last, as though it were a novel or a play, in order to follow the implicit development of the action, a progress of awareness" (xi). If Kunitz is right, then *Obscenities* is an enterprise comparable to both Peter Bowman's *Beach Red* and Dick Shea's *vietnam simply*.

Casey's language, according to W. D. Ehrhart, is based on "the truncated, matter-of-fact speech rhythms that mirror the Vietnam grunts' favorite phrase: 'There it is'—no further explanation offered" ("Soldier-Poets" 248). This language is brutally spare and frugal, and often Casey himself is invisible: only a tape recorder, it would seem, playing back a conversation overheard. "National Guardsman" is a revealing example.

> I'm going to finish
> Getting my degree
> And get a job
> With some brokerage firm . . .

The speaker has escaped the Vietnam war by joining the National Guard. Although the scene is not literally given, it is clear in the white space of the page: basic training (because only there would a draftee like Casey, eventually headed for Vietnam, intersect with a National Guard soldier in this way). The

Vietnam war is apparently very advanced because the speaker's contempt, unimaginative as he seems to be, could only reflect public opinion around or after
Tết 1968. What really clinches this poem as an authentic portrait is Casey's
natural modulation of speech, the way it depicts the National Guard soldier:
arrogant, self-aggrandizing, sarcastic, unkind, but also probably a perennial
loser (there is a good bit of self-delusion, wishful thinking, and ignorance in
his assertion that the Wall Street "interviewers will cream in their pants"—
a boy whistling in the dark). The speaker closes by setting himself up above
these future grunts who "Will be in the mud / Tough shitsky   you alll / I could
give a sweet fuck" (7). Kunitz exhibits a great deal of appreciation of Casey's
strategy: "How beautifully he listens, and with what a fine ear for speech
patterns!" (x).

Casey's mode is essentially documentary, writing a kind of "docupoetry," in
Deborah Holdstein's neologism (60). What he documents is "obscenity" after
"obscenity," moving through his Army service, from basic training, through
military police training, then to Vietnam, and back. One recurring obscenity
he records is the Army itself, the utter boredom and feeling of uselessness in
Army life, as in, for example, "Paco"—a military policeman who is sent to
investigate an alleged theft of personal property. Eventually, Paco radioes in
his report.

> Ten-twenty that last ten-twenty-four
> (Disregard, ignore, shitcan that last assignment)
> The dude
> Found his dust   (12)

That is, he found his money (said by Paco with disgust). What surfaces in this
poem is Paco's frustration at the 10–24 *interruptus,* a break from the boredom
of patrolling the quiet Army post—potential excitement, perhaps an arrest—
now anticlimactically frustrated. Casey's craft as a storyteller is indicated by his
parenthetical intrusion to translate the MP radio jargon. In the sequence "Dis-
regard, ignore, shitcan," the speaker's groping for the right word to indicate
Paco's disappointment, as he moves from officialese to colloquial language,
sets up the sarcastic tone of the final two lines and demonstrates Casey's own
frustration at the jargon and the Army which spawned it.

When Casey moves his theater to Vietnam, however, *Obscenities* shifts into
high gear. Kunitz allows that the book's power may arise "perhaps partly
[from] the inherent excitement of his material" (x)—yes, this is what we in the
cheap seats really want to hear about. The poems up to this point are meant

only to introduce us to the Casey which the poet projects to be our ears and eyes, and to teach us how to read a Casey poem, essentially to listen. "A Bummer" encapsulates the historic realities of the war. A convoy of armored personnel carriers cutting through a farmer's "rice paddies" is interrupted by the landowner "hitting the lead track / With a rake." Here we have the crucial mise-en-scène of the Vietnam war: the confrontation between the massed might of the American military and the unarmored body of the Vietnamese noncombatant. In more places and in more times than Mỹ Lai in March 1968, the results were tragic. Here, there is a certain heroism invested in the farmer, but a heroism curtailed with pathos in the inevitable reprisal: the track vehicles moving "side by side / . . . Instead of single file." In the midst of all this, we see the names emblazoned on the vehicles: "Hard On, Proud Mary / Bummer, Wallace, Rosemary's Baby / The Rutgers Road Runner / . . . Go Get Em—Done Got Em." Casey's litany gives us a composite image of the Vietnam war as well as America in the 1960s: sex (the inevitable tie between sex and war); rock 'n' roll (Creedence Clearwater Revival *and* Tina Turner); drugs (the bummer of a "bad trip"); racism (the infamous governor); movies (a satanic cult and an Antichrist); Saturday morning cartoons (tied here in significant parody to the name of a university); and the military mission (American "stick-to-it-iveness"—killing rationalized as an operation). The close of the poem, according to Kunitz, is "the closest [Casey] comes to a generalization—one of the few times his voice is even slightly raised" (x).

> If you have a farm in Vietnam
> And a house in hell
> Sell the farm
> And go home   (26)

Of course, this advice is useless to the farmer; he is both "in Vietnam" and "in hell" (from the grunt's perspective). Only Casey and other Americans have the choice to "go home." "A Bummer" dramatizes the hopeless situation in which the Vietnamese have been trapped. The slang "bummer" also means *something bad in general,* and here the title indicates with the indefinite article that this sort of encounter is repeated again and again. And if this scene is a microcosmic model of the war as a whole, then the title is a tersely eloquent critique.

"The central obscenity of Michael Casey's book *Obscenities,*" according to Stephen Spender, is "that life is not the reasonable friendly open decent American thing he thought it was, but rather what the Americans are doing in

Vietnam" (4). Spender suggests that this "central obscenity" is expressed in "On Death." The scene painted is of a dead body on a city street, attended by a variety of passersby: "School children" and "adults" as well as a grieving woman who "Wails / And pounds her fists." The most powerful portion is the description of the body, covered by flies.

> It   like made of wax
> No jaw
> Intestines poured
> Out of the stomach
> The penis in the air

The speaker closes by stating, "I don't want in death to be a / Public obscenity like this" (53). "The wish expressed in the last lines," Spender asserts, "instead of being perfectly reasonable, as any young American might expect it to be, suddenly appears a hope only, and perhaps a selfish one at that" (4). Yes, being within the shooting war holds the possibility of sudden death, and the speaker is apparently unable to commiserate here with the dead as well as the grieving. "Public obscenity" also refers to the overall war effort. The people take this all in stride, since it has become a common occurrence, clichéd. It is revelatory to read the last lines as "I don't want [my] death to be [in] a public obscenity like this [war]."

The achievement of *Obscenities* is Casey's distillation of his experience in Vietnam into "the hard core of the observed and the experienced. . . . hard pellets of poems, leaving perhaps a bitter taste of irony, of hatred (especially for the military), and of a kind of gentleness toward the victims" (Spender 6). In terms of prosody and language, Casey's success is in his abrogation of any and all poeticism. Spender proposes:

> It would be truer perhaps to say that Casey and some of the other writers in Vietnam were "anti-poets" than that their work is "anti-poetry." For what it really shows is that almost every preconception of what a poem should be can be thrown out and yet the result be poetry. (3)

Perhaps this is the finest praise one can give Michael Casey: that *Obscenities*, after it has all been said, *is* poetry.

David Huddle: Experiments in the Sonnet

David Huddle, in "Tour of Duty"—a sonnet sequence that opens his 1988 book *Stopping by Home* (a book made up largely of sonnets)—posits a project diametrically opposite to Casey's, addressing the question of traditional poetry's inability to surmount Vietnam's intractability as poetic subject by experimenting with received form and colloquial language. Huddle's poem "Nerves" is a good example.

> Training I received did not apply
> because Cu Chi District was not Fort Jackson.
> Funniest thing, they had dogs like any-
> where, used them for sandwich meat, I ate one
> once, but I guess you want to know if I
> ever shot somebody—didn't—would have—
> curious about it, but my job gave
> one duty, to ask questions. I'd lie
>
> if I said some weren't women, children,
> old men; I'd lie too if I claimed these
> memories weren't part of my life, but then
> shame is natural, wear it, every day
> think of bursting from sleep when mortars dropped:
> crazy run to a dark hole, damp sandbags.   (3)

An earlier version of the poem contained several hyphenated broken rhymes—the former opening lines rhymed "Training I received did not apply be-" with "Funniest thing, they had dogs like any-" and lines 10–11 formerly read ". . . I'd lie too if I claimed my mem- / ories weren't part of my life, but then"—indicating Huddle's spirit of innovation in tackling the sonnet (Villani 40). In the more recent version, Huddle opts for a more conservative approach, but the fact that he abandons the rhyme scheme, ending with an unrhymed couplet when the mortar attack begins, is brilliant—a subtle reminder that even the poet is human, poetry a human endeavor. In addition, the poem evokes both the weirdness of the Vietnam-war experience and the usual frustrations of readjustment into the World, despite distances in time and thought—clearly the speaker is writing this in recall, from the vantage point of America in the 1980s.

In the same way as Casey, Huddle relies on the memories of his own Vietnam tour, investing them with an authority founded on the believability of the speech rhythms in his work. A major difference between the two poets, however, is that Casey intrudes into the text only rarely to deliver a judgment, whereas in Huddle's sonnets, one has a clear sense of the poet—from moment to moment, from line to line—keenly evaluating the moral import of the material at hand, and often this judgment is conveyed through the rhyme scheme (that is, what words are made to rhyme with each other in emphasis) and the lineation (what sense is postulated either by the moment of abeyance, of fateful suspense, which can occur at an end-stopped line break or by the sense of silent hurry implicit in enjambed lines). A helpful example is the sonnet "Work."

> I am a white, Episcopal-raised, almost
> college-educated, North American male.
> Sergeant Tri, my interpreter, is engrossed
> in questioning our detainee, a small,
> bad-smelling man in rags who claims to be
> a farmer. I am filling in the blanks
> of a form, writing down what Sergeant Tri
> tells me. This is dull. Suddenly Tri yanks
>
> our detainee to his feet, slaps him twice
> across the bridge of his nose. The farmer
> whimpers. Tri says the farmer has lied and waits
> for orders. Where I grew up my father
> waits at the door while my mother finishes
> packing his lunch. I must tell Tri what next.   (5)

There is almost a protonarrative signaled by the end words: *almost / male / engrossed / small / be / blanks / Tri / yanks // twice / farmer / waits / father / finishes / next*. Sets of lines are intriguingly revealing: the speaker is *almost male;* Tri is *engrossed* and *small;* the speaker finds himself to *be blank* (i.e., bored); *Tri yanks twice* on the *farmer* then *waits; father finishes;* and what *next?* Not too far off the mark. Rhyming pairs are themselves interesting: that the speaker is *almost* while Tri is *engrossed* and that the *blanks* of the speaker are contrasted with Tri's *yanks* imply that Tri is a man of action, while the speaker is somehow less so, made to seem more passive—a comment on Vietnamese versus American; that Tri strikes the farmer *twice* and then *waits* for a cue implies, however, that the American is expected here to uphold what the Vietnamese does—whether moral or not; from the pair *farmer/father* we might infer that the speaker feels the farmer is a kind of father figure, someone to be respected; and the extremely slant line of *finish* and *next* emphasizes the speaker's inability to know how to "finish," what to do "next." The surface narrative is patently clear, and the speaker is unable to reconcile the quotidian realities of his father's life (what he does for work, how he gets his lunch) with the absurd surrealities of his own life at work in Vietnam, even at this far remove in time, sitting at the poet's word processor in the 1980s.

Throughout "Tour of Duty" the speaker is always the same—a thinly disguised version of Huddle himself—so that the sonnet sequence is in some ways an autobiography. If this is a memoir, what we have is really a moral autobiography, and as the poems unfold, we watch the growing maturity of the speaker, his increasing awareness of the realities involved. The speaker as FNG stumbles through stereotyped events, made so by his own stereotyping thinking. In "New York Laundry," for example, the speaker's penchant for romanticized intellectualism lands him into a well-traveled misunderstanding about truth and the apparent: "Fell in love . . . [and] constructed dense / monologues on individuality / nature, the body politic, for this / silent laundry girl who always seemed about / to smile." He swiftly discovers a truth not only applicable in Vietnam but also universally, that the ingenue's demeanor may hide something else altogether. "A buddy of mine set me straight one day, said / . . . those Cav guys praised / the quiet ways of my little Co Tran, / battalion candidate for Short-Time Queen" (5)—"Short-time" as in the stateside slang "quickie."

The last sonnet, "Vermont," poignantly underlines the speaker's bitter final lesson about appearances.

> I'm forty-six. I was twenty-three then.
> I'm here with what I've dreamed or remembered.
> In the Grand Hotel in Vung Tau one weekend
> I spent some time with the most delicate
> sixteen-year-old girl who ever delivered
> casual heartbreak to a moon-eyed GI.
> I am trying to make it balance, but I
> can't. Believe me, I've weighed it out.
>
> rising that morning up to the cool air where
> the green land moved in its own dream down there,
> and I was seeing, the whole flight back to Cu Chi,
> a girl turning her elegant face away
> after I'd said all I had to say.
> This was in Vietnam. Who didn't love me.   (11)

This poem encapsulates the dilemma of memory: juxtapositions freed from
time and disallowing resolution. Here, the painful rejection by the "most delicate . . . girl" becomes entangled with the lyric image of Vietnam as a "green
land . . . in its own dream down there," almost as if no war is occurring. But
the girl is not delicate, she is "casual"—even cavalier—about "heartbreak,"
and the "green land" is in fact tormented. Under the placid, attractive face lies
a hard and deceptive, even lethal, essence. And the final line highlights this
inherently American loss of innocence (cf. Melville's conception of reality as a
mask to be pierced); "Who didn't love me" of course refers directly to the girl,
but placed as it is in the line, the enticing syntactical ambiguity implies that in
fact it was Vietnam "who didn't love me" and by extension didn't love all of
America.

Huddle's obvious concern with language is emblematized through his treatment of prostitute pidgin in "Words."

> What did those girls say when you walked the strip
> of tin shack bars, gewgaw stores, barber shops,
> laundries and restaurants, most all of which
> had beds in back, those girls who had to get up
> in Saigon before dawn to catch their rides to Cu Chi,
> packed ten to a Lambretta, chattering,
> happy in their own lovely tongue, on the dusty
> circus road to work, but then what did they say?

In the opening octave, the speaker tries to enter the lives of these girls, romantically imagining their lives apart from prostitution; but he ultimately finds
himself trapped by the actuality of the language they use toward him.

> *Come here, talk to me, you handsome, GI,*
> *I miss you, I love you too much, you want*
> *short time, go in back, I don't care, I want*
> *your baby, sorry about that, GI,*
> *you number ten. . . .*

The problem is the same as that dramatized by Pratt in "Words and *Thoughts*";
the pidgin is so specialized that it prevents any true human communication,
at least for the speaker. The girls are able to express their barely disguised
contempt for the GI: "*I want / your baby, sorry about that, GI, / you number
ten*" (i.e., the worst). Even in the World and in the present, the speaker cannot

pierce through the language: ". . . A history away / I translate dumbly what those girls would say" (9). Clearly, the Vietnam war is a continuing tragedy of language, even after the fighting has ceased.

The central concern in veterans' poetry about Vietnam between aesthetic and antipoetic modes is the nagging notion that traditional war poetry (rhymed, metered, formal) may imply a glorification of war, as Kunitz has argued in his introduction to Casey's *Obscenities*. "Owen, Sassoon, and the others were extremely conscious of being poets," Spender recalls. "They carried their poems with them into the trenches and loaded their kit-bags with romantics or classics" (3). Huddle, in his sonnet "Cousin" (dedicated "for John H. Kent, Jr., 1919–1982"), deals with this conflict of image between the world wars and the Vietnam war.

> I grew up staring at the picture of him:
> oak leaves on his shoulders, crossed rifles
> on his lapels, and down his chest so many medals
> the camera lost them. He wore gold-rimmed
> glasses, smiled, joked about fear. He told true
> stories that were like movies on our front porch:
> he'd fought a German hand to hand. The word
> *courage* meant Uncle Jack in World War Two.
>
> Ten years from my war, thirty from his, we
> hit a summer visit together; again
> the stories came. He remembered names of his men,
> little French towns, a line of trees. I could see
> his better than mine. He'd known Hemingway!
> I tried hard but couldn't find a thing to say.   (11)

For Uncle Jack, WWII is a warm pastiche of glory, of camaraderie, of European quaintness—clichés readily accessible throughout the culture, especially in the cinema. The speaker, as a creature of this culture, can readily apprehend these culturally naturalized norms of war—national imperative, war's allure as crucible of manhood—but the memory of the Vietnam war persists in being a denaturalized myth, and becomes inexpressible. There is, however, a mode of expression: the poem. In order to function as an appropriate vehicle for the subject of Vietnam, however, the poem's own conventions, tied as they are to the accepted forms of Uncle Jack's realities, need to be revised. Casey and the other antipoets choose to reject traditional conventions altogether. Huddle chooses to keep certain conventions (the consensus on rhyme, form, and meter:

the poem as a specific kind of bottle) but dispenses with standard poetic language (altering what goes into the bottle). And what Huddle puts into this bottle called "Cousin" is a language that avoids all glorification ("he'd fought a German hand to hand" is said in offhand manner). Huddle's simple, direct language admits finally that there isn't "a thing to say."

Basil T. Paquet: Aesthetician Extraordinaire

Basil T. Paquet, unlike Casey and Huddle, attempts to keep *both* poetic conventions and heightened language, painfully conscious of his work as poetry in the highest literary sense. As Spender puts it, Paquet has a "greater literary self-consciousness" than other Vietnam-veteran poets, with his "ambitions which derive from an idea of poetry based on past examples and which exercise claims on the future" (3). If Casey's focus is on speech patterns and antilyrical compression, Paquet's attention is paid to lyric diction, to metaphor, ambiguity, wordplay, to sensuous rhythm and emotional texture, *but* without any sacrifice of the same devotion to the documentary and the personally realistic as Casey.

Paquet has not published a collection of poetry, but his poems have been published in the *New York Review of Books, Freedomways, Midwest Magazine, WIN Magazine, New Times, Long Island Review,* and *Jamaica Arts Review* (Ehrhart, *Mercy* 111). His poetry has also been anthologized in *Winning Hearts and Minds, Carrying the Darkness, Vietnam Anthology,* and *Unaccustomed Mercy.* He has completed a novel about Vietnam, and his fiction has been included in the short-story collection *Free Fire Zone.* In reference to *Winning Hearts and Minds,* Ehrhart suggests that, "Of the dozen or so poems Paquet contributes, three or four must rank as among the very best Vietnam war poems yet written. Literate without being literary, Paquet was, at the time, far and away the most skillful and practiced of the soldier-poets" (247–48).

As an echo of Wilfred Owen, the sonnet "Christmas '67" illustrates Paquet's method.

> Flares lit the night like a sky
> Full of Bethlehem stars.
> Dark wings against a darker sky
> Laid down red ribbons and bars
> Of bright crashing metal
> To warn of the on-coming
> Assault of men, the long battle

Filled with cries of "in-coming,"
That sent them crawling about
Into the pocked earth, waiting for the promise
Of thudding hosannas, like a gathering of devout
Moths, aching for the flames, but frozen by the hiss
And whistle of mortars and rockets sliding
Down their air pews in a choiring of dying.   (*Winning* 36)

In this poem, Paquet applies the Shakespearean sonnet form—the ultimate love lyric—to war. Paquet's poetic territory and concerns here are reminiscent of the themes and diction of a poem like Owen's "Anthem for Doomed Youth" in which religious language is distorted into the usages of war. In "Christmas '67," Paquet juxtaposes the religious accouterments of Christmas against the horrors of battle, resulting in an irony expressed by the opening image: illumination flares compared with "Bethlehem stars." The Christmas decorations of these men under fire are "ribbons and bars / Of bright crashing metal." Rather than angel choirs, Paquet gives us instead artillery's "thudding hosannas." The difference between this poem and Owen's is that in Paquet's no comfort is found in either lyric imagery or the symbology of Christmas; there are only screams in the night—"a choiring of dying."

"Easter '68" similarly distorts the associations of Easter: resurrection and the renewal of spring.

I have seen the pascal men today.
Long past rising to a passion
they sucked their last sun
through blued lips,
buttressed their intestines in handfuls . . .

The medic-speaker strains, especially in a phrase like "pascal men" (the word *paschal* made somehow less sacral), to grant these dying men some transcendence, but the only Easter he can glimpse is "broken Easters of flesh / girdled in fatigue strips": no longer whole men but only fragments. The penultimate image is striking, a crescendo of hope and subsequent despair:

red arching rainbows of dead men
rising like a promise
to give Jesus the big kiss
and sinking down—

There *is* no renewal, no transcendence, no resurrection, no promise. The speaker is left earthbound, unsolaced, weighed down by the dying around him, the suffering he is unable to assuage: "only my breath on their lips / only my words on their mouths" (*Winning* 37). In "Anthem for Doomed Youth," Owen subverts the language of religion but subsequently replaces it with a consecration of landscape. In "Christmas '67" and "Easter '68"—two poems whose dates frame the most savage fighting of the war during Tết 1968 (itself a Vietnamese megaholiday)—Paquet's subversion of religious language is unremitting and unrelieved, all promises of spiritual transcendence only broken ones.

It may be that "broken" is a word which begins to point to a characteristic obsession of Paquet's, an understandable obsession given his job (or "military occupational specialty"—MOS in militarese). Paquet was a medic in Vietnam. In "Basket Case," Paquet attempts to understand empathetically how it feels to be castrated (or "traumatically amputated" as Caputo might remind us).

> I waited eighteen years to become a man.
> My first woman was a whore off Tu Do street,
> But I wish I had never felt the first wild
> Gliding lust, because the rage and thrust
> Of a mine caught me hip high.

What Paquet postulates here is that the innermost feelings of a person, the complexities unacknowledged in conscious thought, can be conveyed by lyrical language. This persona more than likely would not have articulated his "wild / Gliding lust" and "the rage and thrust / Of a mine" in those same terms, especially lying in a hospital bed. Here is how a poet using Casey's characteristic mode might have rendered these same thoughts in laconic grunt lingo: "Only got my first piece at eighteen. Boom-boom short-time off Tu Do street. I'd of never had it, if I'd known a motherfucking mine would blow my balls away." Such an antipoetic method relies on the empathy of the reader, that the reader will be able to intuit the deeper feelings that underpin the words. Paquet, resorting to lyricism, attempts to voice these underpinnings.

> I felt the rip at the walls of my thighs,
> A thousand metal scythes cut me open,
> My little fish shot twenty yards
> Into a swamp canal.
> I fathered only this—the genderless bitterness
> Of two stumps, and an unwanted pity

> That births the faces of all
> Who will see me till I die deliriously
> From the spreading sepsis that was once my balls.

(Winning 20)

In analyzing Casey's work, Felstiner has pointed out how "the war's full insanity" is semaphored by "everything he does not say" ("American Poetry" 11). Paquet, on the other hand, tries to say it *all* but with memorable and disciplined sophistication. Thus, when his speaker uses the word "balls" at the end, the sudden explosion of the colloquial brings home the true significance of "genderless bitterness" and "spreading sepsis."

In several startling poems, voices lift waveringly from beyond death. "Morning—A Death" alludes to the strophic-antistrophic movements of ancient Greek verse. The opening, subtitled "Turn—Character 1," is a dramatic monologue of a medic speaking to the dead.

> I've blown up your chest for thirty minutes
> And crushed it down an equal time,
> And still you won't warm to my kisses.
> I've sucked and puffed on your
> Metal No. 8 throat for so long,
> And twice you've moaned under my thrusts
> On your breastbone. I've worn off
> Those sparse hairs you counted noble on your chest,
> And twice you defibrillated,
> And twice blew back my breath.

The medic, in weary and overburdened exhaustion, admits: "You are dead just as finally / As your mucosity dries on my lips." The antistrophe, "Counterturn—Character 2," is in the voice of the dead soldier, who ironically enough has wished for the death that the medic has been so heroically trying to postpone: "I'd sooner be a fallen pine cone this winter / . . . Cut down running my ass off at a tree line. / . . . I bought the ticket, I hope I drown fast, / The pain is all in living." The third section, "Stand—Character 1," returns to the medic who hauntingly echoes the opening thought of the second section: "I'd sooner be in New England this winter / With pine pitch on my hands than your blood." A further irony here is that, since the dying man had briefly envisioned himself as a "pine cone," the medic even in New England can never be free of the dead man, recapitulated as "pine pitch." The close is a fervent wish on the medic's part for the ability to make life rather than be a midwife to death. "I'd so much rather be making children, / Than tucking so many in" (*Winning* 22–23). The title is a wordplay on "mourning a death," but here the deaths are so overwhelmingly various that this particular death is only *of* a morning.

And the dead speak in other Paquet poems. In "Graves Registration," we listen to the voices heard by the graves registration (GR) specialist—the military counterpart to the civilian mortician. The scene is battlefield carnage, and the corpses, both Vietnamese and American, begin to speak to the GR specialist as he waits for the GR truck in the sun with the corpses. " 'I remember a cloud / against the flares. / I was high as a mother. / It looked like a fish' " (presumably from a GI whose last moments occur in drug hallucination); " 'Laughter shredded in my mouth. / I felt my throat rip in a choke, / the earth heaved with flame' "; and more. The most striking is a Vietnamese voice:

> "The brightness of sun
> caught this morning
> in his red fist
> the smashed flowers
> of our faces,
> licked the wetness
> the drying surprise
> from our petal-eyes
> and reeled on."   (*Winning* 62–64)

Spender finds in these lines a "poetic peasant idiom" but finally a pathetic fallacy: "giving the dead peasants the voice which is really that of the conscious-stricken [*sic*] American who sees them as a kind of embodied (dead-bodied) poetry" (3). Nevertheless, it is only partially a confession of guilt on the part of the speaker (or some version of Paquet himself); it is also an attempt to make human connections, to transcend the boundaries of self.

Paquet is at his best when he writes in an elevated style, as in a set piece of self-reflexive writing in the opening section of "Morning—A Death," where the medic, in a flight of linguistic fancy, envisions his lifesaving in terms that call attention to the poet's own prosodic obsessions.

> I've scanned the rhythms of your living,
> Forced half-rhymes in your silent pulse,
> Sprung brief spondees in your lungs,
> And the cesura's called mid-line, half-time,
> Incomplete, but with a certain finality.

At first, this writing seems gimmicky, but there is an unavoidable honesty
here—a sense that the poet is organically feeling that these stutters of life *really
are* cognate to prosody. The use of the term "spondee" evokes the rhythm
of the dying man's pairs of long exhalations; the "cesura" with its barrier of
white space is an adequate image of the momentary halting of life. What finally
rescues this risky writing is the sheer imaginative force of the lines which
follow.

> The bullet barks apocalyptic
> And you don't unzip your sepulchral
> Canvas bag in three days.
> No rearticulation of nucleics, no pheonix,
> No novae, just an arbitrary of one-way bangs
> Flowing out to interstitial calms.
> The required canonical wait for demotion
> To lower order, and you wash out pure chemical.
>
> (*Winning* 22)

This elevated diction is not merely highfalutin. The barrage of lexical complexity is meant as an antidote to the jargon stream, a faith in the fireworks of
language and of composition, not merely what Orwell has decried as the "gumming together [of] long strips of words which have already been set in order
by someone else, and making the results presentable by sheer humbug" (134–
35). The unavoidable echo here to the sentence "you wash out pure chemical"
is Randall Jarrell's closing line in "The Death of the Ball Turret Gunner"—
"When I died they washed me out of the turret with a hose" (144)—an important parallel of the dehumanizations of two wars.

One of the processes that Paquet's poems accomplish best is the engagement
of the imagination to the unbelievability of the Vietnam war, its intractability
as poetic subject. "They Do Not Go Gentle" is emblematic.

> The half-dead comatose
> Paw the air like cats do when they dream,
> They perform isometrics tirelessly.
> They flail the air with a vengeance
> You know they cannot have.
> After all, their multiplication tables,
> Memories of momma, and half their id
> Lies in some shell hole
> Or plop! splatter! on your jungle boots.

> It must be some atavistic angst
> Of their muscle and bones,
> Some ancient ritual of their sea water self,
> Some blood stream monsoon,
> Some sinew storm that makes
> Their bodies rage on tastelessly
> Without their shattered brains.   (*Winning* 3)

The title refers to Dylan Thomas's famous exhortation affirming life and the pursuit of it. In Paquet's Vietnam, however, this primal urge is reduced to the body's momentary life after a shell hits, mere corporeal inertia. Diction here implies an intellectualized rationality: "comatose," "isometrics," "id," "atavistic angst." But the lasting impression is of "multiplication tables, / Memories of momma" smeared "plop! splatter!"—American intangibles concretized by onomatopoeia. The point is that Paquet sets up a tension between the quotidian realities of the World with the incredible commonplaces of the 'Nam. Here, it is a tension of diction, of words imported from widely varying sets of connotation, what Brian McHale has called, in postmodernist writing, "Lexical exhibitionism. . . . words which are by their very nature highly conspicuous, self-foregrounding as it were: rare, pedantic, archaic, neologistic, technical, foreign words" (151). The inference we might draw is that through his diction Paquet is forging a metastyle, a metapoetry which partakes of characteristic late-twentieth-century literary modes—postmodernism.

D. F. Brown: The Fragging of Language

The most relentlessly postmodernist of Vietnam-veteran poets is D. F. Brown, in whose poems a certain fragmentation of language occurs, a fragmentation closely resembling the avant-gardism of Language Poetry. I submit, however, that Brown's poetic project ultimately surpasses the experiments of the Language Poets to date; because Brown focuses on the Vietnam-war experience, his innovations on Language Poetry methods may have a greater ideological impetus than those poets whose only subject is language itself. As Philip Beidler argues, "the necessary historical and mythic self-deconstitutions of American vision after Vietnam [are the bases] upon which only can be built truly creative projects of necessary historical and mythic self-reconstitution" (*Re-Writing* 5). In other words, the war and its disruptions can be the ground for new experimentation. According to Beidler, this phenomenon is occurring on all literary fronts: the "breadth of the enterprise" of Vietnam-veteran writing has "frequently embraced and enlarged the forms and strategies of postmodernist new writing" (*Re-Writing* 5). I propose that Brown is on the proverbial cutting edge of such experimentation.

The so-called Language Poets often differ widely in individual theories of poetry, but they share certain assumptions. Witness, for example, these manifestos by the founders of *L=A=N=G=U=A=G=E* (the journal whose title originated the label): Charles Bernstein has proposed that poetry should refrain from "making the language as transparent as possible" because the "movement . . . toward opacity/denseness [can] actually map the fullness of thought and its movement" (70); Bruce Andrews, Bernstein's coeditor, has delineated a poetry of "echoes, harmonies, overtones, but not the principles of organization. . . . [A c]onfusion of realms, profusion of events and interplay on the surface [so that the] subject has disappeared behind the words only to emerge in front, or inside them" (34). The central point is that a poetic of the sort that Bernstein and Andrews champion centers not on subject or the poet's consciousness or poetic form or even syntax but rather on the slipperiness of signification and on the free play of language as an end in itself.

Literary critics writing on D. F. Brown's work assert his devotion to breaking new ground, to innovating poetic conventions and prosodic methods. Jack Marshall's introduction to *Returning Fire* (the 1984 winner of the San Francisco State University Poetry Chapbook competition) points to Brown's

> jumpcuts in syntax, staccato phrases, abrupt compressions of time and distance, a tense urgency and keen anxiety revealed in the ostinato of repeated and broken-off rhythmic patterns; hesitation, attempts at rephrasing, readjusting vision as the syntax threatens to collapse under its burden and instead creates a packed density, razor-sharp edges which omit whatever does not contribute to the evocative, sensuous fabric beaten thin by the pressure of enjambed feeling. (10)

The book's opening poem, "Bluto Addresses the Real," seeks to establish this mode for *Returning Fire,* displaying Brown's characteristic use of fragmented language.

> This is where what then
> happens and who signifies.
> Pulling covered, over again
> and again realize. How long
> it is left in no higher order

than grammar. Education
works they like to say
tell us better
builders waiting to
construct erect. Go on.

Simple as buckshot it's happening.
Under your feet. Don't turn
around. It's yours.

This early Popeye stuff.
Before they automated
animation. Look up!

You have to grab before
it gets away or how

to say it, what
I want.   I love you   (15)

The presence of the words "happens" and "signifies" in the seemingly non-
sensical opening lines telegraphs that we are in poststructuralist territory—
a realm wherein actuality and meaning are segregated, one from the other.
Lorrie Smith has pointed to Brown's "compaction and use of ambiguous syntax and line endings to suggest multiple meanings"; her example is the phrase
"tell us better," which "might be an imperative demand for a 'higher order'
of truth, or it may be modifying 'builders.' " The close of the poem can then
be read, according to Smith, as a "note of possibility that 'the real' might be
retrieved . . . (the 'real' war rescued from the reductive distortions of 'grammar' and 'education')" ("Resistance" 60). Reality in this poem is ultimately
"semiotic, eluding the fixity of symbolic language and residing in the gaps between words and actions" (Smith, "Resistance" 59)—and this is essentially a
thematic concern of the entire book.

Smith has also noted that "a recurring opposition in the book—us and
them—[suggests] the existence of 'something else,' a higher order, somewhere
beyond what 'they say' and somewhere within what 'we know' " ("Resistance" 59–60). This notion of opposed groups of people can ultimately help us
decipher Brown's code in this poem if we focus on the title, "Bluto Addresses
the Real." Bluto is of course a character in the Popeye cartoon mythos; his "I
love you" at the end may be addressed to the viewer of the cartoon, so that
the "Real" in the title is *us*. This poem's startling discovery is that we have a

fictional character breaking the convention of that fiction and speaking *out* of the fiction: hence, a metacartoon. The implication is that we may ourselves also be trapped in some fiction, and perhaps we are. The secret is to try to break out, to pierce through the medium (in our own case, ossified language) to full understanding—in the same way that Bluto, as the eternal bully, discovers in an epiphanic flare at the end of the poem his full humanity: that he can love.

This "breaking-out" is what Brown attempts to do in this book: to pierce through our own blindnesses, especially those imposed by language, to an order of knowledge somehow more profound. Although Brown *may* subscribe to Language Poetry methodologies—and "Bluto Addresses the Real" is a convincing argument for such an allegiance—he has nevertheless, in his specialization of subject, another far-reaching agenda. Brown's reductive deconstruction of language is a method reminiscent of the practice of "fragging" in the Vietnam war—the assassination of a dangerously ineffective officer. Fragging, according to its relentlessly pragmatic logic, is self-defense, a reseizing of control over one's life; similarly, Brown's fragging of language is a way to re-control that language, to force it to say what he *means* to say, to avoid whatever its centuries-old baggage of blood-and-guts glory may imply.

One way to reseize language is through experimentation with syntax. Brown's poem "Illumination," by fragmenting the sentence, dramatizes the feeling of nakedness experienced by the grunts—the anxiety of being decoys.

> no sunrise here   three layers of green
> give a day a lime glow   evening lasts five
> grey minutes   the dark lasts all night
> lighting a smoke marks the spot for anybody
> everything is a dead giveaway
>
>   the new L T dreams up some movement
> he has to see   he is truly possessed
> has been crying for his girl   she is all
> he needs but a little light in the jungle
> will make it   go away   he radios base
> crank up the 105's   fire illumination
>
>   a we-know-they-know-where-we-are-at
> I hope we don't find them   I've been there
> seen the pictures   (*Returning* 29)

This poem's title gives us its method: the syntactical chunks are equivalent to illumination rounds, while the spaces between the chunks represent darkness made even darker by the fact of illumination rounds having passed through. As the chunks materialize their light and pass, the reader experiences incremental knowledge, understanding a bit more after each chunk. What finally accretes is the horror that illumination brings: the angst of "we-know-they-know-where-we-are-at"—causing anxiety because the illumination round has *not* revealed *where-they-are*. Of course, "illumination" also refers to the Vietnam veteran's incremental insights about the war, those realizations back home in the World of how dangerous the war had personally been and how that peril had been increased by our own technology, our leadership, and ourselves. If the treacherous, self-injurious technology of the Vietnam war is complicit with traditional language, then syntactic devolution in these poems functions finally as a revolution against the military-industrial complex. As Jerome McGann has argued, Language Poetry "engages adversely with all that means to appear authoritative, fixed, and determined. . . . So false and self-conflicted seem the ordinary public forms of discourse . . . that the artistic representation of such discourse must . . . activate a critical engagement" (272).

Brown's poem "When I Am 19 I Was a Medic" exhibits in its title's fragmentation of verb tense a conflation of past and present—Vietnam and America—in an attempt to "bring the war home":

> All day I always want to know
> the angle, the safest approach.
> I want to know the right time
> to go in. Who is in front
> of me, who is behind.
> When the last shots were fired,
> what azimuth will get me out,
> the nearest landing zone.

In this first strophe, we see a grunt perched on the edge of angst, relying on safe information, what will save his life. The mixing of tenses, especially "were" and "will" seen as consecutive, emphasizes the synchronicity of these feelings: the speaker experiences them in his present life as strongly as he did in Vietnam. In a sense, he is *still* in the 'Nam. In his waking life in the World, he is continually governed by the overreactions of war. His anchor in life is

> . . . all my stuff:
> morphine, bandages at my shoulder,
> just below, parallel, my rifle.

> I sleep strapped to a .45,
> bleached into my fear.
>
> . . . .
>
> . . . saying my wife's name
> over and over.

In this dreaming/waking world, ritual and habit become watchwords. The speaker is keenly aware of his enhanced wisdom: "I can tell true stories / from the jungle." But the point is that he does not, because such stories, the camaraderie of grunts,

> . . . our sense of humor
> embarrasses me. Something
> warped it out of place
> and bent I drag it along—

The "true stories" become only a burden because their truth seems, to those who were not present, only "warped" and so the speaker is "bent" by the continually conflicted truth which demands to be said but which also seems warped. And the war goes on, driven by the invisible but omnipresent "they."

> Now they tell me something else—
> I've heard it all before
> sliding through the grass
> to get here.   (*Returning* 26)

One aspect of this "they" might be the government giving its own people misleading information (that is, "what azimuth will *not* get me out"), but in fact the word "they" refers to *all* mendacious and misleading people—those whom the speaker, because of his combat experience, can always distinguish. The point is the terrible burden of the Vietnam war: its double-edged responsibilities, the feeling of knowing too much.

Again and again, this sense of the war pervading quotidian American life is invoked. "First Person—1981" is a personal statement recording "these days" which are like

> a pale green gnarl
> roots and vines
> searching for sunlight

> through
> this tangle   (*Returning* 35)

In its plain admission "I get through these days" we see that the poem really is about survival, but a survival which is hampered severely by a lack of light, a tangle of impediments. And not the least of these daily impediments, at least for the poet, is everyday language.

Brown's title *Returning Fire* "is characteristically ambiguous," notes Smith, "(as a verb, shooting back; as an adjective, the fire which keeps reappearing in memory)" ("Resistance" 59). To these I would add—bearing in mind the syntactical ellipses Brown favors—a further ambiguity in the title as a gerund phrase with one preposition or another left out: either "returning IN fire" or "returning TO fire." The first phrase implies that the Vietnam veteran returned to the World while still immersed in the "fire" of Vietnam, a mind-set not easily expunged, and the second suggests a recapturing of the war experience by returning in memory to firefights (and other moments) in Vietnam.

My second revision of the title, "returning TO fire," a potentially cathartic return to combat, is what Brown attempts in the book's title piece, "Returning Fire." The poem's beginning—"what we think / we remember"—implies the shifting notions of what exactly those memories are (and mean) and what we can reconstruct. By returning in memory to Vietnam, Brown suggests, one can "take any way back" and end up slogging "down a hot tropic / trail to good soldiers." The mise-en-scène is a group of grunts "slopped in mud." In extreme empathy, Brown and we wish to rescue them from danger; we hear them speak with "tongues so pure / and gone to god" that

> you want them
>   to slip from green
>   clothes wet boots
>   with plenty hot water
>   you would steam off mud
>   get them ready for bed

"Brown goes against all the macho stereotypes and ideals of our culture," asserts Smith, "by imagining himself as a nurturing figure putting his 'children' to bed" ("Resistance" 63). Of course, the speaker realizes the all-too-real dangers of the Vietnamese jungle, and for him such a phrase as "putting his 'children' to bed" can also have multiple meanings, not the least of which has to do with the "death" of these " 'children.' " The close of "Returning Fire" reveals that it is in effect an elegy for a doomed patrol.

>   they never come back
>   soaked off into jungle
>   they rise only
>   in the rough
>   second growth
>   that follows   (*Returning* 20–23)

The "second growth" may refer to the "Second Coming" of Christ, when the dead will rise from the earth; it may also refer, however, to the continuing growth of the jungle. Beyond these, the most important signification of that phrase may be the "second growth" which occurs in the mind of the poet as well as of the reader—a "second growth" of meaning and understanding.

The poem "Still Later There Are Memories," as Smith astutely asserts, "permanently defers the moment when [war] stories will make sense, since there is no 'now' to help us locate 'later' " ("Resistance" 61–62). In part 1 of the poem, we find

>   Another buddy dead.
>   There is enough dying—
>   Gary Cooper will
>   ride up, slow and easy
>   slide off his horse
>   without firing a shot
>   save us all.
>
>   It is a matter of waiting.
>   We grow old counting the year
>   by days, one by one
>   each morning ritual marks
>   one more, one less—
>   the plane has yet to land.   (*Returning* 45)

The eternal deferment of war stories is tied to a betrayal by myth: the cavalry has not arrived, "the plane has yet to land." This opening portion of the poem, set in Vietnam, records the inevitable feelings of stasis and anomie accompanying the one-year tour. The American high command invented the short tour

to ease the soldier's mind, but the actual psychological effect, as many have
recorded, was the opposite—a growing dread as the year slows interminably
to its close. When, in part 2 of the poem, the setting moves to America, we see
that the counting of days does not cease, and neither do the feelings of anomie:
"a decade / recounting days since." And of course "recounting" is another
word for "telling a story," but here the sense is limited to enumeration, so that
"telling the story" can never occur. The end of Brown's poem is the "later" in
which there *are* "war stories"—really *one* war story: "nobody / comes away
in one piece" (*Returning* 46). This is the final and overwhelming sense of *Returning Fire*—the tragedy of the war—some die, some are wounded, but all
are affected.

In his work beyond *Returning Fire,* Brown's stylistic connections with Language Poetry remain vital and vivid. In 1988, Brown published a ten-page
poem entitled "The Other Half of Everything" in the final issue of *Ironwood.*
Lorrie Smith suggests that this "intricate, eight-part poem . . . marches ner-
vously across the page," pointing out "the poem's fluid richness," a "lyrical
plenitude [that] opens it to the flux and indeterminacy of history" ("Resistance" 64–65).

"The Other Half of Everything" is laced throughout with biting sarcasm
and irony.

> Nobody loses sleep over Nam anymore? Did
> they? Did you? No one refers to Nam as a
> theater of war like they did for the second.
>
> "Chinese Border War"
>
> Act II, scene i. Tropical version.   ("Other Half" 175–76)

This brief passage tweaks all sorts of loose ends: the way mainstream America
has conveniently shelved the Vietnam war, especially in contrast with WWII;
the irony of the military usage "theater"; and a reminder of how, for the
Vietnamese, war with the United States is only a brief interlude in a several-
millenia-long war with China, as well as how, during the advisor period, many
Americans conversely thought of the war as only a border dispute. Such lines
as "Think Nam was a theme park / for working class kids" and "Like the
movie, but no music and it stink" focus the bitter realities of the actual war
into stark contrast against its representations in popular culture ("Other Half"
176, 179). Brown also underlines the ongoing omnipresence of the military-
industrial complex: "Expect to live at peace in the heart of a / military empire.

Every day martial pumped / at you. White lines in your blue sky" ("Other Half" 180). Instead of clouds, contrails. To consider Brown's long poem in this way, through snippets, is to misrepresent its overall impact, however. The "lyrical plenitude" to which Smith points is enmeshed in Brown's Language Poetry method, an accreting multiplication of seeming non sequiturs, a jump-cut montage of apparently unrelated images. Witness one entire section:

1.
You almost have to lie. By now we got so much shit
on this we don't hear otherwise. Lies. Free floating terror. Viet Nam vets. Free fire zones. You
heard it all. You know the tune.

I, for one, am dropping constraints. I'll hold it
to language. More mischief, less mystery.

Just words. A split infinitive.

You don't have to take it on the chin.
Leave the darkness to Springsteen.
I know the tune.

Any time now is going to be twenty years since.

Not always New Year's Day. Not January First.
Beyond counting. One at a time. Down. Per
day, a year older. Per annum yield.

It do take great clots of peanut butter.

And where does music fit?
Between hand grenades and H bombs?
In the past perfect?

What distance the need?
Ben cranks the right nut off the bike's rear wheel.
Dug in slightly, he opens the gears, lifts the. . . .
You can still call it a bike. You couldn't ride it.
He is thinking about the war but his hands are busy.
He holds on. It's cool. He unscrews the valve. De-
flates, hums. 1969. Plei-ku Province. 82nd Combat
Engineers. Sixth bridge out Q L 19. East. This is

the third time he has helped replace it and the N L F
isn't waiting for them to finish. This is first person. The first, at least, he killed with a shovel.

Outside the wire melody doesn't work.

You're waiting for something to happen.

It's your life. You forget you're waiting.
You forget what law this makes.

Whose song which night?   ("Other Half" 172–73)

This section of the poem calls attention to the inadequacy of daily, complacent
language to express the Vietnam-war experience: the slipperiness of signification implied by "Split infinitive" juxtaposed to "free float- / ing terror" (in
fact, a split present participle, hence a near miss); the gap of meaning between the grammatical term "past perfect" and the unavoidable imperfections
of Vietnam past; the "call it a bike" which is the Vietnam veteran's imperfect
reconstruction of the war through a mechanistic reconstruction of memory;
the deconstruction of time in "per day, a year older" coupled with existential
anomie ("You're waiting for something to happen. // It's your life. You forget
you're waiting"); and so on, and so on. Somehow, through some deep under-
current of signification, some subtle subtext of subconscious memory, some
rich vein of underground language waiting to be mined, a gossamer thread of
meaning emerges here, but a thread nevertheless. Brown's work, especially in
his use of cut-and-paste montage, collage, and bricolage, resembles Language
Poetry in a great many respects, but it is finally something different altogether.
The fact of his focus on Vietnam as subject is the source finally of that gossamer
thread of meaning. In his book-in-progress, *Assuming Blue,* Brown is perfect-
ing this thread-of-meaning/collage/cut-and-paste method in long poems such
as "A Little Fire in Burgerland," "Napalm Elegy," and of course "The Other
Half of Everything."

Brown achieves his complex poetic effects by "fragging" ordinary language,
even ordinary poetic language. " 'The understanding syntax provides retards
the understanding I desire,' " he writes. " 'Combat is something else, and to fit
it to grammar is to deform it and offer it up as possibility to understand' " (from
a letter quoted by Smith, "Resistance" 59). Brown's relentlessly deconstruc-
tive fragmentation of language is therefore intended to denaturalize war from
linguistic apprehension and thus from human understanding; only through such
breaking of expectation and pattern can we even begin to comprehend war.

Phrased as simply and unambiguously as possible, war is unspeakable, and the intricate, postmodern, fragmentary maze of Brown's poetry, in profound paradox, linguistically re(as)sembles the harrowing experience of the Vietnam combat veteran.

Coda: The Jargon Stream Is Still *with* Us

During the Gulf war, *Newsweek* documented the latest buzzwords in the 1990s version of the military jargon stream, somewhat gleefully and without any apparent memory of the disinformative tautology of official language in the Vietnam war. In its issue of January 26, 1991, *Newsweek* cited an example of a military buzzword that was particularly revelatory in its dehumanizing connotations—the phrase "Collateral damage"—translated as "civilian casualties" (6). In the February 4, 1991, issue of *Newsweek,* the Pentagon spokesman for the Desert Storm campaign, retired Lieutenant General Thomas Kelly, was reported to have said when asked about the rumor that Saddam Hussein had executed disobedient military commanders, "Well, he does have a very dynamic zero-defect program" (19). Whether or not Kelly had his tongue in his cheek, it is clear that the jargon stream is—to rephrase an old cliché—"alive and well and happily married in Washington." The master trope of the Vietnam veteran who resists duplicitous language—as represented by Casey, Huddle, Paquet, and particularly Brown—is an ultimate harbinger of hope.

Thomas Merton's argument that the deceptively euphemistic language of the Vietnam war points to "symptoms of a national—indeed worldwide—illness" (100) and that the only language which can oppose the jargon stream is the idiom of revolution—"racy, insolent, direct, profane, iconoclastic, and earthy"—is problematized by this idiom being *simultaneously* a "language of power," itself ultimately mired in "self-enclosed finality" (118). These poets' linguistic experimentations, their attempts to create an anticognate to the "city on a hill," are the ineluctable offspring of the "New Babel" which constitutes official Vietnam-war language. Their antibabble is more fluent and truth-telling than any jargon stream—a revolutionary lingo that is not finally a "language of power" (in Merton's formulation). In the face of a declining general audience for contemporary poetry, the question is whether their revolution will reach the people.

FOUR. NEW GENERATION, NO GENERATION

In 1973, the year American troops left Vietnam, Richard Slotkin published *Regeneration Through Violence,* a study of psychomythic motivation in the American West. Slotkin's archetype involves "the American hero [who] is the lover of the spirit of the wilderness, [but whose] acts of love and sacred affirmation are acts of violence against that spirit and her avatars." The basic narrative is an "initiation into a new life or a higher state of being" (*Regeneration* 22), generally revolving around the rescue of a woman imprisoned by Indians; the mythic structure is "an intimate conflict between male avatars of wilderness and civilization for possession of the white female captive" (*Regeneration* 179). The basic rewards of this conflict are "self-creation and self-renewal through the hunt" (*Regeneration* 477) and the advancement of civilization into the frontier. Slotkin points to the self-creative example of Deerslayer killing an Indian in battle and receiving his new identity as Hawkeye from the dying warrior. There occurs, however, the western hero's dilemma: by rescuing the woman and extending civilization into the wilderness, he accepts her ethics and destroys his life on the edge of the frontier; therefore, if the "ethic of the white woman is finally the only acceptable one, the impulse that originally led the hunter to seek the dark female spirit of the wilderness must be corrupt. . . . The hunter myth resolves these dilemmas in the symbolic action of the killing of the beast" (*Regeneration* 553). A classic example, proposes Slotkin, is Ahab's hunt of the whale in *Moby-Dick.* Essentially, these mythic structures "provided a fictive justification for the process by which the wilderness was to be expropriated and exploited" (*Regeneration* 554). It is important here to point out that regeneration through violence is an essentially macho myth,[1] especially in the ways that women are objectified as either captive/treasure or sentimentalized as some "dark female spirit of the wilderness."

The mythic formula of regeneration through violence, as a construction of machismo, is readily transferable to the context of war. Ron Kovic recalls his childhood fascination with the western. "I made my first Holy Communion with a cowboy hat on my head and two six-shooters in my hands" (39). As he got older, his focus moved to "war movies with John Wayne and Audie Murphy"; at the close of *To Hell and Back,* Audie Murphy "jumps on top of a flaming tank that's just about to explode and grabs the machine gun blasting it into the German lines. He was so brave I had chills running up and down my back, wishing it were me up there. . . . It was the greatest movie I ever saw in my life" (43). He and his friends "turned the woods into a battlefield. We set up ambushes, then led gallant attacks, storming over the top, bayonetting and shooting anyone who got in our way." Kovic and his best friend then made solemn promises to join the Marine Corps when they grew up, turn themselves into "the heroes we knew we would become when we were men" (44)—sui generis.[2]

The ubiquitous presence of John Wayne in these narratives is also indicative: the western hero regenerated into the war hero. It is of course important that John Wayne's and Audie Murphy's war is WWII. As Lorrie Smith argues, "The 'story' of World War II . . . has meaning for our culture as a heroic quest, and it forms a coherent narrative in which the soldier's sacrifices are redemptive" ("Disarming" 90). Thus, when Wayne's character dies after his campaign in *Sands of Iwo Jima,* it is intended that we see the sacrifice as fitting and mythically regenerative. Tim O'Brien learned about "the Second World War . . . from men in front of the courthouse. . . . Nothing to do with causes or reason; the war was right, they muttered when asked, it had to be fought" (*If I Die* 13). Rightness here is synonymous with cultural regeneration.

Using WWII rhetoric as a model, the American government used the "regeneration through violence" mythic structure to "advertise" the Vietnam war.[3] Given the elements of the formula as defined by Slotkin, we uncover an absurd equation: the "white woman captive" is represented by South Vietnam, the role of the savage captor (read "Indian") is played by North Vietnam, and the "man without a cross" (Hawkeye's name for himself as a *pure* white in the *Leatherstocking Tales*) is the United States. "The characters and scenario were immediately recognizable to Americans, not because of their knowledge of world politics but because of their familiarity with frontier legends," asserts Margaret Stewart. "In the Vietnam war, the American people were offered an opportunity to relive their original adventure—to recapture at the founding of a foreign nation some of the heroic glory they associated with the settling of America" (*Ambiguous* 4–5). Characteristically, LBJ urged American victory with the words "bring the coonskin home" (Slotkin, "Dreams" 53), a phrase that reverberates with both the western myth and racist overtones.

For many Americans stationed in Vietnam, the western myth and its attendant "regeneration through violence" mind-set, disseminated via the cultural imagery encapsulated in western-movie and war-movie roles portrayed by Gary Cooper, John Wayne, and Audie Murphy, constituted a glorified model and motivation for gung-ho behavior and thinking. Michael Herr records how some grunts would engage in foolhardy heroics

> when they knew that there was a television crew nearby; they were actually making war movies in their heads, doing little guts-and-glory Leatherneck tap dances under fire. . . . They were insane, but the war hadn't done that to them.

The source for their belief in the regenerative power of violence was popular culture—"We'd all seen too many movies, stayed too long in Television City. . . . It was the same familiar violence, only moved to another medium" (209)—the medium of real death, real war.

Earl E. Martin's poem "The trouble with me is I used to believe" recalls how images from popular culture invaded his play as a child: ". . . I used to believe in Audey Murphy heroes / and causes that were actually worth fighting / and killing over." The distortion of Murphy's first name is an orthographic way of pointing out how young the boy is—maybe eight or nine? In the barnyard, dug into a haystack with his BB gun, he wreaks havoc on the livestock: "bang got the bull in the balls / that will teach those dirty Japs" and "bang got a chicken in the wing / look at her run for cover." Martin's narrative carefully reconstructs the child's imitation and emulation of what he conceives as heroic action:

> as i dash to the next stack
> throw a clod of dirt
> it explodes in front of the barn door
> i dive for it.

As he is setting an "explosive charge," he hears the voice of myth urging him on: "Sergeant Rock hollers at me out of a comic / to hurry with the fuse / 'OK Sarge.' " Bringing us back to the present, Martin admits, "I was playing the same game / when I hit Nam / until Nam hit me" (*Demilitarized* 142). The import is clear: Martin's faith in popular-culture war myths and whatever images of regeneration they offered him affected his judgment and actions in Vietnam, literally endangering his life.

Robert Borden's "Meat Dreams," a long work made up of thirty-two lyrical and narrative sections, records a year's tour in Vietnam. In section 7, "Waiting," Borden reports the intrusion of TV into his thoughts as he sits in a landing craft, anticipating battle on a beach:

> How can I believe
> there's real death
> on that beach
> when I know a commercial
> is imminent?
>
> Who's sponsoring this?
> Let's have a brief message
> of importance from
> some local dealer,
> let me hear someone say
> that Coke is the real thing,
> let me hear four out of five doctors
> recommend something
> for pain relief   (Villani 64)

Borden's juggling of TV commercial lingo here is effective, because it highlights the speaker's feeling of incredulity at the situation as well as his genuine desire that it be only a TV show, after all. He wants "Coke [to be] the real thing," not the impending firefight; he wants to be reassured by "medical authority" that there is such a thing as "pain relief" for wounds to come. The speaker's priority of realities—TV is more real to him than the beach he is about to attack—points to the deadly lure of its escapism, at the same time that the poet's stance as controlling genius satirizes TV and all popular culture.

TV and movies were not the only factors that influenced the Vietnam-war soldiers to believe in "regeneration through violence"; their general youth was also a contributing factor—Baritz points out that the "average age of the American soldiers in Vietnam was just over nineteen. In World War II, the average age of the GIs who were in for the duration was about twenty-six" (282). The soldiers' age, coupled with their American lifestyle, meant that there "had not been enough hardening experiences which could have tempered them for the most demanding event of their young lives," in the words of Charles Anderson, a Marine officer who found that "a surprising number [of grunts] seemed shocked to find . . . that when human beings get shot they bleed and scream and turn blue and sometimes die" (174). Another effect of the age of grunts is their "playfulness"—Vietnam as a playground. One grunt remembers that

> during my first fire fight in Nam, I was giggling. We got pinned down by some VC with an automatic weapon. Our machine gunner opens up. The next thing I hear is, "Oh boy, I got 'em. Man, did you see his fucking head fly off?" A kid'll do that. Nobody in the unit was over twenty one. (Baker 91)

The conjunction of youth and play is a common theme in many poems by Vietnam veterans. David Hall's long poem "The Ambush of the Fourth Platoon" plays on the youth of American combatants. The platoon's thirty men "make a bulging classroom / a football scrimmage / with bodies to spare"; their "muscles / . . . ought to be churning / after footballs." The speaker remembers "a simpler time" when he played war on his front lawn, littering it with "dead neighbor children" and then gracefully receiving "clean shots to the belly" until it was time to eat supper. After a brief but furious firefight, the speaker hears the wounded around him:

> . . . squeal[ing]
> like children fallen
> on a gravel playground.
> O God
> who knew it would hurt this bad?

This scene is in deliberate counterpoint with the childhood memory because *playing* war was the only "preparation" the speaker had had for the actual war. The speaker wants to extract himself from the situation at the expense of *anyone,* even his own family. "It's not me / it's not me / it's my sister / my brother . . . / it's anyone else / in this mud / but me." What is underlined here is the speaker's immaturity, wholly unprepared for the consequences of his presence in Vietnam. The speaker is forced to mature rapidly, in mere minutes; the urgency of the moment is indicated by the lines, "Somewhere / someone is shooting / someone in the head." Moments before he is killed by someone with "fish on his breath / as he leans above me," the speaker's mind drifts to his eighth-grade teacher, "Mrs. Porter [who] said God would never allow / the Communists domination over / a Christian people." His last thought is to address her again:

> Mrs. Porter
> expect a rattling of your windows
> some terrible night:
> we have much to discuss
> and we both have much
> to learn.   (14–20)

Whether the speaker really expects to avoid execution or already envisions himself a ghost, he nevertheless wants to set things straight: castigate Mrs. Porter for his lack of readiness, apprise her of the falsity of her religious patriotism. The fact of his certainty ("expect a rattling") reveals his youthful optimism—an optimism which reveals the speaker's faith in regeneration—no matter how ill-conceived.

Certain aspects of military policy in the Vietnam war, however, conflicted with the soldiers' belief in regenerative violence. One was the controversial "one-year tour" (thirteen months for Marines). "The idea behind the one-year tour," writes Myra MacPherson, "was to make fighting in Vietnam more palatable." This was a reaction from the experience of WWII soldiers who were in *for the duration*—that is, until the war ended or they were killed or wounded—suffered from "a sensation of 'endlessness' and 'hopelessness' so depressing and widespread in its effects" (MacPherson 52) that the military command felt a circumscribed period might be preferable. From a tactical standpoint, however, the one-year tour meant that the soldiers were less skilled. One grunt recalled:

> Toward the end of my tour, when I started knowing what I was doing in the jungle and started knowing what to do under fire, it was just about time to go home. . . . I'm going to be replaced by a guy who is as green as I was when I got here, and by the time he gets good at it he's going to be replaced by a guy who is green. (Santoli, *Everything* 43)

Besides the one-year tour causing soldiers to be less effective, there was the unforeseen effect of the *short-timer's syndrome*—a "self-oriented outlook," as Anderson describes it. "During the first half of the tour troops were concerned with their own combat efficiency; in the latter half, they worried about their own survival first and their combat functioning second" (192). The "one-year tour," as Herr noted, caused "Such odd things [to] happen when tours are almost over. . . . a man [who] is down to one or two weeks. . . . becomes a luck freak, an evil-omen collector, a diviner of every bad sign. . . . he will pre-

cognize his own death a thousand times a day" (91). Although officers stayed
in-country for the same length of time as enlisted men, they were rotated in
and out of the combat zone after six months or less; Baritz notes that this
"led to the conviction that the grunts knew better than anyone else, especially
better than the six-month wonders, the shake-'n'-bake lieutenants, how to stay
alive" (292). Since a few months in the boonies was not hardly enough time for
these officers to learn their jobs, "It was . . . a teenage war led by amateurs"
(Baritz 311).

"Rifle Number," section 24 of Borden's "Meat Dreams," humorously underlines the numerology of the short-timer:

> "What's your rifle number?"
> The sergeant asked.
>
> I told him:
> "Seven, sixty-nine,
> double-O seven."
>
> "Don't fuck around," he said,
> "gimme your rifle number."
> "I just did."
>
> He grabs the rifle
> from me and reads:
> "Seven, sixty-nine,
> double-O seven."
>
> *Days left in Vietnam:* 99   (Villani 65–66)

The humor is compounded here of the pop-culture significations of these numbers: "seven" is often a "magic" number in folk contexts (one is reminded of a
blues refrain: "I'm the seventh son of a seventh son"); "sixty-nine," of course,
has scatological meanings, but here it is also the year during which Borden is
in Vietnam; and "double-O seven" refers to the unkillable James Bond. It is
lucky enough, we might presume, simply to have a rifle with such a mystic
number, but to have the numbers invoked on the day one becomes a "two-digit
midget" can be only a good omen.

The short-timer's concern with numbers and what Herr has pointed to as
the multiple precognitions of one's own death is "brought home" (literally) in
section 32, "Meat Dreams":

> *Days left in Vietnam: 0*
> It is my twentieth birthday
> I have died
>   died
>   died
> I have died a thousand times
> without ever being part
> of a column total

Here the numerals themselves—"*0,*" "twentieth," "thousand"—are not the only numbers; there is also the stairstep enumeration of the repeated word "died." And, of course, the most grisly and revealing numbers mentioned are the "column total," alluding to a brigade commander's board listing body counts and kill ratios. "I am as dead / as the corpses you tally," Borden writes, "the numbers ringing in my ears, / so why do you not count me / when I stand up to be?" The "counting" here is double-edged because it refers not only to the returning soldier's guilt at surviving but also to American society for not valorizing the veteran. The speaker admits that he is not as eloquent as telegrams which can express "in twenty-five words or less" to parents that "their government issue / human being is no longer / a functional item." Borden's diction reflects and parodies a quantifying approach to language, where phrases act as counters, placeholders, like terms in an algebraic equation. The closing irony of the poem is a linguistic rebellion against such numbering:

> Oh say can you see
> by the dawn's early light?
> I have seen so much
> by the light of so many
> bleeding, lacerated dawns,
>
> . . . .
> I have thought to myself
> so many times
> that I was witnessing
> the twilight's last gleaming
> on those pock-marked hills,
> I have taken so many malaria pills,
> heard so many brief messages
> of impotence,

been bought and sold
over the counter of dead bodies . . .

Borden's invocation of the "sacred" words of the American national anthem is
a fireworksy attempt to reinvest value and meaning into these words—as such,
it is simultaneously parodic and reverent. The world of TV has been turned
on its head here. Commercials ("a message of / importance" from section 7)
have become "messages / of impotence"; not only is Borden satirizing TV,
but he is emphasizing the speaker's loss of reference in the real world, so that
all importance is ultimately impotent (and thus not regenerative). The closing
lines are an ironic gloss on the western myths foisted by popular culture:

> I am America's sacred cowboy
> riding off into the sunset
> after a job
>   well done/
> *Yippee-yi-o-K.I.A.!*
> *Roll out the cannons*
> *and we'll have a blast!*
>
> "Gooooooooooooooodbye,
> Vietnam!"   (Villani 66)

The sarcasm is heightened by Borden's distortion of popular song lyrics. The
"ki-yay" of the old western-song yodel is changed into the abbreviation for
"killed in action"; "barrels" are replaced by "*cannons*"; and "*blast*" inserts a
tone of impending danger, superseding "barrel of fun." At the end, Borden's
poem turns into a threat leveled at the banality of the World, and his parody
of the Armed Forces Radio greeting seems almost too glibly lighthearted, as
if to imply that Vietnam is something one can never say goodbye to, something that always threatens to explode, to "blast." For Borden, the possibility
of regeneration is finally an empty promise.

   The way in which people went to Vietnam and returned also complicated
the utility of the "regeneration through violence" myth. Once there were fighting units established in Vietnam, each individual replacement went overseas
alone and then, one year later, returned to America alone. One WWII veteran
explained the difference: "in World War II . . . you were assigned to a unit—
I was with the same unit virtually during four years [and] when you came
home on a boat, you had a couple of months and all you could talk about with
your pals . . . was what you were going to do" (Horne 121). Thus, the sol-

dier in Vietnam, going and coming home, was deprived of a certain degree of camaraderie (also a problem from the tactical viewpoint because of a reduced esprit de corps for teamwork) and an adjustment period, a time of decompression. On the subject of returning home, " 'I was killing gooks in the Delta and seventy-two hours later I'm in bed with my wife—and she wonders why I was "different," ' says one warrant officer" (MacPherson 64). The military itself shared in the general society's neglect of Vietnam veterans by speeding them out of military jurisdiction.

Another conflicting factor in the expectation of regeneration was the character of the fighting itself. In WWI, the battle lines were entrenched, literally carved into the ground; in WWII and Korea, battle lines were fluid but tangible—newspapers would show maps indicating where the fronts were, and it was possible to determine how the war was going by looking at the terrain taken or lost. In Vietnam, there were *no* lines. "There was no pattern to . . . patrols and operations," Philip Caputo remembers. "Without a front, flanks, or rear, we fought a formless war against a formless enemy who evaporated like the morning jungle mists, only to materialize in some unexpected place. It was a haphazard, episodic sort of combat" (95). This sort of warfare prohibited any potential sense of regeneration. The western hero was defined by his terrain, by the fact of the settlers advancing behind him as a front, but as John Hellmann points out, in Vietnam "the American hero has somehow entered a nightmarish wilderness where he is allowed no linear direction nor clear spreading of civilization" (111). R. L. Barth's "From the Forest of Suicides" emphasizes this ambiguity through allusion to Dante's *Inferno:*

> The foliage
> blackens
> with night-
> fall,
> dissolving
> to a knotted,
> gnarled
> landscape.
>
> Cold winds
> sough up
> the reverse
> slope.
> Like wailing

> voices,
>
> the leaves
>
> call us home.   (*Soldier's Time* 56)

The suicide's punishment is to grow into a tree in a forest full of suicide trees
which moan and lament their fate. The implication in Barth's poem is that the
"knotted, / gnarled / landscape" which prevents any lining up of anything with
anything is a suicidal terrain, a "reverse / slope," a terrain that invites suicide
through seduction.

The "gnarled landscape" is of course not only a physical space but a mental
and spiritual inscape as well—the strange uncertainties, distorted cause and
effect. Jon Forrest Glade's poem "Blood Trail" illustrates the strange causality
of a blood trail that is not only inscribed in the language but leaps through
bureaucratic terrain and lodges finally in memory. "I had a man in my sights /
and I pulled the trigger"—Glade's language implies a straightforward logic, a
tangible connectiveness of causality and casualty. But, instead, the target un-
expectedly gets up and "run[s] like a wounded deer." At the end of the blood
trail is only "an abandoned pack" with "love letters" sent by "a woman in the
southern provinces" and turned over to "Intelligence."

> Which meant she was arrested,
>
> beaten, raped, locked in a tiger cage,
>
> forced to eat her own excrement
>
> and beaten again.

And whether or not the woman would confess, yield useful information, the
only certainty on which the speaker can count is her execution. Where Glade's
rational, logical language ends up is a twisted syllogism:

> It was a funny war.
>
> I shot a man.
>
> I killed a woman.   (27)

Such distorted certainties and moral ambiguities drained any faith in the naïve
logic of regenerative violence.

Another source of deadly ambiguity was trying to determine who was Vietcong and who was not. "Unlike members of the North Vietnamese Army, the
VC wore no uniform," Charles Anderson writes. "VC looked like civilians,
and civilians looked like VC. Many grunts then considered all Vietnamese

active Viet Cong, 'just to make sure' " (185). According to one grunt, "You can't tell who's your enemy. You got to shoot kids, you got to shoot women. You don't want to. You may be sorry that you did. But you might be sorrier if you didn't. That's the damn truth" (Baker 213). W. D. Ehrhart's poem "Guerrilla War" lists several reasons for this kind of attitude: "Nobody wears uniforms. / They all talk / the same language." On top of these similarities, they carry "grenades / inside their clothes." All are suspect: "women . . . young girls, / and boys." Repeated twice is the speaker's statement that

> It's practically impossible
> to tell civilians
> from the Vietcong;
>
> after a while
> you quit trying.   (*Tired* 12)

What makes this poem work is the simple-spoken, rational voice of the speaker; it is on one level a defense of no longer "trying" to distinguish civilians from combatants—with all the tragic consequences for the civilian which that decision holds. But the voice here is so ingenuous that it convinces. The thorny question is this: if such a levelheaded person could come to this decision, what might we intuit about the absurdity of the situation or the stupidity of the speaker's commanders?

It is important to recall that the myth of "regeneration through violence" is based on *racial difference*—"the myth recounts the regeneration of the soul and the attainment of salvation through . . . violent confrontation with the powers of nature, equated with the forces of darkness" and to "the Puritan the Indian represented the dark forces" (Slotkin, "Dreams" 47, 41)—so that the result is racial violence, race war, genocide. A Japanese journalist in Vietnam, fired on by American helicopters, reported that " 'They seemed to fire whimsically . . . even though they were not being shot at from the ground nor could they identify the people as NLF. They did it impulsively for fun, using the farmers for targets as if in a hunting mood. They are hunting Asians" (Katsuichi Honda quoted by Higgins, 85–86). This viewpoint[4] is supported by the unofficial "mere gook rule." Caputo describes a briefing from his commander: " 'Look, I don't know what this is supposed to mean, but I talked to battalion and they said that as far as they're concerned, if he's dead and Vietnamese, he's VC' " (74). And this was early in the war—Caputo was in the first Marine unit emplaced in Vietnam—later this "rule" metastasized. Here is another rule to "determine" if a Vietnamese was friend or enemy: "no fire [should] be directed at unarmed

Vietnamese *unless they were running*." (Caputo 74). Such "rules" were easily distorted, and Vietnamese were often entrapped into running.[5]

How some American soldiers felt about the Vietnamese often falsely encouraged grunts to believe in the regenerative potential of military violence. Sometimes, Americans were encouraged not to think of the Vietnamese as people: "In some platoons, to call the enemy a 'Vietnamese' was punishable by 100 sit-ups. Call it gook, slant, slope, dink, gink, zip" (Felstiner, "American Poetry" 10). Jokes, sayings, and songs contributed to the dehumanization of Vietnamese: slang like "Squirrel hunting. Cong-zapping. Turkey shoot," or dead Vietnamese referred to as "Believers" or, if they were napalmed, "Crispy-Critters" (Gibson 142–43). Larry Rottmann's poem "S. O. P." satirizes this kind of anti-"gook" humor:

> To build a "gook stretcher," all you need is:
> Two helicopters
> Two long, strong ropes,
> And one elastic gook.   (*Winning* 53)

The poem's "black humour," Caroline Slolock suggests astutely, contains "a taunting delight in the details of torture . . . and the point of its irony seems to be not disapproval of what it describes but rather ridicule of both humanitarian values . . . and of the hypocrisy of official military instruction" (109). Slolock is absolutely right; the poem's title especially indicts the military establishment which gave the troops Standard Operating Procedures—how to take a prisoner under the Geneva convention, for example—without enforcing their usage.

The problems that grunts encountered in how to deal with Vietnamese, how to distinguish between civilians and combatants, were aggravated by military policy: *body counts, attrition, search and destroy,* and *free fire zones.* In a "formless war against a formless enemy," as Caputo phrases it (95), where terrain taken or lost was no index of the progress of the war, military command devised the "body count" as a way to quantify the war (a direct concomitant of technowar, since statistics allowed the use of computer analysis). One result of the policy, affecting such tangibles as promotion or time in the rear, was that soldiers, from low-ranking grunts to commanders, would lie. One soldier recalled his anger on realizing

> our casualty reports in the *Stars & Stripes* were being falsified. In every case, I *knew* what the total was . . . but the numbers were always reported as less. We falsified the enemy casualties. Why not falsify our own? I began to realize the extent of the lie, all the kinds of lies. (Baker 146–47)

Such impersonal policy surely increased the grunts' dehumanization of Vietnamese. But the more tragic ramification is the irresistible temptation to *make* some bodies to count—the "mere gook rule" would not only sanction such killings, but they would in turn bolster the entrenchment of the "mere gook rule" in grunts' thinking. A concept related to body count was "kill ratio": enemy casualties contrasted with American casualties. This only increased the killing; as the number of American deaths grew, there was a corresponding arithmetical need for the other term to increase at an even greater rate—hence, more and more killing of Vietnamese (enemy or not). As Baritz emphasizes, "Keeping the war's score by the arithmetic of kill-ratios and body counts puts an irresistible premium on good numbers" (296).

Slotkin has demonstrated, in his discussion of regeneration through violence, the mythicizing connection between body count and frontier "trophies":

The trophies [western heroes] are perpetually garnering have no material value; their sanctity derives from their function as visual and concrete proofs of the self-justifying acts of violent self-transcendence and regeneration that produced them. So the Indians . . . garnered trophies as proofs and reminders of their battle valor and as kernels around which to build their names and the myth-tales of the tribe. In Vietnam it was called the body count. (*Regeneration* 564)

The rationale underpinning body counts and kill ratios was General Westmoreland's overall strategy of *attrition:* "kill as many guerrillas and North Vietnamese troops as possible. Then they would quit. Then we would win" (Baritz 178). This strategy was not only unimaginative, it was a nonstrategy. Clark Clifford set out to discern the general American war strategy when he became secretary of defense in 1968; discovering that our only strategy was to kill—attrition—he wrote, " 'after these exhausting days, I was convinced that the military course we were pursuing was not only endless, but hopeless' " (Baritz 184). The effect of this strategy on troops was demoralization. One GI recalled how he felt: "What am I doing here? We don't take any land. We don't give it back. We just mutilate bodies. What the fuck are we doing here?" (Lifton 33). An Army platoon leader described his resulting sense of worthlessness.

I never had the opportunity to directly save lives. My responsibility was to kill and in the process of killing to be so good at it that I indirectly saved my men's lives. And there's nothing, nothing, that's very satisfying about that. You come home with the high body count, high kill ratio. What a fucking way to live your life. (Santoli, *Everything* 131)

"Search and destroy," the tactic that shored up the attrition strategy, was also equally unimaginative. In reality this was a decoy tactic—go out and get ambushed, then bring the technowar machine to bear on the ambushers. Gibson discusses it in terms of management and labor, an assembly-line mind-set.

> United States military officers conceived of themselves as business managers rather than combat leaders. Enlisted men were seen as a kind of migrant labor force of only marginal importance. They were marginal in that artillery, jet fighter-bombers, and helicopter gunships were officially responsible for producing enemy deaths, while infantry and armored cavalry became the "fixing force." (121)

In this argument of commodification, the grunt was the cheap currency, cheap labor, since more could be procured through the draft. Grunts in the field intimately understood this link between business and search and destroy. Jon Forrest Glade relates sighting "two NVA soldiers / . . . cooking their morning rice" while he and his platoon were being inserted into the A Shau Valley via helicopter; as the enemy disappeared into the jungle,

> The gunship peeled off
> and raked the jungle
> with rockets and gatling guns.
>
> It was business as usual.   (26)

Of course, this phrase is merely slang about routine occurrences, but the fact that the title of the poem is also "Business as Usual" emphasizes the connection with business, with work, with market commodities. And yet, search and destroy, in terms of business principles, was not good business; a grunt explained the tactic's

> enormous logical fallacy. You send a patrol out in order to get it ambushed, in order to mark a target with a smoke rocket from a helicopter so jets can come in and napalm the area. . . . The VC were smart enough to know that it was going to take two or three minutes at fastest to get a Huey out there, so they could kill a couple of people and split before anybody ever got there. We proceeded to mark the target. . . . Meanwhile the VC were eating their hamburgers in Danang. (Santoli, *Everything* 72–73)

In fact, the enemy became adept at using American search-and-destroy tactics for their own purposes. A CIA case officer in Vietnam explained how the enemy could "make a political point within the country to show American vul-nerability, [by] rais[ing] the level of activity: you take more casualties, people see more body bags leaving" (Santoli, *Everything* 177). In the same way that the United States was using a semiotic of destruction by sending North Viet-nam messages in the form of bombs, North Vietnam sent the United States messages in the syntax of dead Americans.

One way that the high command found to decrease American deaths (theo-retically) and "help" the soldiers tell which Vietnamese were friendly and which were Vietcong was the "free fire zone," which James Kunen has called an "existential strategy."

> The free fire zone creates order in chaos, creates its own meaning. One simply delineates an area, or "zone," in the countryside, and *declares* that anyone in that zone is a "Vietcong." No one can be in that zone and *not* be a "Vietcong," by *definition*. In fact, if a peasant who is definitely *not* a "Vietcong" should stray into that zone, he *becomes* a "Vietcong," because, once again, *everyone* in an FFZ *is* a "Vietcong." Therefore, the American troops and pilots and naval gunners need not concern them-selves with tedious decisions about whether it's OK to fire. They may fire freely, at "targets of opportunity," that is, anything that moves. (249)

Kunen continues by pointing out that Vietnamese who are not in the free fire zone are not by counterdefinition *not* Vietcong—that is, those outside the zone may *also* be Vietcong. "The obvious solution to this problem is to keep moving the free fire zones around, so now everyone here is 'Vietcong,' now every-one there, now there" (249–50). Notwithstanding the moral implications of such a procedure, the strategic repercussions were problematic enough—as more civilians are killed, more nonpartisans would join the guerrillas. Thus, in killing nonpartisan Vietnamese, Americans were augmenting rather than decreasing the forces against them.

In "Free Fire Zone," Serigo [Igor Brobowsky] documents the killing asso-ciated with the zone and the grunt's resulting dehumanization of the Viet-namese. In the scene, an old Vietnamese man's "brittle white hair touched gently by the wind" does not save him from destruction:

> And begging you fall down on your knees
> and raise your wizened hands in supplication
> to what stands mute in us, and cold to all your needs—

The old man stumbles "into the empty field beyond," driven by the Americans' indifference, and "flame comes blazing . . . from the sky." At this point, the speaker asks, "I wonder why / you ever bothered / ever being born" (*Winning* 88). What Serigo paints for us here is murder: the Vietnamese man driven out of his village (presumably outside the free fire zone) *into* the zone, to be executed. The speaker's tone as he describes the death is chilling in its impartiality, almost as if the old Vietnamese has been killed by accident or by an "act of God"; clearly, the self-delusion is that some other agent besides the speaker (perhaps bureaucracy itself) has committed the actual murder. In fact, Serigo calls attention to the moral bankruptcy of the speaker, who ultimately blames the old man for the situation and the murder.

Interestingly, Westmoreland—in reaction to his subordinates' perception that the terms "search and destroy" and "free fire zone" could be misunderstood to the detriment of American credibility—changed the names: search and destroy became "search and clear" or "reconnaissance in force"; and free fire zone was changed to "specified strike zone" (Gibson 186–87). But in practice they remained the same. In fact, such semantic distortion was a commonplace in the higher command. Kunen cites " 'Let's Say It Right,' " a memo from MACV (the Military Assistance Command, Vietnam) to the Armed Forces Vietnam Network:

> "VC Tax Collectors," it instructs, is an "Incorrect Term." The "Correct Term" is "VC Extortionists." Similarly, "South Vietnam" should always be called "The Republic of Vietnam," whereas "The Democratic Republic of Vietnam" must always be referred to as "North Vietnam." . . . No more "body count"—we're not so bloodthirsty. What we count now is "enemy deaths." A great deal is not to be said at all. The use of American troops "to bait the enemy" is an "Incorrect Term." The correct term is "never to be used." (361–62)

The phrase "never to be used," of course, conjures up the specter of George Orwell's *1984,* in which the language Newspeak is designed "not only to provide a medium of expression for the [official] world-view . . . but to make all other modes of thought impossible" (303). In fact, Orwell had already prefigured the Vietnam war. A piece of subversive literature within the novel describes "a warfare of limited aims between combatants who are unable to destroy one another. . . . [and] involves very small numbers of people, mostly highly trained specialists, . . . on the vague frontiers whose whereabouts the average man can only guess at"—an adequate summary of the early Vietnam war (or any insurgency, for that matter). Later events of the war are also described by this description: "such acts as raping, looting, the slaughter of children, the reduction of whole populations to slavery, and reprisals against prisoners . . . are looked upon as normal, and, when they are committed by one's own side and not the enemy, meritorious" (*1984* 186–87).

American troops *did* commit atrocities such as those listed by Orwell, and routinely, it would seem. Anderson remarks:

> When Americans now think of atrocities, the My Lai massacre comes to mind. But murder was not the only type of atrocity, and My Lai was certainly not the first, only the most widely publicized. There were literally tens of thousands of incidents of malicious intent and atrocious result. Most did not involve murder and only a handful were ever followed by any attempt at redress. (177)

Stephen Miller describes a tunnel rat finding a woman in a tunnel:

> You were pregnant when I
> shoved you into the light.
>
> .   .   .   .
>
> They asked you questions.
> You did not answer.
> They tied your hands
> behind your back
> Your shoulders stretched
> forward to hold your belly
> even as we pulled
> out the machete.   (8)

The speaker in this poem is reticent, his expression truncated and blunt. The end of the poem holds out the possibility that the "machete" may only be a scare tactic to extort a confession or tactical information, but the poem's title has already brought home with sledgehammer force the actual result: "Caesarian / Army Style." The matter-of-fact language here is both confession and witness that such events were commonplace.

The apathy of the American people in failing to believe that such atrocities occurred is tantamount to such actions being "looked upon as normal," to use Orwell's phrase, and certainly there is some hawkish portion of the American public which thought them "meritorious." The commission of atrocities was in fact condoned, even predisposed, by American policy. "The emphasis on body count and the strategy of obliteration typified by the free fire zone explain why the GI is likely to be ordered to commit war crimes," Kunen suggests. "His training and the psychological pressures of a horrible and absurd situation explain why he is likely to obey" (252).

Part of this "horrible and absurd situation" is the fact of long periods of utter boredom between the brief excitements of firefights. "Every day you're out on patrol. . . . walking around in little geometric triangles. Go to this checkpoint, go to that checkpoint, go here, go there. . . . before long you're a fucking zombie" (Baker 100). In the rear, typically there were the limitations of either having nowhere to go (for leisure) or when there was somewhere (a town, perhaps), having the command circumscribe when one could leave the base area or where in town one could go. In either case, gone were such distractions as drive-in movies, bowling alleys, shopping malls, and other typically American outlets.

Perry Oldham's "Evening Pastimes" illustrates this sense of extreme ennui.

Read *Arizona Highways* at the Service Club.

Play ping pong at the Service Club.

Watch movies at the "drive-in."

Sit on top of the bunker and get high.

Sit in the hootch and get drunk.

Go to the EM Club and get drunk.

Play cards.

Tell stories.

Read.   (29)

Caputo refers to this condition as "a spiritual disease called *la cafard* by the French soldiers when they were in Indochina. Its symptoms were occasional fits of depression combined with an unconquerable fatigue that made the simplest tasks, like shaving or cleaning a rifle, seem enormous" (68). Charles Anderson observes that in the midst of such overwhelming depression, "For some, committing an atrocity offered welcome relief from the boredom" (183).

Peer pressure is also one of the factors that contributed to the situation. This pressure is not, however, the kind generally associated with teenagers, where peer pressure is applied psychologically, although of course such psychic coercion was obtained; pressure of this sort in the war was backed up by weapons. One grunt admitted:

> I don't know what I would have done if I had been faced with that sort of thing. I don't think I would have taken part in it, but I also don't think I would have tried to stop it. That would have been encouraging your own sudden death. These are the guys who get in fire fights with you. It would have been too easy to get blown away. (Baker 190)

The dangers were not only from one's peers but also from one's superiors. At the National Veterans' Inquiry, one witness testified that he had brought atrocities

> "to the attention of the major. . . . [but] he was there participating himself. I did not go beyond the major because you don't rock the boat in Vietnam, because it's a very lethal place to be. . . . you'd be surprised how many sand bags you can fill and how many dangerous missions you can go on if you start rocking the boat." (Kunen 187)

Ehrhart's poem "Hunting" illustrates the spiritual numbness which accompanies such a moral situation, a numbness which has become a commonplace of the Vietnam war. The speaker's focus is concentrated on the "front and rear sights / form[ing] a perfect line on his body" while suppressing the thought "I have never hunted anything in my whole life / except other men" and thinking instead about "chow, and sleep, / and how much longer till I change my socks" (*Tired* 13). Ehrhart illustrates with precise clarity the mechanism of denial that allows the reduction of human being to target: first, the focus on the technical aspects of soldiering; and second, the active repression of thoughts which may threaten to unbalance one's hard-pressed equanimity. In his poem "Time on Target," Ehrhart combines these aspects with the gee-whiz attitude of an American naïf. The poem again begins with the technical paraphernalia of artillery: "intelligence reports," "a list / of targets," and the speaker's bemusement that through this list he, "a corporal, / could command an entire battery." The possibility of coming to terms with the actual human cost of his "list / of targets" arises when, on patrol, the speaker encounters "the ruins of a house," next to which "sat a woman / with her left hand torn away; / beside her lay a child, dead." The truth of the matter, the awful enormity of the "list / of targets," is immediately repressed, and the speaker along with "the fellows in the COC" are exhilarated by the knowledge that "all those shells we fired

every night / were hitting something" (*Tired* 12–13). The poem's tripartite setting—the isolated COC, the ruined house, and again the COC—calls attention
to the fact of repression (a necessary posture in the combat zone), the antiseptic isolationism of technology, and the possibility of existential refuge within
one's job. But from a retrospective viewpoint outside the combat zone, we are
captured by the woman's plight, and the poem's double-edged irony functions
as both sarcastic comment and self-judgment.

The plain fact, finally, is that there were soldiers in Vietnam who took great
pleasure in killing "gooks." One grunt recalled, "I started to enjoy it. I enjoyed
the shooting and the killing. I was literally turned on when I saw a gook get
shot. . . . if a gook got killed, it was like me going out here and stepping on a
roach" (Baker 85). Herr's catalog of killers thus seems no exaggeration: "redundant mutilators, heavy rapers, eye shooters, widow-makers, nametakers,
classic essential American types, point men, *isolatos* and outriders"; to Herr, it
was apparent that "they were programmed in their genes to do it, the first taste
made them crazy for it, just like they knew it would" (34–35). Elsewhere, he
writes, "The mix was so amazing; incipient saints and realized homicidals, unconscious lyric poets and mean dumb motherfuckers with their brains all down
in their necks" (30).

This complex mix of pressures, repressions, and atrocities easily elides into
the myth of regenerative violence—the racist argument that the victims are
only "gooks," after all—but the possibility of self-creation and self-renewal in
personal and psychological terms must have seemed increasingly dubious. On
the national level, clearly, atrocities had the opposite effect.

Beginning in the 1980s, as more and more veterans revisit Vietnam, poems
written in Vietnamese voices have increasingly appeared—an approach pio-
neered in 1972 by Basil Paquet, as in "Morning—A Death" (*Winning* 22–23).
Rottmann's poems spoken by "Voices from the Ho Chi Minh Trail"—the title
of a poetry reading Rottmann gave at the 1992 national meeting of the Popular Culture Association—are a good example. In these poems inspired by his
1990 return to Vietnam along with other Vietnam-veteran writers, Rottmann
attempts to speak for the Vietnamese who have not had a voice in the American
cultural context. "A Porter on the Trail" seeks this mainstream attention by
alluding to Walt Whitman. The speaker is one of the North Vietnamese haulers
who transported supplies along the Ho Chi Minh Trail under the most primitive
circumstances, carrying matériel on bicycles and by foot.

> In 1966,
> when I started down the trail,

> I carried a copy of
> "The Poems of Walt Whitman"
> in my rucksack.

The porter ranks Whitman's "Song of Myself" with the Vietnamese national epic, *Kim Vân Kiêù,* and cannot understand "how a nation / that gave birth to Walt Whitman, / could also produce / napalm and Agent Orange." Finally, the porter gets a chance to discuss "Song of Myself" with someone who would surely be conversant in Whitman.

> One day, near Khe Sanh, we captured a G.I.
> I was excited, and asked him about
> "Song of Myself."
> But the American said
> he'd never heard of Walt Whitman.   ("Porter" 16)

Rottmann's wry, laconic sense of humor is at its best in this poem. The incisive irony in a Vietnamese knowing more than an American about Whitman is an acerbic comment on a country that has lost touch with its cultural richness.

Elliot Richman's chapbook *A Bucket of Nails* collects persona poems in the voices of different Vietnamese characters (e.g., "The Ballad of a V.C. Truck Driver Who Skinned Frogs and Became Enlightened" or "The Ballad of an Old Vietnamese Woman Who Lives Along the Saranac and Picks Wild Flowers That She Plants in the Snow"). Although Richman is not a Vietnam veteran, his poems on the war muscularly assert an authenticity of witness. The short poem "Jungle Ambush in Monument Valley" is a fascinating example.

> We ambushed the American squad with their own claymores.
> Afterward we finished them off with rifles and bayonets
> and stripped the bodies for cigarettes and weapons.
> I smoked a Marlboro spotted with blood, but did not care.
> The war had made me hard. I thought of a John Wayne
> movie I had seen in Saigon. John Wayne
> wore a white hat and killed Indians.
> This war would be different. The Apaches would win.   (16)

That Richman has his Vietnamese speaker allude to western myth and the regeneration theme (particularly by making the Vietnamese soldier a "Marlboro man") is a stroke of genius, demonstrating how the John Wayne mind-set could be subverted and undermined. At the same time, the speaker's identification with "Apaches" emphasizes the racist, genocidal parallels between the American West and the Vietnam war.

Race Relations Among Americans in Vietnam

African Americans in Vietnam encountered special problems which Euro-Americans did not. Infantryman Stan Goff recalls that when he first entered the Army, "word was going around, and it wasn't a quiet word, that blacks were being drafted for genocidal purposes. Just to get rid of us—to eliminate the black male" (Goff and Sanders 11). Wallace and Janice Terry point to the statistics of black Americans in the armed services.

> Eleven percent of the American population, blacks always died in Vietnam at a greater rate. In 1965 and 1966, blacks were 23 percent of those Americans killed in action. . . . In 1967, blacks were 20 percent of the combat forces, 25 percent of the elite troops, and up to 45 percent of the airborne rifle platoons; 20 percent of the Army fatalities were black, 11 percent of the Marine. By 1968, the war's peak year, 14 percent of the U.S. combat deaths were black. (Horne 167)

According to these statistics, the percentage of blacks killed in action was always higher than the overall African American percentage in the national population; Wallace and Janice Terry argue, however, that "there was little to support the charges" that African American soldiers were "being unwillingly used as 'cannon fodder.' Most black soldiers, in 1966 and 1967, were anxious to prove themselves in combat and agreed that the war was worth fighting to halt the spread of communism" (Horne 168). That there were more African Americans in combat arms than support positions Wallace and Janice Terry explain by pointing out that "fewer blacks than whites possessed the preparation and training for entrance into more highly skilled occupations such as electronics, and thus they ended up carrying guns or pushing brooms" (168).

Charley Trujillo, in *Soldados,* reports that statistics on the numbers of Latinos who served in Vietnam are hard to collect, but the "Department of Defense has estimated that 83,000 Hispanics served in Viet Nam"; he also cites Ruben Treviso's estimate that "twenty percent of Latinos that went to Viet Nam were killed and thirty-three percent were wounded" (vii). Trujillo's conclusion is that "there is more than a strong suggestion that Chicanos throughout the nation fought and died in disproportionate numbers in Viet Nam" (viii). One Marine

said his "platoon was about sixty percent minority—Chicanos, Blacks, Puerto
Ricans and Indians" (80); an Army grunt recalled: "our unit, out in the field,
was eighty percent minorities: Blacks, Chicanos, Indians and Puerto Ricans.
It seemed like it was the minorities who were always the infantry guys and
the other people (whites) who had the rear jobs, maintenance, clerks and desk
jobs. I got to see plenty of that over there. . . . My whole squad was made up of
Chicanos" (86). Other oral histories in *Soldados* attest to similar experiences.[6]

Leroy V. Quintana, the premier Chicano Vietnam-veteran poet, published a
collection of poems on the Vietnam war entitled *Interrogations* in 1992. Like
Michael Casey's *Obscenities,* Quintana's book chronicles a soldier's journey
through the military gauntlet, from "Armed Forces Recruitment Day" in high
school through basic and advanced training, to service in the 'Nam and eventual return to the World. Quintana's style is Spartan, terse, and replete with
deadpan humor, most often satirical. His poem "Jump School—Detail" is a
revelatory example:

> Saturday morning detail.
> The Sgt. handed out
> swing rakes.
> The grass
> tall behind,
> between,
> the barracks,
> waiting.
> Mexican lawnmowers,
> he called them,
> chuckling.   (*Interrogations* 27)

That racism resides in the soldier's superior, albeit defused by the sergeant's
"chuckling," emphasizes the institutionalization of that racism within the military hierarchy. Given that the speaker is a Chicano (since the continuing speaker
in these poems seems strongly autobiographical), the soldier is portrayed as
being caught on the horns of a dilemma, suspended between the insult and
the laughter. Quintana's humor is marvelously controlled: first, the speaker's
Chicano identity wittily makes the epithet "Mexican lawnmowers" literal,
thereby disarming to some extent the sergeant's insult. Second, the phrase
"swing rakes" puns on the military slang "swinging dick"—especially via
consonance with the collateral phrase "swinging Richard" (indicating also a
pun on President Nixon's name). Since "swinging dick" is the military's rough

equivalent of the more elevated term "everyman" (as in the usage "every swinging dick"), Quintana's point wryly extends the position of the marginalized (in this case, the Chicano soldier) outward to *all* (male) soldiers. If all "swing rakes" are "Mexican lawnmowers," then every swinging dick is Mexican too, if only in terms of metaphor. Quintana's re-situation of the marginalized into the center is recapitulated throughout the book in his unsentimental focus on portraits of ordinary soldiers. The genius of *Interrogations* lies finally in Quintana's portrayal of his own maturation into a voice of witness and conscience. At the same time, his laconic style connects him to a tradition of activist poets from the Chicano Renaissance of the 1960s and 1970s; many of these poets wrote predominantly in similarly terse, matter-of-fact, short, and punchy lines: Alurista, Leo Romero, and the young Gary Soto, for example.

Unlike the oral histories of African Americans and Latinos collected in *Bloods* and *Soldados,* similar information about Native American and Asian American veterans is much more difficult to find. According to Tom Holm, "American Indians who fought in Vietnam have received little or no notice [and they] have not been included in a single general study of Vietnam veterans." The estimate Holm cites is "over 42,000 American Indians served in Vietnam between 1966 and 1973"; if that figure is acceptable (and it may be too low, since it probably does not include Native Americans from non-reservation areas), it would mean that about "one out of four eligible Native Americans served, compared to one out of 12 in the general population" (57–58). Clearly, Native Americans (like African Americans and Latinos) bore more than their share of the war effort and suffering. Holm also points out the particular dangers Native Americans encountered in the war: "the 'Indian Scout Syndrome' [assumed] that Indians were more stealthy and could utilize their senses of sight, smell, touch, and hearing better than non-Indians"—this stereotype endangered many Native American grunts who "walked point more than any other member of their respective units" (62).

Joan Arrington Craigwell's poem "Dark Angel" delineates an African American nurse's experience with patients of different races. The poem opens with "a white boy / crying in the darkness" who "won't care that my skin is black." The speaker becomes "the Mexican's dark madonna" but also "the bitch / who cut off the best part of him." Her Native American patient "sees the Great Spirit / even though he has no eyes." The African American is a "Black boy running in the big race / you'll never run again." The topic of Asian descent is only mentioned in the question: "who is the enemy? / Is he yellow or black / red, brown or white?" Significantly, the speaker wonders "Or could it be that it's me?"—clearly, the enormous responsibilities of triage ("I don't want to decide who should die") and the accumulating sense of guilt as patient after patient dies has antiregenerative ramifications. One weakness of this poem is its essentializing of the racial representatives, but its close reveals a genuinely resonant self-realization—"I hear them call / try to save them all / with a touch and a little white lie" (*Vision* 75–76)—the closing words "white lie" spoken by a black speaker are a reverberating commentary on the Vietnam war as a "white lie" rooted in racism.

That Asian Americans are not mentioned in Craigwell's poem indicates how Vietnam veterans of Asian descent are even less visible than other minorities—in terms of both artistic representation and scholarly study. In the *Vietnam Generation* issue entitled *A White Man's War: Race Issues and Vietnam,* the brief prologue to the "Bibliography of Literature on Asian Americans and the Vietnam War" indicates that some "85,000 Americans of Asian descent served in the military during the Vietnam War era; if the percentages were evenly distributed . . . the number of Asian Americans who are veterans of the Vietnam War should be around 30,000 or about 1 percent of the total Vietnam veteran population." The dangers which these people exclusively faced are obvious: "Asian American women serving in Vietnam were liable to be mistaken for Vietnamese women, and thus, for Vietnamese prostitutes. Asian American men were in danger of being mistaken for the enemy in the field" (158). I know of only *one* Asian American Vietnam-veteran poet, Lily Lee Adams. She served as an Army nurse in Cu Chi during the war. Her poetry will be discussed in the following chapter, but here I will include an excerpt from one of her oral histories: "when I was in civilian clothes and walking around the compound with a guy, the other guys would just assume I was a whore"; even Vietnamese "old ladies would get angry, thinking I was a snooty city Vietnamese. . . . After a while I came to hate the word *gook*. And I hated *slant-eyed* and *slope-eyed* and *yellow skin*. . . . Because, for me, you were talking about real people" (Marshall, *Combat Zone* 221–23). Peter Nien-Chu Kiang has taken an important first step in collecting oral histories from Asian American veterans with his article "About Face: Recognizing Asian and Pacific American Vietnam Veterans in Asian American Studies."

An interesting sidelight, apropos of the Native American and Asian American presence in the war, was a commando program which highlights racist attitudes and a total lack of imagination among the American high command. Yoshia Chee, a Hawaiian who is a mix of Chinese American and Native American, reports being a member of an elite unit.

In Okinawa they were forming special groups called Peregrine Groups, made up of all Asian-Americans. Out of the 200 that started in my class, only twenty-five of us finished. All Asians. We got regular Special Forces

training plus lots of endurance exercises. A lot more intelligence training.
And more hand-to-hand combat. We spoke a lot of French. We were supposed to learn Vietnamese, so we could really live off the land. It would
have been nice if we were fluent in the language, but we weren't. We
didn't have enough time, and it's a hard language.

We were supposed to fight on the same principle as the peregrine fal-
con. It comes out of the sky at 200 miles an hour, gets its prey, and takes
it back to the young ones. That was the whole idea: Come in fast, do your
shit, and get out. The theory was that being Asians or half-Asians, we
would look like the Viet Cong, live like the Viet Cong, and think like the
Viet Cong. If you think like them, you can beat them at their own game.
(Maurer 352–53)

No plan hatched by the military could have been more fallacious and unwork-
able. As Chee notes, "that was a big mistake. How can you take somebody out
of Chinatown in Seattle, and expect him to beat the Viet Cong when he doesn't
even speak the language?" (Maurer 353). The shortsightedness of this program
is based on racist blinders: the assumption, "once an Asian, always an Asian,"
without regard to the fact that Asian Americans are most often *fully* American,
true cultural Americans with more than likely no spiritual, linguistic, or attitu-
dinal connections to an Asia which may, for some, be several generations in
the past.

The pitting of Asian Americans against Asians is a reminder of the segre-
gation of "friendly Indians" from "hostile Indians" in American cultural and
literary history. In James Fenimore Cooper's mythos, Chingachgook and his
doomed son Uncas are "good Indians," while the Mingos who work for the
French are the "bad Indians." John Hellmann, recalling Leslie Fiedler's notion
of the American hero's "harmonious relation with nature and a dark 'natural'
man" in *Love and Death in the American Novel,* has pointed out the character type of the "symbolic dark younger brother" (31, 33) in an Indochina
novel as early as *The Ugly American,* by William Lederer and Eugene Burdick,
published in 1958. Of course, cognate examples already exist in American literature and popular culture—Hawkeye and Chingachgook; the Lone Ranger
and Tonto; Huck Finn and Jim; Ishmael and Queequeg, even the (Hispani-
cized) Cisco Kid and Pancho. Fiedler has articulated the stereotype: "male
protagonists [find] adventure and isolation" in such places as "an island, a
woods, the underworld, a mountain fastness" where each hero discovers "a
male companion, who is the spirit of the alien place, and who is presented with

varying degrees of ambiguity as helpmate and threat" (181). For Cooper, the ambiguity is clarified by splitting the Indian into Uncas and Magua in *The Last of the Mohicans*. This tendency of characterization also appears in Vietnam-veteran poetry, fitting if the American experience in Vietnam is in fact rooted in the western myth of "regeneration through violence." A typical example is Jim Costilow's "Sgt. Tieu" (and the poet, revealingly, tells us in a parenthesis to the title that the name is pronounced "Two"): "Yes, I spent my combat time / In Nam's climate so sublime" where "of all the ones I knew, / the finest was a guide named Nuyen Bien Tieu." They had their differences— "Tieu was ugly and not too tall"; "He had his own ideas, / . . . It was hard for us to work together." The climactic moment comes in a firefight when the speaker is wounded and, despite their differences, Tieu "Picked me up like I was dead" to be carried to safety even though bullets "tore right through his breast." In Costilow's rather forced verse, we see the classic pairing which is, although Costilow may probably be unaware, racist in its condescension against the "dark younger brother," its forcing him into the mold of "helpmate." The crucial tip-off is the ending, in which the speaker claims, "And I'll never, ever meet again, / A finer man than you are, Sgt. Tieu" (Topham, *Vietnam Heroes IV* 29–30). One cannot help but note the rhythmic and metric similarity of the name "Sgt. Tieu" with the sonic shape of the name "Gunga Din"; and of course Costilow means to update Kipling here. In either case, the "dark younger brother" is a sacrifice.

A version more interesting in its compassion for the Vietnamese partner is David Huddle's "Sergeant Dieu" in *Stopping by Home*. Here are the opening four lines of "Them":

> Sergeant Dieu, frail Vietnamese man,
> once sat down with me, shirtless, on my bunk
> and most astonishingly in my opinion
> (not his) squeezed a pimple on my back.

The "dark younger brother" here is postulated as an equal—*not* a younger brother at all, but merely another man. Given the French colonialist history of Vietnam, Huddle may also be punning on the French word for "God," so that the poet may be upholding the Vietnamese as moral superiors. The poem is therefore about the speaker's discovery both of the otherness of Vietnamese but also essentially of their worth. The speaker had also shared in the characteristic American stereotyping.

> My first trip to the field, I saw Vietnamese
> infantry troops, loaded with combat gear,
> walking the paddy dikes and holding hands.
> I was new then. I thought they were queer.

Clearly the speaker, in the present, no longer thinks so, since he apologizes by saying "I was new then." The sonnet's closing sestet emphasizes its message:

> Co Ngoc at the California Laundry
> wouldn't say any of our words, but she
> explained anyway a Vietnamese treatment
> for sore throat: over where it's sore inside
> you rub outside until that hurts too. That
> way won't work for American pain. I've tried.   (9)

Huddle is advocating empathy and trying one another's ways as a method for coexistence. He certainly doesn't deny that the "treatment / for sore throat" works; it just doesn't work for Americans. The important part is that "I've tried."

A phenomenon related to the "dark younger brother" syndrome is the combination of the light hero and the dark counterpart within the same character, "the democratic balance of self-reliance and self-restraint . . . possess[es] a dark underside of passionate conflicts, longings, and anxieties" (Hellmann 56). In *American Myth and the Legacy of Vietnam,* a publicity still from the film *The Deer Hunter,* showing the character Michael on jungle patrol, is displayed with this caption: "With headband, streaked face, prominent knife, and background of thick foliage, the protagonist of *The Deer Hunter* evokes the frontier hero who becomes like an Indian to fight Indians" (Hellmann 39). There are, in Vietnam, at least two widely variant versions of this "becoming like an Indian" stereotype exemplified in real life. One grunt, who later deserted to Sweden, recalls his escape from military life into the countryside:

> I wasn't a soldier anymore, I was part of the village. I was wearing Viet-
> namese clothes. I felt as if I was doing something different, I was serving a
> purpose there, not like the purpose I was sent to Vietnam for. I was really
> getting to know these people. In the village we got up pretty early. We ate
> some rice. There was some water buffaloes about the village. We would
> head out into the rice paddies, and the women would do their little chores.
> I wasn't used to doing this, but I really felt that I belonged. (Lane 62)

Inevitably, when the authorities come to bring him back into the military fold, he tells them, " 'I would rather be with them than be with you. You don't act like my people, not like the people I grew up with in the States. Something has happened to you' " (Lane 63). The point, of course, is that it is he who has changed; the changes he thinks he notes have been implicit, potential in America even when he was there—it is merely that Vietnam has brought these dangerous tendencies fully to the surface. The changes he does note in himself are that he has been somehow and somewhat "Vietnamized."

Stephen Miller has portrayed this "Vietnamization" of Americans in a prose poem, "Catch a Falling Star":

> After shooting people, I had a nervous breakdown. It was easy to quit. Just walk away from my post. The jungles were full of refugees and accommodation abundant.
>
> My host was an old Vietnamese man who took me home after we introduced ourselves over a waterhole at dawn. I stayed at his place for several days watching the slow green and black dressed humans sludging their way across rice-paddies, wondering what we had in common.
>
> The old man and I smoked a lot of opium and worked out in the fields every day. It was funny being out there and watching him knee-deep in his little square, foraging for food with a peeled branch bearing a flattened piece of shrapnel. Afterward, toward evening, we would return to his house and sit beneath the thatched bamboo while his wife served us fish-rice and tea. (13)

This poem exhibits the important elements of common work, food, and sharing of cultures (represented by opium)—what is gained is peace and tranquility, a different sort of regeneration. Of course, as we just saw in the case of the deserter's narrative collected by Mark Lane, this regeneration is also belied by the military machine's jealous and inevitable redress.

The ungentle side of Americans "becoming" Vietnamese is a renegade impulse that can involve atrocious violence. Earl E. Martin, for example, describes such a grunt: "nineteen and mean / four ears / strung and hung / about his neck"—emptied by the atrocity of his experience, he is a "gun with boy in hand" (61) who is dead to the World (American sensibility) and lives only for violence. In this poem, the themes of atrocity, boyhood, and lack of regeneration are focused into a single image: the renegade warrior. One of the recurrent legends in the war told of the "white Cong"—a white Army deserter who defects to the Vietcong. Sometimes he is an African American soldier. One Chicano grunt recalled seeing "Salt and Pepper":

> these two American Marines, one black and the other white, who had turned traitor. . . . I was looking around with my binoculars and saw six gooks with black pajamas on, a white dude and a *mayate* [a black man]. . . . They wouldn't let us open up on them. The Viet Cong even stopped and looked at us. One of them was a white son-of-a-bitch, blond hair, and the *mayate,* blacker than black. (Trujillo 177)

In this narrative, we see a fascinating folkloric version of the motif of the white hero and dark sidekick as renegades. Geoffrey Stamm's poem "The Red Sash" describes the discovery, after a firefight, of "a tall black dude" among dead bodies:

> An Army deserter,
> Who led a Viet Cong squad,
> Wearing a long red sash
> Around his waist.

The speaker confesses that he had always been convinced that this deserter was in battle "Not against us, / But for freedom" (14), and that he would have wanted the name of the "black dude" included on the Vietnam Veterans Memorial—an interesting transformation of the regeneration theme—violence for an allegedly good cause.

A fascinating oral history is provided by an African American grunt who styled himself as "Montagnard Man" (a reference to the Montagnard tribes in the mountains of Southeast Asia—for example the Hmong and the Mien—against whom some Vietnamese were racially prejudiced).[7]

> The Vietn'ese, they called me Montagnard, because I would dress like a Montagnard. I wouldn't wear conventional camouflage fatigues in the field. I wore a dark-green loincloth, a dark-green bandana to blend in with the foliage, and a little camouflage paint on my face. And Ho Chi Minh sandals. And my grenades and ammunition. That's the way I went to the field. (Terry 251)

The making of Montagnard Man was an experience right out of early American captivity narratives—a crucial aspect of the regeneration-through-violence myth. On patrol, his squad found an American soldier: "His arms and legs tied down to stakes. And he had a leather band around his neck that's staked in the ground so he couldn't move his head to the left or right." He had been skinned and left to die in the elements, just as if these grunts were in the wilds of some *Hollywood*-style Apache territory. The soldier was in a horrifyingly pitiful condition—"You can see the flesh holes that the animals—wild dogs, rats, field mice, anything—and insects had eaten through his body" (Terry 248)—and asked to be killed; the black grunt, as the man in charge, was the one who had to give the coup de grace (a term that belies the actual horror and existential misery that would attend the final gunshot). What drives him over the edge of civilization (and metaphorically into the frontier, Indian country) is "com[ing] across American bodies, black and white. . . . Markings have been cut on them. Some has been castrated, with their penises sewed up in their mouth with bamboo" (Terry 250). And the Montagnard Man himself begins to mutilate bodies, resulting in a twisted version of "regeneration."

> I collected about 14 ears and fingers. With them strung on a piece of leather around my neck, I would go downtown, and you would get free drugs, free booze, free pussy because they wouldn't wanna bother with you 'cause this man's a killer. It symbolized that I'm a killer. And it was, so to speak, a symbol of combat-type manhood. (Terry 251)

As he himself stated it, "I was becoming a animal" (Terry 247). The irony occurs when, back in the World, he enters a grocery store owned by a Vietnamese in his own neighborhood. The proprietor recognizes him, "Yeah, me know you. You Montagnard Man," and he says, "Ain't that some shit? . . . He's got a business, good home, drivin' cars. And I'm still strugglin'. . . . When the Vietn'ese first came here, they were talkin' 'bout the new niggers. But they don't treat them like niggers. They treat them like people" (Terry 263). The supreme irony is that the regeneration he felt as an outgrowth of his violence in Vietnam is not lasting—he has not been regenerated at all—his blackness and all the societal ills that are projected upon that blackness still imprison him in the United States.

The enemy often used racial divisiveness to split Americans. A Lurp (a member of a Long Range Reconnaissance Patrol [LRRP]) recalled "Hanoi Helen," a North Vietnamese radio personality who would broadcast to Americans,

> got on the air after Martin Luther King had died, and they was rioting back home. She was saying, "Soul brothers, go home. Whitey raping your mothers and daughters, burning down your homes. What you over here

for? This is not your war. The war is a trick of the Capitalist empire to get
rid of the blacks." (Terry 41–42)

This kind of psychological warfare was not only directed through words. An
Air Force policeman recalled that in the field after King's assassination, "To
play on the sympathy of the black soldier, the Viet Cong would shoot at a
white guy, then let the black guy behind him through, then shoot at the next
white guy"; one result of this selective fire was racist: "the reaction in some
companies was to arrange your personnel where you had an all-black or nearly
all-black unit to send out" (Terry 172–73). On the other hand, an armor specialist remembered, "When I went over to the 101st Airborne, I heard stories
that the white guys would stay close to the black guys in the field because they
thought the VC and NVA didn't shoot at the blacks as much as the whites"
(Terry 218). Infantryman Bob Sanders recalled, "For the first time in my life, I
saw total unity and harmony. . . . in the Nam, man, out in the field we were just
a force of unity and harmony. We became just one person. When I first got to
the Nam, I saw a lot of prejudice and shit like that. But Charlie had a tendency
to make you unify in a hurry" (Goff and Sanders 131). There were stories of
close friendships between blacks and whites in the boonies. Montagnard Man
remembered having "a white guy in the team. He was a Klan member. He was
from Arkansas. Ark-in-saw in the mountains. . . . I was the first black man
he had really ever sat down and had a decent conversation with. . . . Arkansas
and I wind up being best friends." During a firefight, Arkansas and another
white soldier were hit—badly—"Arkansas had ceased breathing. And I start
to pounding in his chest and hollerin', 'Dear God, please don't let him die.' "
Although his fellow grunts advise him that Arkansas is beyond help, Montagnard Man continues trying to revive him: "I'm stompin' on him. And he started
breathin' again. And I pulled him from out of the water and dragged him to
the helicopter. . . . Arkansas and the other dude survived" (Terry 246–47).
Evidently the Vietcong and North Vietnamese propaganda campaign directed
at the African American soldier improved black/white relations in the field,
ironically.

The situation was radically different, however, in the rear—the territory of
the REMFs (rear echelon motherfuckers). According to one African American
Lurp, "In the rear we saw a bunch of rebel flags. They didn't mean nothing
by the rebel flag. It was just saying we for the South. It didn't mean that they
hated blacks. But after you in the field, you took the flags very personally."
This reaction was fueled by perceived inequities in the field: "we felt that we
were being taken advantage of, 'cause it seemed like more blacks in the field

than in the rear" (Terry 40). A black Navy radarman remembered a completely different war. "Cam Ranh Bay was paradise, man. I would say, Boy, if I got some money together, I'd stay right here and live, I wasn't even gon' come back to the United States. I was treated like a king over there. It was no war" (Terry 266). Race relations, however, belie this sailor's image of "paradise."

> The only serious fighting at Marketime was between black guys and white guys. . . . there would be nothing but Confederate flags all over the place. And one time they burned a cross. And like some of the brothers was getting beat up. And we were more or less head hunting, too. Payback. (Terry 267)

According to one Army medic, racial problems did not occur only in the rear; there were occasional problems in the boonies. "The black/white relationship was tense. I saw a couple of fistfights. . . . I saw this happen in the field, as a matter of fact. . . . When you see racial incidents developing and weapons lying around, it gets pretty tense" (Santoli, *Everything* 72).

Not surprisingly, African Americans in Vietnam created enclaves—self-created, self-imposed, self-enclosed—where they could regenerate by celebrating black culture. According to correspondent Donald Kirk:

> Turn left off one of the main streets leading to the gates of sprawling Tan Son Nhut air base and you find where it's at in Saigon. It happens on "Soul Alley," where the brothers get together, get close, real tight and rap, let it all out, and none of the rabbits or lifers, as career military men are inevitably known, dares bother them. Check it out, dig it. . . . The brothers, almost all of them enlisted men in olive drab fatigues, stroll down the alley while soul music blares from the little bars and clubs, and some of them settle down for a game of cards in the few hours before night falls. (Pratt, *Vietnam Voices* 483)

The empowerment that African Americans felt in enclaves like Soul Alley manifested itself politically through radicalization.[8] A white Marine corpsman recalled:

> the time that Muhammad Ali refused to go in the service and became a hero. The blacks in the battalion began to question why they were fighting Honky's war against other Third World people. . . . I began to notice certain radicalization pressures going on there. Many Southern blacks

changed their entire point of view by the end of their tour and went home
extremely angry. (Santoli, *Everything* 72)

When he arrived in Vietnam, Stan Goff met other black soldiers who provided
him with a sense of community—especially in terms of politics:

> just because I was black, they were going to protect me like a brother,
> like a real brother. . . . Brothers are really not that close back here [in
> America]. It was amazing how the blacks were organizing among them-
> selves over there. They . . . tried to orient me toward Charlie and toward
> the white men and why I was there. . . . how the government was using
> us blacks. (Goff and Sanders 29)

"At some point in their tours," Anderson writes, "most blacks came to feel
that in Vietnam they were being used to fight 'whitey's war' " (164).

This radicalization was manifested through day-by-day appearance and action. "Blacks fought to wear ballooning Afros and black-power bracelets,
woven, it was said, from the shoelaces of dead comrades," MacPherson reports. "They would give each other the dap—an elaborate finger-popping,
hand-slapping ritual with African origins that could take several minutes, depending on how many blacks were together" (562). Perceived by the predominantly white command as rebellious and threatening, such actions would often
result in punishment or jail for blacks. In July 1971, journalist Donald Kirk
interviewed African American soldiers in Soul Alley.

> "If you pulled all the blacks out of Vietnam, you'd have the biggest revo-
> lution you've ever seen in the United States," says [a] brother whom I
> meet in one of the bars off Soul Alley. "You better believe," he goes
> on, "when Nixon pulls us out there won't be no more United States. The
> blacks know demolition. The blacks know how to shoot. We're gonna use
> all that stuff 'back in the world.' " (Pratt, *Vietnam Voices* 485)

MacPherson records that in the sixties many people assumed that, when blacks
in the 'Nam returned to the World, they "would merge with black radicals with
frightening results" (568). For the most part, this organized revolution[9] did not
occur, although there were individual cases where grunts joined the Black Pan-
thers (Terry 14) or even set up Robin Hood-type robberies. An Army rifleman
used his infantry skills to "commandeer and hijack [a] mail truck" carrying
"regular monies going from the post office to the Treasury Department to be
burned. . . . I couldn't understand that money's going to be burnt when people

is in need" (Terry 105). The important point, however, is that the Vietnam war became an important impetus within the civil rights struggle in Vietnam as well as in America—not only because of the complexities of black/white relations in the war, but from the simple fact that so many African Americans had been taught how to bear and use arms. This situation is an exceptional case in which regeneration did arise from the context of Vietnam, a cultural regeneration of the African American community, although the fact that the feared revolution by black grunts combined with American radicals did not take place may be an index, finally, to the lack of personal regeneration accessible to the African American soldier.

Four poets have addressed the theme of regeneration (or lack of it) in the Vietnam war: Horace Coleman, McAvoy Layne, R. L. Barth, and Gerald McCarthy. Coleman's poetry addresses the racial situation of African Americans in Vietnam, and then transcends this condition through solidarity. Layne's book, *How Audie Murphy Died in Vietnam,* is an allegorical, darkly humorous take-off on many things, including *Pilgrim's Progress.* In *A Soldier's Time* Barth declares his descent from Wilfred Owen and his contemporaries by writing of Vietnam in tightly ordered, rhymed, metered, formal verse. McCarthy's *War Story* chronicles an infantryman's tour in the 'Nam and then demonstrates the effect of that experience in the World.

Horace Coleman: Brothers in the 'Nam Transcended

Besides his collection of poems entitled *Between a Rock & a Hard Place,* Horace Coleman has published poems in various journals and periodicals—including *American Poetry Review, Kansas Quarterly, New Letters,* and *In These Times*—and in such anthologies as *Demilitarized Zones, Peace Is Our Profession, Carrying the Darkness, Unaccustomed Mercy, From A to Z: 200 Contemporary American Poets, Leaving the Bough: 50 American Poets for the 80s,* and *Speak Easy, Speak Free* (*Mercy* 49).

Coleman's poem "OK Corral East / Brothers in the Nam" captures the racial situation in Vietnam, interestingly seeing it in terms of the Hollywood western. The poem opens in an African American enclave:

> . . . Khanh Hoi down by the docks
> in the Blues Bar where the women
> are brown and there is no Saigon Tea . . .   (*Mercy* 49)

The title, according to Ehrhart's note, is "a play on the 1957 Hollywood movie, *Gunfight at the OK Corral*" (*Mercy* 53); here, the archetypical western town is not, however, Tombstone or Dodge City or Laramie or Old Tucson, but Khánh Hòi. The setting is a bar, not the Long Branch Saloon, but a "Blues Bar" where the Vietnamese women have been selected because they are dark. What we have is some sort of simulacrum of the urban ghetto or the black rural South. "Saigon tea" refers to the nonalcoholic drink bartenders serve to Vietnamese prostitutes so that they can drink with GIs without becoming inebriated, hence maximizing their income for a night; here, its lack implies that in Khánh Hòi women do not "hustle" the grunts. Most important in the first stanza is the fact that this setting is a place where bonds between blacks grow stronger— that these soldiers are "getting tight" refers on one level to getting drunk, but on a more profound level it translates as the argot of becoming better friends, growing closer. Coleman then introduces the law:

> the timid white MP has his freckles pale
>
> .   .   .   .
>
> he sees nothing his color here
> and he fingers his army rosary his .45

Here, however, we have no Wyatt Earp or Marshal Dillon; instead, the lawman is a scared "kid" ("timid," "freckles pale"). That he "fingers . . . his .45" is a threatening moment, implying a possible racial confrontation, since "he sees nothing his color here." But this is not America, "not Cleveland or Chicago," and the law cannot intimidate these black soldiers:

> we have all killed something recently
> we know who owns the night
> and carry darkness with us   (*Mercy* 49)

Interestingly, the power of the blacks in the penultimate stanza is shown by a comparison with the Vietnamese, recalling Vietcong propaganda about the Vietnam war as a war of white against nonwhite. The threatening ambience of the final stanza is aimed not only at the "white MP" but ultimately at the World: control over life and death has endowed these blacks with the power of "the night / and . . . darkness"—that is, the blackness of the universe.

The end of the war is, for Coleman, problematic for the black soldier (regardless of any empowerment accorded them in the war context). "A Downed Black Pilot Learns How to Fly" bristles with ironic humor:

> "now that the war is over
> we'll have to kill each other again

> but I'll send my medals to Hanoi
> and let them make bullets
> if they'll ship my leg back and
> if they mail me an ash tray
> made from my 4FC they can keep
> the napalm as a bonus. Next time
> I'll wait and see if they've declared
> war on me—or just America."   (*Demilitarized* 158)

This is an interesting comment on warmaking in America: the idea that since *this* war is over, another must be waiting in the wings. The objects to be traded back and forth—medals for the lost leg, an ash tray for napalm—elicit a sarcastic laugh. The sobering implications, however, come from the speaker's alienation within American society as a "black pilot": the reawakened realization of racial enmity (the "we" who will "kill each other again" are blacks and whites in America) and the alienation of self from country in the closing two lines as index of the disenfranchisement of African Americans in the World.

Coleman's poetry does not merely involve African American issues. He deals as well with the commonplaces of the Vietnam war. Surrealism is captured in "Night Flare Drop, Tan Son Nhut," set during Tết 1968 (notable in the point of view of the characters within the poem because of the customary annual truce period but more notable with the hindsight of history because the Tết Offensive was the turning point of the war). The details of the scene are magnificently and memorably drawn: "Roman candles chase tracers / Little rockets bark at dancing dragons"; during

> . . . a colorful fire fight
> Six Vietnamese MPs
>   eager to watch
> run into a mine field
>   and throw yellow confetti for yards . . .

Coleman's laconic irony works double duty here: "yellow confetti" refers to the grisly fragmentation of these "Vietnamese MPs" caught in mine explosions; but as diction, "yellow confetti" underlines the poem's carnivalesque ambience. The "night flares" from the title provide equally surreal details: "magnesium tears that / burn deep holes in the night." In contrast to the carnivalesque aspects of Tết (and of the ongoing attack), Americans are shown in fear, hiding: "in 100 P alley . . . Americans [are] afraid to come out of their rooms" and "off duty pilots . . . / stand in front of the air conditioners /

sweating." This poem describes Vietnamization—not the official sense of it—
but a more organic version, in which the hegemony of America is driven into
siege by the unity of the Vietnamese (North and South) in celebrating Tết.
Even Saigon, the traditional stronghold of colonial power, is besieged by Tết
(as it literally was during the Tết Offensive). And the night flares, "magnesium
tears," are ineffectual, finally, because "the dark / like the VC   always comes
back" (*Mercy* 50)—they both evince the power of nature.

Coleman's poem "In Ca Mau" (the point in South Vietnam farthest from
the DMZ) illustrates how Americans are imprisoned, entrapped by the war
and its hidden dangers: "the Americans in Ca Mau eat tin-skinned food / play
prostitute roulette clap / . . . with rifles under the bed," a claustrophobic existence in contrast with the expansive movements of the "women [who] sweep
the canal with their oars." Whereas "the people race bicycles on Sundays,"
the Americans who feel endangered "ride six to a fast jeep." They are even
besieged by their own technowar machine; the "five-hundred-pound bombs"
dropped to "pacify the forest of U Minh" reverberate and shake the sides of
the "yellow tent O Club of Ca Mau." With characteristic overkill, "they hunt
communist water buffalo / with quad .50s and infra-red," but the Americans
realize nevertheless that only "one bullet / makes a helicopter a shotgunned
duck" (an ironic reference to the rituals of "regeneration through violence" en-
acted in American swamps and duck blinds). The point of the poem is that the
American presence in Vietnam is only one brief period of occupation within
thousands of years of warfare with China. When the "Americans / leave . . .
the women [will] sweep after them in Ca Mau" (*Mercy* 51–52). The people
will take it all in stride.

Coleman's most striking "us vs. them" poem is "Remembrance of Things
Past"; in this work, he begins by alluding to Baudelaire:

> mortars are
> the devil coughing
> napalm?
> Baudelaire never had
> such flowers
> such bright fleur de lis
> such evil

These flowers refer not only to the technology of "mortars" and "napalm" but
(and perhaps more strongly) to the human response to such technology.

> claymores
> shatter more than bones

> when they attacked we
> killed them dreams and all
> we thought
>
> we fired artillery   they
> shot hatred back

The point is that the Vietnamese, even without retaliatory technology, inflict worse damage: psychological, emotional.

> when we burned their bones
> they loathed us still   dying
> still trying to get their crisp
> black fingers on our white throats   (*Mercy* 51)

In a marvelous touch, the adjective "black" is attributed to dead and dying Vietnamese, and the living Americans are all "white"—note that Coleman uses here the word "our." All Americans, black and white, feel the opprobrium of the Vietnamese, even as they burn, and are united in the "whiteness" of the World. But this unity is finally a solipsistic, dangerous union, always on the edge of death.

Coleman's poems bridge the best aspects of the aesthetic and the antipoetic modes; his lines crackle with precise, arresting imagery and aesthetically pleasing turns of language, without the poeticizing of war which the antipoet would avoid. Along with the antipoet, Coleman wants to demonstrate the senselessness of war, and his particular message is that Americans, with their claustrophobic xenophobia in Vietnam, their overreliance on technowar, could not have won. The only result is that the American soldier must "carry darkness" (*Mercy* 49)—it is significant that Ehrhart titled his anthology *Carrying the Darkness* after Coleman's phrase. For Coleman, this "darkness" is ultimately not worth the trouble, the death, the suffering: there is finally no regeneration in this "darkness" nor in the act of "carrying" it.

McAvoy Layne: Mourning Audie Murphy or Not

W. D. Ehrhart, in his benchmark essay surveying poetry by veterans, "Soldier-Poets of the Vietnam War," describes Layne's "novel-in-verse," *How Audie Murphy Died in Vietnam:*

> In 227 very short and often bleakly humorous poems, Layne traces the life
> of his fictional Audie Murphy from birth through childhood to enlistment

in the Marines, then boot camp, a tour of duty in Vietnam—including capture by the North Vietnamese—and finally home again. . . . None [of the poems] is longer than a single page. Though few, if any, could stand up alone without the support of all the others, their cumulative effect is remarkable and convincing. (249–50)

Out of these 227 poems,[10] Ehrhart picks "Guns" as a sample:

> When the M-16 rifle had a stoppage,
> One could feel enemy eyes
> Climbing
> His
> Bones
> Like
> Ivy.   [98, unpaginated]

This is perhaps the best lyric in the entire work, because its form reflects its sense masterfully. Almost all of Layne's poems in this verse novel are shaped this way—long lines funneling down into single-word lines—some in fact are only columns of words with one word per line. Here, the break of the long first line followed by a slightly shorter line graphically dramatizes the jamming of the rifle, and the file of words at the end is a typographic representation of the Vietcong looking up and down his body, a target—"Climbing / His / bones."

The poem "More on Aloha," in describing Audie's return from R&R, visualizes a letterform:

> Everyone wore starched khakis,
> Shined shoes
> and shaved
> For the flight back to Vietnam,
> Everyone except Audie,
> Who
> Wore
> An
> Aloha
> Shirt.   [127]

This poem is shaped like a letter "F." Given the fact that the poem refers to Audie's lack of military "repair," what we have here in the letter "F" is the

"F-word," the word *fuck* (or maybe *fuck-up*). If Audie had been in the army, this letter would have been the first part of the graffiti acronym "F.T.A."—which has been variously translated as "Fuck the Army" and "Free the Army" (though the first version is probably more widespread); whether or not such an expression was used in the Marines, in which Audie has enlisted (beyond such expressions of "Green Mother" or "The Crotch" for the Corps), his nonconformity takes on ideological significance.

One more instance in which the form aids the meaning of the poem is "Ten October—a dream."

> Ten October was everything.
> In an exclusively temporal war,
> One becomes nothing more than his rotation date,
> Without which
> One becomes merely
> 2245631,
> KIA,
> WIA,
> Or
> MIA.   [143]

Here, the stack of words is constructed of the choices one has in the combat zone: life as a number or nonlife as a casualty (and these come in three varieties—killed, wounded, and missing).

Ehrhart's description of *How Audie Murphy Died in Vietnam* as a "novel-in-verse" lends it too much of a sense of continuity. There is very little sense of the passage of time in the book, at least not in a fluid way. Essentially, Layne gives us aphorism after aphorism, anecdote after anecdote, each of which is set in later and later moments. But only near the end of the story do the moments combine into a reconstructible stream. In some respects, Layne's project here is similar to Peter Bowman's in *Beach Red*—to reproduce in a novel-in-verse the maturation of a soldier—but their prosodies are diametrically opposed. Layne is laconic, terse, elliptical, understated, where Bowman is loquacious, exuberant, hyperbolic. In his understatement, Layne's project is perhaps more closely allied to Dick Shea's *vietnam simply*—also a verse novel—but with even more terseness than Shea brings to bear.

Layne's aphorisms are generally highly elliptical. The title of the following example is "Sex Drive of the eighteen-year-old American Male":

Second
Only
Perhaps
To
The
Thrust
Of
The
Saturn
Five.   [14]

The form is meant to represent both the Saturn 5 rocket and the (symboli-
cally) upright penis of the "American Male." "Thrust," therefore, in all its
scatological force, embodies both motion and emotion, body and ache.
     Layne's vignettes are often wryly ironic; witness "New Guy":

In November
An F-4 Phantom pilot
Spotted a company-sized unit
Crossing a stream,
And dropped a load of 250 lb. bombs
On Mike Company, 3/3.
The largest piece of the radio man
They could find
Was the radio.
It was understandable,
The
Pilot
Was
New
To
Killing.   [97]

The humor of the piece pivots on the phrase "It was understandable"; as the
reader reaches that line, the immediate impression is that what was "understandable" is how the radio is in better shape than the radioman—made of
tougher materials, protected by the radioman's body, or perhaps the radioman
had placed it on the ground but was himself standing. What the reader discovers
in the word-column, however, is that the speaker is actually excusing the pilot's

action as an FNG's mistake—and, of course, this is done so offhandedly that we are convinced there would be no consequences of military justice to the pilot for his "understandable" error. The linguistic category for this mistake is an interestingly "understandable" set of self-reductive oxymorons: "friendly fire" and "friendly casualties."

The Audie Murphy in this novel is *not* the WWII Audie Murphy—war hero and movie star. Instead, he is a "Baby Boomer" presumably named *after* the famous hero. Of course, Layne, given the fact that his protagonist is named Audie Murphy, is leveling a critique merely within his title—*How Audie Murphy Died in Vietnam*—that is, how heroism and the opportunity for heroism did not obtain in the Vietnam war. In some sense, of course, even though this novel is plotted skeletally and the characters are really quite sparsely developed, the very fact of the character Audie's name brings a lot of pressure to bear on him either to be heroic or to rebel against that image.

In fact, what happens to Audie is that he is delayed three days past his DEROS (date of expected rotation from overseas) because the weather keeps helicopters from flying into his base. When he finally gets a lift from a medevac chopper ferrying out wounded (Audie is slightly wounded himself), "He began to feel an emotion new to him, / A / Mother's / Son's / Worry / For / Brother" [172]—a sense of responsibility for his friends back in the combat zone—and he "hopped the next Huey back to the field" [173]. Eventually captured and imprisoned in Hanoi, he is nominated for a Silver Star. Shortly afterward, his wounded arm becomes virulently infected, and the North Vietnamese fear it will need to be amputated. Because of this medical condition, he is offered freedom, but he wants to take the rest of the American prisoners back to the World with him. He asks:

> "Look, we both know what my situation is,
>   What will it take to get the rest out of here?"
>
> "The conditions, Corporal Murphy, basically
>   Are complete American withdrawal,
>   And severance of American support
>   For the Saigon regime."   [195]

Audie asks to talk to the president of the United States by telephone. As might be expected, this becomes great TV news, and the networks vie for the coverage. When the day of the phone call comes, the entire world is listening— all regular TV programming has been preempted. The poem "On 'Lasting' " contains his message:

Mr. President, we realize here
That you are pursuing an honorable & lasting peace.
But, Sir, the war seems to be the only thing
That is lasting.
That is why my parents cannot accept the Silver Star.
The medals should be given to the peace makers
And the planners for a better world,
They should have the Silver Stars.
And I would like to ask that all the campaign
Ribbons being worn today be sent to Washington
To rest.
And that America become the first civilized country
Of the world
To stop the awarding and wearing
Of
Commendation
Medals
For Killing."   [215]

Audie's speech is occasioned by his maturing sense of what it is to be heroic—
here, he is attempting to save not only his immediate friends, but all people
who will be killed in all future wars. (In fact, this sort of action has taken place
in real life, when Ron Kovic "crashed" the Republican National Convention
where President Nixon was about to accept the nomination again in order to
interrupt his speech with certain simple questions [162–69].) The president's
reply to Audie is formulaic: "Corporal Murphy, hopefully / This conversation
will open yet another channel, / Another avenue, / By which we can pursue
the elusive goal / Of peace" [216]. The title of this section indicates Audie's
response to the president: "Checking Out"; he checks out of the Hanoi Hilton,
but he also checks out of America altogether. Ribbons from all over South
Vietnam are mailed to Washington. But we finally see Audie peeling himself
an orange in some "Friendly / Clearing" [227] in South Vietnam (not "home
again," as Ehrhart suggests, although perhaps South Vietnam is now Audie's
home, or home is now wherever Audie is); at the same moment, "Bobby Taylor," a draft resister in Canada is also peeling himself an orange, "Waiting /
To / Come / Home" [228].

Layne's closing poem, "The End," steps out of the sequence and speaks
to us in Layne's own voice: "So / If / You / Think / This / Is / The / End, /

You're / On / The / Wrong / Page" [229]. Layne sets up an endless loop, because this literally *is* the end, but the sense of the poem demands you to turn the
page. The next page, blank, drives you back to "The End." Ad infinitum. What
Layne wants to invoke here is a sense that the dialectic of war and peace is
never-ending. But he also is telling the reader that Murphy's lack of immediate
success in procuring peace is only a temporary setback; this is not the end—he
will get peace. This is not doublethink. It is possible to hold both of these ideas
in mind by remembering that any step toward peace is always made by a single
individual, and that all of us must take that step in order for peace really to
happen. That is finally Audie Murphy's and Layne's achievement: the exercise
of one's life and opportunity for a noble cause. And this exercise, couched as a
verse novel, is at bottom an antipoetic enterprise, but in epic proportions.

R. L. Barth: The Vietnam War's Neo-Formalist

R. L. Barth's *A Soldier's Time: Vietnam War Poems* is unique among books of
poems by Vietnam veterans for two reasons: (1) the predominance of poetry
written in rhyme and meter using inherited poetic forms and (2) its treatment
of *two* conflicts—the French war that ended in 1954 and the American war
that followed. In his approach, Barth's foci have been largely historical, on
the one hand relying on literary history and on the other relating personal, and
ultimately social, history. His literary ancestors are indicated by the dust jacket
blurbs from two poets who are accomplished formalists in their own right:

> Barth's best lines have a classical ring to them: it is as though Lucretius or
> Martial had been reincarnated in the uniform of the U.S. Marines.

> R. L. Barth has done for the Vietnam War what Owen, Blunden and
> Sassoon did for World War I [with] poems whose conscientious and clear-
> sighted craft does full justice to the seriousness of his subject.

The first is from X. J. Kennedy, the second from Timothy Steele; both reliable
readers, they carefully and knowledgeably assert Barth's connections with the
writers they mention. The most revealing clue about literary forebears comes
from Barth himself. His prologue poem entitled "Reading the *Iliad*" begins:

> Volume and desk, coffee and cigarette
> Forgotten, the reader, held in Homer's mind,
> Looks upon Greeks and Trojans fighting yet
> Or heroes and footsoldiers, thin and blind,

Forced-marching for the Styx. But suddenly
Stunned by the clamor under smoky skies,
Boastings and tauntings, he looks up to see—
Not the god-harried plain where Hector tries

His destiny, not the room—but a mountain
covered with jungle; on one slope, a chateau
with garden, courtyard, a rococo fountain,
And, faces down, hands tied, six bodies in a row.

(Soldier's Time 11)

Barth's incredible range of vision encompasses distant ages and locales. Interestingly, it is poetry which binds Greek myth, Vietnam's absurdity, and the reader sitting at a desk. The dramatic situation of the poem underlines the Vietnam dilemma: the reader (and we probably ought to read here *the poet*) is unable to enter imaginatively into Homer's "god-harried plain" without the intrusion of Vietnam, a Vietnam with the incongruity of a French chateau ensconced in jungle made even more incongruous (or perhaps historically more correct) by the image of "six bodies in a row." The implication is that Vietnam seeps into everything one does.

But what this poem reveals about Barth's influences is similarly startling. Here, he points back to the beginnings of Western literary art while using, very comfortably, English poetic forms, to wit, alternating quatrain stanzas in iambic pentameter: the *heroic* or *elegiac* quatrain (itself a revealing choice). An amazing synthesis of form and content, the poem already telegraphs an expectation of approach and attitude to the subject *through* the choice of form. Barth's skill in carrying off the pentameter is substantial; no slave of the iamb, he deliberately peppers the lines with trochees and dactyls. The rhythmic texture is therefore varied and nimble. Clearly, without mentioning his debt in this poem, he is beholden to Wilfred Owen and other WWI poets, if only in his prosodic approach to the subject. "A Letter to the Dead" unveils Barth's conscious identification with these writers:

The outpost trench is deep with mud tonight.
Cold with the mountain winds and two weeks' rain,
I watch the concertina. The starlight-
Scope hums, and rats assault the bunkers again.

You watch with me: Owen, Blunden, Sassoon.
Through sentry duty, everything you meant

Thickens to fear of nights without a moon.
War's war. We are, my friends, no different.

(*Soldier's Time* 32)

In this respect—of being "no different" from these writers—Barth sets himself up as different, or at least distant, from his fellow Vietnam-veteran poets,
perhaps even apart from David Huddle, who tinkers with the sonnet. As Kunitz
has argued, Barth's fellows "can no longer respond to rhetorical flourishes and
sentiments borrowed from the poets who fought . . . in the earlier wars of the
century" (Casey vii). Barth's project is to recuperate formal verse and render
it applicable again to the subject of war, particularly the Vietnam war(s).

   The first section of *A Soldier's Time* is entitled "Dienbienphu Besieged."
Barth's interest in French Indochina is in the people, the individuals caught up
in the siege at Diện Biên Phủ. The poem "March 1954," for example, features the voices of Colonel Charles Piroth and Major Paul Grauwin. Piroth,
an artillery officer, committed suicide at Diện Biên Phủ because of his perceived loss of honor in underestimating General Giap's use of artillery. The
first section, "I. From the Command Post," describes the situation immediately after Piroth's death by grenade and asks the question: "A suicide, he fled
the battlefield. / For what? Events rebuking vanity? / Outmoded honor?" (16).
The middle section, "II. Colonel Charles Piroth," seeks to answer these questions in the colonel's own voice. We overhear a conversation between Piroth
and another officer, probably Major Grauwin, whose speech is rendered below
in italics:

   "*Please spare us further mention of Verduns.*
   Colonel, what if the Viets do *have guns?*"

   Why if they do, they'll be on reverse slopes—
   How transport over crests? with men and ropes?—
   And such trajectories as they'll require
   To hit the fortress when they open fire . . .
   Well, they've no gunners with experience.

   "*But say that Giap's lost his common sense*
   And drags his guns to face us."

                    Then we'll see
   Muzzle flashes, my counterbattery
   Smashing the Viets. Give me half an hour.

(17, emphasis mine)

Clearly, Piroth made an error of underestimation which the Americans would also make later: disbelieving that vast amounts of supplies and matériel could be moved literally by hand and foot, as on the Ho Chi Minh trail. Piroth later realizes that he will never locate the enemy batteries:

> . . . there's no sighting, nothing of the source
> Of heavy shells that, smashing, crashing, force
> Algerians to the ground, shatter the thin,
> Jerry-built bunkers, Legionnaires within,
> And churn the gunpits where Moroccan crews
> Wrestle the 155s through bloody ooze . . .
> My counterbattery? We blindly aim,
> As blindly fire . . .
>
> What's left of my good name?   (17–18)

"III. Major Paul Grauwin" relays that officer's evaluation of Piroth's actions:

> A loss of faith? a loss of nerve?
> A nervous breakdown? That will serve
> The needs of military fashion.
> The truest loss is our compassion.   (19)

Grauwin here creates the "official version" for Piroth's death (by suicide—a self-fragging), and the phrase "needs of military fashion" already prefigures the American mistakes of creating official yet false reports to the public. The terseness of Grauwin's response indicates through its brevity how he has lost, truly, his compassion for Piroth.

In terms of formalist technique, Barth in this poem modulates his verse forms to accompany his message. Section 1, in unrhymed tercets, dramatizes the chaos at the command post after the suicide. Section 2, literally spoken from the grave, broadcasts, in its stentorian iambic pentameter couplets, the almost Shakespearean drama and pretentiousness of the aristocratic Piroth's failure. Section 3, in a "humbler" tetrameter, expresses Grauwin's more plebeian sensibility and dramatically undercuts Piroth's bombastic section through its conciseness.

The remainder of the "Dien Bien Phu Besieged" poems are comparable to "March 1954" and are spoken by various voices: a telegrapher; "internal" deserters singing a marching song beginning "*We are the Rats of the Nam Yum*" (20–21); a French civilian steeling himself to death with the soldiers in a sonnet; the besieged soldiers speaking in alternating quatrains to the "Dead Heroes"; free-verse excerpts from the notebook of the commander of Diện Biên Phủ; soldiers preparing for the last stand: "At 0100 we fix bayonets" (26); couplets spoken by General Navarre, the commander of the French forces in Indochina; and "Lessons of Indochine" spoken by French troops, now prisoners of war—all executed in elegantly crafted poems.

Many of the poems in "American Indochina," the second part of the book, are from the viewpoint of an American grunt, characterized as "I." Barth, however, begins the American section with a disclaimer: "Patrolling silently, / He knows how men will die / In jungles. I am he. / He is not I." Barth herewith claims that the speakers of the following poems are not R. L. Barth. To paraphrase: *I am the one who, patrolling silently, knows how men will die* (i.e., I am claiming an omniscient perspective), *but at the same time, the omniscient narrator I am projecting is not the real me.* A strange disclaimer. Is Barth worried that these poems will be taken as personal narrative rather than fiction? Perhaps, given the mixing of memoir with the fictional by various writers and witnesses of the war, Barth may feel the requirement for such a disclaimer.

"A Letter to My Infant Son" deals with the question—a thorny one among Vietnam veterans—of what to answer when one's child "will ask me / To tell war stories. How shall I answer you?" The speaker recalls hearing stories from his "best childhood friends, / Two brothers"—WWII stories they heard from their father; "each night I worked / Through [the stories] closely, casting and recasting them / In varied forms. Always I was the hero." The poem, a "letter" written *"from Da Nang"* (according to the epigraph), indicates that the speaker is in the war zone as he writes, and he realizes that

> War is not the story
> That you would have me tell . . .
>
> .   .   .   .
>
> . . . True courage is
> Hidden in unexpected terms and places:
> In performing simple duties day by day;
> In sometimes saying *no* when necessary . . .

The speaker understands that the child "will not comprehend the rot, / Disease, mud, rain; the mangled friend who curses / The chance that saved him." The only decision the poem can offer is "How shall I answer you, if not with silence?" (38–39). This is an understandable dilemma, which is a reminder as well of the American tendency to forget historical lessons. The answer to the child's question is really one which lies outside this poem—in the fact of the book of poems itself. *A Soldier's Time* is Barth's best attempt at telling a war story, measured and deliberate, in order *not* to be as clear as possible. When the child is older, the poems will suffice.

"Office of the Dead" maintains an equanimity of voice that belies its message.

> Death's mostly distant here of late
> And random with the seediness
> Of plain bad luck—nothing like Fate.
> But the dead are neither more nor less:
>
> Just dead. I check their metal tags
> For eight hours, till my duty ceases,
> "Body-counting" the body bags.
> I do not have to count the pieces. (51)

The boredom of the Graves Registration specialist here underlines his distance from the enormity of what he does. Hidden within the line "I do not have to count the pieces" is the unsaid, pregnant point of this poem: that somewhere out there, away from the GR point, are people who are committed not only for "eight hours, till my duty ceases." This poem resembles in sentiment Michael Casey's poem "The LZ Gator Body Collector"—the speaker who says, "I had gloves on then" (Casey 56) to assure the reader that in his handling of a dead woman's body he was protected from contamination—at the same time that he is "protected" from understanding the enormity of her death.

"Fieldcraft," the closing poem of "American Indochina," honors the knowledge gained by grunts after a long time in the field—the knowledge which, as the one-year tour progresses, is only substantive when a grunt is "short" and which cannot be passed on to FNGs.

> At last, the senses sharpen. All around,
> I listen closely. Under the dull sound
> Of distant artillery, and the shrieking planes
> Diving with napalm; under the dry crack
> Of automatic rifles; at the back
> Of consciousness, almost, one sound remains:
> Mud sucking at bare feet as they are going
> Between the rice shoots. Nearly silent. Knowing. (67)

Barth's use of enjambment underlines the sense of this poem. Except for the end of the first line, each of the lines is severely enjambed until we come to the colon at the end of line six. Essentially, the movement of the poem narrows, funnellike, to the colon that then points forward to the closing couplet, in which the essential (almost epigrammatic) wisdom is contained. The colon therefore acts as a fulcrum for the poem—on one side, technowar and the FNG, and on the other, the wisdom of *mud*. Mud—a compound of earth and water—is the precinct of the Vietnamese soldier, as Captain Linh, commander of the Cu Chi tunnels, has suggested (Mangold and Penycate 66–67), and so to know mud is to begin to beat the Vietcong. Of course, the one-year tour militates against Americans knowing this essential truth until it is time for them to leave.

The closing poem, part of a closing section entitled "Epilogue & Coda," is called "Two for Any Memorial Day."

> I.
> Young soldiers without campaign ribbons standing
> At attention; vets staging a mock landing;
> Then speeches; gun salutes; taps—
> all for these
> Poor troopers who are finally at ease?
>
> II.
> Observe the rites now: politicians
> And Legionnaires, all rhetoricians,
> Declaiming from the dais glories
> They've sucked from war's nostalgic stories.
>   Here's what Christ meant when he said,
>   *Let the dead bury the dead.*   (73)

Barth's purpose in writing the book is ultimately uncovered here: to forestall "war's nostalgic stories" and desentimentalize all Memorial Days forever. In this project, Barth hearkens back at least to e. e. cummings. A poem like " 'next to of course god america i" (268) essentially deals with the same subject and occasion as "Two for Any Memorial Day."

In furthering his antiwar message, cummings experimented with received, traditional forms—often through grave distortion—so that the form frequently collapsed or exploded under the innovation. The devices of formal verse, after all, have centuries of poeticism behind them; even Owen and Sassoon (to name two of Barth's admitted influences), when they used inherited forms, found them working somewhat against their purposes. Owen "wanted above all to depict the senseless horrors and inhumanity of war," observes Kunitz, "but . . . the elevation of his style inevitably exalted his agonists-in-khaki" (Casey vii). In Barth's work, something of the same sort obtains; his almost classical use of forms, of rhyme, of meter, seems somewhat ill at ease with his proclaimed project. The "elevation of his style" carries its own connotations of glory and heroic sacrifice within it, separate from any debunking to which Barth may lay claim. Barth, for the most part, steers himself away from colloquial language, except in one or two poems, and even there, he uses all the machinery of traditional prosody. And his command of this machinery is impressive. The overall effect of the poems (which I would conjecture Barth did not ultimately intend) may, however, share the problematics Owen encountered in his war poetry: the possibility of exaltation. All that aside, Barth's literary aestheticism underlines his significant achievement.

Gerald McCarthy: The Endless Search for Catharsis

Gerald McCarthy's collection, *War Story: Vietnam War Poems,* published in 1977, eschews any sort of exaltation. "War Story," the opening section of the book, is composed of short, numbered lyrics that are occasionally haiku-like in their intensity. W. D. Ehrhart again provides a good introduction. The twenty-two poems of the opening section "are set mostly in the war zone, but as the book progresses, the poems become richer and more haunting as the full impact of the war slowly settles in upon the former Marine" (255).

"War Story"—a series of short lyric poems spoken from the viewpoint of a single speaker—describes the chronological progress of the speaker's tour. Lyric number 1 (also titled "Med Building") is fairly typical in its use of irony to establish the absurdity of Vietnam.

> They brought the dead
> in helicopters and trucks
> and tried to piece the bodies back together,
> shoved them in plastic bags
> to be sent home.
> Sometimes there was an arm or leg
> leftover,
> it lay around until the next shipment;
> they made it fit in somewhere.   (8)

The import of this poem has to do with the technowar machine's treatment of soldiers as objects, essentially as counters. As long as the equations balance— that is, the right number of arms and legs in a body bag, whoever they belong to—then all is right with the high command. McCarthy demonstrates his craft here by dropping "leftover" in a line by itself, so that the word itself seems left over—isolated, fragmented from syntax.

The images of number 7 are phrased in stateside associations:

> Flares in a night sky
> lighting up the place
> like a football field.
> Ammo belts
> strung over shoulders,
> I remember the time
> I was a newsboy
> with the sunday morning papers,
> throwing the headlines.   (14)

Here, McCarthy uses an image unfamiliar to civilians, follows with a neutral line to buffer the transition, and then relates the image to some familiar aspect of American life—the procedure occurs twice. But it is the ending line that resounds, as the unexpected turn of phrase focuses the poem for the reader. Certainly, what the speaker now throws in Vietnam, bullets and grenades and other projectiles, are the stuff of "headlines"; what is most important, however, is the speaker's limited stock of associative memories—still a youthful preoccupation with football and paper routes.

McCarthy is characteristically laconic in his narration of atrocities. Here is number 9:

> They shot the woman in the arm,
> four of them
> raped her
> and killed an old man
> who tried to interfere;
> and later killed the woman too.
> She was the enemy.   (16)

What surfaces here is the speaker's numbed sensibilities, the easy capitulation to the excuse that she was Vietcong. A helpful contrast is a brief excerpt from

Walter McDonald's "Interview With a Guy Named Fawkes, U.S. Army." The speaker, Fawkes, is telling a reporter "you tell them this":

> . . . tell them kiss
> my rear when they piss about
> women and kids in shacks
> we fire on. damn.
> they fire on us.
> hell yes, it's war
> they sent us for.   (*Caliban* 15)

McDonald's poem is ostensibly a direct quotation out of a reporter's interview. Its anger is directed by Fawkes through the reporter to America, to people who are not supporting the grunts (in Fawkes's view). In other words, the utterance is deliberately immediate. In McCarthy's poem, we hear the "war story" in precisely the way it might have been told at the time, offhand and understated, without anger. The implied subtext of this poem, therefore, is the poet's later quiet outrage which drives him to write it—the need to point to what happened as cold-blooded crime.

McCarthy's number 11 underlines Vietnam's bizarre mundanities.

> Hot sun,
> I walk into a whorehouse
> pay the girl
> unbuckle my pants
> and screw her
> sweat sticking to my fatigues
> small legs grasping my back
> her slanted eyes look up at me
> as I come.
> Outside the tin-roofed hut
> another GI waits his turn.   (18)

That the visit occurs at noon, that the prostitute has "slanted eyes," that there presumably are lines of men waiting outside the hut—all of these may be strange to the middle-American sensibility, familiar though they may be within the context of the grunt.

As do other poems by Vietnam veterans, McCarthy's work often capitalizes on a popular readiness to apprehend filmic allusions. In number 13, itself entitled "War Story," the speaker is pinned down with his platoon and thinks: "We wait for the word / to move out / and nobody *changes the reel,* / we don't get time for *intermission*" (20, emphasis mine). In number 15, "Sniper," the speaker is hit and tries to comprehend it all by relating the situation to a western.

> Goddamn.
> Knocked backward, rolling to one side
> it happens all at once.
> He's got me.
> The arrow sticks in my chest
> and in the distance I can hear the bugles,
> the pounding hooves.   (22)

This retreat to cinematic associations seems endemic to firefights in the poetry of Vietnam veterans. In number 21, the speaker, now at home in the World, finds himself isolated and unwanted during some holiday devoted to the memory of fighting men—the Fourth of July, perhaps, or Memorial Day, even Veterans Day. The speaker is chagrined to find that

> The bank is closed.
> The movie marquee says: John Wayne in…
> I realize
> I am a communist.

Even out of the war zone, the persistence of cinematic association—even within a logic of rejection and rebellion—nevertheless drives the speaker's thought process. More significant, however, is the speaker's identification with the enemy, arising from feelings of alienation.

Number 22, "Voyeur," the closing lyric of "War Story," relays the speaker's sense of disconnectedness, of being unable to make connections with those around him.

> The women rise from the water
> wading through the surf,
> shaking the water from their hair,
> caught in the moonlight,
> bodies thousands of wet drops.
>
> I can hear them laughing
> above the roar of ocean;

> talking to one another
> lying down on the beach.
>
> They stretch themselves
> warm breeze a blanket
> beneath the stars.   (29)

This poem is reminiscent of the ending of T. S. Eliot's "Love Song of J. Alfred Prufrock," when Prufrock says, "I have heard the mermaids singing, each to each. // I do not think that they will sing to me" (7). The girls on the beach are as distant and ephemeral to McCarthy's speaker as the mermaids are to Prufrock; the difference, however, is that the speaker's gulf is more poignant since he is separated from "his own kind"—perhaps these are girls in his own hometown—unlike Prufrock who is (at least on the surface of the poem) alienated from mermaids, another species standing perhaps for lost romanticism. The hallmark of McCarthy's series is their psychological genuineness, couched in a movement from blunt intensity to melancholic lyricism.

The rest of the poems in *War Story* reveal a continual rootlessness, an inability to connect, a sense finally of helplessness. In the short lyric "Ambuscade," the speaker cannot help but associate hunting deer with the war.

> In the distance
> the deer watch us.
> We cross a field
> and follow their tracks
> in the woods.
> The sound of water
> falling over sheets of limestone
> calls us from silences.
> Dark filters through the trees,
> there is no way home.   (39)

The "sound of water" is the speaker's desire here to be seduced by the woods, to belong finally to *something* if not someone, to finally escape the alienating world of "silences." But this is finally impossible also because "Dark" obscures the woods and the way. The final line, "there is no way home," implies an inexpressible ache of unbelonging; although the speaker assumes there is a home, not only is it unreachable ("there is no way . . .") but it may not even exist ("there is no . . . home").

"I'll Bring You a Frozen Chocolate Pie" is a frightening poem partly be-

cause of its subject matter—a speaker trapped in adolescence and considering
rape and molestation (hence the title, a bribe for a child)—and partly from its
half-surrealistic tone, implying the instability of the speaker's mind:

> OK, I surrender.
> I'm twenty seven & feel funny
> buying a tube of Clearasil
> at the corner drug store.
>
> Sometimes I sneak a few comic books
> or the latest copy of Skin magazine.
> I drink cokes forever.

(The "tube of Clearasil" is clearly an index to the speaker's lack of emotional
maturity but may also point to the acne that is often a symptom in Agent
Orange poisoning.) The speaker reveals that his friends are worrying about him
and that he has been going to confession: "the priest said: how many times? /
Oh, it was good afterwards / walking into the daylight." The signs are there: he
can divest himself of guilt and therefore of responsibility—which under other
circumstances might be harmless—but here we get a hint of deeper desires.

> In alleyways I wait
> for young high school chicks
> who've taken a wrong turn somewhere.
>
> I get so hungry
> I eat the fingers on my hand.
>
> When the screaming stopped
> I was lost in morning,
> there were a line of boats
> slipping beneath the water.
>
> When the screaming stopped
> she was lying there
> & I could not wake myself.   (46)

The slippery atmosphere of the closing three strophes is disturbing. Are these
dreams? Or is there within the poem a literal woman "lying there" somewhere, and we have been witnesses to some murky atrocity? The only thing
we can know for sure is that this speaker is completely disconnected from
any sense of human community—though he is sane enough to postpone his
friends' alarm—and he is clearly on the edge of his self-control (if he has not

actually already violated that boundary). The implication, although this is not made clear within the poem but rather by the book as a whole, as the grounding context for the poem, is that the Vietnam-war experience has led to this condition.

The best poems in *War Story,* however, are those in which the speaker is a close approximation of McCarthy himself. One of these, driving in its honesty, is "The Sound of Guns," which begins with the bleak imagery of winter— "December's cold . . . / a spider's web frozen white against the glass"—and endless roads—"The highway runs past the brown fields / all the way west to Omaha, and just keeps going." The poem continues:

> At the university in town
> tight-lipped men tell me the war in Vietnam is over,
> that my poems should deal with other things:
> earth, fire, water, air.
>
> . . . .
>
> At nineteen I stood at night and watched
> an airfield mortared. A plane that was to take
> me home, burning; men running out of the flames.
>
> Seven winters have slipped away,
> the war still follows me.
> Never in anything have I found
> a way to throw off the dead.   (64)

Discussing this closing stanza, John Felstiner asks, "How do you judge lines like these? . . . While the first line may be a poeticism picked up in high school, the last two have a profoundly somber dramatic power, which you would think had been precluded by winters that 'slipped away' " ("Bearing" 33). In fact, the point of the stanza, and the entire poem, is that time heals nothing. The memories of "an airfield mortared"—the sense of frustration and utter betrayal at the destruction of the "plane that was to take me home" coupled with the relief that the speaker had not yet boarded the plane, was not one of the "men running out of the flames"—are still fresh, still evocable in such immediacy. The assumption made by older, "tight-lipped men" is that it is possible to forget Vietnam, to regenerate oneself; the reality is that the guilt and the resistance of the Vietnam war to amnesia are so heavy that Vietnam *is* "earth, fire, water, air" to this speaker. This assertion is the ultimate point of *War Story:* that war stories from Vietnam not only can never be forgotten, but also need to be kept alive, current, in order to make the world a better, more peaceful place.

A final observation about McCarthy's poetic method: he uses all three modes—antipoetic, cathartic, aesthetic. The poems set in Vietnam tend to be antipoetic, using a blunted, spare, terse language to underline the senselessness of the war. The poems depicting readjustment outside the combat zone take on a surrealistic edge, but flash lyrically in moments of aesthetic beauty, in bravura flights of description: "The day splits open: tongues of steel flash / in sunlight, broken stumps in a marshland" (59); or "a pair of woman's breasts / thrust out / like piers along the shore / that catch the force of storms" (45). But throughout the entire book, the prevailing mood is one of catharsis, or at least the quest for some cathartic experience. The final poem in the book, "The Warriors," opens with the bulldogged persistence of this quest—"What survives / is the will to survive"—despite the vicissitudes of life, of pain, of ache of memory—"What continues is the dust. / . . . a moth trapped in the light / outside a window" (66). And yet, at the end, when it has all been said, McCarthy points to the ultimate inaccessibility of purgation: "We come back to ourselves / too often / the ghosts in their grim circle" (69). Catharsis remains out of reach, but the striving for catharsis also remains—as duty, as healing, as life. Again, the endless search for regeneration and the continual frustration. But always the search.

Coda: Poetry, Politics, and (Un)Regeneration

An important consideration here is the widespread American (artistic) perception of some sort of DMZ between poetic and political language. In an issue devoted to this "conflict," *Poetry East* defined the opposed camps.

> For the sake of discussion, let us divide poetry into two general types, personal and political. . . . When the personal poem fails to transcend its individual egoistic dream of reality by connecting itself to the outer world, it becomes solipsistic. When the political poem fails to transcend the public arena of issues and dogma by connecting itself to the inner world of the poet, it becomes rhetorical. (7)

Carolyn Forché's essay "El Salvador: An Aide Memoir" clearly outlines the battle lines: "Stress of purity generates a feeble estheticism that fails, in its beauty, to communicate. On the other hand, propagandist hack-work has no independent life as poetry" (6). But Forché and the editors of *Poetry East* are giving us only the north and south poles of this world of discourse; of what lies in between, Forché's own book is a clear example. Richard Peabody writes, "I

don't find Carolyn Forché's *The Country Between Us* worth very much poetically. As a political document it's compelling. [But] I want the power of the
words. Not the power of the sermon" ("Red Pen" 53). Dev Hathaway, on the
other hand, finds it "a book I admire for beautiful shaping in a number of
political poems. . . . Even a seemingly reported prose poem, "The Colonel," is
stunning . . . a poem cut like a diamond, not just recounted as a horror" ("Red
Pen" 50). Their disagreement is not merely a question of taste, but an index
to the cultural split between the political (seen as hackwork) and the apolitical
(seen as art).

In an essay titled "Remarks on Political Poetry," James Scully has condemned "this tendency to separate aesthetic quality and political poetry into
mutually exclusive categories . . . Assertions that politics and poetry don't mix
are not disinterested statements but political interventions in their own right"
(*Line Break* 3). As far as Scully is concerned, there is no way that poetry can
avoid being political "insofar as it bears a set of assumptions about the organization and priorities of life. . . . Even its silences—sometimes especially the
silences—have political content" (4). The solution of the problem lies within
the self, the poet's own, both projected and actual, by reconciling a tug-of-war
between solipsistic and polemic, between private and public arenas. Forché
roots commitment in the act of writing—"What matters is not whether a poem
is political, but the quality of its engagement"—as well as in the person—"We
are responsible for the quality of our vision, we have a say in the shaping of our
sensibility. In the many thousand daily choices we make, we create ourselves
and the voice with which we speak and work" (6).

The example of Vietnam-veteran poetry clearly demonstrates Scully's and
Forché's assertions. It is possible both to write out of political convictions, as
an essential base for the poem itself, and to write good poetry. This was the
guiding premise behind the seminal anthology of poetry by Vietnam veterans,
Winning Hearts and Minds: War Poems by Vietnam Veterans. Editors Larry
Rottmann, Jan Barry, and Basil T. Paquet bucked the literary establishment
with this book; unable to find a commercial publisher, they formed their own
independent publishing house, 1st Casualty Press. It was only after "the Press
was able to sell [the] first edition of 10,000 copies and run into a second edition
of the same number within six months" (Slolock 108) that commercial publishers took interest, and eventually McGraw-Hill took up the anthology. All
in all, 45,000 copies were printed, and the book sold very well. As Slolock
points out, 1st Casualty Press "had been able to prove that creative literature
could have a wide appeal, and that a small press with largely political rather
than literary or commercial connections could succeed" (108).

The "Note to the Reader" at the end of *Winning Hearts and Minds* advises the reader to *use* these poems "for practical things, like fund raising, inviting contributors to this volume on talk shows, inviting one or more of these poets to address your group, your next rally, meeting or other event. . . . Use copies of this poetry to decorate your home." The editors suggest that the consumers of this poetry should "Read it aloud / Recopy it / Dramatize it / Give it as a gift / And sing it!" (*Winning* 116). This advice is, in its own way, revolutionary. The point is that this poetry is not meant to be merely ornamental but also practical—that is, utilitarian. With complete unabashedness, Rottmann, Barry, and Paquet have established an "open door policy," issued an invitation to the general population to "use" (and it would be hoped, enjoy) poetry—a remarkable achievement.

Undeniably, this open invitation is in itself a political, propagandist act. However, what readers are invited into, the editors propose in their introduction, is a collection of poems "arranged as a series of shifting scenes which describe, in rough chronological order, a tour of combat duty in S.E. Asia. The poems, which span a period of the last ten years, also chronicle the GI's growing emotional and moral involvement with the people and the land" (v). In other words, the poetry is not ostensibly presented as polemic or didactic literature but as an entry into the personal feelings and motivations of the American soldier in Indochina. What is important here is the *personal* focus, the kind of orientation called for by Forché and Scully. It is out of this emphasis on the personal that the public and political must arise.

Spender reminds us that "Yeats complained about certain English poets during the First World War (he meant Wilfred Owen and Siegfried Sassoon) that they wrote as officers identifying their own feelings with the suffering of their men. He condemned their work as 'passive suffering' " (3). Rottmann, Barry, and Paquet propose, even further, that

> Previous war poets have traditionally placed the blame directly on others. What distinguishes the voices in this volume is their progression toward an active identification of themselves as agents of pain and war—as "agent-victims" of their own atrocities. . . . [with] the conviction that there is no return to innocence. (v)

Stan Platke's poem "And Then There Were None" illustrates this. The line "A world safe for democracy" is imaged as an empty promise pointing forward to a deformed second coming, a prophecy rooted in the Bible—". . . when he came / Everyone was dead." Armageddon, annihilation: the American mis-

sion of world security transmuted into the end of the world. Platke proposes
that each person needs to take responsibility for contributing to that potential
eventuality: an admission of personal collusion.

> Yea as I walk through the valley of death
> I shall fear no evil
> For the valleys are gone
> And only death awaits
>
> And I am the evil   (*Winning* 101)

The poem's ending is a revision of a motto inscribed on flak jackets across Vietnam—"*Yea, though I walk through the Valley of the Shadow of Death I shall
fear no Evil, because I'm the meanest motherfucker in the Valley*" (Herr 87)—
itself a revision of what is probably the best-known Judeo-Christian psalm.
Platke's version recharges, breathes new life, into this cliché because, in his
revision, the self-acceptance is no longer macho posturing but a realization of
the evil within the self, the *heart of darkness* theme that such critics as Tobey
Herzog have uncovered in literary and artistic representations of the Vietnam
war: the heart of the matter awakened by violence.[11] "These veterans have shattered the American myth of regenerative innocence," Rottmann, Barry, and
Paquet claim (v). The commission of violence, in itself, does not engender any
sort of regeneration; it only engenders guilt. It is only in the admission of that
guilt, that collusion in evil, that the disaster Platke augurs may be avoided.

PART TWO. THE WORLD

I went from a free-fire zone to the twilight zone.
MARK BAKER,
from an unidentified veteran, *Nam,* p. 262.

Thinking about Vietnam once in a while, in a crazy kind of way, I
wish that just for an hour I could be there. And then be transported
back. Maybe just to be there so I'd wish I was back here again.

MARK BAKER, from an unnamed veteran, *Nam,* p. 319.

Day

I'm nose deep
sandbags and bodies
above me
& below
a rat scurries thru the litter
of c-rats & pockets of the dead
another veecee throws a satchel charge
at my bunker
missing
a sandbag blown into my face
as my wife knocks at the bathroom door
"Are you done in there?"
so I finish
dress
work the day out
& wait for
the night

BILL SHIELDS,
Nam: Selected Poems, p. 12.

FIVE. WHEN ADAM
COMES MARCHING HOME—
WHAT ABOUT EVE?

The cinema character Rambo has swiftly grown into archetypal proportions, a post-Vietnam warrior who persists in winning the Vietnam war *this time,* again and again: first, on the homefront; then in the second movie, back to Vietnam to rescue MIA/POWs; and in the third installment in Afghanistan, a missionary extension of the Vietnam-war mentality outward into the world. Rambo is only one of the newer fictional characters in a long hagiography of mythic figures (both imaginary and biographical) glorifying war; the list includes John Paul Jones, the defenders of the Alamo, Audie Murphy, a multitude of John Wayne characterizations, and so on.

These mythic figures are all versions of R. W. B. Lewis's myth/image of the American Adam: "the authentic American as a figure of heroic innocence and vast potentialities, poised at the start of a new history" (1). Lewis focuses this definition by referring to "a radically new personality" represented as:

> an individual emancipated from history, happily bereft of ancestry, un-
> touched and undefiled by the usual inheritances of family and race; an
> individual standing alone, self-reliant and self-propelling, ready to con-
> front whatever awaited him with the aid of his own unique and inherent
> resources. (5)

The important thing to notice here is the limiting focus on *masculine* self-reliance. Feminist critics have attempted to diversify the Adamic myth (and by extension, the larger myth of America as a New World Eden) by envisioning the possibility of an American Eve. Judith Fryer's *The Faces of Eve,* for example, attempts to feminize the masculinist compartmentalization of female characters into dark and light; "the faces of Eve" Fryer writes, "emerge as the images of woman in the nineteenth century: the Temptress, the American Princess, the Great Mother, the New Woman" (24)—an attempt to diversify female representation archetypally. In *The Land Before Her,* Annette Kolodny essays "to chart women's private responses to the successive American frontiers and to trace a tradition of women's public statements about the west" (xi) by uncovering the exclusion of women from Adamic potential. "In the idealized wilderness garden of what R. W. B. Lewis calls 'the noble but illusory myth of the American as Adam,' an Eve could only be redundant" (5).

Although Lewis's mythic image pertains to the nineteenth century, there can be no doubt that there is a twentieth-century cultural assumption that the Adamic ideal is attainable as well as real, and the classic example is the rise of the Rambo figure, a collective wish by some large portion of America that it is possible to be "emancipated from history," essentially to *start over.* And starting over is a universal fantasy made particularly American by the fact of expansive landscape—that there is always another *place* where no one knows you and you can begin again. Clearly, in Vietnam, there were American troops who believed in the possibility of starting over—"If they kept their date with the Freedom Bird they could *forget everything that they ever saw or did in the Nam*" (Anderson 180, emphasis mine). Both male and female veterans placed their faith in such forgetting—in other words, a recapturing of the state of being "untouched and undefiled," as Lewis had described the Adamic ideal (5).

The real situation of returning Vietnam veterans, however, was that they were unable to forget. Saddled with their histories, they were nevertheless thrust into the role of "an individual standing alone" not because of any Adamic pretensions of their own, but because they were ostracized by American society. One grunt recalled:

> I got back to the World, but this wasn't the World that I had left. . . . I did not fit into the real world anymore. For that twelve months in the Nam, I used to sit down and imagine what I would do in the World when I got back. I'll be with this woman, I'm going to do this and that. I came back to the World and I see people rioting about Nam. People hated GIs for being in the Nam. They was blaming us. I flipped out. I couldn't believe it. (Baker 288)

This feeling grew in the returning veterans almost as soon as they disembarked on American soil. "There was a revealing false rumor," writes Baritz, "that antiwar critics were shooting vets as they climbed out of their planes. It is a mass delusion, of course, but thousands of vets claim that they were spat upon when they first arrived home" (319). Therefore, if the veterans felt themselves "individual[s] standing alone," they did not feel "self-reliant and self-propelling" but only naked and exposed in this strange new place, the World.

The Vietnam veteran faces two arenas of problems, external and internal. The external plane involves actual rejection, whether "spit upon" or merely ignored; whereas the internal involves questions of adjustment and forgetting, psychological trauma as well as guilt. In an untitled poem, Bert Allen illustrates through his imagery the externals of returning home. The "war hero" unmet, unnoticed at the airport, is represented as "an island of army green / surrounded by whirling waves / civilian colors"; the only way he can be "carried through city streets" is by hailing a cab, a ride which makes him painfully aware that there is no hero's parade, but only "the march of pedestrians /. . . when the light turned green" (*Demilitarized* 38). Allen's focus on the color "green," especially since the "war hero" has left a country of such vivid greens, dramatizes the diminution of the Vietnam veteran, suddenly "surrounded by whirling waves" of nongreen. W. D. Ehrhart's poem "Coming Home" relates a similar experience and the thoughts which attend it. At the airport in San Francisco the speaker is relieved that there are

> no more corpsmen stuffing ruptured chests
> with cotton balls and not enough heat tabs
> to eat a decent meal . . .

But when he asks a young woman "to sit / and have a coke," he is dismayed that her reaction is far from what he expected. "She thought I was crazy; / I thought she was going to call a cop." The full strangeness of his situation is brought home by the formulaic greeting he receives on boarding his plane to Philadelphia—" 'Thank you for flying TWA; / we hope you will enjoy your flight' "— his apparent inability to heal the rift between two worlds, that of "corpsmen stuffing ruptured chests with cotton balls" and the other where one could hear " 'Thank you for flying TWA.' " As the poem continues, the speaker's sarcasm and frustration grow, despite the outward surface of the poem's quiet tone:

> No brass bands;
> no flags,
> no girls,
> no cameramen
>
> Only a small boy who asked me
> what the ribbons on my jacket meant.   (*Tired* 16–17)

Allen's "march of pedestrians" and Ehrhart's negative litany—"No brass bands; / no flags, / no girls, / no cameramen"—dramatize the profound disappointment many veterans felt in an America that no longer celebrated its heroes in open limousines forging through downtown oceans of ticker tape. The final note of the poem, the possibility of more soldiers in the future to undergo such loss—imaged by the small boy's interest in the speaker's ribbons—stresses the speaker's hopelessness.

Even more devastating, of course, are the internal problems: the rejection not by others but by oneself, the trauma of guilt. Doug Rawlings's poem "Medic" dramatizes these internal issues.

> medic medic
> if you can
> come help me
> wash this blood
> from my hands
>
> pour cologne
> on this stink
> give this rotting breath
> some
> eternal listerine
>
> stop his screams
> from tearing through
> my dreams my dreams
>
> come help me
> file it all away
> pilate it all away
> on an airplane
> going home   (*Demilitarized* 3)

Rawlings strains overmuch here to be literary—allusions to Pilate and to Lady Macbeth, the assonantal and consonantal echoes of "file it" and "pilate," the pun on "pilot"—yet under the melodrama lurks the real pain of the speaker, suffering rooted in experience and in nightly dreams. What makes this speaker's plight especially poignant is his attempt to "file it . . . away" all during the flight to the World, calling attention to the speed with which veterans were sent home, often within thirty-six hours of leaving the war zone. "To civilians sitting at a desk in Washington, this idea seemed both efficient and altruistic," claim Joel Brende and Erwin Parson. "But for many of the young men, transformed by a year in Vietnam, it proved disastrous. . . . thrust too quickly into an environment that was frequently insensitive and even hostile" (72–73).

Even when the reception at home was warm and positive, the veteran's internal contradictions would still intrude. The opening lines of Peter P. Mahoney's poem "The Airport"—"Crumpled green uniform / . . . Scuffed shoes, stubbled face"—already hint at the speaker's internal chaos. His self-image, however, is somewhat different: "I emerge from the bird's womb / The returning warrior." The reference to the "bird's womb" is a thinly veiled wish for rebirth, for the American Adam's characteristic "emancipation"—especially here, since the "bird" is an airplane, a technological artifact reminiscent of technowar machinery in Vietnam. The phrase "returning warrior" is also a veiled wish; these words are loaded, carrying age-old expectations of welcome and lionization—the son as a victorious figure. What follows is an understandable bit of melodrama, both family and veteran wishing for myths—"Soldier-son, hero-brother / I stand tall in their eyes"—a momentary attempt to recapture old, outworn ideals. The family illusion is that because their son has not been wounded ("unscraped / By war's steel"), he is therefore unscathed, but the speaker understands that "All wounds do not pierce the skin" and struggles to control himself at his family's unwanted, overwhelming sympathy. The phrase "By war's steel" is a poeticism which indicates yet once more the speaker's need for some sort of traditional redemption. The dialectic of this poem is between the language of an earlier culture, in which the possibility for regeneration was acknowledged, and the language of Vietnam readjustment, which is honestly set forth by the closing lines: "My pain will be theirs / soon enough" (*Demilitarized* 13). The family is also unredeemed by the son's experience; in fact, as an element of danger and conflict is implied by these lines, the family will share, perhaps physically if not merely psychologically, in the son's trauma and guilt.

The internal pressures often surface in the form of dreams and nightmares. For example, Montagnard Man—the U.S. Army paratrooper who, as we saw in the previous chapter, styled himself a Montagnard scout—recalls in dreams the soldier he found dying, staked out.

I still have the nightmare twelve years later. And I will have the nightmare twelve years from now. . . . I think that I made it back here and am able to sit here and talk because he died for me. And I'm living for him.

I still have the nightmare. I still cry.

I see me in the nightmare. I see me staked out. I see me in the circumstances where I have to be man enough to ask someone to end my suffering as he did.

I can't see the face of the person pointing the gun.

> I ask him to pull the trigger. I ask him over and over.
> He won't pull the trigger.
> I wake up.
> Every time. (Terry 265)

Such dreams are only part of what has come to be called posttraumatic stress disorder syndrome (PTSD). The first defining characteristic is "exposure to recognizable stressor or trauma"; while this generally refers to "live combat," it is also possible that "a variety of stressors" may be involved, including "extreme weather conditions; loneliness; culture shock." The second characteristic of PTSD is the "reexperiencing of trauma through flashbacks, nightmares, or intrusive memories"; this category of symptoms is probably what many people associate with veterans, especially because of the ways they have been portrayed in the media. Third, PTSD is shown by "emotional numbing to or withdrawal from the external environment": inability to become excited about things, problems with personal relationships, feelings of life not being worth the trouble. Finally, there are "PTSD-related symptoms, including hyperalertness, sleep disturbance, survival guilt, memory impairment, and avoidance of situations that may elicit traumatic recollections" (Card 104).

These adverse personal problems are reflected as well in poetry by Vietnam veterans. The poem "Rice Will Grow Again" by Frank A. Cross, Jr., illustrates the links between events that occurred in Vietnam and nightmares. The opening scene depicts Mitch, a grunt on patrol with his platoon, and a farmer wading through his rice paddy:

> Mitch was steppin light
> When he saw the farmer . . .
>
> .   .   .   .
>   Rice shoots in one hand,
>   The other darting
>   Under the water
>   And into the muck
>   To plant new life.

The contrast between the farmer and Mitch is telegraphed by the placement of lines on the page; as the poem begins, Mitch's lines begin at the left edge, and those pertaining to the farmer are indented. The contrast dramatized by the structure of the poem has to do with life and death, with generation and destruction. Mitch "Rip[s] the farmer up the middle / With a burst of sixteen" because the farmer's privilege and capability is "to plant new life." The ultimate contrast is between America and Vietnam: who engenders? who destroys? As the poem continues, the dying farmer, "rice shoots / Still clutched in one hand," speaks: "Damn you / The rice will / Grow again!" Even at his death, the farmer's curse revolves around new life, emphasizing the eventual victory of life over death (and figuratively of Vietnam over America). At the close, the poem's setting shifts to the United States:

> Sometimes,
> On dark nights
> In Kansas,
> The farmer comes to
> > Mitch's bed;
> And plants rice shoots
> > all around.   (*Demilitarized* 19–20)

This poem is not only about the farmer's "haunting" of Mitch, though on one level it is, as the alternation of indentation shows—the farmer's lines now on the left, Mitch's on the right. The closing of the poem is not only a circling about of the farmer's prophecy, that is, that the loss of the war also haunts Mitch at night. More important, the farmer's planting of "rice shoots / all around" is a sign of "new life," implying that Mitch may also have the chance and the capability of engendering and growing. That Mitch's dream is not violent implies that acceptance of his guilt can occur, and that his recovery, at least, is possible.

In "The Weight of the Sheets," Jon Forrest Glade describes the experience of a vet who feels he has exorcised his Vietnam-war nightmares, insisting "I'm all over that now." The incident that sets up the poem's context begins with the speaker considering the purchase of a machete in a military surplus store:

> but its hilt fit my hand
> just a little too well,
> and old memories
> broke through barriers
> that were disappointingly thin.

What immediately follows is a flashback to Vietnam, and the speaker declines the purchase, repressing his memories deeper. The master touch here is that Glade does not describe the content of the speaker's nightmares, but rather hints at his nightmare scenes from an external viewpoint: "my wife says / I curse and cry / and talk in my sleep." The poem then closes with the veteran's admission of his difficult readjustment.

> And I know for a fact,
> that sometimes my scars
> cannot bear
> the weight of the sheets.   (48)

Unlike Glade, R. Joseph Ellis in "Memory Bomb" deals not so much with nightmare as with waking memories intruding on everyday life. The poem opens with vivid memories of the surreal landscape of Vietnam.

> The incredible greens, almost sinister
> in their growing. The flowers, red or yellow,
> silk-like, sick-sweet and potent. And with
> their shells of fine art, the insects
> dancing insanely in the gross heat.

These memories are bombs because they explode into the speaker's day, engendering there a complete takeover, the speaker's waking life usurped first by the physical, tangible flavors and sensations of Vietnam. It is more difficult to recall people: "faces edged with fear," "foolish, brave talk," "lies," and "panic spreading like fog"; instead, it is easy to remember "Death [as] / The lecher on the nude beach." As John Felstiner points out, Ellis tries "for figures of speech to verify what haunts him" until "Finally Ellis moves from both the physical and the personal memories into three metaphors for the way memories persist in him":

> A sleeping seed waiting to grow.
> A piece of metal itching to travel.
> A book of pictures dying to be seen.

Felstiner notes that the "satisfying rhythmic progression" of these lines could serve as an adequate closing. "But something disruptive is still at work, and 'Memory Bomb' goes on for seven more lines, poetically haphazard, of agonized premonition" ("Bearing" 32–33). In the poem, the speaker fears that "The bomb of memory will explode / into a red, hot thing" (*Demilitarized* 14) and that this explosion, irresistible, will consume him. Clearly, in this poem and the previous two ("Rice Will Grow Again" and "The Weight of the Sheets"), the vivid connections between the Vietnam of memory and the dream/nightmare/vision of the present cannot be severed.

Drugs, which became an inescapable part of military life in Vietnam, especially near the end of American involvement, inevitably surfaced in the World. Frances FitzGerald has in fact suggested that these drug problems may be "the revenge of the Indochinese":

> the heroin, unlike anything else the Vietnamese sold the American soldiers, was of excellent quality—white as ivory and of such purity that it would cost a small fortune to support a habit of it on the illicit market of the United States. . . .
>
> The United States might leave Vietnam, but the Vietnam War would now never leave the United States. The soldiers would bring it back with them like an addiction. (423–24)

Don Receveur's poem, "Doper's Dream," set in Vietnam, paints a vivid portrait of gothic horror.

> The mind
> becomes an
> oil-slicked pool
> of night time
> liquid
> under the oil
> dark shapes
> struggle and mate,
> small still-born
> terrors
> rise toward the surface.   (*Winning* 98)

The unconscious, imaged here as an "oil-slicked pool," comes very close to the surface of the conscious mind, threatening to explode its "small still-born / terrors." The poem may be melodramatic and perhaps clichéd, but it is effective in evoking the hopelessness of the "doper," the sheer terror of believing in no other reality.

Rawlings's poem "Mainline Quatrains" evokes this situation transferred to the World.

the shadow of a man glides down the road
dressed in dust and wrapped in grays
bent earthward beneath an invisible load
he moves silently through his endless days

alone in the night he sits in his rented room
searching his arm for a heavenly vein
placing his soul on a silver spoon
he finds his religion in the candle's flame

his prayers throb to the beat of his blood
his wounds scream for their pinch of salt
his body sways and flows with the flood
he plunges into the deepening vault   (*Demilitarized* 67)

The horror of Rawlings's poem is not in the internal terror of drug addiction but its external waste. He portrays a life without purpose, except for the purpose envisioned in the second quatrain: the fix. The addict here only takes charge of his actions in the second stanza; in the other two stanzas, he is swayed and buffeted, driven by an "invisible load," by his "wounds scream[ing]," by his "body . . . flow[ing] with the flood." The final action of "plung[ing] into the deepening vault" may not be a voluntary choice, after all, but merely a fall. Unfortunately, Rawlings's choice of rhymed quatrains works against the poem, because he is forced into certain word choices by the rhyme. "Invisible load" is prompted by "road" when a more apt (and more tangible) metaphor is called for; "flood" and "vault" are likewise clichéd and imprecise but actuated by "blood" and "salt." In the middle stanza, however, the slant rhymes *room / spoon* and *vein / flame* are marvelously executed, and that stanza alone is worth the price of admission, driving home the point of the poem with a vengeance through the resonant diction of "heavenly," "soul," and "religion."

The issue of drug addiction, both in Vietnam and back in America, is a complicated one. The "most salient point," according to Myra MacPherson, is that *"Vietnam was the direct cause of their heroin use* . . . For many, heroin was self-medication in a violently oppressive setting, in a war that had lost all meaning." American armed-forces policies against smoking marijuana may have helped move soldiers toward heroin, which was not "as loud" in GI slang—that is, it was less detectable because it could not be smelled. Also, MacPherson continues, "some among our so-called friends—highly placed Laotians, Thais, and South Vietnamese—were making a killing in drug trafficking." American heroin users were widespread among all racial groups—"some 68 percent who used heroin in Vietnam were white"—so that heroin use became a " 'social activity' " (573–74). Although many of these users did not ultimately become addicted to heroin, the stereotype of the Vietnam veteran as "drug-crazed" had been established and so, whether or not they were drug addicts, many veterans were plagued by this junkie image when seeking jobs, making friends, or just surviving. One veteran recalled applying for a job which required a physical.

> The doctor and I were talking and when he found out I was a veteran he asked me if I went to Vietnam. After that he started looking me over like something has got to be wrong. When he was taking my blood pressure, he took my arm and lifted it up and started looking it over. . . . I knew what he was doing, but I tried to ignore it. Then he grabbed the other arm and. . . . I said, "Get your hands off of me, man. The physical was going all right up till now."
>
> He was looking for tracks and it pissed me off. . . . I told them what they could do with that job. (Baker 286–87)

Vietnam veterans often faced insensitive civilians like this physician. Charles Anderson suggests that the "veteran took the mountain of ennui he found in America as evidence that the hometowners didn't really care what he had gone through in the previous year, didn't care about the buddies he lost or those still there when he came home. Such extreme apathy was inexcusable" (160). As Anderson continues to point out, these people were in fact equally apathetic about Vietnam before the veteran went there; the change has occurred within the veteran's psyche, but that in itself, even if acknowledged, is no solace. Perhaps even more infuriating were the interminable questions that the Vietnam veteran was forced to answer—or at least listen to. "Why couldn't they just say, 'I don't give a damn about what you did, about your friends who got zapped,' " suggests Anderson, "instead of faking their concern and asking their questions while their real concerns were elsewhere" (161–62). W. D. Ehrhart's poem "Imagine" recalls such questions:

> Had he been in battle?
> Had he ever been afraid?

As the speaker tries to answer these ever-present (and identical) questions, he understands the only things that the questioners can envision:

>   Newsreels and photographs, books
>   And Wilfred Owen tumbled
>   Through their minds. Pulses quickened.
>
>   .   .   .   .
>
>   When he finished speaking,
>   Someone asked him
>   Had he ever killed?   (*Tired* 19)

The poem dramatizes the lack of communication between the questioners and the veteran; the civilians are never able to visualize Vietnam in its actuality, but only in received notions of the world wars. Ehrhart leaves the worst question for last, not only because the questions were inevitably asked in this order (as he records in his memoir *Marking Time*), but because it is the most disturbing; it sets the veteran up as something different from the ordinary person, different from the questioners. As Ehrhart recalls his college days after the war, "I was Swarthmore's real live Vietnam veteran. I was a specimen. A curiosity. I was a freak in a carnival sideshow" (*Marking Time* 11).

One of the greatest problems encountered by veterans returning from Vietnam is difficulty in loving, in being intimate. One grunt revealed an extreme feeling of this sort in therapy. "If I'm fucking, and a girl says I love you, then I want to kill her . . . [because] if you get close . . . you get hurt" (Lifton 271). Joel Brende and Erwin Parson suggest that such difficulties begin "in Vietnam where it was necessary to keep one's feelings under control at all times. Losing control over feelings could mean instant annihilation for the soldier and his unit" (104). Inevitably, the very fact of being in a war zone has tremendous effects on soldiers' psyches and emotional systems. Feelings of guilt and loss also affect the veteran's self-esteem, further hampering his ability to love. A "basic inability to mourn and grieve is also a source of deep emotional problems," Brende and Parson write. "Veterans who lost close buddies now find it difficult to get close to others" (105). These feelings occur with lovers or spouses as well as with children. Brende and Parson record the case of a veteran, Jim, who had experienced PTSD symptoms until he got married, at which time they diminished. However, Jim began to have problems again when his wife became pregnant. "He slept with two knives and a pistol under his pillow, and unintentionally attacked his wife during nightmares." It turns out that Jim had been forced to kill a Vietnamese child who was carrying concealed explosives. "Jim had not known for certain that the approaching child was booby-trapped. What he remembers of the incident, after it was discovered that the child had in fact been booby-trapped, was a virtual 'carnage' in which several civilians were killed" (111). Jim was suffering from a double conflict: first, he had an unshakable fear that "children cannot be trusted"; second, he felt simultaneously that "children are innocent and must be protected from 'people like myself, people who could kill children' " (112). Clearly, these dysfunctions can be complicated and difficult to diagnose, much less counsel and heal.

Perry Oldham's "The Happy Warrior Returns Home" is a frightening example of such intimacy problems as imaged in poetry.

> He has the moon
> He's wearing heavy shoes
> He's got the blues.
>
> He comes in drunk as a pig.
> And she lying on the bed
> Her belly big
> Her face shining with grease.
>
> There they sit. Like a bomb waiting to go off.
> They are sitting on the bed.
> He is leaning forward, elbows on knees.
> She holds herself near him
> But there is a little space between them.
> They remain so for a long time, side by side
> Without talking.   (*Demilitarized* 34)

There is a tremendous sense of anticipation here, almost as if disaster is imminent, unchangeable. This sense of imminence is accomplished partly by Oldham's abandonment in the last stanza of the rhyme scheme set up in the first seven lines. Oldham expresses this doomsday feeling clearly with the line "But there is a little space between them"; what volumes are said in that "little space"! John Felstiner has pointed out the function of understatement in Oldham's work. "The century's wars have exhausted adequate poetic response, so that only a drastic understatement leaves the subject intact. And sometimes an entire poem omits what it might have said" ("Bearing" 35). This poem is an eloquent example.

Such problems with intimacy also affect the veterans' children. On this subject, poetry by Vietnam veterans has dealt with their children in America as well as with (their) children in Vietnam. Doug Rawlings has written an example of each, printed on facing pages in *Demilitarized Zones*. The poem "Jen" celebrates nature and Rawlings's feelings of being again at one with its cycles.

> the birch splits
> its own bark
> the snake its skin
> the child leaps
> into the woman
> she always has been
>
> nothing is new and
> nothing is changing
> the birch is the bark
> the snake the skin
> the child the woman
>
> the seed, flowering,
> dies back into the earth
> the child, growing,
> turns forward
> toward her new birth.   (*Demilitarized* 32)

We are given a miniature chain of being here—plant, animal, human—but even more interesting, this chain is reminiscent of the Genesis creation myth: tree, snake, Eve. Instead of a Fall, however, what Rawlings posits is a circle, a new faith in life and (we read between the lines) love. Rawlings's poem "A Soldier's Lament," however, is diametrically opposed:

> They came every day
> to sit
> beneath the barbed wire
> They came to sell us
> what they would:
> a comb
> a medal
> a ring
> a sister
> if they could

At the end of the first stanza, we readily assume that these sellers are typical Vietnamese, and that the list of objects being sold indicates to what depths of morality they have sunk.

> They came to torture us
> these children of the dust
> to torture us
> with their eyes
> with their lies
> with the hatred in their eyes
> the ice in their smiles
> the wretchedness of their lives

The first clue the reader is given that we are to take special notice is the phrase "children of the dust"—the name given by the Vietnamese to the abandoned children of American servicemen. So the "torture [done] with their eyes" has to do with those eyes not being Asian, but rather a mixture of "slant" and "round," to use the argot of that war. The "hatred in their eyes" and "the wretchedness of their lives" are a double insult and revenge aimed at the fathers who have abandoned them—the Vietnamese treat these Amerasian children with great contempt, calling them *bụi đời,* the "dust of life."

> They came and now
> they will not go
> They came and we
> cannot live as before
> They came and now
> our souls
> blister and burn
> above the fire
> of children's curses   (*Demilitarized* 33)

The anaphoric echoes of the phrase "They came," repeated three times, chimes the guilt of the absent fathers, visited here on the American soldiers who are the speakers of this poem, because whether or not they are the biological fathers, they share in the blame (as perhaps do American noncombatants) because of the American presence in Vietnam.

Horace Coleman, in his poem on the Amerasian children of Vietnam, "A

Black Soldier Remembers," sets the scene with careful craft. The "Saigon daughter" is glimpsed in the "dusty square," implying at once the Vietnamese phrase for Amerasian children. That the girl is near "the Brink's BOQ/PX" and the "ugly statue of / the crouching marines" immediately identifies her both with the American presence (the BOQ/PX) and their effect on the Vietnamese (the statue); the "crouching marines" are a memorial to South Vietnamese combatants, but their demeanor and their equipment indicate American influence. In the closing stanza, we see the speaker and his "Saigon daughter" through the eyes of nearby "amputee beggars" who sneer, we might guess, because the man and girl are the "same color and [have] the same eyes"; the tragedy is that they can offer each other nothing. In a way, he has already given her *too much.* "I have nothing she needs but / the sad smile she already has" (*Mercy* 52). Their relationship (whether they are *truly* father and daughter or only figuratively so) is a synecdoche for the relationship between America and South Vietnam—the first *literally* created the second and then abandoned it.

Stan Platke's poem about Amerasian children, "Fathers Day, 1975," tells us by its date that these children have been twice betrayed, first by the American retreat and then by the fall of South Vietnam. The poem begins in the characteristic way American troops were spoken to by many Vietnamese: "Say GI / Did you get your Father's Day card today." These children "Born of desperation / Born of lust / Or born of both / But born of you" have the "blue blood / Of America / Running through their veins." The conventional wish of such a greeting card might say "I wish I knew you," but the one the speaker receives (whether figuratively or not) reads:

> "You number fucking ten, prick
> I hope your penis rots off
> I hope your testicles dry up"

The poem then follows this curse with a sarcastic "Happy Father's Day" (*Demilitarized* 153). The poem is an attempt to awaken America, to remind the country that there are consequences which follow actions, and that the Amerasian children in Vietnam are consequences which have not been taken care of. Interestingly, the curse of the children is couched in terms of castrating these fathers, that is, removing from them the ability to engender; as a comment on the nation, this is tantamount to removing U.S. ability to wield force in the world.

One focus of Vietnam-veterans' issues in the World has been the Vietnam Veterans Memorial dedicated in 1982. Public controversy arose over its symbolism. While veteran Jan Scruggs was organizing fund-raising, the "antiwar movement . . . seemed poised to launch an intellectual and political assault" on the Memorial movement. Veterans themselves were divided. Newspapers "found it curious that the vets wanted to link the words 'honor' and 'Vietnam.' Most quoted bitter, angry veterans who considered the [honor] to have been 'too little, too late' " (Scruggs 29, 39). When the Memorial design had been chosen, "a Vietnam vet" appeared before the federal Commission of Fine Arts and "called Maya Lin's design a 'black gash of shame' " ("Vietnam Veterans Memorial" 567). Although many veterans have now accepted the Memorial as an appropriate and moving commemoration, Ehrhart still has misgivings in his poem "The Invasion of Grenada":

> I didn't want a monument,
> not even one as sober as that
> vast black wall of broken lives.
> I didn't want a postage stamp.
> I didn't want a road beside the Delaware
> River with a sign proclaiming:
> "Vietnam Veterans Memorial Highway."
>
> What I wanted was a simple recognition
> of the limits of our power as a nation
> to inflict our will on others.
> What I wanted was an understanding
> that the world is neither black-and-white
> nor ours.
>
> What I wanted
> was an end to monuments.[1]   (*Tired* 71)

Ehrhart's forte throughout the entire body of his poetic work is his voice, the calm voice of a compassionate, politically devoted, caring person. These are the qualities that carry through in this poem, with its quiet and subtle force. He uses anaphora to set up the poem's bipolar structure: the things "I didn't want" and "What I wanted." The first half of the poem is rooted in concrete tangibles: "the wall," "a postage stamp," and "a road." The line break after "Delaware" is interesting because it mythically calls up George Washington, and we recall that the Washington Monument is within sight of the Vietnam Veterans Memorial. We wonder what George Washington would have thought of all this: the Vietnam war, the veterans, the hawk/dove schism of the country, the Wall. In the second half of the poem, we hear Ehrhart the speechmaker rather than the poet, as he calls for a "simple recognition / of the limits of our power"; the poem is nevertheless a graceful speech. The simple eloquence of the last couplet—its easy language and rhythm—lends great power to Ehrhart's message.

Gerald McCarthy also voices his criticism of the Vietnam Veterans Memorial in "The Hooded Legion"; this poem's epigraph from poet laureate Joseph Brodsky, "let us put up a monument to the lie," indicates McCarthy's complaint:

> There are no words here
> to witness why we fought,
> who sent us or what he hoped to gain.
>
> There is only the rain
> as it streaks the black stone,
> these memories of rain
> that come back to us—
> a hooded legion reflected in a wall.
>
> Tonight we wander weaponless and cold
> along this shore of the Potomac
> like other soldiers who camped here
> looking out over smoldering fires into the night.
>
> What did we dream of
> the summer before we went away?
> What leaf did not go silver
> in the last light?
> What hand did not turn us aside?   (*Shoetown* 27)

When water wets the black granite of the Memorial the names reportedly seem to disappear. Perhaps it was this phenomenon which inspired McCarthy's lament that the Wall is a sad alternative to soldiers having gone to Vietnam in the first place. And yet the poem is ambivalent; even Washington's soldiers may have felt their lot unjust as well when they "look[ed] out over smoldering fires into the night." McCarthy's poem is not only a call for a more fitting reminder than this Memorial of the sociopolitical underpinnings of the war, but a bittersweet realization that each individual's involvement in the Vietnam war is finally a product of circumstance and coincidence—an entropic catastrophe which could have been turned aside by a gesture, a look, a word, a "leaf [going] silver / in the last light."

The Wall eventually took on mythic significance in its eerie ethereality, in its reflective surface seeming to become a Carrollesque temporal/spatial/ metaphysical boundary between the living and the dead, America and the Vietnam war, the World and the 'Nam. In such a context of duality and dialectic, the Wall eventually became a source of daily community as combatants and survivors, veterans and nonveterans, would meet and commingle, would leave mementos, letters, pictures. Janet Krouse Wyatt's poem "We Went, We Came" illustrates the dualistic thinking which has become a hallmark of the Vietnam war: "We went to the war; / We came back to chaos." In a litany of statements accompanying the duple movements toward and away from Vietnam, Wyatt demonstrates the loss of innocence, pairing the earlier "innocent and forgiving" with the later "embittered and intolerant." "We went alone and open; / We came back alone and isolated." Although Wyatt's logic may be too simplistic in its relentless redoubling, the close of the poem illustrates the importance of the Memorial as an alternative to the destructive trend of this duality: "We went to the Wall; / We came back away with hope" (*Visions* 151).

Bill Shields's poem "miles of bones" goes beyond such a positive (albeit sentimental) view of the Wall.

> 58,000
> the number of Vietnam
>
> veteran suicides . . .
> it equals the names
>
> on the Wall
> today: 7/09/91 8:10 p.m.

Shields's inclusion of an exact time marks the moment, giving it a genuine urgency, and calls attention to the fact that "tomorrow / we'll exceed it" (65– 66). As much as the Memorial may foster healing in some veterans, the plain fact is that Vietnam-war deaths continue, apparently unabated. As D. F. Brown has written, "nobody / comes away in one piece" (*Returning* 46).

Brown's phrase implies that everyone walks away from (the Vietnam) war in fragments, whether metaphorically, spiritually, mentally, or literally—in physical terms. Walter McDonald's poem "Veteran" casts light on such personal fragmentation.

> I get as far as the park
> this time.
> Spectators queer as animals
> circle me like a campfire.
> They hope I'll fall.

Leaves lie in the park
like tiny bombs
ready to explode. Someday
someone raking
will strike a fuse.
We'll all be killed.

My stumps itch
inside their legs,
lightweight aluminum
clump clump. One of my arms
goes out of control, shifts smoothly
like a transmission, salutes.

They think I'm
shooting a bone
at them. I'm trying
to turn back. They're closing in,
this is Da Nang, their eyes
rake me like AK-47's.   (*Burning the Fence* 32)

McDonald's persona in this poem is not only hampered by physical injuries; he
has clearly been spiritually and emotionally scarred by Vietnam and, as such,
is an appropriate representative of *all* Vietnam veterans. The poem is most poignant as well as most ironic when the veteran, who is obviously trying to heal
himself, loses control and throws an involuntary salute. The phrase "shooting
a bone" is appropriately and masterfully ambivalent here, with its sexual overtones, the combative connotations of "shooting," and the deathly allusions of
"bone." In this persona's psychological alienation, space and time collapse:
"this is Da Nang, their eyes / rake me like AK-47's." For this veteran, the
World is as dangerous as the 'Nam.

  Alan C. Lupack's "Army Experience" is one of the more interesting poems
dealing with the overall experience of the Vietnam veteran in America because
of its use of blackness as metaphor.

I was a Black man
sold into slavery

. . . . . .

Now that I've learned their dark white ways
they send me weak and wanting
into the world.

> Does the strength return,
> my Black brothers,
> before the soul despairs?   (*Peace* 86)

The identification of the entire African American experience with that of the Vietnam veteran is both startling as well as revealing. It may emphasize the "master / slave" mentality held by the high command toward the grunts (cf. James Gibson's view of the search-and-destroy operation as essentially a management/labor situation, in which labor was considered expendable). More interesting, however, is the resulting equation of veterans with blacks—not just African Americans, but all oppressed peoples. And "Black" here can refer to the cultural associations which the color black carries in Western symbology: death, mourning, evil; so "my Black brothers" can also be read as an apostrophe to those who share with the speaker this identification with death (as killers and killed) as well as evil (whether attributed by others or acknowledged by the self). Lupack's metaphor is a huge catch-all conceit with a multiplicity of facets; as such, it mirrors Richard Wright's assertion that the black is America's metaphor.

The remainder of this chapter will focus on three particular poets—Bill Shields, Steve Mason, Marilyn McMahon—and their responses to the position of the Vietnam veteran in America, as well as on the first anthology of women's poetry on the Vietnam war, Lynda Van Devanter and Joan Furey's *Visions of War, Dreams of Peace,* which unveils a communal vision of female veterans' experience during the war and its aftermath.

Bill Shields: "Post-Vietnam Stress Poetry"

Bill Shields is an angry poet—a shaman of pain. In several publications, including the *Samisdat* issue *Post Vietnam Stress Syndrome* (1988), *Drinking Gasoline in Hell* (1989), his selected works collection *Nam* (1989), *Human Shrapnel* (1992), and as a contributing editor to the newsletter of the *Vietnam Generation* journal, Shields has excruciatingly dissected posttraumatic stress disorder syndrome, which he discriminatingly focuses as "post-Vietnam stress syndrome."

The majority of Shields's poems deal with the personal aftermath of the Vietnam war, but he also has written vivid and memorable poems on being in-country in characteristically laconic, understated language. The poem "When a Man Explodes" sarcastically compares the event with a "cat with a firecracker up its ass" and "a bucket of human / thrown for ½ acre" (*Nam* 3). The title "My Easter Poem" turns out to be about a Saigon prostitute ("she'd been peddling her ass since age 11 / 2 blocks from Saigon's Soul Alley"), for whom apparently there can be no rising, no salvation—"her baby [who] watches / from a basket as momma turns tricks" is mysteriously negated by the end of the poem—"Her baby? // she has no baby" (*Nam* 4).

Shields's poems on being a Vietnam veteran in the World emphasize repeatedly and with immense force how the war continually re-arises, intersects, and explodes the vet's everyday American existence, intruding into every facet of life—"The firebase / behind the couch" ("In Country," *Nam* 22). In the poem "Wife," the speaker is unable to tell his wife that during coitus "the bones shook & my blood pumped wildly" not because of sexual excitement but because of "the tiger grass beginning to seep / up thru the sheets"; the conflation of worlds is hammeringly brought home by the description of "my hand pawing the nightstand / for a weapon & coming up with the kid's copy / of Dr. Seuss" (*Nam* 14). The implied comment which rebounds here is that somehow American presence in the Vietnam war was also something out of a Dr. Seuss universe. The confusion of one's children in America with the enemy in Vietnam is especially harrowing. The poem "8 Years Ago" begins with an apparent attack by a Vietnamese child—"she had me dead on my feet / the grenade . . . in those little hands"—but when the speaker reacts in fear, "the urine running down my legs," the child says, " 'Do it again / daddy' " (*Nam* 18).

Shields reserves special sarcasm for the subject of Agent Orange. In his poem "Inappropriate," the speaker is "forever coming home to the sweet arms / of Agent Orange" (*Nam* 29); another poem is ironically entitled "Better Living Thru Chemistry" (*Nam* 31). As I pointed out in an earlier chapter, Agent Orange is Shields's particular demon because of his apparent tragic family history with dioxin poisoning; at his daughter's hospital bedside, the speaker imagines "the bruises / from countless IV's ran up her arm / & straight back to Vietnam" (*Nam* 34). The title of this poem, "A Tour of Duty," implies that Shields's daughter is also a Vietnam vet, and, by extension, the children of all Vietnam veterans are in particular "disabled / Nam vets" ("VFW," *Nam* 10).

American society's reactions to the Vietnam veteran in the aftermath of the war is also a frequent, vituperative theme in Shields's poetry. In "phoenix" (a particularly revealing title because he had been assigned as a Navy SEAL in Vietnam to the Phoenix program), Shields begins by admitting "I'm tired of writing these goddamn poems" because of public apathy; instead, he would "rather leave the door open / here at 512 South Fifth Street tonight / & give 'em a seat in the bunker / of my nightmares" (*Drinking* [3], unpaginated). Even current sympathy for Vietnam vets (which Shields evidently feels is hypocritical and "too little, too late," as they say) receives sarcastic attention: "you walked out on our funeral years ago / & now, in fashion, you've lined up / to be pall bearers at the local heroes hill" ("drinking gasoline in hell," *Drinking* [5]); "now they drag their adolescent children to the movies / to see how the Vietnam war really was   in 1989," and the speaker is "still not talking," preferring to continue his "years of silence & self-annihilation" ("years," *Drinking* [6]).

The society's climate of gradual warming toward Vietnam veterans as well as George Bush's opposite declaration that the Gulf war had "exorcised the specter of the Vietnam syndrome" are, for Shields, ultimately meaningless: "after all these years, I don't care / if you can forgive me because // I'll never forgive myself" (*Drinking* [12]). The title of this poem—"there is no metaphor for the pain"—clearly explains Shields's attitude toward the question of aesthetics in Vietnam-war poetry. For him, literary value is equally meaningless in the face of Vietnam-related horror. In a poem with the ironic title "Saving Grace," Shields calls attention to the impossibility of art in the context of the Vietnam war.

> there was no poetry
> in a dead Viet Cong
> with a cock
> in his mouth
> holding a cigarette
> in a napalm black hand
> but goddamn
> did we ever
> take pictures
> of 'em   (*Nam* 1)

Evidently, aestheticization of the Vietnam-war experience is, for Shields, not only a dangerous falsification but ghoulish. To call Shields an antipoet is not to say that he cannot use highly aesthetic description and metaphor; for example, in "The Minutes Become Years," he describes an enemy soldier whose "newly-dead body" is kept "dancing [by] the impact of each bullet" as "flimsy as a scarecrow / in a tornado / his blood misted around his dancing feet" (*Nam* 26)—a tremendously evocative and artful metaphor. Spender's description of an important characteristic among earlier Vietnam-veteran poets certainly applies to Shields: "the self-abnegation of these writers who seem to care for nothing except giving voice to a particular infinite agony packed into a transitional moment" (3). Shields's deliberate choice to avoid traditional aesthetics is a decision as brave as his continuing courage to live despite the terrible guilt and nightmares that, from the evidence of these poems, plague his days.

One reviewer of an anthology of Vietnam-war poetry refers to poets who "ache with wounds that will never heal" (Primm, Review 78). Shields may belong among these, but what is significant is his dogged insistence on facing and mastering his pain, like a shaman, in order to save others. A fitting example is his poem "jingoism," which responds to the Gulf war "against a virtually unarmed enemy":

> How many Iraqi children died with our metal in their bones?
> I'm not going to make a nineteen year old kid a hero
> for having the innocence to kill
> I have two Purple Hearts myself
> for being young and stupid
> & that is not an excuse
> to fill a coffin   (66)

Shields's authority to be a spokesman on war and postwar experience is significant and must not be ignored.

Steve Mason: "Poet Laureate"

Steve Mason's books entitled *Johnny's Song* (1986), *Warrior for Peace* (1988), and *The Human Being* (1990) have established a stellar reputation for him within vet circles; the Vietnam Veterans of America have declared Mason their poet laureate.

Mason's forte is the long poem. In *Johnny's Song,* the shortest poem is a full two pages, while the remainder run from six to sixteen pages. In his work, Vietnam is more of a presence than a fully evoked place; Mason's concern with Vietnam is in its effect on veterans and on the nation. Each poem therefore meanders from subject to subject in an easy, talky language without much embellishment or metaphor. This is not to say that his writing is not purposeful, but only easygoing. Perhaps the best way to characterize Mason's work is that each poem seems suited for delivery to a large audience as a kind of personal narrative or reminiscence. In fact, many of them were exactly that: "The Wall Within" was delivered as part of the dedication of the Vietnam Veterans Memorial in 1982; "Closure: A Much Needed War" was "shared in New York City on May 7, 1985," as Mason puts it, after the dedication of the New York Vietnam Veterans Memorial (*Johnny's Song* 1–18, 87).

"The Last Patrol" is the only poem in *Johnny's Song* which contains an extended section set in Vietnam. It opens with a reminiscence of Mason's childhood.

> In my neighborhood (when I was a kid)
> we didn't know how to cure it,
> but we knew how you *got* it,
> "Walk around all day
> in your wet bathing suit
> and you'll get Polio!"
> That's it—
> We were ahead of the scientists
> by about eight years!
> Jeez, we were smart.
>
> We also knew how to avoid
> the second most dreaded injury
> in the whole world,
> "Don't pick that up by yourself!
> You'll get a HERNIA!!!
> or worse—the unspeakable
> DOUBLE (cross yourself) HERNIA!!!
> AARGH"
> Forget about that no one
> ever knew anybody who had one
> (or both)
> it was enough that grandmothers
> shrieked against them—
> and if they shrieked
> we listened.

This extract demonstrates Mason's style. He certainly does not follow either the aesthetic or the antipoetic strains we have noted in Vietnam veterans' poetry so far. This text is in fact more like a stand-up monologue; there are even clues on how to deliver the material ("cross yourself"), clues which are a comedian's (or political speaker's) guide to "working a room," an audience. The lines are not predicated by either meter or Projectivist "breath units"; the line breaks are, quite frankly, also clues to the person who delivers this to an audience: they are often points at which the speaker might pause for maximum audience effect. There are no recognizably repetitive patterns of syntax; no discernible patterns of sound telegraphed by rhyme, alliteration, assonance, consonance, and other sonic devices; no ambiguity or paradox, for the most part, but certainly a well-developed sense of irony and sarcasm. In other words, there are almost none of the usual signposts used to identify, classify, and analyze poetry, except that Mason rarely reaches the right margin of a page. The power that Mason's poems have is an implied stage presence (conveyed by his system of clues for stage delivery) and a folksy honesty that endears him to audiences (both in person and in print). His expression and humor broadcast a pleasant personality which has, not too far below the surface, levels scarred by the Vietnam war. As such, Mason is an attractive, charismatic figure, a spokesman for Vietnam veterans, a cathartic presence.

To continue with "The Last Patrol," Mason admits that he reenters Vietnam in his memory when "I just get tired of waiting for me / to be like me again," especially since "like some of you I was born there." At times like these, he feels "ready to slip under the wire / for one last patrol," and late at night "I am gone— / . . . past the concertina / on the downward slope / of my nightly fears. . . . a one man / search and recollect mission." Then Mason discusses *killing chickens* ("Where I come from kill a chicken / spend the rest of your life / in reform school. . . . the first thing I ever killed / was a man."), *baseball, stickball,* and finally "Madam Tich's / little boy, Nguyen, anyway / who came to kill me one afternoon / . . . and brought his own duck with him / as an appetizer"—what is immediately apparent here is Mason's sarcastic sense of humor. The scene is a "church in the rain / (on this side of the canal from Cambodia)," and Mason takes pains to describe it:

> Through the storm the church looks
> like a shadow
> and in my mind it has ever remained so.
> That night when we were ambushed,
> I was certain it was the only building
> left standing between Kien Phong Province
> and Augusta, Georgia.
>
> . . . .
> . . . the support beams,
> pitifully decorated with faded
> pink crepe paper
> scalloped and twisted by some long gone
> custodian of the faith.
>
> . . . .
> . . . the dais was covered
> with flat sheets of uncut

> French grape soda cans
> and on the podium an erect
> decapitated statuette of Christ stood
> (the head placed gently at the base).

It is the next morning after a firefight, and Mason's men are bivouacked within the church. "After several sharp words from me / they reluctantly gave up the torture / of two hapless captives," and then Mason senses the presence of Nguyen outside at the door of the church; "his wounds were atrocious." Mason sits with him, gives him a soggy cigarette, and strokes his hair; " 'Toi com biet,' (I don't understand) / he whimpered. / . . . He was in unbearable pain." Nguyen nods toward Mason's pistol.

> Back inside the church
> the muffled "puff"
> which blew Nguyen's lights out
> was barely discernible
> above the rain
> (but for me it still echoes).

Mason reenters the church, and speaks "to the Christ head / 'Toi com biet,' " in existential perplexity. He turns to see one of his men

> holding Nguyen's duck over his head
> like a trophy—
> raising my head to the rafters
> I howled like a mad dog,
> "ANYBODY FOR A LITTLE STICKBALL!?"
>
> (*Johnny's Song* 29–43)

Okay. The story may be a true one; I have used "Mason" here rather than the conventional "speaker" to refer to the "I" character because Mason, I believe, is speaking very much in his own voice, rather than as a projected fictional narrator (as much as one can speak in one's own voice in literature, at any rate).

The narrative uncovered by Mason's "search-and-recollect" mission is his mise-en-scène. The moment when he administers the coup de grace to Nguyen is the moment of Mason's awakening into experience, into an ambivalent and ambiguous manhood. The term coup de grace (with all its connotations of genteel militarism) is therefore wholly appropriate here, as it usually is not in the Vietnam-war context, as in, for example, the Montagnard Man's killing of the staked-out soldier to "put him out of his misery." The killing of Nguyen is *not* a choice offered to Mason as an Army officer if he had been "going by the book." He should have radioed for a medevac chopper or somehow tried to save Nguyen's life—again by the book. The decision launches him from innocence into experience, and this is why so much of the poem is centered on humorous anecdotes of childhood. "The Last Patrol" is not only a search for the ramifications of that fateful event; it is a search for Mason's lost childhood. At that moment when he turns away from the Christ head in the church, he knows already that he has severed himself violently from that childhood of stickball and shrieked warnings from grandmothers, and so he bellows into the air, in a frantic grab at that childhood sliding so swiftly into the irretrievable past, " 'ANYBODY FOR A LITTLE STICKBALL!?' "

The poem also serves a purpose in the book as an entity. Mason understands his audience: Vietnam veterans and those who have an interest in Vietnam. He therefore has to establish his claim to speak as an authority—homegrown and colloquial, but nevertheless an authority—then he has to show that he has paid his dues. To that last question in the list of questions that Ehrhart so despises, Mason can reply, "Yes. I saw him. I held him in my arms. I did it to ease his pain." Since Nguyen is not an American or a "friendly," there is none of the ambiguity which Montagnard Man's coup de grace (if you can call it that highfalutin term) causes him in nightmares. Which does not mean, however, that Mason does not have his regrets over shooting Nguyen ("the muffled 'puff' / . . . for me . . . still echoes").

There are other moments as powerful in *Johnny's Song*. "The Wall Within" speaks of a metaphorical "wall within" on which are recorded all of a person's sorrows, losses, regrets—our inner "Wall" which we must face before we can be whole. In that poem, the movement to raise that external "Wall" in Washington, D.C., is called "an act of spontaneous / moral courage [whose] like may never / have been seen on any battlefield / in the history of mankind" (*Johnny's Song* 18).

"Angry Little Poem of Spring" is a self-conscious, occasionally self-indulgent rant about "the keen sense of justice and appropriate moral outrage," according to Mason, "which have become characteristic of the Vietnam veteran." Here is a portion:

> The world is getting ready
> to replenish itself
> and two, would-be admirals
> are dancing a technological,

mating dance in the Sea of Japan.
It's the one they choreographed
for opus Armageddon
(in c-sharp for lute, metal and water)
that's the one with the really great chorus
at the end (when the sea gives up its dead)
and the rest of the world goes
down
the
drain . . .

But that's not what made me mad.
It was the pentagon applauding,
GOOD SHOW! that pissed me off.   (*Johnny's Song* 69–70)

There are poetic moments in Mason's work when his writing reaches a measure of intellectual complexity, sound texture, rhythmic music, and honest profundity. For example:

The veteran swings between
murder   and   suicide.
His journey is the plain geometry
of conscience;
a pendulum's arc
tracing across the face of the sky
a child's smile
which asks the unspoken question,
"Who speaks for the little ones?"
                    ("The Casualty," *Johnny's Song* 79)

Or:

. . . let no grim, graybeard of a god
speak again to us of glory
by bodycount.   ("The Casualty," *Johnny's Song* 86)

There are eloquent turns of phrase in these excerpts—for example, "opus Armageddon / (in c-sharp for lute, metal and water)" or "the plain geometry of conscience"—and conscious use of such sonic devices as alliteration in "grim, graybeard of a god." More important, however, if Mason's sense of irony *is* "characteristic of the Vietnam veteran," then his achievement is to give these veterans a voice. As poet Andrew Gettler has written of *Johnny's Song,* "I'd dip into Steve Mason's clear, straightforward verse—not only to reassure myself that, yes, it *could* be set down, could be told (and told well) to others—but to come, however slowly, to the realization that *I was not alone*" ("Johnny's Song" 14).

The book closes with "After the Reading of the Names," in which we hear of Johnny, "Johnny went off to war / and Johnny didn't come home." Johnny is an "everytroop," so to speak, and the occasion of the reading of the names, to Mason, is "Johnny's Song." The poem closes, "as much as I love the words / I've come to really hate the music . . ." This poem illustrates the worst impulse of Mason—a tendency toward unadulterated sentiment. Perhaps this arises from the relative brevity of this poem, so that Mason does not have the room to weave in the reminiscences and other raconteur's embellishments that he uses to flesh out his longer pieces. It might even be more apropos to say of Mason that he is basically sentimental about the Vietnam veteran and the Vietnam-war experience, and his best work arises only when he is able, through breadth, to temper that sentiment through the texture and play of his verbal embroidery.

Warrior for Peace is introduced by Oliver Stone, who won an Oscar for directing the Vietnam-war movie *Platoon.* These poems are generally shorter than those in *Johnny's Song,* or they are much, much longer—ranging from a single page to forty-three pages. Mason seems more self-conscious about being a "poet" in this book; he has even included a sonnet addressed to Yuri Schevchenko, a Soviet army sergeant who died in Afghanistan—"Sonnet for a Dead Brother." In this poem, Mason alludes to the popular belief that the war in Afghanistan was the Soviet Union's Vietnam, such that Schevchenko is as close to a Vietnam veteran as Mason can find in a Soviet citizen. "Internationalist combatants" is the term he coins to bind the two of them together. Essentially, the wisdom this poem offers is expostulated in the closing couplet: "Afghans, Viet Cong, you, me, all the others— / we were all poor men, better met as brothers." Mason advances here a fairly eloquent proposal for peace, a proposal which bypasses national boundaries as well as governments.

As a sonnet, this is adequate work. Here is a sample quatrain, beginning with a question attributed to the dead Schevchenko's father:

> "What nation . . . and what good cause in time
> lists the cost of any war in human terms?"
> Governments do not record in human rhyme,
> nor newspapers print simple truth from rice berms.

(Warrior 22)

Mason writes about two-thirds of the poem in a fairly regular pentameter, lapsing for a third of the poem into hexameter. This may be defensible in the final couplet, if he meant to write alexandrines for effect. The rhyming words, though almost always full rhyme, are interesting (particularly the pair *glory / Yuri*). Only once does the rhyme scheme lead Mason astray: to rhyme with "terms" in the quatrain quoted above, Mason forces the diction "rice berms," when the more proper choice (rhyme aside) might have been "rice paddies"— that is, the fields themselves rather than the dikes surrounding the fields.

There are, however, several places in *Warrior for Peace* when Mason sinks completely into sentimentalism. One example, from "A Perfect Pink Belly":

> And your kisses are mad things.
> Alive. With wet little minds
> of their own.
> Snorting, sniffling, giggling things—
> intent on the mischief of pure joy . . .
>
> Chrumpff! To the belly!!
> Phrumph! Phrumph!! Hey! ChicgaChicga!!
> To the soft, powdered underchin.
> Much laughy sounds and a little spit-up.
> Gosh, life is good!   (*Warrior* 25)

Purely sentimental. Worse than anything in his first book.

In his third book of poems, *The Human Being*, one poem registers a significant advance beyond "Sonnet for a Dead Brother" in terms of bridging abysses of national enmity. This poem, "Uncle Ho," addresses Ho Chi Minh as a fellow poet (with an epigraph from Ho Chi Minh's poems) and as a figure of respect. As with Yuri Schevchenko, Mason sees commonalities with Ho Chi Minh: "there are dreams . . . you and I shared all along— / the simple dreams of children growing strong / not fearing the madman's yoke or hangman's rope." In this excerpt, we can glimpse Mason's closer attention to versifying devices, such as the end rhymes *all along / growing strong* and the internal rhyme of *madman's yoke* with *hangman's rope;* there is also repetition of syntax and sense in the latter pair: the parallelism of *madman's* and *hangman's* (two possessives, one a victim and the other a victimizer) as well as of *yoke* and *rope* (both instruments of punishment which encircle the neck).

Mason attempts to empathize with his former enemy, recalling Ho Chi Minh's wish "to be cremated / and your ashes set in an urn / beneath the bamboo house / you chose over the mansion" and lamenting (presumably *with* Ho Chi Minh) that

> . . . the Soviets treated you
> like a Muscovite hero.
> I pray for you that one day
> they will let you rest in peace
> instead of lit-up in a glass cage . . .

The poem closes with a "little present" which Mason leaves for Uncle Ho: "A little rag doll / which belonged to a flower of Vietnam." In this poem, this is the only place where Mason bows toward the sentimentality found in his earlier two books. The phrase "flower of Vietnam" overly romanticizes and essentializes the girl who had owned the doll (or even objectifies this girl as woman). But the closing lines end with an image rather than the moralizing statements that often end his poems from the earlier two books.

> I hope this day,
> not on this earth,
> you and she are one.
> That you will chase
> the black and white clouds together
> and hold hands as the Little Bear
> dances over the Red River.   (*Human* 108–10)

Mason's language here is nondescript, even pedestrian. There is still in his verse a great deal of abstraction and direct, not-so-artful statement. In these three books, nevertheless, there is a sense of the incremental development of a poet, as long as Mason resists his strong urges toward the sentimental.

Oliver Stone, in his introduction to *Warrior for Peace*, claims Mason's work "chilled me to a bone I thought would never again be touched by poetry." No "bullshit or pomposity." No political division between "left and right." According to Stone, Mason is "a goddamn walking-around Poet—in the true barbaric meaning of the word—a bard, a prophet crying out in the wilderness, our Homer come home to remember us (to make us not forget) the ten *fucking* years the Trojan Wars ate us *and* this country up the ass" (*Warrior* 9). Here is Mason's final allure: he is "one of us"—just an ordinary guy. Mason is therefore on the populist side of the consistent and insistent rebellion against intellectualism that has flourished in the United States at almost all levels of life since Andrew Jackson's presidency and more than likely before. This means that Mason *could be* a force. If he *is* a poet and if he thinks of himself as such, is there any way that he can advance the state and reputation of poetry in this country? Especially among the general public, which has very little awareness that *any* poetry has been written since Frost or maybe even Longfellow? Could he do this by example, say, by fulfilling Stone's promise that Mason is "our Homer"?

Oliver Stone's hype of Mason as "a prophet crying out in the wilderness" images Mason as a type of Adamic figure; yet such a poem as "The Last Patrol" suggests that Mason himself has not come away from the Vietnam war "untouched and undefiled," Lewis's phrase defining the American Adam (5). The value of Mason's oeuvre lies in the cathartic release his poems offer to fellow (male) Vietnam veterans. According to Andrew Gettler,

> *Johnny's Song* is a book that embraces, with such seeming effortlessness, not only the pain of vets, the futility of that (or of *any*) war, the hollowness that haunted (and still haunts) so many of us; but also those who were left behind to grieve, those whose grief didn't truly begin until *we* came home. It extends as much sympathy and understanding as any of us can ever offer anyone. ("Johnny's Song" 14)

This response is from the viewpoint of a male veteran. The feminist response to Mason's work is in diametric opposition. In her article "Back Against the Wall: Anti-Feminist Backlash in Vietnam War Literature," Lorrie Smith points to these lines from *Warrior for Peace* as an example of "the misogyny which is a mainstay of popular Vietnam war literature and film" (115):

> All American men my age
> suffered the bad luck and ill-timing
> of drawing Vietnam and women's lib
> in the same ten years!
> Sort of like getting hit by a truck
> the same day they told you
> about the stomach cancer.   (*Warrior* 93)

"Evidently, we are meant to smile wryly in sympathy," Smith writes, "but the female reader (excluded from most war texts and assaulted by many) can only wonder if she is the truck or the tumor." Not surprisingly, Smith calls Mason "a cross between Chuck Norris and Rod McKuen [whose] lugubrious ramblings have little to offer the serious reader"; she labels his poetry a "slick commodity of popular sentiment" ("Back" 120). (It is a damning comment on the American publishing industry that a "slick commodity" is published over the many other fine poets—Vietnam veteran or not—simply because of a cynical assumption that Mason's "popular sentiment" will sell.)

In response to both Gettler and Smith, I will register my faith in Mason's general feelings of sympathy, as revealed by the gradually developing sophistication of his sensibility from book to book; although he may not become a feminist, Mason can at least develop a sensitivity toward the women in his audience. At the same time, the evolution of his poetry, although slow, leads me to be optimistic that Mason is committed to transforming his work into something more than a sentimental, "slick commodity." The question is whether he can accomplish this before his reputation within (academic) poetry circles is completely eroded.

Dream Visions: Poetry by Women Vietnam Veterans

Sharman Murphy, in her eloquent essay "I Thought My War Was Over: Women Poets of the Vietnam War" in the March 1991 *Poetry Flash,* asks why "there *aren't* many women whose work we associate with the U.S. war in Viet Nam. . . . Where might we look to find women's war poetry? How do we understand their silence/silencing?" In her own search for these women poets, Murphy admits, "the pickings are slim" (1). *Visions of War, Dreams of Peace* is the mainstream, New York publisher's response to Murphy's central question: the *very* first anthology of poems on the Vietnam war exclusively by women who were *in* Vietnam.

In her landmark study *The Remasculinization of America,* Susan Jeffords proposes that "the arena of warfare and the Vietnam War in particular are not just fields of battle but fields of gender, in which enemies are depicted as feminine, wives and mothers and girl friends are justifications for fighting, and vocabularies are sexually motivated" (xi). It should be no surprise that in narratives about the Vietnam war, male bonding is therefore emphasized, argues Jeffords, and "to insure that the value of the masculine bonds is maintained, women must be effectively and finally eliminated from the masculine realm" (*Remasculinization* xiii).

Such exclusion of women has occurred in the poetry of the Vietnam war as well, particularly among veteran poets. W. D. Ehrhart, who edited the definitive anthology of Vietnam-war poetry entitled *Carrying the Darkness,* admits his own complicity in this exclusion of women; in his foreword to *Visions of War, Dreams of Peace,* Ehrhart recalls that *Carrying the Darkness* contained "only five poems by women, and . . . none of them had been in Vietnam"

(*Visions* xvii). Ehrhart's other definitive anthology, his collection of the twelve "best" veteran poets, *Unaccustomed Mercy,* contains no women at all. The "official," established canon of "soldier-poets" is a macho stronghold.

Visions of War, Dreams of Peace lays siege to that stronghold, as the first women's anthology of Vietnam-war poems. Of the forty poets published by Lynda Van Devanter and Joan Furey, three are Vietnamese, three are Vietnamese American, six are American civilians (including a musical entertainer, Red Cross workers, an American Friends Service volunteer, and an antiwar activist—the writer Grace Paley—who traveled to North Vietnam in 1969). The rest—twenty-eight poets—are all veterans, military nurses. These women writers challenge the American culture's typically macho representation of the Vietnam war by grounding their work in the female body—a populist version of *l'écriture féminine*—and through a feminist (re)vision of the literary tradition of the *dream-vision* poem, piecing the hopes of individual women into a quilt of healing and reconciliation.

It is important at this point to note that many poems in *Visions of War, Dreams of Peace* are not of high literary quality from the viewpoint of traditional aesthetic standards. "Many of these poems are awkward and sentimental, many rely on limp rhymes, many wear their hearts on their sleeves," poet Sandy Primm observes (Review 78). Although Primm's estimation is accurate, it is important to note that in the context of women's war poetry, this realm of evaluation is always problematic. Susan Schweik asserts, "the question of bad poetry means always the question of bad (or good) poetry *for whom?"* (*Gulf* 17); according to Schweik, it is possible for a poem to earn "its literary value paradoxically, by defying literary value" (*Gulf* 21). We have seen this phenomenon already in the antipoetic strain of Vietnam-veteran poetry, but here the question involves gender difference: inasmuch as these poems validate female experience and feminist sisterhood, they are valuable, and the question of literariness is beside the point. It is certainly the fault of a patriarchal publishing/literary industry that these women did not have the benefit of earlier women war poets as models.[2] Perhaps, like many male Vietnam-veteran poets, they would have rejected these predecessors, but it would have been helpful to know that there *were* women writing poems on/in/about war in the twentieth century. Nevertheless, there are many fine poems (by any standard) in *Visions of War, Dreams of Peace.* What cannot be denied is that these poems are important not only from the perspectives of feminist validation and publication history (noting that this is the first collection of women's poetry on Vietnam), but also because these poems ultimately reveal much about the representation of the Vietnam war in American culture.

The most persistent American cinematic Vietnam-war representation, as
many have noted, has been Rambo—an Adamic figure; in the first two
Alien movies—thinly disguised Vietnam allegories in which an elusive enemy
whomps space-age technology but fails against good old-fashioned pluck—
Sigourney Weaver's spacewoman is transformed into a Ramboette, bare biceps
and trusty machine gun. Granted that such a representation is indeed empower-
ing for the female movie viewer, *Visions of War, Dreams of Peace* nevertheless
offers a radically different image for the Vietnam war: an image of the woman
who braves horror and fear, who is later haunted in dreams and in waking moments by memories of war, but nevertheless a woman who remains a nurturer
and not a Rambo clone. And yet the women writers in *Visions of War, Dreams
of Peace* have also been irrevocably marked by war. Jane Marcus, writing about
WWI, suggests that "wars destroy women's culture, returning women to the
restricted roles of childbearing and nursing and only the work that helps the
war effort" (129). With the advantage of hindsight, we know that the Vietnam
war, while it upholds Marcus's statement, was also more ambiguous than that
(if only in the context of wide antiwar protest). The poems in *Visions of War,
Dreams of Peace* reflect and refract all of that ambiguity.

   An interesting representational phenomenon, keeping in mind Jeffords's assertion about remasculinization in Vietnam narratives, is a reversal of the
Rambo image—a feminization of the male combat soldier. *Visions of War,
Dreams of Peace* is peppered with such descriptions: "His was the smooth soft
skin / of light blond hair and ruddy cheeks" (33); "every man who has died, /
had the same last word on his lips—/ 'Mother' " (40); and, in poem after
poem, the recurrent scene of a nurse sitting by the bedside of a dying soldier—
a stranger—holding his hand and perhaps telling him a "little white lie" (76).
More often, however, the recurrent image is of the fragmented male body:

> . . . there was a handsome, blond soldier.
> I grabbed at flesh
> combing out bits of shrapnel and bits of bone
> with bare fingers.   (14)

"It was your arm, leg, lung, brain, heart / I knew most intimately" (45).

> . . . I never
> pulled someone's hair
> for fear it would be in my hand,
> with the scalp and skull attached.   (112)

"I snip an annular ligament / and his foot plops unnoticed into the pail, / superfluous as a placenta after labor has ended" (30). Marcus has noted that the "fragmented bodies of men are reproduced in the fragmented parts of women's war texts" in World War I (128). The fascinating common thread in these Vietnam poems, however, is the woman's intimate, *hands-on* connection with the male fragmented corpus—devastating moments for future nightmare and memory. But the more obvious cultural note here is how the particularly American segmentation of the female body in slasher films or in TV advertising (Budweiser and bikinis, say)—how this "cut-and-paste" masculinist process is transferred to the male body in these war poems from the woman's perspective.[3]

In turn, what grounds as well as counteracts such horrific experiences for these poets is the woman's body. Note, for example, the ironic metaphor in the excerpt quoted above which begins "I snip an annular ligament"; the amputation of a soldier's foot is imaged by Dana Shuster as a terrible reversal of childbirth—what has been born in that moment are "phantasms of his footless future" ("Mellow on Morphine" 30), while the foot is "superfluous as a placenta" shed by the woman's postpartum body. Ann Rosalind Jones, in her essay "Writing the Body," argues that "if women are to discover and express who they are, to bring to the surface what masculine history has repressed in them, they must begin with their sexuality. And their sexuality begins with their bodies, with their genital and libidinal difference from men" (366), following the lead of Julia Kristeva, Luce Irigaray, and Hélène Cixous. Elaine Showalter, refining her notion of a "gynocritics," points to "the importance of the body as a source of imagery" as long as writers are cognizant "that factors other than anatomy are involved in it. Ideas about the body are fundamental to understanding how women conceptualize their situation in society [mediated] by linguistic, social, and literary structures" ("Wilderness" 252). Although these other structures complicate the idea of a discourse arising from and rooted in the female body (particularly Showalter's warning about "the crude essentialism, the phallic and ovarian theories of art, that oppressed women in the past" ["Wilderness" 250]), there is nevertheless a force implicit in such writing: "a powerful alternative discourse seems possible: to write from the body is to re-create the world" (Jones 366). In *Visions of War, Dreams of Peace,* a body-oriented poetic informs and empowers much of the writing.

In these poems, the body-centered woman's perspective is revealed again and again. What it is like to be a woman veteran, to be in Vietnam, is addressed in physiological (and by extension, psychological and emotional) terms which no man can *truly* understand. Lily Lee Adams demonstrates:

> Being a vet
> Is like
> Losing a baby
>
> No one says
> Anything to you
> And you don't
> Say anything to them.   (*Visions* 123)

In this short but powerful poem, Adams dramatizes the Vietnam vet's silence—
both choosing to be silent but also being silenced by a society, a culture which
wants "to exorcise the specter of the Vietnam syndrome" (as George Bush
couched his perception of the effect of the Gulf war on historical memory)—
but, more important, Adams uses as her central motif *miscarriage,* a solitary
disaster centered within the woman's body, something no man has ever experienced. At the same time, Adams envisions a female audience which has
(potentially) felt this experience and emotion.

Often in these poems, the focus on feminine anatomy serves to highlight the
subconsciously learned acceptance of patriarchy by these women who were,
after all, mostly in their early twenties during the war. Here is an excerpt
from Lou McCurdy Sorrin's "Short 1968–1990" (a reference to the slang term
which designates someone about to exit from the military or, in this case, about
to rotate home from Vietnam):

> See how I strut
> and sashay my butt
> just a bit.
> .   .   .   .
> Thinking about wearing a miniskirt
> perfume
> long hair
> being a round-eyed girl
> back home.   (*Visions* 142)

The references to "strut[ting]," to "sashay[ing] my butt," to "wearing a mini-
skirt / perfume / [and] long hair" point up the speaker's prefeminist frame
of reference, at least within the temporal and spatial location of the poem.
The line "being a round-eyed girl" aptly shows the young nurse's unconscious
appropriation of the anti-Asian slang of "slant-eyed"—a masculinist objectifi-

cation of women, after all, given that the term typically was used by American soldiers to refer to Vietnamese prostitutes. Sorrin's point in "Short, 1968–1990" is that, although she *physically* left Vietnam, she has never been *psychologically* able to leave. She has brought Vietnam with her back to America, and it has been twenty-two years, with no end in sight.

Physiology notwithstanding, there are also the emotional and psychological scars borne by these women—and perhaps the more harrowing of these is the persistence of memory. One reason many of these women undergo these harrowing memories is their job as nurses: all the hand-holding and brow-wiping of dying soldiers. "I went to Vietnam to heal / and came home silently wounded," writes Dusty, "feeling your pain, which never eases" (*Visions* 117). In "Hello David," Dusty describes her vigil at the bedside of a dying patient, a soldier named David.

> I will stay with you
> and watch your life
> flow through my fingers
> into my soul.

That's the moment of truth. The "life / flow[ing] into my soul" means the nurse becomes charged with an awesome responsibility: having to live *for* David. The problem is that, whereas earlier she tells David "I will . . . give you something / for your pain," the nurse will have no one to nurse her in turn: "So long, David—my name is Dusty. / David—who will give me something / for my pain?" (*Visions* 43–44).

Such intimate moments as soldier-nurse and soldier-patient shared in the 'Nam are inaccessible to the woman veteran back in the World. The problem is stereotype. Diane Carlson Evans writes, "I don't go off to war / So they say / [because] I'm a woman," but this overly easy categorizing is belied by her question: "Who then / Has worn my boots?" (*Visions* 95). Norma J. Griffiths revealingly asks:

> The "Vietnam Vet"
> people instantly conjure
> their own picture
> in their mind
>
> Is it ever of
> a woman?   (*Visions* 94)

Worst of all, the woman veteran feels betrayed by the multitudes she healed
at such personal expense in Vietnam. An excerpt from Sara McVicker's poem
"Saigon?" illustrates:

> If one more guy
> asks me if I was in Saigon
> or Da Nang
> I think I'll scream.
> Or maybe pop him in the nose. . . .   (*Visions* 130)

The woman veteran therefore finds herself ineffably isolated—from other
women, from other veterans (particularly the male ones), and from such therapeutic mechanisms as vets' "rap sessions." Ironically enough, the speaker's
frustration is directed at wanting to appropriate masculine violence as resolution—the poem is thus to some degree aimed at a masculine audience, unlike
Adams's "Being a Vet Is Like Losing a Baby."

But the most devastating scars are those which are both within the soul as
well as literally inside the body: ovary as mine field. Marilyn McMahon's poem
"Knowing" recalls that during the war, nurses (like grunts) were unaware of the
dangers of Agent Orange and hence did not ask their patients "where they had
been, / . . . whether defoliation / had saved their lives. / I did not know to ask."
But the price that has been paid in the following decades, back in the World,
is impossibly high, as the speaker chooses to forgo motherhood: "I choose not
to know. . . . / If snipers are hidden / in the coils of my DNA" (*Visions* 187–
89). In one sense, this woman has been "unwomanned"; she can no longer be
a mother, even though it *is* her own personal choice. The woman's very body
has now become a battlefield, and the poet is to some extent a lifelong POW.

The overall effect of *Visions of War, Dreams of Peace* is a variety of voices
and identities, reflecting the editors' desire to have the entire book speak for a
silent multitude, for all the women who have gone to Vietnam. Van Devanter
and Furey hope "that the reception given these works will encourage more
women to write and publish, be reviewed, criticized, and proclaimed. These
women need to be heard" (xxiii).

Feminist critics have long noted the similarities between an inclusive writing
project such as *Visions of War, Dreams of Peace* and the traditional quilting bee.
Showalter argues that "metaphors of pen and needle have been pervasive in
feminist poetics" and the "patchwork quilt has become one of the most central
images in this new feminist lexicon," suggesting that "a knowledge of piecing,
the technique of assembling fragments into an intricate and ingenious design,

can provide the contexts in which we can interpret and understand the forms, meanings, and narrative traditions of American women's writing" ("Piecing" 224–27). The architectonics of *Visions of War, Dreams of Peace* resemble the quiltmaker's art. The poems are not grouped by poet, but pieced together into blocks named thematically: "Visions," "Recollections," "Reflections," "Awakening," "Healing," "Lessons," and "Dreams."

The thematic frame of "Visions" and "Dreams" (as reflected by the book's title) suggests the genre of the *dream vision*—typically a poem which explicates a vision of transcendent import that somehow resolves a profound spiritual crisis. The crisis in these poems is the place of woman in the context of war. As Jeffords argues, "The [Vietnam] war and its representations have been success-fully employed as vehicles for a renewed sense of American masculinity [which is] equally excluding, and more significantly, equally damaging to women and those who are the subjects of masculine domination" (*Remasculinization* 169). One might argue that the Gulf war has accelerated this process. The impor-tant point, however, is that women are excluded, isolated, marginalized, and thereby trivialized. The book flip-flops the margins into the center through the poems' focus on sexual difference and on patriarchal tyranny. The quiltlike effect of the book is a tapestry of memory, a collective personal history that moves from nightmare visions of Vietnam through reflection and reconciliation and finally to an ability to face the future, rather than to look backward into the Vietnam of memory. *Visions of War, Dreams of Peace* is therefore a col-lective dream vision stitched from individual dream visions, a hopeful dream of the possibility of peace (within each person and throughout the world), but nevertheless a hope quilted from the nightmare crises and eventual resolution of women at war.

A similar project has been attempted by Wendy Wilder Larsen and Tran Thi Nga in *Shallow Graves*—a jointly written book of poems. A similar sense of hope obtains at the end of that book, but the reconciliation offered by their collaboration is belied by the way Tran Thi Nga's passionate verse novel/autobiography overshadows Larsen's naive and lackluster poems. As Murphy notes, Larsen's poems reflect "a heightened American schizophrenia: an 'inno-cent' racism, the irrelevance of good will in the context of resultant violence, the distance between calm affluence and the ravages of war" (4). In contrast, the reconciliatory impulse is more successful in Van Devanter's and Furey's anthology.

This sense of renewed hope and reconciliation in *Visions of War, Dreams of Peace* is also rooted in female experience: motherhood. Van Devanter's poem "For Molly" recasts the archetypal father-son question:

> What did you do in the war, Mommy?
> Hazel eyes shining brightly
> Pony tails bobbing softly
> One pierced earring and an orange juice mustache.

The daughter asks about a veteran's empty shirtsleeve and then tells her mother a story about a "good war" in which "nobody got guns or dead." In this story and in her child, the mother finds hope. "Little girl with dreams so peaceful / Alphabets and clowns and people / I don't want you growing up too soon" (*Visions* 204). This closing line harbingers two opposing viewpoints: first, that children may inevitably grow up to be warlike (or at least *be in war,* as we have seen women closer to the front lines in the Gulf war than military women in any other American war), and second, that there may still be time—if we act soon enough—to train children to continue to be peaceful, to retain their natural tendencies toward peace. This second perspective is the final note which *Visions of War, Dreams of Peace* would have us believe in and practice. As Norma Griffiths writes, "Let us think no more / of 'the war to end all wars' " but rather "of the Peace to end all wars" (*Visions* 201).

Reacting to the myth of the American Adam and its attendant matrix of a New World Eden, Annette Kolodny's feminist response was to point out that the "psychosexual dynamic of a virginal paradise meant . . . that real flesh-and-blood-women—at least metaphorically—were dispossessed of paradise" (*Land* 3). Because of this dispossession, Kolodny claims, women were "understandably reluctant to proclaim themselves the rightful New World Eve" (*Land* 5), particularly in the context of a forest wilderness, but when settlers reached the open, expansive prairie, the "American Eve had at last found her proper garden [because] parklike and flowered expanses alternating with stands of trees . . . seemed to offer nothing of the claustrophobic oppression of a wooded frontier" (*Land* 8). On the prairie, therefore, women "proclaimed a paradise in which the garden and the home were one" (*Land* 6). Similarly alienated and excluded from the male vet's Adamic fantasies, the female Vietnam veteran encountered a comparable situation: she must create her own space in the landscape of Vietnam (and, for our purposes, in the literature of the Vietnam war). In *Visions of War, Dreams of Peace,* the arrangement of the poems into a narrative of healing, from trauma to recovery, may thus be imagined as cognate to the garden/homemaking enterprise of the American Eve, especially in light of the poems near the end of the anthology that focus on motherhood and children. Such orchestration on the part of the editors may be seen therefore as the enactment of a traditional social script and hardly a challenge to the patriarchy that underpins war.

Few poets in *Visions of War, Dreams of Peace* really take on the patriarchal system. Sharon Grant, for one, is clearly aware of the conflicts between feminine realities and the war's masculine projections. The stanza "If this is a war, / why am I swaying in a hammock / painting my nails coral, / planning a tan?" in the poem "Flashback" (*Visions* 9) is not merely a statement of the absurdity of the Vietnam war; it also juxtaposes the violence concurrently occurring in the not-so-distant jungle with the speaker's self-beautification—the interesting irony here is that both the war and the woman's nail-painting and tanning are related to masculine desire. A WWII poem cognate to this is Mitsuye Yamada's "Minidoka, Idaho":

> In Minidoka
> I ordered a pair of white
> majorette boots
> with tassels from
> Montgomery Ward
> and swaggered in
> ankle deep dust.   (*Camp Notes* 26)

The speaker, a girl imprisoned in a relocation camp, is twice oppressed here by patriarchal institutions—the overt actions of the U.S. government and the covert effects of male constructions of femininity. In *Visions of War, Dreams of Peace,* Grant contributes "Dreams That Blister Sleep," one of the more consciously poetic performances—an unrhymed villanelle—which contains the lines "You strip-searched the mama-sans for the man. / You didn't know about sisterhood then" (*Visions* 59). In this poem, we have an admission of guilt and collusion in wartime patriarchal domination of the Vietnamese woman and (the speaker can now admit) the American one as well.

Another contributor to *Visions of War, Dreams of Peace* who takes up a feminist stance is Dana Shuster. In her poem "Like Emily Dickinson," Shuster imagines Dickinson "tucking tight little poems / into the corners and crannies / of her father's home" and parallels this imagined action with her remembrances of patients: "I tuck their names / into the crevices / of my crenelated heart." The names—"Lonnie from Tennessee," "Danny from LA," "Chief the Ute," "Pocho from Arizona," "Skeets from somewhere," and "The boy with no name"—are almost the clichéd every-ethnic-group squad of soldiers. It is important to notice here that Dickinson is imaged *within* "her father's home," but to situate herself the speaker inverts the locational imagery: the male names are tucked within her "crenelated heart," a heart with battlements, a fortress. Thus, the traditionalist, patriarchal situation of Dickinson protected

by her father is inverted, but the speaker ironically takes on a military sem-
blance in protecting her charges. Nevertheless, we must remember that Dickinson's seclusion is a rebellion that enables her to write, whereas the speaker's
"tucking" only increases her own pain and memory, her "penance time."

> Emily in white,
> I in green,
> we do our work
> endure and abide
> tucking away the hurt
> saving it for the time
> when alcoves need airing
> when corners need cleaning
> when hearts need healing
> when there are no more
> empty corners
> convenient to fill.   (*Visions* 74)

Shuster is keenly and painfully aware here of the limiting role allowed to the
woman in American culture: to be always "tucking away," always "saving it,"
always sacrificing herself, always "cleaning" and "healing." The very fact that
these tucked-away names *are* aired in this poem, however, implies that all the
corners in the heart were filled. Just as Dickinson's poems were published, ex-
cavated from the "corners and crannies," this speaker's fullness of heart drives
her to write, and that in itself is an act of revision, already moving toward
feminist expression.

In "Grandfathers Rocking," an unrhymed sonnet written twenty-two years
after "Like Emily Dickinson," Shuster speculates how the patriarchal systems
of war are passed on, envisioning grandfathers on "sagging front porches /
spinning out glories of battles" for boys as if in ancient ritual.

> Is this the way it is vectored through time,
> this fervor to offer their anonymous blood
>
> . . . .
>
> in the name of dark urges most dare not articulate?
> Or is it perhaps a Y-linked pandemic
> never isolated because researchers are male?   (*Visions* 165)

The latter question's imagination of a masculine conspiracy to hide a biological male pathogen—warlike tendency as a disease—is a truly angry feminist

stance, worlds (and words) of vast difference from Shuster's earlier "tucking away" of the feminine.

Although I would have preferred the poems in *Visions of War, Dreams of Peace* to have been more strongly feminist, more rigorously (re)written, the book's very presence is enough of a statement in itself. As Van Devanter and Furey attest, "This book is the earliest venturing out of some . . . hidden writings. The women whose poems are included here are absolutely courageous in their sharing of their innermost thoughts, feelings, pain, and growth; before, during, and after the Vietnam War" (*Visions* xxii). Certainly the "earliest venturing out" of male veterans' verse in *Winning Hearts and Minds* also occasioned many poems that do not finally stand up to rigorous literary analysis. What *is* significant is that these poems have surfaced and been published— that these women poets are "absolutely courageous," relentlessly honest, and unabashedly direct about *their* war. For the individual poet and each individual reader, female or not, the bottom line of *Visions of War, Dreams of Peace* is the possibility and actuality of catharsis and release. Now that the silencing of women veterans' poetry—a silence inextricably interwined with that traditionally imposed on women by patriarchy—has been broken, the macho canon of Vietnam-war poetry (and by extension, of all Vietnam-war literature) can never be the same, has been forever revised.

Marilyn McMahon: "Wounds Heal from the Bottom Up and the Outside In"

Of the twenty-eight Vietnam veterans whose poems appear in *Visions of War, Dreams of Peace,* the most accomplished writer is Marilyn McMahon. Her work is a personal complement to the communal project of catharsis that the anthology takes up: McMahon's poems are also concerned with the process of catharsis and healing. Besides the poems in Van Devanter's and Furey's anthology, her work has appeared in two chapbooks, *Works in Progress* (1988) and *Works in Progress II* (1990). The very titles of these books adumbrate her focus on healing as process, as work in progress.

In "Wounds of War," we encounter the therapeutic method in McMahon's poetic project:

> *Wounds heal from the bottom up*
> *and from the outside in.*
> *Each must be kept open,*
> *must be probed*
> *and exposed to light.*

> *Must be inspected*
> *and known.*
>
> (*Works in Progress* [2], unpaginated)

Each of her poems, "inspect[ing] and know[ing]" wounds of memory, is therefore an excavation, akin to psychoanalysis, a psychic debridement (a surgical term for the removal of dead or contaminated tissue). The etymology of the word *debridement* reveals its appropriateness in this context—the term derives from the Middle French word *debriser,* to unbridle—so that we might say McMahon's poems are meant to free the psyche, relieve the self, from the bridle of malignant Vietnam-war memories. McMahon is thus a poet of the Vietnam-war aftermath, a healer of veterans' hearts and minds.

There are wounds and there are wounds. "Wounds of War" chronicles physical damage—a "shell fragment" which "invade[s] his heart / his lungs, his liver, his spleen," and an infected wound which "becomes a greenhouse / for exotic parasitic growths"—as well as psychic, spiritual wounding—a Vietnamese woman whose family and livelihood have been destroyed ("rockets blew away her home and rice paddy"), the nurse whose "days are haunted / by the texture of blood / the odor of burns / the face of senseless death," and the vet who "stares at the gun he saved, / . . . desperate to stop the sounds / and the pictures" (*Works in Progress* [1–3]). The salient purpose here is to detail and probe these wounds of memory in order for healing to occur—a painful and courageous process.

There are the wounds of male domination. The prose poem "In This Land" sets a woman and a man on a "beach for play: smooth sand, gentle waves," she reclining in "a lawn chair, aluminum with yellow webbing, exactly like those in Mom's backyard," while he "sits in another, green." Although the setting is Vietnam, the scene is pastoral, serene, unmolested by the "noises of war: helicopters, jets, boat engines; tanks, APC's, jeeps, Hondas." Their respective roles are revealed by their speech—"his deep voice, sharing items of interest to colonels, and her soft voice, responding to his rank and masculinity"— a tableau of traditional gender roles, focused on the man as subject, and the woman as object (her "dress is sleeveless, short, sunflower yellow"), as adornment, as well as "admirer—the assigned role of her sex for hundreds of years." Although the man drones on, speaking "of helicopter crashes, and botched rescues," the woman only "listens with the part of her brain not otherwise engaged." Into this scene of complacency, comfort, and patriarchal tyranny, the war intrudes, making even the landscape hostile (as perhaps it truly may be): "The ocean is foreign, alien, violent." The tide is bringing three bodies in "flight suits, swollen with three days submersion." The significance of the poem is that the quotidian complacencies of life, the expected easy American routines, will not obtain. The woman's world is shattered; she sees the bodies as isolated colors—"White. Blue. Black. Khaki"—and she is "Ice cold." At the end, the scene remains essentially the same, but the final word reverberates thunderously: "Empty" (*Works in Progress* [5–7]). The war is here represented as a black hole, as a ravening monstrous maw, and the woman's Americanness, her habituated feminine role, her very essence, are all brought into question on the edge of the abyss. The poem "In the War Zone" unveils Vietnam (both the country and the war) as a destructive, rapacious place/time:

> Frightened people in the ditches
> numb people in the trenches
> angry people in the streets
> lonely people in the bars
> shattered people in the hospitals
> and unmarked graveyards.
>
> There are many, many body bags
> in the war zone.   (*Works in Progress* [16])

In either case, oblivion (the empty beach or the "many body bags") becomes the master trope, and the poet's job is to point out the void and vacuum for others to avoid.

Frequently, McMahon's subject is complacency and its dangers. In "July 20, 1969," she meditates on synchronicity—"On the moon," "In Seattle," and "In DaNang"—the three sites typographically imaged in the poem by separate columns. On the left, we see Neil Armstrong's famous step: "On the moon, one man / stepped from a small / metal craft / bounced lightly on the / ladder, and out onto the dusty ground." In the center, we see "Mom and Dad / watch[ing] on their TV" the moon landing, presumably, with the doors of the house "propped open to catch / the breeze." On the right, we see a firefight between "a squad of Marines" and "8 guerillas [*sic*] / . . . aim[ing] their launcher / at . . . the expected / in-bound plane." As the poem closes, all three columns (and their dramatic situations) are funneled into a new central column where we see the "in-bound plane" landing:

> 163 American servicemen,
> Commander Betsy Jackson
> and I filed
> down the ladder.
>   (*Works in Progress II* [1–2], unpaginated)

The different strains are braided here into a single momentous instant: the speaker's entry into the war zone is equated to the moon landing as something unprecedented, a reference point after which nothing can ever be the same, after which the complacent scenes of the earlier middle column can never be (re)lived.

The speaker of these poems, at this moment on "July 20, 1969," is thrust into a place/life/condition in which faith, grace, and religion become problematic. The ironic title of the poem "Dying with Grace" calls attention to different deaths: an "eight year old boy . . . kicking a soccer ball / . . . met by two bullets / from an automatic machine gun"; the boy's grandmother "who was rail-thin at 35" and "who fell asleep in the refugee camp"; the "young man / once from Brooklyn" who killed "12 of the enemy / before he was felled by a grenade." And also the dead not *in* Vietnam—the male veteran who "dies of the cold in a park / across the street from the White House" and the woman veteran plagued with "nightmares / of choppers full of wounded / and dead" who jumps "from the Golden Gate bridge." Did all of these dead "die with grace?" (*Works in Progress II* [9–11]). The speaker does not answer the question directly, but the answer is clearly no. In the poem "Confession," McMahon contrasts the Catholic sacraments of childhood ("Three Hail Marys, and the Act of Contrition. / I am forgiven. / My soul is pure white") with the emptiness of these rituals as seen by the (former) war nurse: "after ten hour night shift / admissions, transfers, two deaths. . . . Fingernail stained orange— / Betadine prep for an emergency trach," the speaker is present at a group confession:

> My silent catalogue:
> Bless me Father, for...
> I was enraged, wanted to hurt another.
> I committed adultery two, no three times.
> I was proud, would not pray.
> Thirty others forgiven at the same time.

Even in the post-Vietnam-war present, the atrocities continue: "Poison gas in Iran and Iraq. / In El Salvador, disembowelled priests / and two women. / . . . Martinis and handshakes in Beijing / across one thousand bodies." The speaker is left only with questions—"Where is forgiveness / and purification of soul? / Where is communion? and when?"—and with the final decision "I will not pray" (*Works in Progress II* [13–15]). Again, we have the centrality of the Vietnam war—in these two poems, a central cause in the poet's loss of faith, eventually a conscious choice.

In addition, the fact that in "July 20, 1969" there are only two women

("Betsy Jackson / and I") in contrast to "163 American servicemen" indicates a predominant theme in McMahon's poetry: sisterhood and feminist solidarity. The woman on the beach ("In This Land") is in part victimized because she is alone, without female companionship and support. "In the War Zone" dramatizes McMahon's awareness of the (deadly) objectification of women in war.

> In the war zone
> the madonnas
> are pictures in a wallet
> or they are dead women
> suckling infants
> in the ditch at the side of the road.
>
> (*Works in Progress* [15])

In her poem on the Vietnam Veterans Memorial, "Crone," McMahon discovers some of the problematics of sisterhood—a resultant (perhaps unwanted) searching of one's soul and conscience. "An old woman moves close / . . . in the black mirror" and, rather than looking for a name on the Wall, "She peers at my face." The old woman's question "do you get to put a face / a smile   a curl / on one of these names?" is probably directed at eliciting a memory about her loved one(s), but instead entraps the speaker as if the old woman were the Ancient Mariner. "I want to move / but I stand   frozen in her gaze" because "I cannot recall their names." At the end of the poem, the old woman's grief has been somehow assuaged, perhaps by her maternal concern for the speaker—"Her tears have stopped"—but the speaker is herself poised on the edge of catharsis and does not yet feel its healing release *within* the text of the poem. "She waits   eyes locked / watching my tears / still / waiting" (*Works in Progress II* [3–5]). This closing highlights a double purpose of these poems: to offer anyone scarred by the Vietnam war the opportunity of catharsis by making sure that "wounds are inspected and known" but also to offer women vets the special benefits of sisterhood, of shared sorrow in female company, so that the reader can know *I am not alone*. In this way, the female veteran is freed from the delusional solitude and isolation of the Adamic stance and can begin her individual process of healing.

The poem "Knowing," which was treated at some length above, deals with the subject of Agent Orange poisoning. The poem opens with a sense of impending doom hinted at by ambivalent beauty.

> I watched the helicopters
> flying slowly north and south

along the DaNang river valley,
trailing a grey mist
which scattered the sun
in murky rainbows.

These choppers are dusting the Vietnam landscape with dioxin "to destroy / the hiding places of snipers / and ambushing guerillas [*sic*]." Withered and stunted trees give no clue of danger to the nurse, who does not know that her patients— "soldiers burning / from jungle fevers: / malaria, dengue, dysentery"—are passing on an invisible time bomb.

I did not ask where they had been,
whether they or the uniforms I held
had been caught in the mist,
whether defoliation
had saved their lives.
I did not know to ask.

Again, sisterhood is represented as a double-edged blade, revealing through the sufferings of her friends what price must be paid for such innocence—the continuing health problems among the children of nine other women veterans: "Jason's heart defects, and / Amy's and Rachel's and Timothy's. / Mary's eye problems. / The multiple operations / to make and repair digestive organs / for John and Kathleen and little John." Through the pain of her "sister" nurses, the speaker realizes what she can never experience, what has been "removed forever from [her] knowing":

The conceiving, the carrying of a child,
the stretching of my womb, my breasts.
The pain of labor.
The bringing forth from my body a new life.

These lines are couched in a way that makes it appear as if the woman has become infertile, unable to be a mother, but her loss, it turns out, is a matter of deliberate personal choice.

I choose not to know
if my eggs are
misshapen and withered

> as the trees along the river.
> If snipers are hidden
> in the coils of my DNA.
>
> (*Works in Progress* [9–12])

Bravery here involves the voluntary abdication of motherhood in order to pre-serve future generations from invisible "snipers"—Agent Orange mutations. This bravery is morbidly akin to the debridement impetus we have noted in her poetry—the removal of contaminated tissue (in this case, DNA)—but a debridement which is valorized by a self-sacrificing heroism. McMahon's heroism finally negates the macho "heroic innocence" values of the Ameri-can Adam myth (Lewis 5) and validates not some highfalutin conception of an American Eve but rather the ordinary woman placed within extraordinary, awful contexts.

Coda: No Adam, No Eve, No Eden

In his poem "jingoism," Bill Shields refers to American soldiers in the Gulf war having the "innocence to kill"; such is the heritage of Adamic innocence, it would seem. To be an American Adam, Shields might suggest, is to be "young & stupid" (66). As Jeffords convincingly argues in "Debriding Vietnam" and *The Remasculinization of America,* there is a regeneration of (avowed) Adamic innocence in the patriarchal and institutional recuperation of masculinity in post-Vietnam-war America, but at the individual level, both men and women Vietnam veterans are unable to actualize the ideal of Adamic innocence in their own lives. In her poem "In the War Zone," Marilyn McMahon's driving mes-sage succinctly explains why there is no possibility of an Adamic approach or attitude to the war by Vietnam veterans: "There are many, many body bags / in the war zone" (*Works in Progress* [16]). The unavoidable presence of death in the Vietnam-war experience (in the 'Nam and in the World) ultimately de-nies, even prohibits, a self-image or identity which is—as Lewis describes the American Adam—"untouched and undefiled" (5).

SIX. WARRIORS AGAINST WAR

In *The Great War and Modern Memory,* Paul Fussell describes a tripartite pattern discernible in WWI war memoirs.

> The "paradigm" war memoir can be seen to comprise three elements: first, the sinister or absurd or even farcical preparation . . . second, the unmanning experience of battle; and third, the retirement from the line to a contrasting (usually pastoral) scene, where there is time and quiet for consideration, meditation and reconstruction. (130)

Fussell argues therefore that the memoir is more than simple autobiography; it is in fact "the deepest, most universal kind of allegory. Movement up the line, battle, and recovery become emblems of quest, death, and rebirth" (131). If this structure is applied to the Vietnam-war narrative's categories, then the in-country period becomes equated with Fussell's middle section: Vietnam = death.

Cornelius Cronin finds "a second, contrasting three-part paradigm in British World War I memoirs":

> first, training and initiation into battle; second, separation from the unit and removal to a safe place (a hospital, or staff duty); third, return to the front. This pattern also involves quest, death and rebirth, but significantly, death is associated with removal from battle and from one's comrades in arms and rebirth with a return to the front. (77)

In the context of the Vietnam war, neither of these mythic structures seems completely apropos. Even if one could somehow sidestep the second term's dangerous ramifications (Vietnam = death), Fussell's third period of "consideration, meditation and reconstruction" in fact very rarely occurred for Vietnam veterans, sometimes arriving at their homes mere hours after they packed their gear in the 'Nam. This lack of "debriefing" or "decompression" has been, as we have noted, one of the causes of readjustment difficulties that have plagued Vietnam veterans. In effect, the vaunted "rebirth" in Fussell's paradigm never took place for many soldiers returning from the Vietnam war.

Although many Vietnam veterans did experience the bonding and camaraderie which Cronin's schema requires, this paradigm is also not representative because esprit de corps was often at such a low ebb in the 'Nam that grunts who had the good fortune to receive a "million-dollar" wound or be transferred to rear-echelon duty for the most part avoided any return to the "boonies." The salient point is that, in either of these paradigms, the third term of the syllogism is rarely (if ever) completed; in mythic terms, this lack of completion contributes to the severe anomie in which many Vietnam veterans still find themselves two decades after Saigon was taken over by the North Vietnamese.

Robert Jay Lifton, in his breakthrough study *Home from the War: Vietnam Veterans, Neither Victims Nor Executioners,* proposes another paradigm based on Joseph Campbell's monomythic structure, *the hero of a thousand faces.* The single face Lifton culls out of the thousand is "The Hero as Warrior [who] follows the heroic life-trajectory of the call to adventure, the crossing of the threshold into another realm of action and experience, the road of trials, and eventually the return to his people to whom he can convey a new dimension of wisdom" (26). In the course of this study, we have been quite close to this mythic territory. Richard Slotkin's idea of "regeneration through violence" is a particularly American version of this Hero/Warrior myth and, as we have seen, the expected regeneration is thwarted, if not at the societal level (so argues Susan Jeffords), certainly at the personal level. Lifton in turn proposes that the reason such regeneration has not occurred has been because of a distortion brought into the mythic structure. "The hero in any myth," he asserts, "becomes the giver of immortality. And the Hero as Warrior incarnates this symbolic quest; he kills not to destroy life but to enlarge, perpetuate, and enhance life" (27). According to Lifton, these regenerative functions of *enlargement* and *enhancement* have been sacrificed for the single function of *perpetuation,* and perpetuation not of life, perhaps, but of the societal status quo:

We then encounter the phenomenon of the warrior class, or what I shall call the socialized warrior. Now the allegedly heroic act, the killing of the enemy with whatever accompanying ritual, is performed to consolidate and reaffirm the existing social order. The socialized warrior thus easily lends himself to the corruptions of patriotic chauvinism. (27)

Focusing this scheme on the Vietnam veteran, it should be obvious that the "existing social order" perpetuated is the technowar machine and its attendant tautological jargon stream of "patriotic chauvinism."

Campbell points out the formulaic cycle of "*separation—initiation—return:* which might be named the nuclear unit of the monomyth."

> A hero ventures forth from the world of common day into a region of supernatural wonder: fabulous forces are there encountered and a decisive victory is won: the hero comes back from this mysterious adventure with the power to bestow boons on his fellow man. (30)

Applying this circular paradigm to the Vietnam veteran's experience, we see that Campbell's category "a decisive victory is won" is not obtainable. In an attempt to claim such a "decisive victory," Richard Nixon argued that "We won the war in Vietnam, but we lost the peace" (165), thereby separating a "decisive victory" in military terms from an "indecisive defeat" in the political realm—a particularly tautological assertion, since the alleged "victory" may be disputed.

When we look, however, at the final term of Campbell's "nuclear monomyth"—particularly "*the power to bestow boons on his fellow man*"—we might note that certain small groups of Vietnam veterans did set about "bestowing boons" on their fellow human beings. That boon has been the antiwar stance from the soldier's point of view. It is possible, therefore, to cast the experience of the Vietnam veteran within Campbell's monomyth if we consider carefully *when* the juncture between the second and third steps of *initiation* and *return* occur. This juncture is found not at the point of DEROS (date of expected rotation from overseas), as might be expected, but rather at the point when the Vietnam veteran begins actively to oppose the war. The period of *initiation* therefore covers military training, departure to Vietnam, combat or other trauma, return to America, and difficulties of readjustment. The point at which the veteran gains "the power to bestow boons" is when enough war experience has been assimilated to reveal the falsity in it—the discovery of being a "socialized warrior," in Lifton's terms. The veteran can then wrest warriorness away from the society and back onto the self, reanimating Lifton's Hero/ Warrior purpose to "enlarge, perpetuate and enhance life" (27). The new quest of the warrior at this point is not to kill but to induce the society to stop the Vietnam war, and eventually all wars, basing this "boon" on the veteran's own experience of war.

Keeping this in mind, we can demonstrate that the two separate "quest—

death—rebirth" paradigms proposed by Fussell and Cronin are in fact workable. Fussell's paradigm—"first, the sinister or absurd or even farcical preparation . . . second, the unmanning experience of battle; and third, the retirement from the line . . . for consideration, meditation and reconstruction" (130)—can be naturalized in this way: (1) military training, (2) Vietnam-war combat folloẃed by alienation in the United States, and (3) antiwar activity. Cronin's paradigm—"first, training and initiation into battle; second, separation from the unit and removal to a safe place (a hospital, or staff duty); third, return to the front [and reunion with] comrades in arms [as] rebirth" (77)—can be seen as (1) military training and Vietnam-war combat, (2) alienation in the United States, and (3) antiwar activity, especially in league with comrade Vietnam vets. The desired end for the warrior is therefore war against war.

"Hell, No, We Won't Go!": The Antiwar Movement

Myra MacPherson has stressed that *"the antiwar element is paramount and cannot be stressed too often. It is the unique facet that colors every aspect of the Vietnam experience"* (45). This movement, in some respects, contributed to the rejection which Vietnam veterans felt upon their return and often felt while they were fighting. Baker documents this feeling: "The real atrocity in Nam was not the fighting. The real atrocity to me was the American people not backing up their troops," recalled one veteran (305). Vietnam veterans became the scapegoats of the public denial of the war. MacPherson claims that "In interviews with hundreds of veterans—from the most successful to the least well-adjusted—I have yet to find one who did not suffer rage, anger, and frustration at the way the country received them" (46).

The civilian movement against the Vietnam war had a poetry movement associated with it, as exemplified by such anthologies as Diane di Prima's *War Poems,* Walter Lowenfels's *Where Is Vietnam?,* and Robert Bly's and David Ray's *A Poetry Reading Against the Vietnam War.* Although these works fall outside the boundaries of this study, since the poems were not written by veterans of the armed forces, it is useful to look at themes exemplified in civilian anti-Vietnam-war poetry.[1] One of the best of these poems is Galway Kinnell's "Vapor Trail Reflected in the Frog Pond."[2] In the opening section, which describes how "In the sky's reflection / in the frog pond the vapor trail / of a SAC bomber creeps," Kinnell sets up a confrontation between the "immaculate" technology of the Vietnam war and Nature, the "frog pond" (poetry by Vietnam veterans, as we have seen, has often criticized technowar through precisely this contrast). Section 2 continues: "And I hear America singing . . . /

the [c]rack of deputies' rifles . . . / sput of cattleprod, / TV groaning . . . / the curses of the soldier as he poisons, burns, grinds and stabs." In this rework-ing of Whitman—"the America-song, a patriotic travesty, a hymn of praise gone deadly and terrible" (Beidler, *American* 73)—Kinnell encapsulates the sixties (even though he was at the time—1966—in the midst of its upheaval): the civil-rights struggle, the inner-city riots, the Vietnam war, and the bur-geoning antiwar movement. "Realizations like these—the perversion of the American idea, and the unreality of the media—show up in countless poems," proposes John Felstiner, but "Kinnell may even be going deeper, toward com-passion for the soldier" ("American Poetry" 5). Section 3 opens in an unnamed Asian locale, undoubtedly Vietnam, where "bones wearing a few shadows / walk down a dirt road, smashed / bloodsuckers on their heel." These walking "bones"—peasants? American soldiers?—are keenly aware that flesh is only flesh, that in death the flesh will be eaten by dogs or by birds. The walkers are portrayed as innocents:

> shoulderblades smooth, unmarked
> by old feather-holes, hands rivered
> by erratic, blue wanderings of the blood,
> eyes crinkled up as they gaze
> at the drifting sun that gives us our lives,
> scrotum wrinkled as it drifts
> over our blazing, foot-battered paths on the earth.
>
> (Bly and Ray 61–62)

In this section, the absurdity of Vietnam the place and Vietnam the war as imaged in the surrealistic terms used so often in poetry by Vietnam veterans also surfaces. The rapaciousness imagined here in "smashed / bloodsuckers," hungry dogs and birds, is balanced against the human being "walk[ing] down a dirt road"—whether Vietnamese farmer or American soldier. In either case, Kinnell gives a complete reversal of the opening: from gentle frogs contrapun-tally set against the furious technology of humans to a rapacious nature tamed by the engendering capacity of the human. This reversal becomes even clearer in the more recent, presumably final version of this poem in which the ending (sans "the scrotum wrinkled as it drifts") reads, "seed dazzled over the foot-battered blaze of the earth" (Kinnell, *Selected Poems* 69–70), evoking edible grain as well as human sperm. "However battered and erratic, there is chance for life," asserts Felstiner ("American Poetry" 6). Such "chance for life" was the ultimate goal of the antiwar movement.

The Vietnam-veteran antiwar movement has been a progression toward the championing of this sort of "chance for life." Felstiner points out that "Kinnell strenuously revised this [third] part of the poem during the years that he was reciting it at rallies . . . [indicating] the failure of the last stanza to compose what it has to say" ("American Poetry" 5). In some respects, this progression was the model as well of the veterans' antiwar movement. There were at least two national groups which eventually organized: the Citizens' Commission of Inquiry on U.S. War Crimes in Vietnam (CCI) and the Vietnam Veterans Against the War (VVAW). Both groups held hearings alleging war crimes. CCI sponsored the "National Veterans' Inquiry" hearings regionally throughout 1970, culminating in a national hearing in Washington, D.C., in December 1970; VVAW opened the "Winter Soldier Investigation" hearings in Detroit on January 31, 1971. Both sets of hearings have been documented, the National Veterans' Inquiry in James Kunen's *Standard Operating Procedure* and the Winter Soldier Investigation in the VVAW's *Winter Soldier Investigation*. Interestingly, both groups at first had worked together (along with Jane Fonda and Mark Lane), but eventually split, so that there came to be two separate investigations. The elder of the two associations is VVAW, which "began inconspicuously in 1967 when six Vietnam veterans marched together in an antiwar demonstration in New York" (Kerry 8). On the other hand, CCI was not initially a veterans' group, having been established by two civilian activists who sought veteran support, but CCI eventually involved many Vietnam veterans. Incidentally, Vietnam-veteran poets were involved in both investigations; Steve Hassett (whose poems appeared in *Demilitarized Zones*) testified in the National Veterans' Inquiry, and Larry Rottmann was a witness in the Winter Soldier Investigation.

"For the first time in this country's history, men who fought a war marched to demand its halt" (MacPherson 55). The hearings conducted in 1970 and 1971 were, because of the limitations of time and funds, relatively small affairs; the Winter Soldier Investigation, for example, involved only about 150 Vietnam veterans (Kerry 8). In April 1971, the "march" MacPherson cites occurred when about one thousand veterans came to Washington to protest the war in Vietnam. They camped on the Mall near the Lincoln Memorial, at first with the government's reluctant permission but eventually against an eviction order that was not enforced. The thousand campers were eventually joined by other veterans who did not camp but stayed in "homes, congressional offices, and in truck and trailer campers" according to a study conducted by Hamid Mowlana and Paul Geffert (Kerry 172–174). The entire group of protesting veterans—including veterans from WWI and WWII—grew to about 2,300, according to

Mowlana and Geffert. This number, however, does not include the spouses and lovers who accompanied veterans, as well as parents and families, especially of soldiers who had been killed in Vietnam.

This mass protest, named "Operation Dewey Canyon III," took place from Sunday, April 18, to Friday, April 23, 1971; parodying the two original Dewey Canyon operations invading Laos, this protest was called "a limited incursion into the country of Congress" (Kerry 26). Its several phases of action included lobbying on Capitol Hill, guerrilla theater in the streets of Washington—where veterans reenacted, in face paint and with toy weapons, atrocities which had occurred in Vietnam—speeches and debates at the encampment, marches throughout the week (including one at the Supreme Court, in which veterans were arrested), a candlelight march around the White House, and a ritual flinging of medals and ribbons on the steps of the Capitol. John Kerry, as a VVAW spokesperson, testified before the Senate Foreign Relations Committee, which met in special session:

> I would like to say for the record, and for the men behind me who are also wearing the uniform and their medals, that my being here is really symbolic. I am not here as John Kerry, but as one member of a group of one thousand, which in turn is a small representation of a very much larger group of veterans in this country. Were it possible for all of them to sit at this table they would be here and present the same kind of testimony.[3] (Kerry 12)

There were other mass demonstrations. In *Born on the Fourth of July,* Ron Kovic records what he calls "The Last Patrol," a convoy of Vietnam veterans and friends which traveled thousands of miles in August 1972 to attend the Republican National Convention in Miami in order "to reclaim America and a bit of ourselves" (158, see 157–69).

Resistance to the war came not only from Vietnam veterans but also from soldiers on active duty. Throughout the Vietnam war there was an ongoing clandestine underground newspaper movement among GIs; such subversive activity was dangerous and held out the possibility of participants being prosecuted for federal crimes. One of the more celebrated cases of resistance by active duty service personnel was the 1969 case against the "Fort Jackson 8" (the group had been known as the "Fort Jackson 9" until one of the accused was discovered to be a government informer). An interracial group of GIs, including soldiers who had served in Vietnam, the Fort Jackson 8 were the leaders of an antiwar group, GIs United Against the War, which had members stationed in Army posts internationally, including Vietnam. The eventual result of the case was that all charges were dropped. Defense lawyer Michael Smith writes,

> The men, in standing firm on their democratic rights, were able to draw wide support both within and outside the Army. Uniting on opposition to the war made it possible to weld both white and black GIs together in an effective organization. The men were good soldiers. . . . [and] conduct[ed] themselves in such a manner they made it possible for the anti-war and civil-liberties communities in the country to come to their defense. . . . The Army, in its heavy-handed attempt to liquidate organized anti-war sentiment, did not calculate that the effort would rebound, as it did, and thrust anti-war sentiment up a new level.

Smith concludes by emphasizing the eventual growth of connections between the soldier-activists and the antiwar protestors; the Fort Jackson 8 "helped reorient the anti-war movement toward recognizing the potential of a new key component, the *new breed of soldier, the anti-war GI*" (Halstead 29, emphasis mine).

The history of Vietnam-veteran poetry reflects the personal development of the Vietnam-veteran antiwar activist in interesting ways. Four anthologies have been published that (generally) constitute the first publication of the poems contained: (1) *Winning Hearts and Minds: War Poems by Vietnam Veterans,* published by 1st Casualty Press and later McGraw-Hill (1972); (2) *Demilitarized Zones: Veterans after Vietnam,* from East River Anthology (1976); (3) *Peace Is Our Profession: Poems and Passages of War Protest,* also from East River Anthology (1981); and (4) *Visions of Wars, Dreams of Peace: Writings of Women in the Vietnam War,* published by Warner Books (1991). Two retrospective volumes have appeared to collect "the best" already published poems: *Carrying the Darkness: American Indochina—The Poetry of the Vietnam War,* published by Avon (1985) and republished as *Carrying the Darkness: The Poetry of the Vietnam War* by Texas Tech University Press (1989); and *Unaccustomed Mercy: Soldier-Poets of the Vietnam War,* also from Texas Tech University Press (1989).

The first four books mirror the tripartite paradigms we have noted in war memoirs. *Winning Hearts and Minds* chronicles the experience of soldiers in the Vietnam war (including a marching cadence to represent military training before departure to Vietnam); *Demilitarized Zones* illustrates the experiences of Vietnam veterans after return to America; *Peace Is Our Profession* represents the radicalization of Vietnam veterans into antiwar protest; and *Visions of War,*

Dreams of Peace recapitulates the entire paradigm, as the title of the book may already hint.

This paradigmatic patterning in these four texts implies that there has always been a close tie between Vietnam-veteran poetry and antiwar protest, particularly in association with VVAW. Jan Barry, the editor of *Peace Is Our Profession,* himself a cofounder of VVAW, chose to minimize this connection and widen the scope of his book by including nonveterans; *Winning Hearts and Minds* and *Demilitarized Zones* had also included civilians, but there were very few compared to the number of veteran poets included. When W. D. Ehrhart compiled *Carrying the Darkness* (which in effect contains and re-envisions the project of the three earlier books by reprinting the most exemplary poems by Vietnam veterans), he echoed and supported Barry's editorial decision to combine the groups by also including a substantial number of civilian poets. As Philip Caputo had suggested, there was a need to set about " 'reconciling the schism created by the war,' " a schism dividing the country between " 'moral conviction, as represented by those who *resisted* the war—and service, as represented by those who *fought* it' " (quoted by MacPherson, 59). *Visions of War, Dreams of Peace* is an even more significant document of reconciliation because Lynda Van Devanter and Joan Furey included works by Vietnamese and Vietnamese American poets.

In this chapter, we will consider *Peace Is Our Profession,* treating only the Vietnam-veteran poets (as we have done with the other collections, particularly *Visions of War, Dreams of Peace*); this will entail some distortion of Barry's overall vision in editing this work, since substantially more than half of the writings included in the book are by nonveterans. However, since the Vietnam veterans included in *Peace Is Our Profession* share in the general spirit of the other writers, and also since Jan Barry is himself a Vietnam veteran (and one of the most outspoken of the vets), I do not believe my concentration on veteran writers is a great distortion. It is nevertheless a distortion insofar as Barry himself has not differentiated the two groups of writers anywhere in the work, except in the notes describing the contributors; this means that this book, as a collective statement against war, is not by any means representative of either camp but of both together, without differentiation.

Horace Coleman's poem "I Drive the Valiant" satirizes the military's way of announcing a soldier's death to the survivors.

> I drive the valiant Blue Valiant
> to the bereft and bereave them
> I say:
>
> Dear Sir or Madam or Mrs, it is my

sad duty to inform you that your
husband, son, brother, father (choice of one)
is dead   missing in action   marrying a Vietnamese
and beloved by all his comrades and commanders

(A. Ground) While on a sweep of the
Central Highland, Saigon bars, DMZ he
threw himself on a whore   grenade   1/Lt
thereby sparing his comrades or
(B. Air) Flying from the MPs, Thailand, Phu Cat
he machine gunned   took pictures of   sprayed
sixteen of the little bastards before
they got his young ass, rendering vital service
before he was rended

The body, head, or other remains may be sent
to the local undertaker of your choice or
viewed at the nearest military installation
with his rank embroidered on it

Gratuities
                    are not necessary   (*Peace* 99)

Fussell has noted this kind of multiple-choice approach to communication in WWI: "The Field Service Post Card has the honor of being the first wide-spread exemplar of that kind of document which uniquely characterizes the modern world: the 'Form'" (185). Nothing was to be written on the post-card except signature and date; all messages were to be chosen from provided phrases, for example:

I am quite well

I have been admitted into hospital
$\begin{Bmatrix} \text{sick} \\ \text{wounded} \end{Bmatrix}$ and am going on well.
                             and hope to be discharged soon.

I am being sent down to the base.   (Fussell 184)

One would construct a message by crossing out all phrases which did not apply; any additions of text would cause the card to be destroyed by censors. Of course, this limited a person from expression beyond the officially sanctioned viewpoint; as Fussell notes, "the post card allows one to admit to no state of health between being 'quite' well, on the one hand, and, on the other, being so sick that one is in hospital" (185). Coleman's multiple choices are hilarious;

one of the funniest is "he / threw himself on a whore   grenade   1/Lt." Coleman's well-made point is the military mind-set's inhumanity and insensitivity along with a critique of the continuing mendacity of language perpetrated by the military.

In keeping with the truce between the resisters and the fighters is Gerald McCarthy's "Marking Time." This poem dramatizes the arrival of a draft evader returning from Canada amid a hubbub of media coverage: "Two flags on the Peace Bridge / . . . A river that spans the boundary / between countries, between freedom and prison." Along with the reporters and cameramen, "US marshalls [*sic*] wait to take their prisoner, / the one clear eye will bring it all back." The title "Marking Time" arises from the parade-field maneuver of marching in place, that is, without moving forward or backward; for the exile in Canada, this implies a kind of stasis, of movement without motion. Of course, the title also refers to the situation of waiting for time to pass, of marking off the days, until the American government allows the exile's return. Bruce Byer, in McCarthy's poem, decides to mark time no longer, to move toward a conclusion. But it turns out the result would be further suspension.

> I want to say that it was yesterday,
> but two years have passed.
> Somewhere in Buffalo he gets out of jail,
> turns to face a new set of charges,
> another courtroom.
>
> This is what remains, these reasons
> that smoulder unnoticed,
> here in the land of victory.   (*Peace* 204)

The phrase "land of victory" is ironic here in a couple of ways. First, the Vietnam debacle calls attention to the phrase's inaccuracy, and, second, Byer seems to have reaped no victory at all; the only victory that may have occurred is the land's (i.e., the government's) victory over Byer, and an empty, self-destructive victory it is.

Joseph M. Shea's "After the Bomb" exemplifies one of the directions Vietnam-veterans' poetry has taken: the jeremiad for peace. The poem opens with "sadness in the land / And silence" broken by an unnatural "blue fire . . . grown in the east." This poem oscillates between a quiet lyricism and overwrought sentimentalism. The silence of the opening stanza is followed by apocalyptic and melodramatic imagery—"From the depths of hell blood welled" and "Vipers . . . slithered"—culminating in a furious prayer whose urgency is telegraphed in capital letters.

LORD, WE DID NOT UNDERSTAND.
LORD, IF WE HAD ONLY KNOWN.
Lord, let the birds sing. We will listen.
Lord, let the grass grow. We will see.   (*Peace* 294)

The return to the quiet of the opening stanza represents repentance. Of course, the poem's circularity forces the reader back to the quiet beginning; and the reminder which Shea is hoping readers will apprehend is that we, in the middle of the 1980s when this was published, are still in the white space *before* the first stanza, so that it is still possible to prevent a nuclear holocaust.

The editors of *Peace Is Our Profession* and *Carrying the Darkness* are perhaps the two most politically committed poets among Vietnam veterans. Jan Barry has yet to publish a book-length collection of his poetry, but he has continued to publish chapbooks of a political nature. According to Ehrhart, "Barry is perhaps the single most important figure in the emergence of Vietnam veterans' poetry, not only for his own pioneering poems but especially for his tireless efforts to encourage and promote the work of others" ("Soldier-Poets" 247). Ehrhart's encomium to Barry certainly applies to Ehrhart himself, with perhaps only the change of the word "emergence" to "fostering"; he has edited three influential and important anthologies of poems by Vietnam veterans. In the rest of this chapter, we will look closely at these two poets as well as at Lamont B. Steptoe, another politically committed Vietnam-vet poet whose chapbook *Mad Minute* dramatizes the African American veteran's experience.

Lamont B. Steptoe: Black Jeremiah

The poems in Lamont B. Steptoe's chapbook *Mad Minute* (1990) focus on all aspects of a soldier's life, from training to combat to return, with the utmost passion being directed at the aftermath of the war through an African American vision and language, tinged by the fire-breathing sensibility of the political activist. The "mad minute" to which the book's title refers is the practice of clearing one's perimeter by simultaneously firing all weapons on automatic in all directions for a full minute; "compulsive eruption, the Mad Minute," writes Michael Herr. "Sometimes we put out so much fire you couldn't tell whether any of it was coming back or not" (62). Steptoe's poem calls the Mad Minute an "Ultimate orgasm / of lead and steel," then compares it to a Wild West image: "Covered wagon circle / punishing slant-eyed Indians" (68). As a metaphor for the entire book, the Mad Minute's operative term is "mad"—in both senses of *crazy* as well as *angry*.

In the poem "On the March," Steptoe portrays himself as "a nineteen-year-old / hard dick po' Black boy / from Pittsburgh, Pennsylvania" undergoing basic training. During a march, "double timing with 150 pounds," the speaker is on the verge of dropping out when "My Native American brother / White-lightning / . . . Apache tough / he grabbed me in the small / of my back / we danced up, danced up, danced up." This memory of brotherhood apparently sustains Steptoe to survive his tour in Vietnam: "My Native American brother / red like Georgia clay / rode me bareback on the pinto pony / of his soul" (4–7). In Vietnam, the sun itself is profoundly affected (or infected) by the war; in "Crossing the Wire," the sunlight is "Cut / to ribbons / on razors edge / it stains the sky / scarlet" (8). In the poem "Parts," the young soldier is at first perplexed by the strangeness of "people / fragile as brown sticks / in black silk skin" but eventually envisions himself as being at one with the people and environment of Vietnam: "I am / part black silk skin / brown stick" and also "I am / the red dust of the moon" (9–11). This is not to say that Steptoe somehow sidesteps horror in his Vietnam experience; he is witness to and partaker in an "Ambush" where "A fifty-one caliber machinegun / cut him in half / like a hoagie"—the enemy soldier eruptively transformed into a thing split in half, only meat, "the half with / the brains and heart / dead on the ground" (12).

It is in the poem "Returnee" that the brilliant and dangerous beauty of Vietnam finally explodes into a hard-edged lyricism.

> After, the golden blood-flecked sky of 'Nam
>
>   .   .   .   .
>
> After, the giant metal dragonflies that chased
> their reflections across ten-thousand
> rice paddies
>
>   .   .   .   .
>
> After, the "meth" and the "opium" and the "grass"
> of this sandbagged world,
> We return home with thunderstorms for sentences
> and shouting typhoons . . .

In the imagination of the veteran back in the World, "night flares illumine the corridors / of our brains." For Steptoe, it is this PTSD, "this post-Nam reality [which] continues to / shift and change," that drives him into his art:

> to utter poetry
> create beauty
> never knowing peace

but building so that someday
others may never know war.   (13–14)

Steptoe's art is rooted in African American speech rhythms, both gospel and
jive. "A Wounded Life" uses repetition for its effect (one can almost envision
the call and response between preacher and congregation in an AME church):
"O' God / I'm poor Black / and crazy / nobody cares / poor Black and crazy /
nobody cares / po' Blk crazie / po' Blk crazie / fo' dey took me / from my
home" (18). Steptoe is echoing and revising, reinscribing, Langston Hughes's
blues rhythms; he is signifying and testifying, improvising on a jazz riff like
Etheridge Knight or Quincy Troupe; like Ntozake Shange or Wanda Coleman,
Steptoe mines the lingo of the streets and transmutes it through outrage into
revolution.

In the poem "Gulf of Tonkin," Steptoe dons the haircloth and dusty robes
of the prophet screaming in the wilderness, a Jeremiah figure.

> I spit in the eye
> of the lie
> that sends sons
> to die
> and causes families
> to cry
> I
> hocker
> dragon spit
> in the face of Congress
> that repeats Vietnam
> like episodes of Mash
> and episodes of Rat Patrol
> and episodes of Sgt. Bilko
> and episodes of Gomer Pyle . . .

Steptoe (writing in 1983, the poem hints) is prophesying the Gulf war almost a
decade early: the intimate, incestuous connections between TV network news
and the American military, creating and packaging images of war in the same
way that Hollywood falsified and prettified war for TV. Steptoe speaks out of
the experience of oppression to give substance to his rant: "I survived / This
black man / survived / to scream these curses"; he enlists the weight of racist,
antiblack history.

> I curse
> you with the ju-ju of Africa
> the ju-ju of my ancestors
> who cursed your southern soil
> while plowing fields
> and chopping cotton
> under the bloody sun
> of American slavery   (25–36)

As David Willson writes in his review of *Mad Minute,* "Steptoe's screams of outrage have never needed to be heard more than now. . . . I hope they are listening in the Pentagon to this prophet poet, but I have my doubts" (15). Apocalypse hangs in the balance.

The poem "On Patrol" describes Steptoe's state of mind in post-Vietnam-war America: "Twenty years later / I still leave home / like I was going on patrol" watching for "snipers and booby traps"; this condition of watchful wariness is not just PTSD, because "Twenty years later / I'm still in at war / because America's at war with me / (or rather the color of me)" (57). The beating of Rodney King by Los Angeles policemen and, following the "not guilty" verdict in the 1992 criminal prosecution of those policemen, the riots—arson, looting, assault and battery, even murder throughout urban America—all of these are battles in Steptoe's war.

Although Steptoe uses African American literary techniques in his art, I submit that his method is mainly antipoetic. Again, I reiterate that I do not mean to say that Steptoe is *not* a poet, but rather that his poetic strategy is to resist lyricizing and poeticizing war (the Vietnam war, class war, race war, any war) through traditional aesthetics. As an artist devoted to prophecy, the rant, the jeremiad, Steptoe is a shaman—a priest figure who runs the gauntlet of death and destruction in order to bring healing and sanity to his fellows, to us. But this shaman is not committed to some otherworldly realm; his work is firmly based on the real world, on memory, on history, on politics, on personal risk. For example, in the poem "Survivors,"

> We fall out of history like dominoes
> tumbling into oblivion
> like sideshow targets
> in deer hunting season   (67)

Steptoe's awareness of history as text, the possibility of history being re-scripted, repackaged, and changed into something antithetical to fact and compassion—this awareness informs his disciplined rant. The shaman risks "tumbling into oblivion," being a "sideshow target," but only in this way can he transform his community for the better. This is "mad" (crazy *and* angry) but relentlessly necessary.

Jan Barry: "Nine-to-Five War" and a Plain Style

Jan Barry's Vietnam is a different Vietnam from the place of free fire zones and Zippo squads. He went to Vietnam in December 1962. Veterans who were first in-country in 1967—like Ehrhart, say—would have been greatly surprised and perhaps shocked that Barry spent half of the first night of his arrival at his base camp riding a bicycle in civilian clothes to a nearby town and back (Santoli, *Everything* 5). And yet, even back then, certain truths about the war were already clear. Barry recalled:

> *we* were the war. If we wanted to go out and chase people around and shoot at them and get them to shoot back at us, we had a war going on. If we didn't do that, they left us alone. . . . There was no war after four-thirty. On Saturday, no war. On Sundays, no war. On holidays, no war. That's right, a nine-to-five war. (Santoli, *Everything* 5)

There are some resemblances here to the search-and-destroy decoy trick, except that Barry's war sounds much quieter. Perhaps because his service was during the "advisors' war," when evidence of the French occupation was more plentiful than it might have been for later American arrivals, Barry's poems set in Vietnam have a greater sense of Vietnam's history and its wars than the work of many other Vietnam veterans, for the majority of whom the personal realism of battle scenes was plainly ahistorical.

Barry's poem entitled "In the Footsteps of Genghis Khan" dramatizes this American tendency to ignore history by underlining not only the fact of continual foreign aggression in Vietnam (as imaged by the separate presences "at Nha Trang" of the "French legionnaire," "the Japanese," "American expeditionary forces," and, much earlier, the Mongols), but also indirectly the Vietnamese hardihood in enduring and surviving each of these invasions.

> Unhaunted by the ghosts, living and dead
> among us
> in the red tile-roofed French barracks
> or listening in on the old Japanese telephone line . . .

These American soldiers go about the duty of establishing a headquarters, "oblivious to the irony / of Americans walking in the footsteps / of Genghis Khan." Even in 1962, the latest year depicted *within* the poem, a future American victory is already proposed as suspect. The likelihood of naïveté and subsequent defeat is supported by the fact of the poem's emphasis on the speaker's age—the period since the Japanese occupation is mentioned as being twenty years, "(a year more than my nineteen)," admits the speaker—an emphasis in the midst of a narrative whose historical range encompasses at least six hundred years of armed struggle. The poem at its close aptly portrays a particularly American type of innocence.

> Unencumbered by history,
> our own or that of 13th-century Mongol armies
> long since fled or buried
> by the Vietnamese,
> in Nha Trang, in 1962, we just did our jobs:
> replacing kepis with berets, "Ah so!" with "Gawd!
> Damn!"   (*Veterans Day* 5)

This view of the war as potentially unwinnable is interesting insofar as this poem is one of the earliest published poems by a Vietnam veteran, having appeared in *Winning Hearts and Minds* fully eleven years before Barry published it in this version in his chapbook *Veterans Day*. The weakest part of the poem is the closing, with its (essentializing) American-schoolboy pidgin Chinese: " 'Ah so!' " Clearly, this is meant to characterize the nineteen-year-old for us, but it also casts doubt on the poet figure projected by Barry behind the surface of the poem as being perhaps too facile, too glib, especially given the " 'Gawd!' / 'Damn!' " split by a line break.

One of Barry's most effective poems is the lyric "Floating Petals."

> See: here the bougainvillea;
> there, the cactus and palm—
>   here: the lotus flower;
>   there, the bomb-shattered bamboo
>
> of viet-nam
>
> severed flowers, sharded fronds:
>   floating in shrapnel,
>   sealed in napalm.   (*Winning* 74)

In this quiet lyric, Barry evokes the variety of exotica in Vietnam as well as the commonplace mundanity of war technology. What makes the poem effective is the poet's avoidance of direct explanation, of overt polemical comment, so that the words "sealed in napalm"—that is, Vietnam trapped in this most appalling of wars—can speak its own piece.

Barry's "Harvest Moon" has a similar restraint; the poem describes familiar homegrown Halloween scenes fraught with entirely different significations. Jack-o'-lanterns "hide candle flames of bamboo villages . . . // glowing behind the orange / decapitated skulls of Asians." There are more tricks than treats. "On a city sidewalk gangs of stick-armed / tricksters steal candy from younger ones," and "down the road / small shapes scatter from a farm / as a field of hay goes up in flames" (*Demilitarized* 139). Barry's point is that the atrocities which occurred in the Vietnam war have been already seeded in America, where "tricksters" in city, town, and country vandalize—but this is more than vandalism, when "a field of hay" burns. In the speaker's mind, this inevitable fact is etched in the equation of jack-o'-lanterns to "skulls of Asians" lit from within by Zippo flames. And Vietnam is now as close as "down the road."

As do many Vietnam veterans, Barry traces his political and perhaps human awakening to the Vietnam war: "Once you were a strange, alien name / far across the seas somewhere. / Then you were a small, damp, green / hostile land." In this poem named "Viet Nam," spelled in the Vietnamese manner rather than the Western conflation *Vietnam,* Barry thanks "my foster, second home" (i.e., Vietnam) for "giv[ing] me courage and hope / in the face of governments gone mad." Barry is keenly aware that he owes his compassion and his personal freedom and realization of choice to the Vietnam war. "You have taught me, foster land / to be not just a man / but a human being" (*Demilitarized Zones* 173).

This poem underscores Barry's abandonment of a poetry based on image and subtlety of language for a more directly polemic and straightforward language—the antipoetic stance—as we have seen so many Vietnam-veteran poets do in admitting the failures of traditional prosody in the face of the Vietnam war. The everyday language Barry chooses is indicative of a political choice to eschew the artistic concerns of poetry and "speak plainly" to Americans, more of them than the small group who pay attention to poetry.

In his two chapbooks, *Veterans Day* and *War Baby,* Barry is unabashedly and purposefully didactic. The poem "Lessons" is a dialogue between father and son—the father a Vietnam veteran who wishes to explain the truth of war to his son. But the son's insistence reminds the father of this son's glee—" 'Nicky's dead! Nicky's dead!' "—during an emergency some years past when the son's younger brother had stopped breathing. The "lesson" learned here is not that of the son learning about war, but the father acceding to his own rhetorical question, " 'when is it going to happen / again?' " (*War Baby* 11–12). In "Veterans Day," a poem set during the dedication of "the Wall," the speaker asks:

> This black marble wall
> may be our most debated war memorial.
> Yet where are
> the marble monuments,
> the flagpoles,
> to the civilian victims
> whom wars are said to be about,
> whom soldiers are said to have fought
> to defend?   (*Veterans Day* 10–11)

This poem clearly does not *want* monuments, but rather calls attention to what "wars are said to be about." Perhaps the most important revelation of these two chapbooks is Barry's heightened personal commitment to these issues—to "peace as our profession," as the anthology of poems he edited suggests in its title. For Barry, therefore, the aesthetic qualities of poems are subordinated to radicalization, perhaps even sacrificed in an effort to speak in a plain language, without the ambiguity which poetry often seeks to foster.

W. D. Ehrhart: Evolution of a Poet

"I find it extremely difficult to sit here and talk about the Vietnam war as art," said W. D. Ehrhart at the 1985 Asia Society conference on literature and the Vietnam war. "I don't give a goddamn about art. I'm not an artist. I'm an educator, and my writing is a tool of education" (Lomperis 32). Ehrhart as poet has the admirable knack of being passionately both artist *and* educator at the same time; as Lorrie Smith points out, "he manages to be didactic without being preachy or propagandistic" ("Resistance" 53). Ehrhart's disclaimer at the Asia Society conference is clearly a political statement, and his poetry as well is an equally political statement which has gained strength and force in poem after poem, as his career as a poet has advanced. From his first poetry book, *A Generation of Peace,* to his most recent, *Just for Laughs,* we can read the dramatic evolution of a poet, and Ehrhart's achievement is indeed substantial and worthy of notice.

Ehrhart most deserves the cognomen "person of letters" among Vietnam-veteran writers because he has published more work in *varying* genres than any other vet—a range that Philip Beidler has labeled "cross-literary, transgeneric, multimedia, including a significant role in the production of Stanley Karnow's *Vietnam: A Television History*" (*Re-Writing* 157). Besides editing the poetry anthologies *Demilitarized Zones, Carrying the Darkness,* and *Unaccustomed Mercy,* Ehrhart has published twelve volumes of poetry, including *To Those Who Have Gone Home Tired: New and Selected Poems* and *Just for Laughs* (on which I will focus generally to illuminate his poetic achievement). Ehrhart's work in nonfiction includes a trilogy of memoirs: (1) *Vietnam-Perkasie: A Combat Marine Memoir* (1983), which narrates his enlistment into the Marines, his thirteen months in Vietnam, and his return to the United States—a work comparable to Tim O'Brien's *If I Die in a Combat Zone* or Philip Caputo's *A Rumor of War;* (2) *Marking Time* (1986, reissued as *Passing Time* in 1989), which chronicles Ehrhart's life after Vietnam, his radicalization, and his protest against the Vietnam war; and (3) *Going Back: An Ex-Marine Returns to Vietnam* (1987), a journalistic account of his return trip to Vietnam with poets Bruce Weigl and John Balaban at the invitation of a former North Vietnamese general. He has also published "Soldier-Poets of the Vietnam War"—a benchmark historical canon-forming survey of the work of Vietnam-veteran poets—and other significant essays on Vietnam-war-related subjects, collected under the title *In the Shadow of Vietnam: Essays, 1977–1991* (1991). His contributions to the scholarship of the Vietnam war include annotating bibliographic citations as a contributing editor to Merritt Clifton's *Those Who Were There: Eyewitness Accounts of the War in Southeast Asia, 1956–1975 and Aftermath* (this work is especially helpful to the scholar of Vietnam-war poetry because it locates poems published individually in journals and other outlets) and a stint as visiting Professor of War and Social Consequences at the William Joiner Center of the University of Massachusetts at Boston.

Ehrhart's poems set in the Vietnam war precisely capture the feelings of being a combat soldier, a grunt in Vietnam. The poem "Viet Nam—February 1967" records the sensations of being newly in-country, an FNG, listing impressions of Vietnam from a fresh viewpoint, from a person not yet numbed or hardened by combat. But these impressions are not random; each quatrain addresses a set of associations: (1) first impressions of weather and smells ("Air heavy with rain and humidity, / . . . Dank smell of refuse"); (2) visual impressions, close as well as distant ("Patchwork quilt of rice paddies"); (3) military technology ("Thundering roar of aircraft on the prowl, / . . . Crackling whine of small arms"); and (4) people ("Ramshackle busses crammed with people / . . . A ragged child stares at passing soldiers" [*Winning* 5]). The syntax of the poem lends to its reception by the reader. The first three stanzas have no predicate and are technically not sentences, giving a flavor of abeyance to the impressions; the closing stanza becomes a sentence only in the last line, and that sentence encompasses the tragedy of Vietnam. This tragic essence is double: first, the juxtaposition of "child" and "soldiers" prefigures atrocities, perhaps even by the speaker; second, the child may "stare" at the soldiers in envy, since he is "ragged," and be dreaming of a time when he too can become a soldier—thereby continuing the ongoing tragedy of war.

This same innocence, sustained and cherished in the field, could have unexpected effects as it coddles and protects the wearer of that innocence from the true magnitude of his actions. " 'Bring me back a souvenir,' the captain called," begins the poem "Souvenirs." During the patrol, the troops find "a Buddhist temple by the trail":

> It must have taken more than half an hour,
> but at last we battered in
> the concrete walls so badly
> that the roof collapsed.

Before the building folds, however, the speaker steals "two painted vases" intended for incense; the poem ends, "One vase I kept, / and one offered proudly to the captain" (*Tired* 8). In this poem, we are shocked by the speaker's ingenuous pride in his gift which has been stolen—but not *merely* stolen, since a temple has been destroyed for it, and obviously the destruction was hard work, since the grunts worked for "more than half an hour." What makes this poem especially poignant is that it is in fact a confession of guilt; in his memoir *Vietnam-Perkasie* Ehrhart records this very event as an actual occurrence (140–42).

Ehrhart also records the harrowing of this innocence, whatever its effects. If FNGs survive, they become hardened and callous. And death, at least, when the grunt is still in the early part of his tour, seems to lose part of its menace: "I'm not going to make it out of here anyway, so what the hell?" Of course, as one's tour wound down, these feelings would change to extreme caution as one came to fear death more and more, perhaps more than before. Ehrhart's poem "Sniper's Mark" reflects this earlier numbing to death and its effects.

> He seemed in a curious hurry
> to burn up what was left
> of the energy inside—

> A brainless, savage flurry
> of arms and legs and eyes.　　　　　*(Tired* 9)

The speaker of this poem—in an innocence much different from that noted in the poem "Souvenirs"—muses abstractedly, and such word choices as "curious" and "flurry" reflect his emotional distance; what the speaker no longer notices is that this is a human being, perhaps even a fellow American. But for the reader, the scene is only too present, partly from the word choice—"brainless, savage"—but perhaps more frighteningly from the word "eyes" as the reader imagines their look of surprise or hurt or desolation. This poem resembles Basil Paquet's "They Do Not Go Gentle" in its theme, but the salient difference is in approach. Here, it is what Ehrhart leaves out that fuels the horror.

Ehrhart also recalls the thoughts of the grunt who, late in his tour, has become obsessed with the horribly unfair dangers surrounding him. "The Next Step" records this point of view, which amounts to an enervating paranoia:

> The next step you take
> may lead you into ambush.
>
> The next step you take
> may trigger a tripwire.

The poem continues in this vein, repeating the refrain "the next step you take" with different consequences—exploding mines, dismemberment, "split[ting] your belly open," sniper fire—until the poem resolves in these closing lines:

> The next step you take.
> The next step you take.
>
> The next step.
> The next step.
>
> The next step.　　　　　*(Tired* 11)

The anaphoric repetition of "The next step you take" dwindling to "the next step" near the end contributes to the sense of growing dread in this poem, and the accumulation of dreadful potentialities accretes into a sense of helplessness leading to indecision. But indecision would be just as deadly here—a paralyzing double bind.

The form of this poem also helps to reinforce its message. If the couplets are meant to resemble footsteps, what happens at the end of the poem when the last line stands alone? Is the speaker also standing alone, frozen in the jungle?

Or has that last step elicited the click of a mine arming itself so that the speaker cannot lift his weight off it? Or is the second step in the unfinished couplet the step which killed the speaker? That these questions are unanswerable (but not rhetorical) helps to give the reader some sense of what this awful feeling of anomie must be like.

Like other Vietnam-veteran poets who underplay their connections to earlier war poets, Ehrhart does not mention the influence of the WWI soldier-poets, especially Wilfred Owen—although we are given a clue in the poem "Imagine" where "Owen tumbled / through [the] minds" of naive questioners (*Tired* 19). Paul Fussell, in *The Great War and Modern Memory,* has noted the unavoidable effects of roadside calvaries or crucifixes for the Allied soldier in WWI (117–20); Owen, for example, has a poem called "At the Calvary Near the Ancre" that imagistically suggests a connection of the war with the Antichrist and the Apocalypse (108). There was also a persistent rumor of a Canadian soldier crucified by the Germans. The theme of the soldier as sacrifice was of course inevitable, and in many poems the private was compared with Christ on the path to Golgotha, "each soldier [seen as] a type of the crucified Christ" (Fussell 119). "Christ," Ehrhart's poem on this theme, reveals a difference in *who* is compared to the sacrificed Christ (friend or foe). The speaker sees a "Crucified Christ [who] did not hang on the cross" and had none of the usual scourges—"nails," "crown of thorns," "open wounds"—except for "a small black hole upon His cheek."

> Today, angelic hosts
> of flies caress His brow;
> and from His swollen body comes
> the sweet-sick stench of rotting flesh.   (*Tired* 13)

Here, the Christ may be Vietnamese, and not necessarily a soldier (Vietcong or NVA)—an intriguing bit of compassion. The conceit is certainly cognate to those of WWI poets—Owen, Siegfried Sassoon, Edmund Blunden, and others. Ehrhart's concerns are the same: the crucifixion of religion itself in the face of war as well as its inability to respond in any useful fashion; the violence perpetrated on the sanctity of the person, but nevertheless the possibility, however slim, of redemption in the war zone.

Ehrhart's method in his poems set in/during the Vietnam war is generally structured on an apprehensible event or scene, evoked through a precision of detail in the setting or of intonation in the speech of characters within the poem. His overall mode is irony—satire, dramatic irony, sarcasm—and this irony often points toward both writer and reader: our guilt and our collusion in the Vietnam war. In poems set in America, however, Ehrhart becomes more discursive, less reliant on scene. These poems are more directly polemic and often rely on rhetorical language. As such, they seem more overtly political, though, of course, all of Ehrhart's work is political, even his substantial body of lyrical poems not directly relating to Vietnam.

"A Relative Thing" is a typical example of this more polemic mode. The poem addresses the complacent American public, imaged here as soldiers' parents: "We are the ones you sent to fight a war / you didn't know a thing about." Subsequent stanzas paint a picture of the war to which Americans back in the World were not privy: "a breastless woman / and her stillborn child"; "We fought outnumbered in Hue City / while the ARVN soldiers looted bodies / in the safety of the rear"; "pacified supporters / of the Saigon government / sitting in their jampacked cardboard towns"; "We have been Democracy on Zippo raids, / burning houses to the ground, / driving eager amtracs through new-sown fields." These impressions are worlds away from those given in "Viet Nam—February 1967." What follows is condemnation:

> . . . we were the instruments
> of your pigeon-breasted fantasies.
> We are inextricable accomplices
> in this travesty of dreams:
> but we are not alone.
>
> . . . .
>
> We are your sons, America,
> and you cannot change that.
> When you awake,
> we will still be here.   (*Tired* 17–18)

There is more than a threat here; this poem calls attention to the ineffable identification between the grunt and the parent back in the World, in America. It is not merely a matter of shared guilt—they are in fact the same flesh.

A great many of Ehrhart's poems are about this sort of self-discovery. In "A Relative Thing," he tries to foster the discovery in others; other poems are about Ehrhart's own burgeoning awareness. A good example is "Making the Children Behave"—its two stanzas set up as then and now, the young speaker's ignorance versus present understanding. The opening stanza recalls "strange Asian / villages" where the only humans, to the relentlessly innocent speaker, are "myself / and my few grim friends"; the closing stanza realizes the possibility of a "strange Asian" viewpoint:

> When they tell stories to their children
> of the evil
> that awaits misbehavior,
> is it me they conjure?   (*Tired* 20)

In this poem, Ehrhart is giving up a former view of humanity for another, moving from xenophobia to a realization that it was really the "strange Asian" villagers who were human and that the speaker is now the bogeyman. This acceptance of the self as bogeyman is another index of the Vietnam-war heritage—the recognition of evil within the self. This poem illustrates as well Ehrhart's personal courage. When he revisited Vietnam, this was one poem he brought—translated into Vietnamese—to show when his Vietnamese hosts would ask for a poem, as he knew they would, since the fact of his being a poet was one of the main reasons he had been invited.

Ehrhart also senses, bitterly, the failure of American myths in his own presence in Vietnam during the war. In the poem "To the Asian Victors," he relates how, as a child, "I learned about Redcoats— / I studied myself, / though I did not know it at the time" (*Tired* 20). This reversal of myths devastated Ehrhart in ways that are not apparent in this poem. When he was interviewed for the documentary *Vietnam: A Television History,* he spoke about his discovery:

> In grade school we learned about Redcoats, the nasty British soldiers that tried to stifle our freedom, and the tyranny of George III, and I think again, subconsciously—but not very subconsciously—I began increasingly to have the feeling that I was a Redcoat. I think it was one of the most staggering realizations of my life that to suddenly understand that I, I wasn't a hero, I wasn't a good guy, I wasn't handing out candy and cigarettes to the kids in the French villages. That somehow I had become everything I had learned to believe was evil. (*America Takes Charge* 5:18)

Ehrhart's revelation here shows not only the influence of the morality play of the American Revolution, but also the influence of war movies and TV shows such as *Combat* in the reference to "handing out candy . . . to the kids in the French villages," so that, while the sacred myths are proving false, they are simultaneously being sustained.

The poem in which Ehrhart makes his own separate peace with (North) Vietnam, finally, is in "Letter," whose epigraph reveals that the poem is addressed "to a North Vietnamese soldier whose life crossed paths with mine in Hue City, February 5th, 1968":

Thought you killed me
with that rocket? Well, you nearly did:
splattered walls and splintered air . . .

This poem is a fusion of the various feelings that memories of the Vietnam war
raise in Ehrhart's psyche in 1976 (almost the tenth anniversary of his almost-
death). One of these feelings is Ehrhart's dismay at the national optimism and
amnesia engendered by the bicentennial celebration.

. . . things are back to normal.
We've just had a special birthday,
and we've found again our inspiration
by recalling where we came from
and forgetting where we've been . . .

Another feeling arises from his nagging difficulties (perhaps slighter now but
still present) in readjusting to America, the inconclusiveness of the U.S. retreat
from Vietnam.

Do better than that
you cockeyed gunner with the brass
to send me back alive among a people
I can never feel
at ease with anymore . . .

The result of the fusion of emotions into poetry is a new hope; "Since nothing in American culture helps Ehrhart assimilate his experience," notes Smith,
"he turns to his enemy" ("Sense-Making" 14). And this new hope is inspired
by the reunified republic of Vietnam and the fact that their guardian spirit is a
poet. He advises his old nemesis, the North Vietnamese soldier:

. . . build houses; build villages,
dikes and schools, songs
and children in that green land

.   .   .   .

Remember Ho Chi Minh
was a poet: please,
do not let it all come down
to nothing.

(*Tired* 34–35)

And yet this hope is *not* certain, since this soldier is the "cockeyed gunner" who *had* missed a clear shot back in 1968, and so Ehrhart's separate peace may be hardly any consolation after all. Such lack of solace is a hallmark of Ehrhart's poetry about Vietnam; one wonders if he will find peace—but certainly a poem like "Letter," which strives consciously to resolve all the relevant issues, is a strong step.

What solace Ehrhart does find is rooted in lyricism, in his love for nature. "A Confirmation," dedicated "for Gerry Gaffney," relates the story of a fishing trip: "Solemn Douglas firs stride slowly / down steep hills to drink / the waters of the wild Upper Umqua." It turns out that Gaffney, who accompanies Ehrhart on this trip, is also a Vietnam veteran, a Marine buddy.

> Both recall, in easy conversation,
> one-man poncho-tents rigged
> side by side in total darkness,
> always you and I, in iron heat,
> in the iron monsoon rains . . .

Despite the fact that years have gone by and "we are older by a lifetime," the pair find that "nothing's changed."

> For we were never young, it seems;
> not then, or ever. I couldn't cry
> the day you went down screaming, angry
> jagged steel imbedded in your knee—
> I knew you would live,
> and I knew you wouldn't be back,
> and I was glad, and a little jealous.

These conflicting feelings from a decade ago do not hamper their easy companionship, and "with an old, eager patience / you teach me how to cast the fly / gently" to land "a fourteen-inch rainbow trout / . . . its tiny heart / beating with defiance . . . / helpless in my hands." In the peace of the Oregon woods, the two reminisce about Vietnam, about "the little shy / flower who always wore a white Ao Dai." What Ehrhart finds in this moment is peace and reconciliation:

> together now, in this small circle of light,
> we bow our hearts to the shadows
> of the Klamath Indians; now,
> and always, in our need.   (*Tired* 41–43)

It is fitting that this poet who is devastated by the failure of American myth to sustain his self-image and his image of the nation finds consolation in a masculine bonding ritual—regeneration through violence (almost; Ehrhart "throws the fish back / in the awkward silence" [42])—a ritual in the mythic forests of the Far West. It is finally the balm of myth which relieves his personal anomie, but only for the moment. "The healing power of love, nature, and friendship may be effective in Ehrhart's own life," admits Smith, but inevitably "such personal consolations are insufficient to counter the force of history or to correct the mistakes of the past" ("Sense-Making" 15).

Another, perhaps more expansive, comfort for Ehrhart may be found in his radicalism, his activism. *To Those Who Have Gone Home Tired,* as Smith has pointed out, "traces one representative veteran's growth from naiveté to disillusionment, anger, and political activism" ("Sense-Making" 14). The book's title poem dramatizes the interlacing of the issues of the Vietnam war with myriad political and humanitarian concerns:

> After the memories of Kent and My Lai and Hiroshima
> lose their power
>
> .   .   .   .   .   .
>
> After the last American dies in Canada
> and the last Korean in prison
> and the last Indian at Pine Ridge
> After the last whale is emptied from the sea
> and the last leopard emptied from its skin
>
> .   .   .   .
>
> What answers will you find
> What armor will protect you
> when your children ask you
>
> Why?   (*Tired* 28–29)

Driven by the hypnotic rhythms of anaphora, this poem postulates the Vietnam war as only one of many fronts for political activism—American aggression, the environment, animal rights, the depatriation of Native Americans, and more—but here they have all come home to roost *in the home,* in "your children['s question] // Why?" And the discovery of this range of political issues is both mirrored and complemented by the poet's own recovery of self; "Ehrhart connects two converging continuums: his personal coming of age and the destructive flow of history" (Smith, "Sense-Making" 14).

In 1985, Ehrhart had the opportunity to return to Vietnam. A return visit, for those veterans who have been able to make one, becomes an important part of their healing from the war; those who have made such a visit and written a memoir (William Broyles's *Brothers in Arms* and Lynda Van Devanter's *Home Before Morning,* to name a couple) inevitably emphasize the cathartic nature of such a journey. Near the end of *Going Back,* Ehrhart remembers his catharsis as an exchange of sensory images, a fitting trade for a poet:

> Now when I think of Vietnam, I will not see in my mind's eye the barbed wire and the grim patrols and the violent death that always exploded with no warning. Now I will see those graceful fishing boats gliding out of the late afternoon and across the South China Sea toward safe harbor at Vung Tau, and the buffalo boys riding the backs of those great gray beasts in the fields along the road to Tay Ninh. Now I will not hear the guns, but rather the gentle rhythmic beat of rice stalks striking the threshing mats. (180)

Many of the poems in Ehrhart's most recent book *Just for Laughs* arise from this experience, but they do not evoke such pastoral imagery at all—nor do they resurrect the ingenuous impressions of the young Ehrhart newly in-country in "Viet Nam—February 1967." For example, the poem "For Mrs. Na" (occasioned by his return to Vietnam) marks the opening of *new* wounds in (the) place of the old ones.

> I always told myself,
> if I ever got the chance to go back,
> I'd never say "I'm sorry"
>
> . . . .
> . . . that was nearly twenty years ago:
> enough's enough.

But facing the five-times-bereaved Vietnamese mother in her home in Cu Chi district is an unexpected confrontation for which no one can prepare.

> . . . here you are.
> And you lost five sons in the war.
> And you haven't any left.
>
> And I'm staring at my hands
> and eating tears,
> trying to think of something else to say
> besides "I'm sorry."					(*Laughs* 23–24)

This poem is so simple, so eloquent in its easy language, that it hardly needs comment. What the experience awakens in Ehrhart is a need for personal recommitment: to find "something else to say / besides 'I'm sorry,' " to find new value, new purpose. In his poem "Last Flight Out From the War Zone" (dedicated to the poet Bruce Weigl, one of Ehrhart's companions on the 1985 visit to Vietnam), Ehrhart glimpses this possibility in his kinship with Weigl:

> I like your resolves—clear and neat
> like a compass and map in articulate hands:
> to get out of the South, forever;
> never to kill yourself; to value
> the moments of the modest present.
>   . . . .
> Friend, we must cling to what little
> the war didn't take: our voices,
> the singular vision, that hard sleep
> from which you jump
> as if you've seen something.
> You have. And I have.

As in "A Confirmation," the poem dedicated to Gerry Gaffney, Ehrhart finds consolation in kindred companionship, this time with two poets (John Balaban had accompanied Weigl and Ehrhart to Vietnam). What Ehrhart finds valuable are Weigl's resoluteness, his devotion to life, and that they share the stigmata of the Vietnam war as well as the "singular vision" it affords. The poem closes, "We will walk point together" (*Laughs* 22); as poets, they will scout the wilderness for the rest of us—"walking point for us into the future . . . cutting new paths in our literature" (Stephens, *Dramaturgy* 143)—seeking what new value and goodness may arise from the Vietnam war. Going back to Vietnam may have offered Ehrhart the hope he had sought but did not find in his "Letter" to the "cockeyed gunner."

The significant impression one draws from *Just for Laughs* is Ehrhart's greater devotion to aesthetics, despite his disclaimer five years before that "I'm not an artist. . . . my writing is a tool of education" (Lomperis 32). As Michael Stephens has observed, "Book to book Ehrhart seems to become a better poet, a finer craftsman" (*Dramaturgy* 144). In *Just for Laughs,* there are frequent allusions to the work of other Vietnam veterans, thus setting up an intertextual poetic network. The poem "In the Valley of the Shadow" describes an existential darkness—"Bent, we drag it with us like a cross" (*Laughs* 15)—

which is strongly reminiscent of Horace Coleman's lines "we know who owns the night / and carry the darkness with us" (*Mercy* 49), which were, after all, Ehrhart's source for the title of his anthology *Carrying the Darkness* to signify the overall poetic experience of the Vietnam war. A similar "title game" may be discerned in other poems in *Just for Laughs*. The title of Ehrhart's poem "Unaccustomed Mercies" alludes to Weigl's poem "Monkey" in which we find the lines "I like a little unaccustomed mercy. Pulling the trigger is all we have" (*Romance* 16), which served as the source for Ehrhart's title for his other canon-forming anthology, *Unaccustomed Mercy;* the poems "A Small Romance" and "Small Song for Daddy" in Ehrhart's *Just for Laughs* mirror and echo in their titles Weigl's poems "Small Song for Andrew" in *The Monkey Wars* and "A Romance" in the book of the same name.

Ehrhart is also more deliberate about his use of prosody. In the poetry published before 1990 he had been a relentless proponent of free verse, but in *Just for Laughs,* he includes poems in rhyme, meter, and inherited forms. In "A Small Romance," which describes a father lulling a daughter to sleep,

> a soft blue light seemed to dance.
> I held you tight, a small romance
> of sleepy child and sleepy father
> singing sapphire songs together   (*Laughs* 41)

The poem's characteristic stanza is the couplet quatrain in tetrameter with a varying mixture of iambic and trochaic stresses. One might argue that the setting here, the bedtime story/nursery rhyme situation, is what elicits the traditional versification, but there are other examples in *Just for Laughs*. "A Scientific Treatise for My Wife" begins:

> The ancients thought the world is flat
> and rides upon a turtle's back,
> or that the planets, sun and stars
> revolve around the earth in crystal spheres.   (*Laughs* 34)

Ehrhart's use of rhyme in these quatrains is sprightly, particularly in his careful sprinkling of half rhymes—*father/together, stars/spheres,* and other rhymes in "Scientific Treatise": *Hawking/daunting* and *physicist/obvious*—a method which connects him with Wilfred Owen as well as Emily Dickinson.

Ehrhart's use of received stanzas is equally significant. Whereas in his earlier poetry he had often applied the verse paragraph, using the stanza break to telegraph a change in topic or in sense, in *Just for Laughs* we find quatrains—both rhymed and unrhymed (e.g., "For Mrs. Na," "Love in an Evil Time")—tercets ("For Anne, Approaching Thirty-five," "What We're Buying"), and couplets ("The Ducks on Wissahickon Creek," "The Next World War"). There are also less common stanzas, for example, unrhymed octets ("Starting Over"), septets ("What Keeps Me Going"), and quintets ("Second Thoughts," "The Children of Hanoi"). One poem in quintets, "How I Live," displays an intricate relationship between rhyme and form.

> I bumped my head on the setting sun.
> The night had only just begun
> and I was dizzy already, reeling
> like a drunk walking on the ceiling
> of a world turned upside down.
>
> A steady star burned above the town
> I thought I lived in, but I couldn't
> find it, and a voice said I shouldn't
> even bother, what with the wind
> rising, clouds piling, tide coming in.   (*Laughs* 77)

This poem (which proceeds twenty lines beyond this quotation) is based on the rhyme scheme *aabbc cddee*—that is, five couplets with the central couplet spanning a stanza break. What Ehrhart gains from these experiments in rhyme and form is the serendipity of enjambment, both lineal and stanzaic—thus artistically complicating his work.

Notable also is Ehrhart's experiment in inherited forms. A villanelle entitled "The Way Light Bends" innovates that form's closing quatrain by *not* joining the two refrains in a couplet but rather installing them as the second and fourth lines of the quatrain to open up a sense-making space in the third line. Ehrhart's experimentation in formal prosody is a fascinating index to his evolving image of himself as more of a poet, an "artist" and not merely an "educator."

Just for Laughs also projects an overwhelming sense and mood through the considerable patterning of image which obtains not only in poem after poem, but also throughout the book. This pattern establishes a consistent virtual reality in which the poems reside—night, dust, smoke, fog, cold rain, winter, a storm, blindness—a universe of darkness, murkiness, low visibility, and therefore indeterminacy, in which fire is a threat (as metaphor for war) and light is potential salvation. That fire and light often coincide indicates the infinitesimal margin of difference between death and life. In "The Way Light

Bends," the light can be either beautiful—glowing "through trees in winter dusk"—or dangerous, the way light can "burst forever when the missiles fly" (*Laughs* 73). The poem "In the Valley of the Shadow" (the title itself is revelatory) gives us the image that "Something out there in the dark / came breathing, stalking, waiting," and the speaker and his companions, lost in the darkness, would "swear / our innocence to God or Satan / for a single drop of sun" (the phrase "God or Satan" again indicates the small differences which obtain). The looked-for salvation is couched in images of fire: "wanting women, girlfriend, mothers / to protect us, to descend in fire / on angels' wings, torch the darkness" (*Laughs* 14–15). But fire also devours; in the apocalyptic poem "The Next World War," a "man with his hand on a trigger / . . . dances on flames [and] / . . . takes the flames in his hands, // into his lungs, his eyes / burning, his hair, on fire" (*Laughs* 74). In "Parade," a sarcastic lament on the honoring of Vietnam vets "Ten, fifteen, twenty years / too late," the speaker asks:

> How many wounded generations,
> touched with fire, have offered up
> their children to the gods of fire?
> Even now, new flames are burning,
> and the gods of fire call for more . . .   (*Laughs* 17–18)

A world replete with "street[s] washed with fire," where a young man can "stumbl[e] through Asia / dropping lighted matches like a fool" ("Who Did What to Whom," *Laughs* 29). A world where "The slow finger of moving light / from the lightship off Columbia Bar / [is] barely able to bore a hole / in the smothering darkness" ("The Facts of Life," *Laughs* 44). A world where "the first / flat gray of early dawn" is a "Small miracle, such magic" ("Winter Bells," *Laughs* 33).

In the face of such overwhelming darkness and despair, salvation is found in *love,* as (often) imaged in light. In "A Small Romance," the love of daughter and father at bedtime ritual is dramatized by "a soft blue light [which] seemed to dance" around the daughter's head, so that the father, once the child has fallen asleep, finds himself both illuminated and illuminating: "to my surprise, / I plucked two sapphires from my eyes" (*Laughs* 41). Ehrhart's daughter Leela, as she sleeps, "begins again / the long night dreaming / darkness into light" ("What Keeps Me Going," *Laughs* 79); at a "toystore" in Vietnam, "two identical warplanes, / flight leader and wingman, / 'U.S. Air Force' stenciled on the sides" are picked up by Vietnamese children who "pretend they are flying, / nothing but light in their eyes" ("The Children of Hanoi," *Laughs* 80). These two examples demonstrate Ehrhart's faith in the regenerative beauty and radiance of the truly young and innocent. The other personal salvation comes, for Ehrhart, from the love of his wife. In "A Scientific Treatise for My Wife," a meditation on the history of cosmologies that ends with "Stephen Hawking [who] postulat[es] ways / black holes disfigure time and space," he tells her, "the universe begins and ends with you" (*Laughs* 35–36). These are topics that can verge on sentimentality, but Ehrhart's voice is so amazingly honest that he never finally falls into the sentimental.

Ehrhart's poem on sentimentality in poetry reveals, in part, how he avoids the sentimental. "The Heart of the Poem" advises: "Split the ribcage open / with a heavy-bladed knife, / a hatchet or an axe." After levering the ribs open, reach in and

> . . . dig until the heart
> seats firmly in your palm,
> like a baseball or a grapefruit,
> then jerk it out.
>
> Get rid of it.
> Sentiment's for suckers.
> Give us poetry.   (*Laughs* 58)

This kind of toughness is what makes Ehrhart's poems tick. At the same time, the particularity of the poem—the precision of a phrase "like a baseball or a grapefruit"—illustrates the basis in real events, textures, personalities which characterizes good poetry. For Ehrhart, the true poet is "all discipline, all muscle, lean and hard" ("The Poet as Athlete," *Laughs* 53). It is just such muscularity in verse to which Ehrhart aspires and achieves.

Over a period of fifteen years, we find Ehrhart's poetry moving from the hard and gritty poems set in Vietnam, through an angst-filled period of soul-searching and nation-searching in America, to the more lyrical aesthetic poems of *Just for Laughs* after his return to Vietnam. Although he has found momentary solace in companionship and in political radicalism branching out from Vietnam, for Ehrhart, it's always back to the war: "Vietnam has remained a permanent condition of my life—as much a state of mind as a geographical location, the turning point, the place where I first began to see and think and learn and question" (*Going Back* 5). Having *physically* gone back, Ehrhart may finally find the consolation he has long sought in future poems in which he can reconceptualize the Vietnam war finally into something (potentially) ameliorative. For Ehrhart, the secret lies in language: "didactic but not dogmatic, lyrical but not transcendental; his plain-spoken, chastising style is appropriate for a moral and political reconception of Vietnam" (Smith, "Sense-making" 15). Tied to this crucial basis in language and voice is Ehrhart's continual commitment to empowerment of the voiceless (as indicated by his indefatigable support of other vet writers), to witness, to conscience. Herein is finally his greatest achievement—literary or otherwise, in poetry or prose—Ehrhart's significant presence as an untiring, ever vigilant voice of conscience.

Coda: Dissident Poetry, Protest Poetry, and the New (Winter) Soldier

That Steptoe, Barry, and Ehrhart, in the final analysis, generally make the very same choice of polemics over poetics (although Ehrhart is ultimately not quite as able as Barry and Steptoe to eschew poeticization) is indicative of a category of political poetry defined by James Scully:

> we should distinguish dissident poetry from protest poetry. Most protest poetry is conceptually shallow. I think of the typical protest anthology: poems in opposition to the Vietnam war or to the coup in Chile. . . . Such poetry is issue-bound, spectatorial—rarely the function of an engaged artistic life, but compensation for a politically marginalized one. It tends to be reactive, victim-oriented, incapacitated, lacking the theoretical and practical coherence that could give it muscle and point. . . . the telltale characteristic of protest poetry is that it seldom speaks the active rage or resolution of people on the receiving end. I mean oppressed and exploited people. (5)

In other words, protest poetry more often actually tells us more about the poet than it does about the situation being protested. "Dissident poetry, however," Scully suggests, "breaks silences: speaking for, or at best *with,* the silenced; opening poetry up, putting it in the middle of life rather than shunting it off into a corner." In such a life-affirming, life-oriented poetry, what is emphasized are "connections—say, between social empowerment and valorization and human definition—that the dominant ideology declares that 'poetry' must ignore or suppress" (5). In light of Scully's distinction, we see that poetry by Vietnam veterans exists in a continuum between these two poles. Steptoe, Barry, and Ehrhart are all enmeshed in the middle of that continuum, although Ehrhart seems to strive more consciously to achieve the ideal of a "dissident poetry." Perhaps Barry and Steptoe, in their total commitment of person to didactic poetry, may also be said to be in the same general camp.

In any case, this ideal of committing one's entire person to a cause, which all three poets certainly do, has been given a name in the context of Vietnam veterans resisting war—John Kerry's conception of a "New Soldier" who "does not accept the old myths":

> the New Soldier is asking America to turn. . . . from false glory, hollow victory, fabricated foreign threats, fear which threatens us as a nation, shallow pride which feeds off fear. . . . the New Soldier is trying to point out how there are two Americas—the one the speeches are about and the one we really are. (Kerry 158–60)

Clearly, this idea of a "New Soldier" is an attempt to create "new myth" (or at least to reconstruct old myths)—a realization of Lifton's call for the removal of the "socialized warrior" whose "killing of the enemy . . . is performed to consolidate and reaffirm the existing social order" to return to "the Hero as Warrior [who] incarnates this symbolic quest; he kills not to destroy life but to enlarge, perpetuate, and enhance life" (27). The VVAW's play on Thomas Paine's words decrying the "summer soldier" as the soldier of expediency, resulting in their term "the winter soldier," is also an attempt to reconfigure myth; but in renewing myth, the VVAW are also returning to the "symbolic quest" motifs. Their "grail" is the ending of the Vietnam war and the punishment of war crimes at the root of national guilt—and as a long-term objective, the abolition of war overall.

The mythic image of the "warrior against war" is certainly not a new coinage, but I submit that it is unprecedented in American culture. The precedent (particularly vis-à-vis poetry) is the British experience in WWI. "Like their forebears of 1914–18," writes Beidler, "the American generation of Vietnam fought a war not of their own making but of the making of politicians and experts, a war of ancient animosities that cost nearly everything for those involved and settled virtually nothing" (*Re-Writing* 3). Vietnam-veteran poets are ineffably aware of this connection. Norma J. Griffiths's poem "Keep Mum" exemplifies this awareness:

> Teach 'im ta fight.
> Teach 'im ta run.
> 'E's doin' a duty.
> Wot mus' be done.
>
> Giv 'im a gun.
> The blood mus' run.

Tis honor and glory
wot mus' be won.

Tell 'im it's freedom.
Tell 'im we've won.
But 'bout the horror,
keep mum, keep mum.   (*Visions* 166)

Griffiths's use of a cockney accent and argot parodies the politicians (or all civilians, Siegfried Sassoon might say) who favor war and, in the context of the Vietnam war, points to that war's parallels with WWI, an Anglo-American lineage. Just as WWI was a major influence in the rise of Modernism and its worldview of fragmented experience, the Vietnam war was a similarly eruptive experience for Americans, an epistemological and ontological crisis inextricably involved in the advent of Postmodernism in America. Fredric Jameson has called the Vietnam war the "first terrible postmodernist war" in which we can chart "the breakdown of any shared language through which a veteran might convey such experience" (84).

We have seen that many Vietnam-veteran poets have given up on the lyric possibilities of traditional poetry in the face of such a postmodern "breakdown of any shared language." Two Vietnam veterans who attempt to engage in "new" mythopoeia still true to the realities of the Vietnam war without abandoning the lyrical aesthetics of poetry are Bruce Weigl and Yusef Komunyakaa, whose work we will consider in the next two chapters. In their devotion and passion, Weigl and Komunyakaa create a true dissident poetry.

SEVEN. BRUCE WEIGL: "USEFUL TO THE WIND"

In "Soldier-Poets of the Vietnam War," W. D. Ehrhart quotes JFK twice: "Most [Vietnam veterans] had been in grade school or junior high school when John F. Kennedy had declared that 'we will bear any burden, pay any price' in defense of liberty," and "In 1963, John Kennedy said in a speech at Amherst College, 'When power corrupts, poetry cleanses'" ("Soldier-Poets" 263, 265). Ehrhart's quotations of Kennedy, read in concert, bracket the Vietnam-veteran poet's situation: the entrapment of history and manifest destiny as well as a faith in the efficacy of poetry—the "burden" borne may be so ineffably heavy that only poetry is salvific. This situation is especially true of Bruce Weigl, a romantic, an innocent, from whom innocence is violently stripped, so that the poems become a quest for the regaining of romance, of simple love.

In the course of Weigl's first four collections—two limited editions published in 1976, *Executioner* and *A Sack Full of Old Quarrels,* followed by two full-length books of poems, *A Romance* and *The Monkey Wars*—the poet we intuit seems to deal with a multitude of themes besides the Vietnam war. In fact, if one were to compute in these four books the ratio of the Vietnam-war-related poems to those unrelated to the war, the answer would be that less than *one* in *four* poems are about the war.[1] And yet, there is an overwhelming impression in these four collections that the Vietnam war is *the* central event that governs a life, albeit a subterranean or, more precisely, subliminal influence. As Weigl writes about Toledo, Ohio, or his grandparents, or the ancestral fields of Eastern Europe, or his marriage to a Japanese American, the ubiquitous ghost of the Vietnam war implies an urgent need for catharsis, purgation, or (to use JFK's term) "cleansing."

Bruce Weigl's poems on the Vietnam war are powerful and effective because he uses predominantly the short lyric—a familiar staple—and keeps his language simple, almost brutally so. Jeffrey Walsh has pointed out how war has emerged into "a distinctive and central element in the modern literary con-

sciousness. Military terrain and situations have become familiar" (1). Weigl
uses our familiarity to "raise the consciousness" of the complacent American, as 1970s argot would term it. In his poems on the Vietnam war, Weigl
forces us to re-view the war through the increasing eloquence and aestheticism
of his attempts to revise his Vietnam-war experience. And each of his poems
is a ritual of "cleansing"—thus Weigl conflates the antipoetic, cathartic, and
aesthetic modes.

A Romance: The Quest for Escape

A Romance contains all of the Vietnam poems from Weigl's earlier chapbooks.
These poems deal with the experience of being in-country and back in the
World in many of the typical ways other Vietnam-veteran poets have dealt with
Vietnam. There is surrealism here: "I remember a flower / a kite, a mannikin
playing the guitar, / a yellow fish eating a bird, a truck / floating in urine"
("Sailing to Bien Hoa," *Romance* 3). There is Vietnam's dislocating weirdness in the inexperienced eyes of a youthful American: memories of riding a
horse in Ohio—"a broken gray mare my cousin called Ghost"—melding with
the vision of "two Chinese tanks . . . their tracks slapping the bamboo like
hooves" until the speaker "did not know for a moment / what they were, but
knew they were not horses" ("The Sharing" 9). There is a reduction of language more severe than Michael Casey's, perhaps an overreaction to the jargon
stream: "There is a hill. / Men run top hill. / Men take hill. / Give hill to man"
("Monkey" 19). There is constant exposure to potential violence, resulting in
a numbing anomie.

> North Vietnamese mines, Vietcong mines,
> French mines, American mines,
> whole fields marked with warning signs.
>
> . . . .
>
> Here is how you walk at night: slowly lift
> one leg, clear the sides with your arms, clear the back,
> front, put the leg down, like swimming.   ("Mines" 33)

This numbness accompanies the soldier back to the World: "One melancholy
ghost after another / parades by my window. / Rain falls like wax beans. / Key
moves in the lock" (38). The title of this poem, "Executioner on Holiday,"
chillingly implies that the veteran, back in America at last, is only on furlough
from killing.

The prevailing impression of most of these quotations from poems may be characterized by the word "dream" or, perhaps more aptly, "nightmare": "there's a new disease, / I don't know if I'm awake or asleep, // one day I'm back in the army, / a nameless private" ("Executioner on Holiday" 38). Catch-22 all over again. Ehrhart suggests that Weigl "seems unwilling—by design or by default, one cannot tell—to confront the war directly, relying time and again on dreams, illusions and surreality. . . . almost as if, even after 11 years, the war is still too painful to grasp head-on" ("Soldier-Poets" 256). In "Him, on the Bicycle," the scene opens "In a liftship near Hue" and below:

> The door gunner sees movement,
> the pilot makes small circles:
> four men running, carrying rifles:
> one man on a bicycle.

Suddenly, in a dislocating wrench as if in dream, the speaker finds himself below, a target—"I'm on the back of the bike / holding his hips"—an amazing epiphanic moment, realizing the humanity of one's enemy. Lorrie Smith astutely compares this scene to a cinematic moment in popular culture as the speaker and the enemy "fly past the battleground like Butch Cassidy and the Sundance Kid" ("Sense-Making" 16). In the closing scene of that movie, the gringo outlaws, surrounded by *federales,* make a last-ditch run for freedom, guns blazing, and we never find out, *within* the filmic text, if they survive. A similar ambivalence obtains in Weigl's text, as the bicyclist disappears "Like a blaze / streaming down the trail" (30)—a "final ambiguous image in which the Vietnamese man may either be literally torched by the gunner or apotheosized in the speaker's fantasy" (Smith, "Sense-Making" 16). This sort of ambiguity becomes a shorthand for a widespread confusion about how the war ended for Americans, the murkiness of result which allows Nixon's tautological summation that "We won the war in Vietnam, but we lost the peace" (165).

The horror, however, occurs more poignantly at the personal rather than national level. The moral murkiness enshrouds each individual, making even the most basic essences untrustworthy. The long sequence, "Monkey," begins by trying to get back to basics.

> I am you are he she it is
> they are you are we are.
> I am you are he she it is
> they are you are we are.
> . . . .

> Good times bad times sleep
> get up work. Sleep get up
> good times bad times.

The speaker, through an obsession with rote and routine, is trying to "fix reality and to fend off memory and desire" (Smith, "Sense-Making" 16). But memory is a plague:

> I don't remember the hard
> swallow of the lover.
> I don't remember the burial of ears.
> I don't remember
> the time of the explosion.

The over-protestation of the repeated "I don't remember" is given the lie by the particularity of things unremembered. The escape from the poem, as Ehrhart suggests, is through a reliance on "dreams, illusions and surreality."

> my monkey my beautiful
> monkey he saved me lifted
> me above the punji
> sticks above the mines
> above the ground burning
> above the dead above
> the living above the
> wounded dying the wounded
> dying.

That the language here mirrors the obsessive simplicity and redundancy of the poem's opening implies that the fantasy is not really much of an escape, and the speaker's repetitions are an attempt to nail down the fantasy *as* escape. The inherent irony is that the "monkey" is of course the Vietnam-war experience itself. "Weigl images the war as a monkey on his back—a tenacious memory, potent and insidious as a drug; a carnivalesque *Doppelgänger,* both intimate and repugnant" (Smith, "Sense-Making" 16). The closing lines of the poem reiterate the inescapability as well as futility of the Vietnam war, all wars.

> Men take hill away from smaller men.
> Men take hill and give to fatter man.

Men take hill. Hill has number.
Men run up hill. Run down. (15–19)

The linguistic redaction (its reductiveness) marks the ubiquity of the speaker's cynicism: Vietnam and America merge, the violence not brought home but rather found there. As Philip Beidler suggests, "our only hope of shaking the brutality is to keep trying to tell the monkey poem for as long as it takes us to get it right" (*Re-Writing* 197).

The mundanity of this marriage of violence and everyday existence can only be borne, Weigl suggests, through a faith in love and the lyrical. The book's title poem is set in a sleazy bar: a "skinny red-haired girl" with a "big mean boy friend" at the inevitable pool table "catches me staring, my lust like a flag." The speaker generalizes the scene with a lament at "wanting women I know / I'll have to get my face / punched bloody to love." The tone of habitual and despairing pathos is relieved, however, by the speaker's realization that he is only one of many: "the thousands of me / out on the town with our impossible strategies / for no good reason but our selves, / who are holy" (*Romance* 6–7). The important conflation here is the welding of self to holiness: the realization and acceptance of one's own worth and grace.

Without such faith, one is doomed, because the world Weigl paints outside the Vietnam war is an ambivalent wilderness rescued only by the lyrical impulse. In "Hand to Hand," for example, there is an extracurricular liaison between a basic trainee and his First Sergeant: "unable to sleep, he comes gentle like so much man, leads me past the fire guard, past fifty sleeping soldiers, pushes his bunk aside, pulls me and we dance and I learn hand to hand brothers, learn the places on the body that betray." This *may* be a rape, telegraphed by the phrases "so much man" and "places on the body that betray." But the speaker endures because the skills of hand-to-hand fighting may save him in Vietnam. And so the poem's ending sensations—"Close my eyes. Open them. Fall violently upward" (5)—imply that the speaker metaphorically "dies" here (the "Fall . . . upward") in order to avoid a literal death (now or later in Vietnam). There *is* a more obvious rape by a pederast:

I was seven and the man who played the trumpet
took me to the roundhouse
where he said the hobos slept,

. . . .

He made me take him into my mouth,
my face rose and fell with his hips

> and the sun cut through boxcars
> waiting to be emptied.   (29)

What enables the speaker to survive is the final image of the "sun cut[ting] through boxcars," a fantasy of rescue, perhaps. The more telling clue, however, is the title of the poem, "The Man Who Made Me Love Him," in the ambivalent choice of the word *love*.

The potential of love and lyricism as escape is dramatized in the poem "Anna Grasa" which describes a homecoming from Vietnam: Weigl's father had a huge metal sign made with "*WELCOME HOME BRUCE* / in orange glow paint / [with] rented spotlights." The speaker is aghast at the naked impropriety of the sign, given his inner feelings of guilt ("my eyes burned").

> But behind the terrible thing
> I saw my grandmother,
> beautiful Anna Grasa.
> I couldn't tell her, tell her.
>
> I clapped to myself,
> clapped to the sound of her dress.
> I could have put it on
> she held me so close,
> both of us could be inside.   (45)

The grandmother's name is transformed into a pun on *grace,* as in the colloquial "saving grace" as well as the more technically religious connotations of the word. The terror of the homecoming scene is *almost* negated by the refuge of Anna Grasa's love, but not quite; the speaker is unable to confess and thus achieve catharsis: "I couldn't tell her, tell her." But for now, for the needs of the moment, her love will suffice. The solace of lyricism is at least possible, if only for a moment.

The Monkey Wars: Bringing Vietnam Home

Ehrhart's complaint that Weigl, in *A Romance,* is "unwilling to confront the war directly" is ameliorated by Weigl's innovation in *The Monkey Wars,* given the context of other poets' use of their Vietnam-war experiences: an assumption and acceptance of responsibility transcending even the antiwar commitment of a poet like Jan Barry or Lamont Steptoe. Michael Casey and other Vietnam-veteran poets have implied that the American soldier was a sort of victim,

certainly active in the violence but also absolved to some extent by the failures of government and some sort of personal anesthesia. Weigl's poems in
The Monkey Wars include the speaker among the guilty, if only through the
penance of memory. The opening poem, "Amnesia," illustrates this sense of
responsibility:

> If there was a world more disturbing than this
> Where black clouds bowed down and swallowed you whole
> And overgrown tropical plants
> Rotted, effervescent in the muggy twilight and monkeys
> Screamed something
> That came to sound like words to each other
> Across the triple-canopy jungle you shared,
> You don't remember it.
>
> You tell yourself no and cry a thousand days.
> You imagine the crows calling autumn into place
> Are your brothers and you could
> If only the strength and will were there
> Fly up to them to be black
> And useful to the wind.   (*Monkey* 1)

Weigl's title here is ironic as well as wishful: a desire to forget about Vietnam
coupled with a concomitant drive to remember, once again to fly in innocence,
"to be . . . useful." Lorrie Smith claims that in this poem, "Vietnam has oblit-
erated the memory of a world before war" ("Sense-Making" 16); this reading
requires that the referent for the pronoun "this" in line 1 be Vietnam. There is
at least one other way to interpret the sense here. I propose that "this" in line 1
refers to America after the war and that the "world more disturbing" is Vietnam. The presence of the comparative adverb implies that not only the past is
disturbing, but the present also is, and it is disturbing precisely *because* of the
Vietnam war having happened (in general and to the speaker). Hence, in this
initial octave of an antisonnet, when the speaker claims "You don't remember
it," he is protesting that he has forgotten Vietnam. But the concrete force of
the description of this inwardly re-created Vietnam belies such "amnesia": the
speaker *cannot* forget. In both readings, Smith's and mine, the important point
is the inability to escape Vietnam. And this is clinched by Weigl's use of the
second person, an accusing finger pointing out that not only the speaker but
we as well "don't remember it"—recall Smith's notion that poetry by Vietnam veterans "dismantles the popular myth that we have regained our national

innocence [by admitting] that U.S. involvement in Vietnam was a mistake" ("Sense-Making" 14).

The acceptance of memory and hence guilt is the pivot into the closing sestet, which highlights the poet's (and our own) responsibility. The ultimate usefulness here is the poet's sacrifice, a determination to face once more the unfaceable "world more disturbing," to wrest from it some boon. The grim yet necessary responsibility: social and personal therapy. As introduction to *The Monkey Wars*, this poem emphasizes Weigl's project: to reintegrate himself into reality, into nature, "crows," "autumn," "wind." The last, as a metaphor for language, is his connection with us, the medium which reminds us of what we must never forget.

"[T]he task of the Vietnam writer [is] to create a landscape that never was," argues Beidler, "a landscape of consciousness where it might be possible to accommodate experience remembered within a new kind of imaginative cartography" (*American* 16). Michael Stephens describes Weigl's "cartography" as a "mythical and violent Midwest [and] a disruptive, war-gutted Vietnamese landscape" ("Combat" 149). Weigl's landscape is hard and elemental, where existence is a primal confrontation with a violent, indifferent world—in traditional terms, a masculine landscape.

Of course, Weigl's landscape is literally a "wordscape," and its salient features are those words he uses most, accreting into figurative escarpments, bluffs, skyscrapers, and mill stacks. Such an accounting of a poet's obsessive words can often be instructive, and so it especially is in *The Monkey Wars*.

The colors Weigl uses are restricted to basic ones: *red, yellow, green, blue, gray, brown*. No indigo here, and certainly no cyan or magenta, much less ochre or obsidian. His fancier colors are relatively plebeian: *olive drab, silver, scarlet, gold*. Of most note, however, is that *white* occurs 17 times, *black* 12 (as compared to the highest count for the colors named above: 7 for *blue*). Weigl's world is essentially monochromatic, with occasional brushstrokes of color.

Interestingly enough, although these strokes may describe "red sun" or "blue water," the sudden splashes of color in this drab landscape are not most often jungle blossoms or midwestern cornflowers, as one might expect, but birds. There are 7 references to the generic word *bird*, with a myriad of types mentioned: *gulls, crows, starlings, chickens, sparrows, herons, egrets, hawks,* and *doves* (and not the homo sapiens variety of the last two). Even monkey, so conspicuous in the book's title and also in *A Romance*, only appears 5 times, and 3 of those occurrences of the word are in a single poem.

It should come as no surprise, therefore, that of the four classical elements, *air* scores 17, while the *combined* total for *earth, water,* and *fire* only comes to 13. And *wing* occurs a whopping 19 times. Of other anatomical words, the most numerous pertain to the upper body: *face* 13, *head* 12, *eye* 11, *arm* 10, *hand* 10. And the words that describe upper-body functions are also numerous: *think* 16, *watch* 13, *see* 13, *sing* 13, *remember/recall* 13. An interesting phenomenon here is the ratio of incidental to deliberate actions: *see* 13 and *look* 2, *hear* 7 and *listen* 1. One inference may be that the poet, in Weigl's cosmos, is to some extent without choice—rather like Alex the droogie who is forced to watch horrific films in *Clockwork Orange*—yet the poet must observe, he must record and contemplate, for he will be asked to remember, ultimately to sing.

That this landscape is masculine is also demonstrable. *Man* occurs 11 times compared to 7 for *woman, boy* 10 to *girl* 8; the most telling, however, is 11 for *father* compared to 2 times for *mother*. The contrasts among Vietnam, America, and Europe are stark; men in America and Europe are farmers or industrial workers, while in Vietnam they are represented by a monk with a "charge / Wired between his teeth and the floor" (23); in Zagreb or Texas, "women thrash wheat" (9) or a "woman finish[es] her song" (27), but in Vietnam, they are a bar girl [with] terrible scars" (14), a "mama san . . . slam[med] to her knees" (26), and a "girl / Running from her village, napalm / Stuck to her dress" (46).

This last image is not an exception; the inanimate verb that occurs most often is *burn* (17 times). And of course references to *flares, fire, blaze, smoke, flame,* "crackling signs" (5) and "crackling / Muscles" (47). Despite this negative aura, however, there are *hope* and *mercy* and *beauty* and *laughter* here; most important, the word *love* appears 17 times compared to 7 for *hate*.

Daniel Guillory, in faulting Weigl for "not offer[ing] many startling turns of phrase" (64), has missed the point. Weigl has deliberately used a plain style so that the "penetrating images of death and suffering," which Guillory himself notes (64), will speak eloquently, without recourse to ornate language. Weigl limits his diction to a small vocabulary of "hard" Anglo-Saxon words as, I propose, an active resistance to the jargon stream, with its "incongruity [to] hide the reality of moral outrage," as Walsh puts it (206). As John Felstiner has proposed, "Washington's need was to sanitize reality and quarantine the fact from the word—precisely what much poetry avoids" ("American Poetry" 10). Weigl wants to reunite "fact" and "word," insisting on the most basic vocabulary, as common a denominator as possible (at what risk to his art, some critics may ask) in order to deflate jargon-stream terms like "kill ratio," "defoliant," and "pacification," to expose their true connotations.

The effective result of Weigl's limited diction is that the obsessive repetitions of the words themselves telegraph, as do repetend words in a sestina or refrains in a villanelle, the author's own obsessive relationship with the subject and thus the reader's need to pay attention. Weigl's recourse to a plain style, however, does not mean that he cannot "turn a startling phrase," as Guillory suggests. Weigl mixes etymologies: "pyramids of pipe"—Latin and Anglo-Saxon; "calligraphy of wings"—Greek and Anglo-Saxon; and "jungle of our indulgences"—Sanskrit and Latin (19, 22, 39). These three examples illustrate sophisticated sound effects, especially the last: assonance (j*u*ngle and ind*u*lgences) interwoven with consonance (the play of *j, l, n, d,* and *g* sounds).

Of course, the final judgment of this book must rest on the poems. The overall ambience of *The Monkey Wars* is an insoluble reagent of loss and hope, concocted in reaction to overwhelming despair. The titles themselves show this: "Song for a Lost First Cousin," "Song of the Lost Private," and "Small Song for Andrew." This last poem describes Weigl's son as "more beautiful / Than the light / Before the light has touched anything" (39)—lines which are indeed hopeful. But this is the high point; this is only a "Small Song," the title claims. More typical is "Song for a Lost First Cousin" which mourns the loss of childhood, the impossibility of continuing an innocent boys' relationship with a gay cousin.

> I couldn't tell you I remembered how we'd stripped:
> Beautiful boys in the shower at the public beach,
> The skin where your suit had been so white
> It burns my eyes to remember.
> Yet we let go now so carelessly
> The minutes break open as eggs
> And when I try to speak
> I only stutter, only lie.   (7)

Loss in the present is foreshadowed by loss in the past. In "Flight," Weigl describes his grandmother's first sight of an airplane in 1919 Zagreb; her father takes the frightened girl

> Into his arms to listen
> To the huge bird, the flight, the shadow
> Burned into wheat.   (9)

The harbinger of technowar, perhaps a World War I dogfighter, is seen as almost a natural phenomenon, but one which is a "dark shape eating air," and it *burns*. An elegy for Weigl's grandfather, "Killing Chickens," is set in

a pastoral Midwest which is already on its way to wasteland. "Red sun . . .
burning out / Past slag heaps of the mill" (15) is the backdrop against which
we see the grandfather's farm. In fact, the grandfather is himself a symbol of
the oncoming desolation of the American landscape.

> . . . In August he didn't feel the fly
> Come into his cancerous ear and lay its eggs.
> He didn't feel the maggots hatch
> As he sat dazed with pills in the sun.   (16)

Middle America in *The Monkey Wars* has fulfilled this prophecy in our own
present: an inferno of "the slag air . . . the flaming steel and the shitty bars /
And the steady grind of a mile of industry" is the setting for the poem ironically titled "Hope" (19). In "Noise," even suburbia—the isolationist refuge of
our century—has been affected.

> Next door the newlyweds
> Scream at each other, three A.M.
> I hate your fucking guts he says . . .   (33)

And finally we find that the wasteland extends even to the country—the mil-
lenial territory of Thomas Jefferson's chosen people, the yeoman farmers.
Hunting is no longer the countryman's heritage to his son; the "good boy" now
must "steal away" from his father to hunt an egret,

> Wiping out from the blue face of the pond
> What he hadn't even known he loved, blasting
> Such beauty into nothing.   (45)

Little hope for the future, it would seem, when even Andrew, Weigl's "son
[who] / Is strong and sure of himself" (29), may grow up to be such a boy—
a hunter who does not understand the intimate connection to quarry. We have
seen the failure of the mythic process of "regeneration through violence" in the
context of the Vietnam war; this poem dramatizes its failure in a post-Vietnam-
war America.

For Weigl, in both *A Romance* and *The Monkey Wars,* there is ultimately
no separation between the landscape of Vietnam and of America; in fact, the
equation extends even to the ancestral landscapes of Europe. This fusion is not
merely occurring within tortured memory; the landscapes are joined by vio-

lence. As Smith rightly argues, "The dark underside of Vietnam is finally . . .
a monstrous exaggeration and a logical extension of the more banal forms of
violence and moral depletion of home" ("Sense-Making" 16). Hence, even
though many poems in this collection do not expressly mention the Vietnam
war as such, they are all illuminated by a spectrum of violence—a spectrum
of minute gradations in which the war is not a different, separate violence but
only the most visible.

These gradations are highlighted by imagistic associations. The "biplane" in
Zagreb is the imagistic precursor to the Huey helicopter in Vietnam. The "fly /
Come into [Grandfather's] cancerous ear" is cognate to a variety of Vietnam-
war commonplaces: the intrusion of the war into American living-room TVs,
the "cancer" of dissension eating into even the bastions of the middle class, the
decay of discipline in the enlisted ranks (e.g., the many incidences of "fragging" in the war; the instances we have seen of atrocity and American soldiers
sliding into renegade primitiveness). The "good boy" hunting the egret, as
Smith has noted, "re-enacts a soldier's naive killing" ("Sense-Making" 17).

These subtle connections among Vietnam, America, and Europe allow Weigl
to evoke the incredible violence of the Vietnam war without the surrealistic
bloodshed or nihilism to which other Vietnam-veteran poets have resorted. To
avoid triteness and overstatement, and yet keep an almost journalistic sincerity,
Weigl roots his poems in realism and subtlety so that they speak softly as well
as forcefully for themselves. For example, "Temple Near Quang Tri, Not on
the Map" tells its muted but harrowing account in a realistic setting:

> Dusk, the ivy thick with sparrows
> Squawking for more room
> Is all we hear; we see
> Birds move on the walls of the temple
> Shaping their calligraphy of wings.

Mentioning "calligraphy" and "carved faces for incense" prepares us for the
monk who "Sits legs askew in the shadow" and is "bent over." Where another
poet may have resorted to gratuitous violence is in the climactic scene:

> We bend him to sit straight
> And when he's nearly peaked
> At the top of his slow uncurling
> His face becomes visible, his eyes
> Roll down to the charge

Wired between his teeth and the floor.
The sparrows
Burst off the walls into the jungle.   (22–23)

What is significant here is what is left out. We do not literally *know* if the booby
trap explodes; the narration's immediacy implies that the speaker is physically
present and close to the bomb. And Weigl makes no direct statement about
either the deviousness of the Vietcong in changing a priest into a bomb or the
callousness of the officer who "wants to ignore" the monk in obvious distress.
But the poem is eminently satisfying because of its emotional completeness,
its simple fluency, and the way in which the opening image of "sparrows /
Squawking" is brought full-circle into that soundless explosion of sparrows.

Smith has proposed that *The Monkey Wars* is "a darker view of the limitations of transcendent and redemptive imagination" ("Sense-Making" 16) and
that "lyric imagination utterly fails to ameliorate or transform the memory of
Vietnam" ("Sense-Making" 17). The seeming tragedy is that of the speaker of
"Burning Shit at An Khe," who regrets:

Only now I can't fly.
    I lay down in it
And finger paint the words of who I am
    Across my chest
Until I'm covered and there's only one smell,
    One word.   (11)

We are reminded of the earthbound speaker of "Amnesia." In "Noise," it is
not only the speaker caged in by the "triangle" of the dramatic scene ("me,"
"newlyweds," and "trainmen"); Weigl himself and by extension all of us seem
trapped by the triple conspiracies of history, of time, of place—Vietnam,
America, Europe—the entire human world:

A triangle of nervous noise
Because the noise in my head too,
The noise is always in my head.   (33)

And the "noise" is not limited *within* the confines of *The Monkey Wars*.
Stephens argues that the book's "violent moments . . . are used to unmask and
to articulate our troubled emotions" ("Combat" 150), eventually pointing to
our own complicity in violence.

I propose, however, that Weigl *does* offer us hope. Smith may be too ready to attest to "the limitations of a lyric response to Vietnam" ("Sense-Making" 14). She closes her argument by citing the poem "Song of Napalm" in which Weigl, sharing a pastoral moment with his wife, remembers a running girl smeared with flaming napalm. The speaker attempts to transform the image:

> So I can keep on living,
> So I can stay here beside you,
> I try to imagine she runs down the road and wings
> Beat inside her until she rises
> Above the stinking jungle and her pain
> Eases, and your pain, and mine.

But the poet finds that "the lie swings back again" because "The lie works only as long as it takes to speak." The girl, forever ablaze, falls

> Into that final position
> Burning bodies so perfectly assume. Nothing
> Can change that; she is burned behind my eyes
> And not your good love and not the rain-swept air
> And not the jungle green
> Pasture unfolding before us can deny it.   (46–47)

The important aspects of Weigl's method to remember here are the sense-laden vibration of air and breath at the end of each poem, as in the exploding sparrows of "Temple Near Quang Tri," and the subtle way connections among Vietnam, America, and Europe are drawn, strings of silence which pierce the white space surrounding each poem. If we listen to the echoes at the end of "Song of Napalm," we see that the horrible image which dominates the poem cannot be supplanted by love and the lyrical, but what is unsaid yet subtly important is that the image of the burning girl does not itself *deny* the "good love" of wives and husbands and children; "good love" nevertheless exists and flourishes. The lines "So I can keep on living, / So I can stay here beside you," and "But the lie swings back again" imply that lyric imagination fails; but Weigl nonetheless *does* "stay here beside" his wife. And *does* continue to write poems, failure of lyricism or no.

Smith assumes that, in more than a decade of writing and publishing poems on Vietnam, "Weigl cannot finally shake his monkey" ("Sense-Making" 17). I suggest that the failed lyric impulse Smith has observed may be part of the artful surface of *The Monkey Wars* and that the vigorous subtext here is an ongoing war with the "monkey"—with no surrender in sight. Although the speaker who is "Burning Shit at An Khe" can only see his own self as "one smell, / One word," Weigl as poet fights such nihilism with his basic, obsessive vocabulary. This grounding in the hardy roots of language may still rescue lyricism; in *The Monkey Wars,* Weigl comes very close indeed to learning once more to fly with the crows of the poem "Amnesia" and therefore to be human. Smith is correct in pointing out that he "guards against the peculiarly American habit of denying history" ("Sense-Making" 18), but Weigl is also fighting a battle to save the enterprise of poetry as something redemptory and "once more useful to the wind." *Song for Napalm,* a collection of his previous Vietnam-related works with eleven new poems, is evidence of Weigl's continuing battle.

Song of Napalm: "Through All That Green Dying"

James Scully's distinction between *protest poetry* ("conceptually shallow . . . issue-bound . . . reactive, victim-oriented, incapacitated") and *dissident poetry* (which "breaks silences . . . opening poetry up, putting it in the middle of life" to connect "social empowerment and valorization and human definition" [5]) is upheld by Weigl's fifth book, *Song of Napalm.* The development of Weigl's work on the Vietnam war has been precisely a movement from *protest* to *dissident* poetry, and the totality of *Song of Napalm* stands as dissident poetry in contrast both to the protest poetry written by earlier Vietnam-veteran poets and to Weigl's own earlier poems on the war. The witness to this is that Weigl is finally able to overcome the ever-present difficulty of earlier poets: how to portray the absurdity and horror of Vietnam without sacrificing lyrical aesthetics. As we have seen through the examples of Michael Casey or Bill Shields, one solution is to eschew traditional lyricism and develop an antipoetry. Weigl succeeds in solving the problem of *poetically* depicting the Vietnam war without concomitant romanticization.

The poem "LZ Nowhere" demonstrates Weigl's aesthetic method.

> Nights I spent on the dusty runway
> under the green liftship
>
> tethered down from the wind of the highlands
> shaping the moonlit field
>
> surrounding us like care.
> I stroked the length of the blades

> those nights
> and moved the rudder and flaps
>
> so it felt like legs parting
> or someone's arms opening to me.   (*Song* 40)

The mixture of machine and sex as an outgrowth of technologically based machismo, imaged repeatedly in chopper gunships and Phantom jets, is evoked
here through the phrasing of "stroked the length of the blades" and "legs parting / or someone's arms opening to me." But the fantasy here is ultimately a
masturbatory one, hence the title "LZ Nowhere," an indicator that the speaker
is lost, despite the relative calm of the scene. Any possibility of hope or solace
or comfort offered by the closing lines is finally an empty promise. Empty
precisely because of the situation: that the liftship's blades *are* blades, that is,
the machine is in fact a weapon. And the sterility of this weapon becomes an
eloquent synecdoche for the ultimate uselessness of war.

  Song of Napalm recombines the Vietnam-war poems from *A Romance* and
The Monkey Wars into a new configuration beyond the original orderings, inter-
spersed with new poems. Divided into three sections entitled "Sailing to Bien
Hoa," "Song of Napalm," and "The Kiss," the overall movement of the book
is roughly equivalent to the emotional development of a soldier in Vietnam:
the loss of innocence and romanticism (the surreal hopefulness of the poem
"Sailing to Bien Hoa") in the cauldron of the 'Nam; the ambiguities and ironies
inherent in the return to the World (imaged through the cynicism and despair
voiced by the poem "Song of Napalm"); and the synthesis and possibility of
hope implied in "The Kiss." This poem conflates leaving for Vietnam with
childhood memory and future salvation. The departure is set in winter, and the
speaker shivers from the cold and "ached / to be away from the love / of those
waving" their goodbyes—then Weigl spins the memory:

> (Once as a boy I was lost in a storm,
>   funnel cloud twisting so near
>   I was pitched from my bicycle
>   into the ditch,
>   picked up by the wind and yellow sky,
>   my arms before me
>   feeling my way through the wind
>   I could not cry above.
>   Out of that black air of debris,

out of nowhere, my father bent down,
lifted me and ran
to the house of strangers.)

Weigl evokes a particularly American brand of innocence by rewriting *The Wizard of Oz*. The innocent does not return home (as Dorothy does in the movie) only to find that the house is empty and about to be swept up into the tornado of history. Instead, the father bears him to safety at a "house of strangers." This complex of allusion and implication points variously to the anticlimactic homecoming of the typical Vietnam veteran as well as to the dangers inherent in a "house of strangers"—in this case, being a foreign interloper in what is actually a civil war. On the day of departure, the speaker is again saved by his father:

on my lips he kissed me hard
and without a word he was gone
into the cold again.
Through the jungle, through the highlands,
through all that green dying
I touched my fingers to my lips.   (68–69)

What creates the margin of safety in the childhood memory as well as in the Vietnam-war tour is the father's literal and remembered presence. The duplicate fantasies of escape in the poem reify into an actual escape through "all that green dying."

This image of the father is different from Weigl's earlier portraits of fathers in poems. In "Fourth of July: Toledo, Ohio," two fathers are shown: next door, the "twelve-year-old kid screaming, / holding up one burnt mangled thumb" has a father who "looks up from the barbecue / and spits out his cigar in disgust." One inference may be that this macho response, tied to patriotism, is in large part to blame for American involvement in the Vietnam war. And so it is telling that "My people are no different: / the old man is inside / listening to Wally and the Walleyes / jam to the 'Beer Barrel Polka' " (*Romance* 4). In "Song of Identities," the speaker's father is set up as closed-minded, unable to reconcile his son's marriage to an Asian American (in other words, an *enemy*):

My father, a good man,
can't look my wife in the face.

> She's Japanese. He was in that war
> on a boat dumping fire
> into people's kitchens.   (*Romance* 40)

The poem "Homage to Elvis, Homage to the Fathers," despite the implications of its title, portrays fathers as ambivalent heroes metaphorically martyred: "our fathers died / piece by piece among the blast furnace rumble" and "Watch workers pass as ghosts" (*Monkey* 41). "Snowy Egret" presents a neighbor boy whose "hard father's / Fists I've seen crash down on him" (*Monkey* 45). Attitudes toward fathers in Weigl's earlier work are at least ambivalent, if not negative. Thus, the wholly positive portrayal of the father in "The Kiss" is an index of hope, of the loss of cynicism. And the kinesthetic playing out of this optimism is entirely fitting, "through all that green dying / I touched my fingers to my lips," as if the father's imprint is not on the spirit or the mind, but rather on the flesh: the physical remembrance of the kiss as well as the father's marking of the son's life through the heritage of DNA.

The final poem, "Elegy," both demonstrates the complete apotheosis of a dissident poetic and also upholds the success of the lyric imagination, not necessarily in ameliorating the experience of the Vietnam war but in celebrating the beauty inherent in the act of remembrance itself. The poem sets up an elegiac tone without glossing over realities.

> Into sunlight they marched,
> into dog day, into no saints day,
> and were cut down.
> They marched without knowing
> how the air would be sucked from their lungs,
> how their lungs would collapse,
> how the world would twist itself, would
> bend into the cruel angles.
>
> Into the black understanding they marched
> until the angels came
> calling their names,
> until they rose, one by one from the blood.
> The light blasted down on them.
> The bullets sliced through the razor grass
> so there was not even time to speak.
> The words would not let themselves be spoken.

> Some of them died.
> Some of them were not allowed to.   (*Song* 70)

One difference between this poem and much earlier Vietnam-veteran poetry
(including Weigl's earlier poems) is the focus on "sunlight" as opposed to the
green gloom of the jungle's triple-tiered canopy. In this sunlight—emblematic perhaps of post-Vietnam-war certainties about the moral malfeasance of
America in the war—the dying is unmistakable. Weigl's brilliant play on language here is the transformation of "angles" to "angels": from the cruelty of a
useless death not understood to a faith in salvific possibility. The crucial close
of the poem implies the optimism offered by distance—emotional, spatial,
temporal—from the Vietnam war. "The words would not let themselves be
spoken" *then*. But since this is *now*, and there are those "who were not allowed
to [die]," the implication is that these survivors have the duty to speak the unspeakable, to right the wrongs. It is possible to read the line "Some were not
allowed to" in a negative sense, calling attention to the difficulties encountered
by Vietnam veterans who returned. I propose instead that Weigl succeeds here
in finding a "light at the end of the tunnel" of cynicism: a purpose and a final
grace. Such affirmation of life and of expression and truth is, after all, the
ultimate purpose of a true dissident poetry.

EIGHT. YUSEF KOMUNYAKAA: "DEPENDING ON THE LIGHT"

Dien Cai Dau is Yusef Komunyakaa's fourth book of poems. Unlike Bruce Weigl, he had not included a single poem on the Vietnam war in his earlier three books because he had been waiting for emotional distance—objective and journalistic—from his 1969–70 Army tour there. George Garrett, in his foreword to D. C. Berry's *saigon cemetery,* proposes that "ordinary judgment [of Berry's poems] must be suspended. We are too close, and the wounds and scars, literal and metaphorical, are too fresh" (viii). It is just such a suspension of judgment that Komunyakaa does *not* want; he wishes his work to be tested with the full rigor applied to all serious literature.

The fact that Komunyakaa waited fifteen years to publish poems on Vietnam differentiates his work significantly from that of other veteran poets, especially those who published in the early 1970s. The difference is not so much that he has achieved a distance from his Vietnam-war experience but rather that the development of his craft has not been inextricably bound up with the Vietnam war, unlike Ehrhart, for example. Komunyakaa comes to this subject with an academic grounding in modernist and contemporary poetics as well as classic surrealism, and his work registers an aesthetic advance not only of poetry about the Vietnam War but also of war literature in general.

An earlier version of *Dien Cai Dau* featured an epigraph from Tim O'Brien —"Imagination is a killer"—a statement which aptly characterizes these poems. Komunyakaa writes on the high wire of language, sans net. He balances clichés ("gung-ho" officers, "Jody," "Shangri-la") against surprises (Viet Cong prisoners "like / marionettes hooked to strings of light" and "Afternoon sunlight / [making] surgical knives out of chrome / & brass). He juggles elite references ("Buddha" and "Björn Håkansson") with popular culture ("Bob Hope" and the "Donut Dollies"). Having survived the killing fields of Imagination, Komunyakaa gives us the irreality which is Vietnam.

Walking Point Toward *Dien Cai Dau*

From his first chapbook in 1977, *Dedications and Other Darkhorses,* through his third full-length book, *I Apologize for the Eyes in My Head,* published in 1986, Komunyakaa's forte has been the counterbalancing of seeming oppositions and incongruities. In his 1984 collection, *Copacetic,* he links the French poet Villon with Leadbelly the blues singer, calling them "two roughhouse bards." Villon and Leadbelly have been "canonized by ballads / flowering into dusk, crowned with hoarfrost," and by the end of the poem, we learn that their true link is being "strung out on immortality's rag" (*Copacetic* 37). The point is clear: these two artists, so separate in century and in reputation, are really quite inseparable when we consider the "bottom line"—the immortalizing quality of art. No matter present categories of rarefied elitism or pedestrian popularity.

In a long poem entitled "1984" in *I Apologize,* Komunyakaa writes, "We laugh behind masks & lip-sync Cobol" (38)—a sentence that brings Eliot's *Waste Land* or Yeats's "Second Coming" home to roost. The phrase "lip-sync Cobol" evokes resonant associations—the mentality of MTV and game-shows, alienation via technology, and our own complicity in contemporary senselessness. Komunyakaa makes the line work by yoking the unyokable; it is after all literally impossible to lip-sync Cobol, much less speak it. But to "lip-sync Cobol" is to abrogate the human and identify with or idolize the machine—a singularly apt comment on our times.

Komunyakaa's method of crunching together the dissimilar works at several levels: in the poem as a whole (as we see in "Villon / Leadbelly"), within a strophe, or even within a line. But the most interesting occurrences are the most compressed—diction. In "1984," the lines "listening all night to a calliope / hoot the equinox" aptly demonstrate this compression (*I Apologize* 39). Etymologically, the phrase is constructed from Anglo-Saxon roots ("listen" and "hoot"), the name of a Greek demigoddess (Kalliope, the Muse of heroic poetry), and the Latin borrowing "equinox." In terms of denotative collocation, "calliope" and "equinox" announce an elevated lexicon as opposed to the more quotidian "hoot." The connotational ambience of these words, finally, imparts charm and sense to the phrase; since we hardly expect a "calliope" to "hoot," our attention is drawn to the word "equinox." Bearing Yeats and Eliot in mind, we realize that our time is one of transition—a verging revolution, a cusp for which we "listen all night." The waiting of the desperate and the powerless, the waiting for Godot, so to speak.

But perhaps the most striking aspect of Komunyakaa's work is the desperate

and rapacious drive of his imagination. The poem "Death Threat Note" from
his 1979 book, *Lost in the Bonewheel Factory,* is a good example.

> Dear Poetry Editor,
> why did it have to
> come to this?
> Walk out any door
> & you will never know.
> Turn any doorknob
> & open the butcher shop.
> The rocking chair rocks by itself.
> A cat paces the windowsill;
> The moon's followed you home.
> Another set of footprints
> surfaces in new snow.
> At any moment
> a steel door slams
> & locks a man in an icehouse.
> In a recurring dream
> I see Weldon Kees' car
> parked on the Golden Gate Bridge.
> I've fallen deeply in love
> with a woman's lovely hands
> on death row. Listen, a knife
> can heal your mouth.
> It's no good to fall
> pointing to the North Star,
> moaning the color of foxfire.
> The meat-wagon runs off
> the road. I do not give warnings.   (*Lost* 33)

On a certain level, this poem is universally appealing as a kind of wish fulfillment; replace for yourself the words "Poetry Editor" with "foreman," say,
or "drill sergeant," or even "department chair." This poem, like all wish-
fulfillment fantasies, is a relatively harmless exercise—except for the tone
which develops in the poem. As it unfolds on the page, we see an almost anaphoric repetition of paranoia and fear. We begin to identify with the plight of
the poor "Poetry Editor" who looks constantly over either shoulder. Normally
innocuous objects—rocking chairs, a cat, the moon, footprints—take on a

deadly aspect. The mystery makes a more overtly dangerous turn: images of steel doors, icehouses, death row, and the meat wagon. No one will know what happened to us, just as no one knows whether Kees actually committed suicide or maybe spent his last years sunning himself on some beach in Mexico. The entire piece is a progression of images, building one upon the other to set the requisite paranoiac mood for the final ironic note, "I do not give warnings." Ironic because of course the whole poem is itself a warning, but a complex one which both warns and assaults by causing such irrepressible anxiety. Ultimately, the accretion of imagined versions of the single threat clinches the poem's argument. The line "The rocking chair rocks by itself" is essentially cognate to "I've fallen deeply in love / with a woman's lovely hands / on death row," but the later line contains the additional subtext: *it doesn't matter what happens to me any more.* Komunyakaa accomplishes this advance of extractable meaning through the juxtaposition of fiercely imagined fragments in a sequential collage.

Reviewers have misunderstood both the import and the rationale of Komunyakaa's montage approach to lyricism, mistaking his surrealistic fragments as, at worst, obfuscation, and at best, a mere "taking on of airs." Rochelle Ratner, reviewing *Copacetic* for the *Library Journal* in March 1984, proposed that "Komunyakaa . . . attempts to be too 'hip' " (494). In October 1987, Matthew Flamm reviewed *I Apologize* for the *New York Times Book Review;* although he admired Komunyakaa "at his best—fierce yet mysterious," Flamm complained that "sometimes [the poems'] obscurity seems no more than hip poetic posturing" (24). In his Vietnam-war book, *Dien Cai Dau,* Komunyakaa finds a different way to imagine fiercely, avoiding any stance that might be taken as "posturing." Flamm also claimed that Komunyakaa "works . . . with an intense distrust of any sort of conventional knowledge" (24); in his Vietnam-war poems, Komunyakaa mines the body of conventional knowledge to make the poems accessible to more readers.

The development of Komunyakaa's Vietnam-war poems dramatizes his odyssey in the writing of *Dien Cai Dau* from an earlier devotion to an intricate surrealism to the accessibility he would need to accommodate the Vietnam war as subject. A useful example is the poem "Losses," published in *Indiana Review* in 1987, and the following year in *Dien Cai Dau.* The earlier version contains forty-five lines, trimmed down to twenty-seven. Some lines from the earlier version:

> Scouting the town's skyline,
>
> He lingers at the flighty edge like a deer;

> always with one ear cocked
> & ready to retreat,
> to blend in with hundreds of greens & golds
> plaguing the hills, poised to
> give in like the slipknot
>
> of a delicate trap rigged against odds.   ("Losses" 154)

And the revised lines in the *Dien Cai Dau* version:

> & now hc scouts the edge of town,
> always with one ear
>
> cocked & ready to retreat,
> to blend with hills, poised
> like a slipknot
> becoming a noose.   (*Dien Cai Dau* 61)

What Komunyakaa edits out is a certain brand of lyricism and metaphor. The reference to the Vietnam vet on "the flighty edge like a deer" is perhaps too judgmental, calling attention to both the antisocial and the animalistic. The phrase "hundreds of greens and golds / plaguing the hills" (while the word "plaguing" may illuminate the vet's avoidance of beauty) is itself too beautiful, too evocative, still too resonant of the pastoral. Replacing "a delicate trap rigged against odds" with "a noose" makes use of the reader's conventional connotations at the same time that it concretizes the "delicate trap." Komunyakaa's method of revision is made even clearer by comparing the tercet

> away from car horns & the landscape of crooked
> things dancing against a neon backdrop
> redder than backfire or blood   ("Losses" 155)

with the resultant revision, "away from car horns & backfire" (*Dien Cai Dau* 61). Again the movement is toward the more concrete and away from the surreal, allowing more of the reader's everyday life and associations to come into play. Other revisions throughout *Dien Cai Dau* are revealing. The title "Like Something from Fellini" is transformed into the readily accessible "Nude Pictures." One poem which does not make it into *Dien Cai Dau* is "Ia Drang Valley," probably because it relies too much on esoteric information: the speaker, a soldier in Vietnam, identifies his own situation with Goya's painting *The*

Third of May, "where I'm shoved against the wall / with the rest of the mute hostages" and "I stand before the bright rifles, / nailed to the moment" (145). Although the poem strikes significant chords of ideology and loss, the Goya connection becomes finally too distant from the ordinary veteran's experience.

While the poems destined for *Dien Cai Dau* were being annealed and purified into their essential narratives, Komunyakaa published a chapbook of Vietnam-war poetry, *Toys in a Field* (1986). Several of the poems in this collection would later end up in *Dien Cai Dau:* " 'You and I Are Disappearing,' " "A Greenness Taller Than Gods," and "Facing It," for example. The interesting thing to note, however, is which poems do *not* reappear in the later full-length collection. One fascinating poem, "Water Buffalo," is told from the viewpoint of the animal who sees himself as "Hung belly, hooves, & asshole, / everything pushing against my bulging eyes. / . . . like a brass foghorn lingering over a river of fire." The water buffalo perceives himself as embattled by an "iron bird . . . with stars falling from its mouth," a "whirlwind machine . . . / hammering the sun gong." The story ends with the bull killed by "silver lances," realizing "Bullheaded dynamo that I am, / I am no match for their fire, / for what's in their hearts" (*Toys* 7–8). Again we have the contrast between technowar and nature, approached in this poem from an unusual and fresh point of view.

In "Le Xuan, Beautiful Spring," the speaker, a Vietnam veteran, accidentally finds "her photograph / torn from a magazine & folded / inside *Sons and Lovers.*" This mystery woman, "in her translucent *ao dai,*" surrounded by "women / wearing fatigues," elicits ambivalent thoughts: other figures in the photograph call her " 'goddamn trouble maker. // Bluestocking,' " but nevertheless "soldiers undress her / behind dark aviation glasses." At the moment of identification, Komunyakaa paints her in surreal imagery:

> Madame Nhu delicate as a reed
> against a river, just weighing the gun
> in her hand? Didn't a blood-tipped lotus
> take root in the torn air? (*Toys* 14)

The ambivalence focused by this poem is intense, an electric interaction of memory, lust, and disillusionment.

In both of these poems, Komunyakaa is still operating in a fiercely imagined and stylized world of charged, almost vortexlike, imagery and sensation. In *Dien Cai Dau,* he moves away from such fireworks and takes up a more reportorial voice, balanced against his characteristic surrealism in order to find a way to convey the commonplace and the bizarre in the Vietnam-war experience.

Dien Cai Dau: **Crazy, an American Soldier**

Its title coming from a Vietnamese phrase signifying "crazy," a label projected onto American soldiers in Vietnam, *Dien Cai Dau* is an odyssey through the Vietnam of memory, with the entire panoply of characters we might associate with the war: the tunnel rat, Hanoi Hannah, enlisted men planning a fragging, "a girl still burning / inside [the] head," Buddhist martyrs, bar girls and mama-sans, Bob Hope, the POW and the MIA, the short-timer, Jody, Boat People, the Amerasian child, the vet turned hermit, the mother who does not accept her son's death, dead grunts, and of course those who returned to the World. These poems are as strikingly lyrical as Komunyakaa's previous work, but in a less manneristic way; the language is similarly toned down in order not to distract from the message. And the poems are more narrative than others of Komunyakaa's oeuvre, lending each depicted scene a slightly journalistic or documentary flavor.

Komunyakaa's characteristic method of balancing opposites and the incongruous is rooted in French surrealism. Critics of surrealism have pointed to "The poet Isidore Ducasse, the 'comte de Lautréamont,' who . . . had provided the classic example in writing of 'the chance encounter of a sewing machine and an umbrella on a dissection table' " (Rubin 19), a serendipitous yoking in whose interstices an immanent, wholly startling signification can well. Komunyakaa has inherited this mode of juxtaposition from the Surrealists, specifically through the poet Aimé Césaire. A typical example is "2527th Birthday of the Buddha":

> When the motorcade rolled to a halt, Quang Duc
> climbed out & sat down in the street.
> He crossed his legs,
> & the other monks & nuns grew around him like petals.
> He challenged the morning sun,
> debating with the air
> he leafed through—visions brought down to earth.
> Could his eyes burn the devil out of men?
> A breath of peppermint oil
> soothed someone's cry. Beyond terror made flesh—
> he burned like a bundle of black joss sticks.
> A high wind that started in California
> fanned flames, turned each blue page,
> leaving only his heart intact.
> Waves of saffron robes bowed to the gasoline can.　(18)

This poem takes as its base a kind of journalistic language, and of course the seed of the piece is the rumor that the heart of a self-immolated monk literally had not burned, a rumor perhaps gleaned from an actual news story. But the poem quickly moves into the contrapuntal surrealistic plane with "the other monks & nuns . . . like petals," setting up a group of images: petals, leaves, and finally pages, reminding us of Holy Writ. (And the phrase "terror made flesh" of course vibrates for Christian readers.) But the Komunyakaa wrinkle here is how the political situation is mystically manifested—American collusion made evident by the "high wind that started in California." The astonishing final image juxtaposes "saffron robes" with "the gasoline can," succinctly summing up the Vietnam war that arises from this volatile situation: "the gasoline can," a harbinger of technology which emblematizes violence and death, becomes a new deity, and all the saffron robes will be ultimately consumed.

Komunyakaa's surrealism varies from that of the other veteran poets' because he does not depict Vietnam itself or the Vietnam-war experience as *literally* surreal, as do many of the other poets. Surrealism has been defined as "the attempt to actualize *le merveilleux,* the wonderland of revelation and dream, and by so doing to permit chance to run rampant in a wasteland of bleak reality" (Gershman 1); in other words, the exploration of the strange, through fortuitous juxtaposition, allows revelation to occur in the midst of the real. Through surrealism, Komunyakaa *discovers*—or perhaps more appropriately, *reveals*—Vietnam and does not only document its *apparent* surreality for an incredulous audience. The book's opening poem, "Camouflaging the Chimera," enacts this process of revelation. The scene is of an ambush where "We tied branches to our helmets. / We painted our faces & rifles / with mud from a riverbank." The soldiers imagine themselves as invisible and still— "We wove / ourselves into the terrain"—almost as if they are made of earth or rock—"Chameleons // crawled our spines, changing from day / to night: green to gold, / gold to black." When the Vietcong come on the scene, they are less attuned, less at one with the earth than these soldiers: "VC struggled / with the hillside, like black silk // wrestling iron through grass." Surrealism in this poem does not function to present Vietnam to the reader as exotica, but rather to underline the existential reality of ambush: the internal psychic state of each combatant. The wish fulfillment of camouflage involves *becoming* the landscape, abdicating one's memories and anything else which might disrupt the illusion—"The river / ran through our bones. Small animals took refuge / against our bodies." The angst of the situation, the impending firefight, is focused by the closing lines "a world revolved / under each man's eyelid" (3– 4)—a revamping of the cliché "my life passed before my eyes." Of course, the phrase also refers to "the world" or everything not Vietnam, delineating each combatant's acute realization that he does not *belong* in this place, that his death here would be literally senseless. The dramatic situation of this poem also acts certainly as a signifier for the entire war, and thus the word "Chimera" in the title serves as a political statement.

The poem " 'You and I Are Disappearing' " (a quote from Björn Håkansson) is a bravura performance highlighting Komunyakaa's technique of juxtaposed images.

> The cry I bring down from the hills
> belongs to a girl still burning
> inside my head. At daybreak
>   she burns like a piece of paper.
> She burns like foxfire
> in a thigh-shaped valley.
> A skirt of flames
> dances around her
> at dusk.
>   We stand with our hands
> hanging at our sides,
> while she burns
>   like a sack of dry ice.
> She burns like oil on water.
> She burns like a cattail torch
> dipped in gasoline.
> She glows like the fat tip
> of a banker's cigar,
>   silent as quicksilver.
> A tiger under a rainbow
>   at nightfall.
> She burns like a shot glass of vodka.
> She burns like a field of poppies
> at the edge of a rain forest.
> She rises like dragonsmoke
>   to my nostrils.
> She burns like a burning bush
> driven by a godawful wind.   (17)

Here, Komunyakaa is performing what he calls "the kind of intellectual wrestling that moves and weaves us through human language." According to

Komunyakaa, "language is what can liberate or imprison the human psyche" (Gotera, " 'Lines' " 220, 225), and this poem dramatizes a speaker who is simultaneously liberated and imprisoned. The speaker here is at a loss to describe this scene fittingly. The charged language grapples with a view that is both unimaginably beautiful and incredibly horrible, all at the same time. The speaker, again and again, tries to find a metaphor that will convey both the beauty and the horror—the dilemma of speaking the Sublime, in Edmund Burke's terms. And the speaker comes enticingly, asymptotically close without finding the ideal phrase. Finally, he simply has to stop. And the final image points a biblical finger: the girl will always burn in the speaker's mind in the same way that the burning bush could have burned forever unconsumed. What really nails this image is the phrase "godawful wind" which puns on "awful God," straight out of the Old Testament, while it resurrects the root meaning *full of awe,* or more properly here, *filling with awe.*

" 'You and I Are Disappearing' " also demonstrates Komunyakaa's poetic ancestry in English, specifically William Carlos Williams and his use of the image. Just as Komunyakaa has been influenced by the Surrealists, Williams had been influenced by Cubist art. Marjorie Perloff notes that Williams's "*Spring and All* lyrics . . . provide verbal analogues of . . . Cubist fragmentation and superposition of ambiguously located planes" (182). In many of these poems, Williams's "images do not carry symbolic weight; they point to no external sphere of reality outside themselves," Perloff writes. "Rather, items are related along the axis of contiguity. . . . In a larger sense, the whole book constitutes just such a field of contiguities. Williams's recurrent images— wind, flower, star, white, dark—are perfectly ordinary, but it is their *relationships* that matter" (186–87). If we ignore for a moment that the signified is "she"—a human being—Komunyakaa's images here are similarly ordinary: "a piece of paper," "oil on water," a "cigar," "a shot glass of vodka," "a field of poppies"; others are lexically more interesting but still reasonably innocent: "foxfire," "a sack of dry ice," "a rainbow," "dragonsmoke." As with Williams's images, it is the "*relationships* that matter"; what drives this poem is the anaphoric repetition of "she burns"—the accretion of which underlines the intrinsic horror of the poem and, by extension, the war itself. The ultimate focus is on humanity and on humaneness.

Many of the poems in *Dien Cai Dau* deal with human response and connection in combat. "Nude Pictures" begins at the end, "I slapped him a third time," only implying the story which comes before: a squad blown up by a booby-trapped girlie magazine, leaving one man who screams and laughs hysterically, drawing rescue troops

> to him like a marsh loon
> tied to its half-gone song
> echoing over rice fields
> & through wet elephant grass
> smelling of gunpowder & fear.

In "2527th Birthday of the Buddha," the typical Komunyakaa opposition is the documentary vs. the figurative; here the conflict is between nature and human intrusion. The morning shattered by the booby trap's concussion "came back together like after / a stone has been dropped through a man's reflection / hiding in a river." The "stone," a semaphore for the explosion, intrudes upon the harmony between human beings and nature—here, the squad and the morning. Now the hysterical soldier intrudes upon the reassembled morning, "like a marsh loon / tied to its half-gone song" (that is, nature gone mad).

The final human intrusion occurs in the arresting closing line: "Lifted by a breeze, / a face danced in the treetops." Literally, of course, this is a wafting scrap of a nude picture, with the face coincidentally framed. On a figurative level, however, the image finally rescues humanity; the lexical territory of "lifted" and "danced" argues for an upbeat ending here. Just as the speaker and the sole surviving soldier hold hands—"He grabbed my hand & wouldn't / let go" (25)—("only connect," as E. M. Forster tells us) so too are human beings and nature harmoniously reunited, if only metaphorically. And yet, such reunion can last only a moment in the murkiness of this war; in this poem, *vision* seems somehow hampered, and *hearing* becomes the predominant sense. Steven Cramer extends this point: "If visual murkiness is Komunyakaa's metonym for the blurred moral outlines of all wars, *Dien Cai Dau* is also charged with the Vietnam veteran's peculiarly anguished knowledge of *this* war's moral ambiguities" (103).

Komunyakaa's devotion to a highly textured language is clearly evident. There are arresting turns of phrase throughout *Dien Cai Dau:* a tunnel rat moves "Through silver / lice, shit, maggots, & vapor of pestilence" (5); the Vietcong are "lords over loneliness / winding like coralvine through / sandalwood & lotus" (8); conspirators plan a fragging, "their bowed heads / filled with splintered starlight" (16); an armored personnel carrier is "droning like a constellation / of locusts eating through bamboo" (19). For the most part, however, the language of *Dien Cai Dau* is a spoken language, in the Wordsworthian sense—it is the extraordinary way in which these everyday words are combined which makes the poems significant.

As Michael Casey does in *Obscenities,* Komunyakaa uses the grunt's language and speech for credibility. In "Hanoi Hannah," however, he places the argot in the mouth of the enemy, to demonstrate the ambivalent ambience of Vietnam; the poem begins with the disembodied voice of Ray Charles "call[ing] from waist-high grass, / & we duck behind gray sandbags." Hannah's voice greets the soldiers:

> "Hello, Soul Brothers. Yeah,
> Georgia's also on my mind."
> . . . .
> "It's Saturday night in the States.
> Guess what your woman's doing tonight.
> . . . .
> "Soul Brothers, what you dying for?"

It is interesting to note here that Hannah speaks not just colloquial English, but fluent black English; her speech is so well-tuned as to be virtually indistinguishable from the American voice who says "Let's see if we can't / light her goddamn fuse / this time." That Komunyakaa is African American generally makes little difference for many poems in *Dien Cai Dau,* but in this poem it is significant because blacks (and hence the poet) are being directly addressed here. Hannah plays Ray Charles and Tina Turner, speaks to "Soul Brothers," and taunts them with Martin Luther King, Jr.'s assassination—"You're dead / as King today in Memphis"—it may well be the speaker's first realization of that event. As this poem shuttles between reported speech and narrative passages, it displays a seamlessness of diction, unlike that of earlier Vietnam-veteran poets like Basil Paquet, who deliberately embattles one set of connotations against another for tension. Here, the everyday diction—"duck behind," "light her fuse," "Howitzers buck like a herd / of horses"—is allowed to rest easy with slightly more elevated phrases—"Artillery / shells carve a white arc," Hannah's "knife-edge song," "We lay down a white-klieg / trail of tracers." But the salient point here is Hannah's intimate command of English and the social nuances conveyed by language.[1] Within the poem's narrative, the soldiers sending Mad-Minute fire and steel outward into the night imagine Hanoi Hannah "falling / into words, a bleeding flower," but her final parting shot—"You're lousy shots, GIs"—underlines her ascendance. The close of the poem transforms Hannah into a chthonic presence: "Her laughter floats up as though the airways are / buried under our feet" (14).

The plight of the veteran home from the war is handled by Komunyakaa differently from other Vietnam-veteran poets, and this variance arises partly from questions of race. Throughout *Dien Cai Dau,* black soldiers remember a different Vietnam: Vietcong leaflets saying, *"VC didn't kill / Dr. Martin Luther King"* (47); the white bars and the black bars on "Tu Do Street" in Saigon (29); the black POW remembering "those rednecks" in Georgia, " 'Bama," and Mississippi to help him through enemy torture (42). But other poems focus more universally on the generic returnee. The poem "Combat Pay for Jody" brings clichés to life, focusing on a soldier and his inevitable encounter with Jody (the folkloric figure back home who "steals" the combat soldier's wife or girlfriend); throughout his tour in Vietnam, the speaker survives because of the memory of his girlfriend: "the molten whistle of a rocket / made me sing her name into my hands." The testimony of a "grunt" for whom the thought of his lover functioned as a chivalric favor preserving him from harm is so common that it becomes apocryphal.

> Her lies saved me that year.
> I rushed to the word
> *Love* at the bottom of a page.
> One day, knowing a letter waited,
> I took the last chopper back to Chu Lai,
> an hour before the firebase was overrun . . .

Similarly apocryphal are the stories of Jody's legendary exploits. Upon the speaker's return "to Phoenix, the city hid her / shadow" and her "used-to-be" tells him, " 'It's more, man. / Your money bought my new Chevy' " (50). In "Combat Pay for Jody," Komunyakaa has composed a vividly lyrical narrative which encompasses the 365 days of the speaker's Vietnam tour and his eventual return to the World. More important, he has created a realistic voice which reenlivens the overworked clichés of military life and which points up the returning soldier's inability to navigate in what used to be his private landscape.

The Vietnam Veterans Memorial, as we have seen, has become an emblem of the readjustment difficulties of the Vietnam veteran, and Komunyakaa's poem "Facing It" (the closing poem in the book) does exactly what its title says—face the monument and what it signifies.

> My black face fades,
> hiding inside the black granite.
> I said I wouldn't,
> dammit: No tears.

I'm stone. I'm flesh.
My clouded reflection eyes me
like a bird of prey, the profile of night
slanted against morning. I turn
this way—the stone lets me go.
I turn this way—I'm inside
the Vietnam Veterans Memorial
again, depending on the light
to make a difference.
I go down the 58,022 names,
half-expecting to find
my own in letters like smoke.
I touch the name Andrew Johnson;
I see the booby trap's white flash.
Names shimmer on a woman's blouse
but when she walks away
the names stay on the wall.
Brushstrokes flash, a red bird's
wings cutting across my stare.
The sky. A plane in the sky.
A white vet's image floats
closer to me, then his pale eyes
look through mine. I'm a window.
He's lost his right arm
inside the stone. In the black mirror
a woman's trying to erase names:
No, she's brushing a boy's hair.   (63)

This poem is literally a reflection about reflections; it is a "facing" of the dualities that govern this everyday life: there and here, America and Vietnam, living and dead, night and day, old and young, white and black. Komunyakaa does not declaim, does not decry; instead, he presents, practically unmediated, a series of images. Like the speaker of " 'You and I Are Disappearing' "—the poem about the burning girl—the poet here is faced with an ineffable scene, but instead of searching for apt metaphors to voice his feeling, he reverts to a reportorial mode. Everything ultimately is point of view, and we are always "depending on the light / to make a difference." This is what Vietnam-war poetry (and all poetry in essence) *must* do—enlighten, give light, illuminate, the better for all to see and see well.

Dien Cai Dau is a breathtakingly original work of art because of the believable, down-to-earth language which speaks the thoughts and feelings of authentic characters, filtered through Komunyakaa's atypical vision. In the last line of *Dien Cai Dau*—a book whose title means "crazy"—a woman is "brushing a boy's hair," an action which affirms sanity and life in the face of the insanity of the war: the love between a mother and child, between two human beings. Writing about Weigl's *The Monkey Wars,* Smith proposes the *potential* of a "salvific poetic vision which might unify past and present, anguish and affirmation" ("Sense-Making" 17). Komunyakaa fulfills this promise in *Dien Cai Dau.* As Weigl does in *Song of Napalm,* Komunyakaa accomplishes a true dissident poetry.

Critical response to *Dien Cai Dau* has been strongly favorable. Cramer asserts that "Komunyakaa makes a major contribution to the body of literature grappling with Vietnam—a poetry that pierces the artificial border between moral and aesthetic engagement" (105). Wayne Koestenbaum argues that *Dien Cai Dau* "renders a kind of experience so extreme it seems to forbid a merely esthetic response" (50) and is "filled with such unsentimental cameos, powerful because foreshortened" (51); he complains, however, that "foreshortening . . . is an ambiguous murky process [which] mystifies the events it seems to describe so lucidly" (51). I submit that this murkiness, this mystification, is part of the Vietnam-war experience, and that Komunyakaa is precisely rendering this slippery indeterminacy.

Komunyakaa's achievement points to the possibility and actuality of self-renewal and solace in poetry by Vietnam veterans. As the body of poetry by veterans moves from mere documentary to self-discovery and personal commitment, from a gratuitous surrealism to a conscientious use of academic surrealistic techniques, future work by Vietnam-veteran poets becomes increasingly able to transcend the paralyzing horror of the Vietnam war. "The true work of the poet after our war," suggests Beidler, is to locate "moments of reflexive epiphany [and] articulate out of such moments the new text of creative supplementation wherein the imagings of history and myth can be contained within some new order of redemptory vision, some whole new poetry of ongoing life" (*Re-Writing* 182). Perhaps, despite evidence to the contrary in the events of the Gulf war, it may be possible to wish with Ehrhart (and Beidler) that JFK's declaration " 'When power corrupts, poetry cleanses' " ("Soldier-Poets" 265) can be more than mere rhetoric.

CONCLUSION.
RADICAL VISIONS EXTENDED

The "radical vision" that Vietnam-veteran poets have developed in order to re-view Vietnam and the war is also shared by Vietnam-war poets who were Vietnam-*era* veterans (service members who served during the war but were not sent to Vietnam) as well as by nonveterans who are intimately knowledgeable about the war—Americans who were either civilian workers in Vietnam or those who are "co-sufferers" of PTSD with Vietnam vets in the immediate family (recall Bill Shields's trope of the child with Agent Orange mutations as a Vietnam vet). Poems which share this radical vision often also break into the three prosodic modes we have noted—antipoetic, cathartic, and aesthetic.

One example is Bryan Alec Floyd, who was in the Marine Corps but never served in Vietnam. According to W. D. Ehrhart, Floyd's "poems are apparently based on interviews with numerous Vietnam veterans, and they ripple with authority" ("Soldier Poets" 252). With sections named after various fictional Marines, Floyd's book *The Long War Dead* is a type of *Spoon River Anthology* set in the war. The poem "Private First Class Brooks Morgenstein, U.S.M.C." portrays, with rare vision, a grunt's retreat into daydream about his wife, a daydream which reaches surrealistic heights:

> He only knew as he held his rifle
> during a sweeping operation
> that next year he would hold her,
> and when he kissed her,
> his tongue would touch hers
> and she would feel
> as though a piece of the sun
> was in her mouth.
>
> . . . .

> During the bad times,
> such as when the platoon was ordered to torch a village,
> he would feel his rage deepening,
> without bottoming out,
> and he would be shaking with fear and shame and ecstasy
> that he was still alive.
> He would make himself think of her,
> and with the thirst that comes from drinking of it,
> his lust would grow and become exalted
> like a great tree,
> and he knew if he made it back
> she could climb his body
> and that he with branches would cover her with himself
> and they would be unable to tell
> how much of him was him
> and how much of him was her.   (61–63)

Continually implied in Floyd's work is his critique of the war. "Floyd's poems have marvelous range," Ehrhart writes, "giving voice to those who supported the war and those who detested it, lashing out with equal vehemence at American generals and North Vietnamese diplomats, the antiwar movement and the failed war." Ehrhart's praise of Floyd is superlative: "He succeeds, like no other poet I know of, in offering the full breadth of feelings and emotions of those who fought the war" ("Soldier Poets" 252). This particular poem offers a surreal brand of catharsis in the grunt's epiphanic merging with his wife—a revitalization of Edenic myth, sans snake.

Another example is Lady Borton, who was sent by the American Friends Service Committee to Vietnam in 1969 to be assistant director of the Quaker refugee programs in Quảng Ngãi, a provincial capital in central Vietnam, for a two-year period. In 1980, she then returned to Southeast Asia for a six-month period as health administrator of a refugee camp housing Vietnamese boat people on Pulau Budong, an island in the South China Sea off the coast of West Malaysia. Borton's memoir, *Sensing the Enemy,* addresses this experience with frequent flashbacks to her 1969 to 1971 stay in Vietnam. She also returned in 1990 to work in Vietnam.[1]

Borton's poem "A Boom, A Billow" demonstrates her personal development of "radical vision." New in Vietnam, she carries a stance of "uninvolved objectivity" while watching "sleek jets" on bombing runs in the far distance; what she hears and sees is similarly distanced: "A boom. / A billow of dark gray smoke. / Napalm." That afternoon, however, she learns her first lesson when she meets a victim of such bombing runs, a boy who "had no nose, / only two holes in the middle of his face. / His mouth was off to the side," the skin on his face and body all "shiny red scar tissue." The most striking detail (from the perspective of the World) is reserved for last:

> One hand was partly usable,
> the fingers of the other,
> soldered to his wrist.
> Napalm.   (*Visions* 13)

This bipartite poem, a "before / after" or "then / now" configuration, is punctuated by the two utterances of the word "Napalm." In the first stanza, the tone of the poem is one of indifference, a reliance on American myths of the government's honesty; the second stanza unfolds in a matter-of-fact way which may superficially seem indifferent but which is finally involved in profound political ways. The antipoetic straightforwardness of Borton's presentation is part of the poem's deliberate art, dramatizing the speaker's (and the poet's) awakening to social responsibility, the demands of a historicized consciousness, and the failure of American myths.

Another example of a nonmilitary veteran who evinces this "radical vision" is John Balaban, a conscientious objector who performed his alternative service in Vietnam as a teacher; Ehrhart has written of Balaban that "he is as much a veteran of Vietnam as any soldier I have ever met" ("Soldier Poets" 250). His poem, "After Our War," underlines his "radical vision":

> After our war, the dismembered bits
> —all those pierced eyes, ear slivers, jaw splinters,
> gouged lips, odd tibias, skin flaps, and toes—
> came squinting, wobbling, jabbering back.
> The genitals, of course, were the most bizarre,
> inching along roads like glowworms and slugs.
> The living wanted them back, but good as new.
> The dead, of course, had no use for them.

Such a nightmare vision necessitates, finally, that we ask some very tough questions, questions which address the very nature of the war and finally of the American government and of American character:

> After the war, with such Cheshire cats grinning in our trees,
> will the ancient tales still tell us new truths?
> Will the myriad world surrender new metaphor?
> After our war, how will love speak?   (16)

In this poem's concern with aesthetics, an interrogation of old myths ("the ancient tales"), we find a self-reflexive questioning of the usefulness of the aesthetic as an ingress to "radical vision," wherein Americans—hawks and doves alike—are offered the possibility of understanding the ramifications of the Vietnam war, both on a personal as well as a national level.

The question of how to accomplish this is familiar to Vietnam-veteran poets who have wrestled with their poetry, occasionally to the edge of their poems' destruction as poems. The actuality of the Vietnam war—its surreal absurdity, its mangling of language, and the incredible variety of literary (and other artistic) responses to the war—has opened up the space for truly postmodern language, narrative, and representation. "This first terrible postmodernist war cannot be told in any of the traditional paradigms," Fredric Jameson observes, calling attention to the "breakdown of all previous narrative paradigms [and] the breakdown of any shared language" (84). Poetry by Vietnam veterans, in its assumption of a "radical vision," suggests that it may be possible to bypass these breakdowns. But in order to be supremely effective, "the poetry of the Vietnam war," as Cary Nelson has suggested, "must consequently risk more, openly contend with its coeval public history, and court its own formal dissolution" (10). Such a dissolution of the necessity for their poetry of witness and warning is clearly the driving desire of each of these Vietnam-veteran poets.

NOTES

Introduction

1. Seven anthologies of war poetry which cover a wide range of times and cultures (including gender) are *Where Steel Winds Blow,* edited by Robert Cromie; *War and the Poet,* edited by Richard Eberhart and Selden Rodman; *Scars Upon My Heart: Women's Poetry and Verse of the First World War,* edited by Catherine W. Reilly; *Chaos of the Night: Women's Poetry and Verse of the Second World War,* also edited by Catherine W. Reilly; *The Penguin Book of First World War Poetry,* edited by Jon Silkin; *The Oxford Book of War Poetry,* edited by Jon Stallworthy; and *The War Poets,* edited by Oscar Williams.

While Stallworthy includes some poems on the Vietnam war, there are several anthologies which are devoted to Vietnam alone: *A Poetry Reading Against the Vietnam War,* edited by Robert Bly and David Ray; *Where Is Vietnam?* edited by Walter Lowenfels; and *War Poems,* edited by Diane di Prima. African American perspectives are not adequately represented in these collections; see *Vietnam and Black America,* edited by Clyde Taylor—this anthology contains not only poetry but fiction and sociopolitical commentary as well. To date, there has been no anthology of Vietnam-war poetry by other ethnic groups. Poetry has also been occasioned by the war in countries other than the United States. An interesting publication, for example, is Edward Kissam's *Vietnamese Lessons*—a small booklet of found poetry from "a U.S. Army Handbook of Vietnamese Phrases"—published in London in 1970 while America's involvement in Vietnam was ongoing.

Vis-à-vis poetry by Vietnam veterans, there have been six major anthologies: *Winning Hearts and Minds,* edited by Larry Rottmann, Jan Barry, and Basil T. Paquet; *Demilitarized Zones,* edited by Jan Barry and W. D. Ehrhart; *Peace Is Our Profession,* edited by Jan Barry; *Carrying the Darkness,* edited by W. D. Ehrhart; *Unaccustomed Mercy,* edited by W. D. Ehrhart; and *Visions of War, Dreams of Peace,* edited by Lynda Van Devanter and Joan A. Furey. These are cited in the text by a shortened form of the title.

It had been my purpose, at an earlier stage of this book, to present within this study at least one poem by every Vietnam-veteran poet. But there is such a large and continually growing body of poems that my earlier intention has not proved practicable. Instead, I will provide here a list of poetry collections out of which I have not quoted within my text: R. L. Barth, *Looking for Peace* (1981, 1985), *Simonides in Vietnam and Other*

Epigrams (1990); Bill Bauer, *The Eye of the Ghost* (1986); H. W. Bingaman, *Reckonings* (1988); Robert Borden, *True Tales and Tall* (1992); Timothy Clover, *The Leaves of My Trees, Still Green* (1970); Horace Coleman, *Between a Rock and a Hard Place* (1977—poems used from this chapbook are cited by reference to their appearance in *Unaccustomed Mercy*); Frank A. Cross, Jr., *Reminders* (1986); Jabiya Dragonsun, *Hit Parade* (1989); W. D. Ehrhart, *A Generation of Peace* (1975, 1977), *Rootless* (1977), *Empire* (1978), *The Awkward Silence* (1980), *The Samisdat Poems of W. D. Ehrhart* (1980), *Matters of the Heart* (1981), *Channel Fever* (1982), *The Outer Banks and Other Poems* (1984), and *Winter Bells* (1988—poems used from these Ehrhart volumes are cited by their appearance in *Winning Hearts and Minds, To Those Who Have Gone Home Tired,* and *Just for Laughs*); Harvey D. Fletcher, *Visions of Nam* (1987); Zook Gaffney, *Eating Little Dogs During the Revolution* (1978); Andrew Gettler, *Only the Mountains Are Forever* (1987), *Zen and the Art of Perfect Desire* (1990), *Footsteps of a Ghost* (1991), and *lurid dreams . . . because we all have them* (1991); Jim Gray, *War Poems* (1986); J. Vincent Hansen, *Blessed Are the Peacemakers* (1989); Terry Hertzler, *The Way of the Snake and Other Poems* (1985); Warren Hope, *An Unsuccessful Mission* (1983); Allston James, *The Mile Away Contessa* (1977); G. P. Johnson, *I Was Fighting for Peace, But Lord, There Was Much More* (1979); Cranston Sedrick Knight, *Tour of Duty* (1986); Yusef Komunyakaa, *Dedications and Other Darkhorses* (1977), *Premonitions of the Bread Line* (1980), *Copacetic* (1984), *February in Sydney* (1989), and *Magic City* (1992); Norman Lanquist, *Angels* (1987); Serge Lecomte, *Crimson Rice* (1990); Walter McDonald, *One Thing Leads to Another* (1978), *Anything Anything* (1980), *Working Against Time* (1981), *Witching on Hardscrabble* (1985), *Rafting the Brazos* (1988), and *Splitting Wood for Winter* (1988—poems used from these McDonald chapbooks are cited in the full-length books in which they appear: *After the Noise of Saigon, Burning the Fence, Caliban in Blue and Other Poems, The Flying Dutchman,* or *Night Landings*); Richard P. Magdaleno, *Vietnam Rose* (1971); John Musgrave, *On Snipers, Laughter and Death: Vietnam Poems* (1993); Michael Robert Pick, *Childhood/Namhood/Manhood* (1982); Stan Platke, *Antietam to Vietnam* (1974); Sandy Primm, *Short Time* (1977); Doug Rawlings, *Survivor's Manual* (1982); Robert Schlosser, *The Humidity Readings* (1981); Richard C. Schulze, *Leatherneck Square* (1989); Bill Shields, *We Killed Like Champions* (1986), *Where I Live* (1986), *Nam Poems* (1987), *Sparks of Hell* (1987), *Post Vietnam Stress Syndrome* (1988), *Post Vietnam Stress Syndrome II* (1988), *Post Vietnam Stress Syndrome [III]* (1989), *Winners and Other Losers* (1989), and *Human Shrapnel* (1992); Paul D. Shiplett, *Dog Ears* (1979); Stephen Sossaman, *A Veteran Attends a July Fourth Barbecue* (1982); Lamont B. Steptoe, *Crimson River* (1984, revised 1989); B. D. Trail, *Flesh Wounds* (1989); Bruce Weigl, *Executioner* (1976) and *A Sack Full of Old Quarrels* (1976—poems used from these chapbooks are cited by their appearance in *A Romance, The Monkey Wars,* or *Song of Napalm*). That these titles and poets appear in this note instead of in the book proper is not meant as a comment on the quality of the poems; the needs of the study simply could not allow for quotation from all of them.

There has also been increasing interest in Vietnam-veteran poetry by journals. *DEROS,* a poetry journal devoted to Vietnam veterans, was published from 1981 to 1987 by editors Lee-Lee Schlegel and Ken Rose. *Chiron Review*'s Spring 1991 number focused on poetry by vets: Kevin Bowen, David Connolly, Jabiya Dragonsun, W. D. Ehrhart, Andrew Gettler, Jon Forrest Glade, Steve Mason, James Soular, Lamont B. Steptoe, and B. D. Trail. As editor of the Spring 1992 issue of *Owen Wister Review* (from the University of Wyoming), Jon Forrest Glade published poems by W. D. Ehrhart, Bill Shields, B. D. Trail, and David A. Willson. With Theresa Brown of the University of Chicago, I edited a thematic issue of the *Journal of American Culture* on the poetry of the Vietnam war, published in Fall 1993. This issue contains poems as well as critical essays. The journal *Viet Nam Generation,* with Bill Shields as a contributing editor, continues to publish poems by Vietnam veterans.

Two Vietnam-war poets who were not military veterans should be noted here: John Balaban and Elliot Richman. Balaban's collections of poetry not quoted from include *Vietnam Poems* (1970), *Blue Mountain* (1982), and *Words for My Daughter* (1991). Richman's collections include *Blastin' Out of Abilene* (1988) and *Fucking in Stupid Hope* (1989).

An interesting project is the American Poetry Press's series of *Vietnam Heroes* and *Vietnam Poems* volumes, containing poems (and sometimes prose) by Vietnam veterans and "friends of veterans": Jocelyn Hollis, ed., *Vietnam Poems: The War Poems of Today* (1983) and *Vietnam Poems II: A New Collection* (1983); J. Topham, ed., *Vietnam Heroes: A Tribute* (1982), *Vietnam Heroes II: The Tears of a Generation* (1983), *Vietnam Literature Anthology: A Balanced Perspective* (1984—contains poems by R. L. Barth); *Vietnam Heroes III: That We Have Peace* (1985), and *Vietnam Heroes IV: The Long Ascending Cry: Memories and Recollections in Story and Poem* (1985).

Also of note is *Viet Nam Flashbacks* (1984)—an anthology of poetry, fiction, and other writing, edited by Jim Villani et al., and published by Pig Iron Press in Youngstown, Ohio. A selection of Vietnam-war poetry is also contained in Nancy Anisfield's *Vietnam Anthology* (1987).

Three bibliographies that are helpful in locating creative literature related to the war are *Vietnam War Literature* by John Newman with Ann Hilfinger (1988); *Writing About Vietnam* by Sandra M. Wittman (1989); and *American Women Writers on Vietnam* by Deborah A. Butler (1990).

2. Korean-war veterans have not produced a significant body of poetry; Keith D. McFarland's *The Korean War: An Annotated Bibliography,* for example, lists thirty-three novels arising from the Korean war, but no poetry.

3. One of the earliest personal narratives, *GI Diary,* was written by an African American veteran, David Parks, but it was not originally well-received by critics. Perhaps since it was published in 1968, when the Tết Offensive first began to escalate public opinion against the war, the literary climate may not have been ready for *GI Diary.* Two more recent oral history collections about African American experience in the 'Nam are *Brothers: Black Soldiers in the Nam,* by Stanley Goff and Robert Sanders, and *Bloods:*

An Oral History of the Vietnam War by Black Veterans, edited by Wallace Terry. Two significant milestones in the collection of Vietnam-war memoirs by minority veterans are Charley Trujillo's *Soldados: Chicanos in Vietnam* and Peter Nien-Chu Kiang's article, "About Face: Recognizing Asian and Pacific American Vietnam Veterans in Asian American Studies." Collecting oral histories from other minority groups—especially Native American veterans—is a project that still needs to be taken up.

Oral history collections that survey Vietnam veterans in general include *Nam,* edited by Mark Baker; *Life on the Line: Stories of Vietnam Air Combat,* edited by Philip D. Chinnery; *Conversations with Americans,* edited by Mark Lane; *Strange Ground,* edited by Harry Maurer; *Everything We Had,* edited by Al Santoli; and *To Bear Any Burden,* also edited by Al Santoli. Corinne Browne's *Body Shop* documents soldiers' experiences and memories as they convalesce in an Army hospital.

Besides the memoirs already mentioned—Caputo's *A Rumor of War;* Kovic's *Born on the Fourth of July;* and O'Brien's *If I Die in a Combat Zone*—other conventional narratives include *Brothers in Arms: A Journey from War to Peace,* by William Broyles; *Once a Warrior King,* by David Donovan; *Line Doggie: Foot Soldier in Vietnam,* by Charles Gadd; *And a Hard Rain Fell,* by John Ketwig; *Chickenhawk,* by Robert Mason; *Where the Rivers Ran Backward,* by William E. Merritt; *Welcome to Vietnam, Macho Man,* by Ernest Spencer; *Phantom Over Vietnam: Fighter Pilot, USMC,* by John Trotti; and *The Courageous and the Proud,* by Samuel Vance. Two high-ranking officers who have published memoirs are David Hackworth (*About Face*) and William Westmoreland (*A Soldier Reports*). A trilogy that deserves special note is W. D. Ehrhart's set of memoirs: *Vietnam-Perkasie, Marking Time* (later republished as *Passing Time*), and *Going Back.* Two military physicians have also published Vietnam-war-related memoirs: *365 Days,* by Ronald J. Glasser and *12, 20 and 5: A Doctor's Year in Vietnam,* by John A. Parrish.

Personal narratives by female Vietnam veterans had been neglected until Lynda Van Devanter published her memoir *Home Before Morning* in 1983. Collections of interviews include *Home Front: Women and Vietnam,* edited by Barthy Byrd; *In the Combat Zone,* edited by Kathryn Marshall; and *A Piece of My Heart,* edited by Keith Walker. Lady Borton (not a military veteran, but decidedly a veteran of Vietnam, having served there with the American Friends Service Committee from 1969 to 1971 and returning to Southeast Asia in 1980 and 1990) has published a memoir, *Sensing the Enemy.*

Besides Michael Herr (*Dispatches*), journalists—photographers and correspondents —have published memoirs and collections of personal narratives, including *Nothing, and So Be It,* by Oriana Fallaci; *Page After Page,* by Tim Page; *Bitter Victory,* by Robert Shaplen; *The Doom Pussy,* by Elaine Shepard; *The Bad War,* by Kim Willenson; and a memoir focusing on combat photographers Sean Flynn and Dana Stone entitled *Two of the Missing: A Reminiscence of Some Friends in the War,* by Perry Deane Young. Fiction writer James Jones published a reportorial memoir, *Viet Journal.*

There have been memoirs written by Vietnamese and Vietnamese Americans, including *Our Endless War,* by Tran Van Don; *When Heaven and Earth Changed Places,* by Le Ly Hayslip; and *A Vietcong Memoir,* by Truong Nhu Tang. Oral histories include James M. Freeman's *Hearts of Sorrow: Vietnamese-American Lives,* Lesleyanne Hawthorne's *Refugee: The Vietnamese Experience,* and Joanna C. Scott's *Indochina's Refugees: Oral Histories from Laos, Cambodia and Vietnam.*

Collections of documents include *Dear America: Letters Home from Vietnam,* edited by Bernard Edelman, and *Vietnam Voices,* edited by John Clark Pratt. The Vietnam Veterans Memorial has also been the focus of attention: *Facing the Wall,* by Duncan Spencer, and *Shrapnel in the Heart,* by Laura Palmer. Another interesting sidelight is the topic of antiwar soldiers and veterans: *GIs Speak Out Against the War,* by Fred Halstead; *The New Soldier,* by John Kerry; and *The Winter Soldier Investigation,* published by the Vietnam Veterans Against the War. The journal *Viet Nam Generation* published a special issue on this topic in 1990: *GI Resistance: Soldiers and Veterans Against the War,* edited by Harry W. Haines.

4. Virak Khiev, "Breaking the Bonds of Hate" (8). This article is significant because its author is a young Cambodian immigrant to America who, at nineteen, is too young to remember the Vietnam war itself but for whom its reverberations and repercussions are nevertheless inevitable: "In America, . . . we don't have to live in the jungle like monkeys, we don't have to hide from mortar bombing and we don't have to smell the rotten human carrion. But for the immigrant, America presents a different type of jungle, a different type of war and a smell as bad as the waste of Cambodia" (8). Virak Khiev's scathing indictment of post-Vietnam-war America demonstrates how inextricably interrelated are the realms of the 'Nam and the World.

5. Kalí Tal, publisher of the journal *Viet Nam Generation,* has argued against the danger of a "total reduction of war to metaphor" (223), a fault she finds in the work of Hellman, Beidler, Myers, and also in James C. Wilson's *Vietnam in Prose and Film:* "to see Vietnam War literature as a continuing process of signification [so that when] the war becomes sign (and therefore not war) we won't have to think about it anymore" (219). Tal's approach is to see the war as "a devastating reality—a series of events taking place on a physical rather than symbolic level" (224). Tal's position is well-taken, but aren't war survivors who encounter "devastating reality" on a "physical level" also unavoidably forced to deal with these events on a "symbolic" plane, either in recollection or in retelling? That the process of symbolization or even signification is an inevitable consequence of working through the experience in memory (and myth)?

6. Vera Brittain is only one poet among a great number of women writers; Nosheen Khan in her study, *Women's Poetry of the First World War,* lists sixty-three women writers on WWI (182–87). Khan's bibliography also notes several anthologies of women's war poetry, including *One Hundred of the Best Poems on the European War By Women Poets of the Empire,* edited by Charles Forshaw, published while WWI was being fought. Catherine Reilly's anthology *Scars Upon My Heart* surveys seventy-nine female WWI poets—both British and American.

7. As she did in *Scars Upon My Heart,* Catherine Reilly has recovered the canon of WWII women poets via *Chaos of the Night,* an anthology which features the poems of

eighty-seven women—all British. Although there is at present no comparable American anthology, the contributions of American women to WWII poetry are addressed
by Susan Schweik's *A Gulf So Deeply Cut: American Women Poets and the Second
World War*.

8. I am grateful to Susan Schweik for the hint in her article "A Needle with Mama's
Voice: Mitsuye Yamada's *Camp Notes* and the American Canon of War Poetry" that
female poetry from the Japanese internment camps will serve as good comparison texts
with poetry by women in WWI and WWII as well as in the Vietnam war. See also
"Toyo Suyemoto and the 'Pre-Poetics' of Internment" and "Identity and Contestation
in Nisei Women's War Poetry," chapters 6 and 7 of Schweik's *A Gulf So Deeply Cut*.

A note about the pagination of Yamada's *Camp Notes:* in "A Needle with Mama's
Voice," Schweik cites page 29 for the poem "Cincinnati"; in *A Gulf So Deeply Cut*,
however, Schweik indicates that "*Camp Notes* is unpaginated" (340n); my version of
Camp Notes has "Cincinnati" on pages 42–43. The copyright page in my *Camp Notes*
indicates three separate printings in 1976, 1980, and 1986—as well as three separate
copyrights by Yamada, also in 1976, 1980, and 1986—evidently these three "printings"
are actually different *editions* with variations in content.

Chapter One. The Wild West Revisited

1. Excerpted from a travel brochure (San Francisco: Pacific Area Travel Association,
n.d.).

2. Kolodny quotes here from Walter Raleigh's "Discovery of Guiana" (1595), as
quoted by Howard Mumford Jones in *O Strange New World*, p. 48; from Robert Johnson's "Nova's Brittania" in Peter Force, *Tracts*, 1:11; and from John Smith, "A Description of New England," in Force, *Tracts*, 2:9.

Chapter Two. Machine in the Jungle

1. I borrow the term "technowar" from James William Gibson's *The Perfect War*.
Gibson's thesis, with which I concur, is that technocratic warfare already contained
and predicated America's defeat in the Vietnam war. Loren Baritz, in *Backfire*, agrees
wholeheartedly with Gibson and points to the hallowed position technology holds in
America's national mythic structure, as emblematized by the cultural image of "Yankee
ingenuity, American knowhow. . . . the tinkerer whose new widget forms the basis
of new industry is nowhere better shown than in our national reverence of Thomas
Edison" (44).

2. Westmoreland's text—a speech he gave to the Association of the U.S. Army on
October 14, 1969—may be found in its entirety as appendix A of *The Electronic Battlefield* by Paul Dickson (217–23). Interestingly, Dickson points to the visionary tone of
the speech as "the violent and hardware-heavy violent equivalent of Martin Luther
King's nonviolent 'I Have a Dream' speech" (71–72).

3. The mechanization and computerization of the Vietnam war grew to such a furi-

ous pitch in the Pentagon that technological proposals soon became patently ludicrous. Dickson records how a plan was tested "to train munitions-carrying pigeons to land on North Vietnamese trucks where they would explode on touchdown." They scrapped the plan, however, when they "discovered that pigeons could not be taught to distinguish a communist truck from a noncommunist truck" and they feared that the North Vietnamese might train their own pigeons, so that "a Red pigeon might intercept an American one and escort it to the nearest parked helicopter (which could only be American or South Vietnamese)." Another experiment, called the "Lava plan," sought "to find the right chemical mixture that could be dropped on the Ho Chi Minh Trail and turn the damp soil to grease (the right mixture was never found)." Engineer Stanley Hirsch describes a particularly humorous proposal: "Did you hear about the sensor we came up with in the shape of a dog turd? Well it was about the size of your thumb and really looked like a turd. We figured that they'd be good on the Ho Chi Minh Trail where trucks and troops would make contact with them. . . . We called it TURDSID because it was a Seismic Intrusion Detector or SID. There was one big problem with it, however, and that was that after a lot of work had gone into it we discovered that there weren't any dogs running around on the Ho Chi Minh Trail so it was later reconfigured to look like a small piece of wood" (Dickson 36–38).

4. For a fuller account of the bureaucratic snafu concerning the M-16, see Baritz (239) and Doleman (40).

5. Secretary Robert McNamara argued that "speed and mobility were essential because a traditional army could not be everywhere it needed to be in a contest with irregular fighters. Air mobility would compensate" (Baritz 254). The official Army line was that "the capacity of the enemy, whether guerrilla or NVA, to apply his doctrines of hit-and-run tactics, surprise, and mobility, could be severely cramped by the helicopter"; in addition to its direct combat role as a gunship, the chopper could serve as "troop carrier, gun tractor, supply van, scout and command ship, and medevac vehicle" (Doleman 38).

6. This feeling of merging with machinery is attested to by pilots in particular. Jet pilot John Trotti recalls: "Before I had been essentially childlike in my love for flying; now I was a precision instrument of destruction to whom flying was an unquestioned but minor skill. I was the weapons system, with a twenty-five ton monster as an extension of my will" (137). That this statement was used as a blurb on the back of the hardback edition of Trotti's memoir makes an interesting comment on the market audience, or at least on the publisher's views on the book's potential readers.

7. Army chopper pilots genuinely cultivated this cultural image, often carrying revolvers, as in Don Receveur's Wild Bill "(Hickok / with a 38 in his armpit)" ("Cobra Pilot," *Winning* 49). *Chickenhawk* pilot Robert Mason inched his own image even further into western myth by carrying "a double-barrel derringer as a secret, last-ditch weapon" in a holster hand-tooled by a Navy boatswain's mate in trade for "a couple dozen folding P-38 can openers from our C rations" (49, 61). Not only the dandy gambler's weapon but the ancient art of barter as well.

8. Cincinnatus (a pseudonym protecting the identity of an Army historian) docu-

ments that planning a "heliborne" attack first begins with helicopters conducting "aerial reconnaissance of the proposed battle area to select primary and alternate landing zones" followed by "a thirty- to forty-five-minute artillery and air bombardment, known as the 'preparation' of the LZ" (75–76). Gibson notes that, before this bombardment could proceed, artillery "had to be 'sighted-in' or 'registered' on the target [which] created high visibility for American forces: 'This registration begins with a high smoke streamer or smoke round, both of which are easily recognizable in the jungle' " (Lt. Col. James R. Ray quoted by Gibson, 104). Therefore, by the time the "heliborne" troops arrived in the LZ, the enemy would have had several opportunities and hours to prepare. In fact, when the second wave of helicopters brought to the LZ "additional artillery . . . for subsequent infantry searches of [the] area" (Gibson 104), the enemy commander at a distance would know how far American troops would patrol by observing what artillery pieces were delivered: "He could determine how far out . . . the G.I.s would move, for he knew such units inevitably stayed within supporting range of their 105mm howitzers. By drawing a 10,000-meter-radius circle around the location . . . he could plot where the noisy, jangling, littering American troops would be conducting operations" (Cincinnatus 79).

9. This especially execrable procedure—the destruction of food—uncovers much about American national integrity: "The U.S. Air Force used American aircraft but Vietnamese *markings* were put on the planes and a Vietnamese was required to fly along in each aircraft. This slight subterfuge was undertaken to avoid problems with international law forbidding destruction of food intended for civilian consumption" (Gibson 230). Operation Ranch Hand was intended to deny food sources to the Vietcong. In fact, the people most affected by defoliation were not our avowed enemy but our alleged friends: "children were the first to die when crops were destroyed. After them came old people. Babies were third in line—they died when the mother's milk dried up . . . Guerrillas who could move when food was short were least affected by crop poisoning" (nutritionist Jean Mayer quoted by Gibson, 231). The overall effect of defoliation on land resources was staggering: "Air Force planes sprayed 18 million gallons of herbicide containing dioxins on some 6 million acres—around one-seventh of Vietnam's total land area, and a much higher proportion of its most fertile cropland and richest forests" (Gibson 225).

10. On defoliation, Army doctor Ronald Glasser reports what one of his patients concluded: "Let me tell you about that defoliation program. It didn't work. No, I mean it. It ain't done a damn thing it was supposed to do. I'll give 'em there are a lot of dead people out there because of it, but not theirs—ours. . . . An AK-47 round is effective up to 1,500 meters and accurate up to 600. So we'll hit an area, like along a busy road, billions of gallons of the stuff, and pretty soon there's nothing except for some dead bushes for fifty or even 300 meters on both sides of where the road or track used to be. So the gooks will start shooting at you from 300 meters away instead of five, only now you're the one that ain't got no place to hide. Ever try running 100 meters or 200? It takes time, and they're firing at you the whole way. And I mean the whole way" (227).

11. See especially Fred A. Wilcox, *Waiting for an Army to Die,* and Robert Klein, *Wounded Men, Broken Promises.*

12. The notion of the bombing as a semiotic phenomenon is upheld by Lyndon Johnson's explanation that "the slow escalation of the air war in the North and the increasing pressure on Ho Chi Minh was seduction, not rape. If China should suddenly react to slow escalation, as a woman might react to attempted seduction, by threatening to retaliate (a slap in the face, to continue the metaphor), the United States would have plenty of time to ease off the bombing. On the other hand, if the United States were to unleash an all-out, total assault on the North—rape rather than seduction—there could be no turning back, and Chinese reaction might be instant and total" (quoted from *The Pentagon Papers* by Gibson, 329). A macho semiotic, indeed—couched in an antiwoman, masculinist language (as is so much of Vietnam-war rhetoric). The various *official* reasons for the bombing include (1) reprisal for an alleged attack on the U.S. Navy (the Tonkin Gulf incident which resulted in Johnson's carte blanche to conduct the war); (2) interdiction of North Vietnam's ability to wage war by destroying military targets (bridges, for example, though civilian targets were certainly also bombed); (3) to disable the Ho Chi Minh trail (which was outside Vietnam altogether, so that eventually air war was redistributed over Laos as well as Cambodia); (4) to demoralize the enemy, (5) as a bargaining counter, that is, to force North Vietnam to negotiate peace; and so on, and so on. In fact, the bombing had the exactly opposite result from that expected by Washington. After more than two years of bombing, a report which was not released to the public revealed that "as of October, 1967, the U.S. bombing of North Vietnam has had no measurable effect on Hanoi's ability to mount and support military operations in the south." The North Vietnamese had also not been demoralized by the bombing; the same report showed that "the bombing campaign has not discernibly weakened the determination of the North Vietnamese leaders" (quoted from *The Pentagon Papers* by Gibson, 355). The bombing had actually hardened the resolve of the North Vietnamese people to continue the war. Pham Van Dong asserted in a TV interview that "the destruction of the North—with all the efforts and all the barbarity of imperial America— only caused the people to be more resilient and more resolute in their determination to resist and to win" (*America's Enemy* 6:15). In the same TV program, North Vietnamese surgeon Dr. Ton That Tung explained how American predictability allowed everyday life to continue: "We always knew when they were about to drop their bombs. For example, in the morning, they usually arrived about ten o'clock, just after breakfast. Then they took a break, and went back to their bases for lunch. Then they came back to drop their bombs again at about three in the afternoon. Since this was the routine, we tailored our schedule accordingly. We began our surgery at about five in the morning, and took a break at nine or ten" (*America's Enemy* 6:17).

13. This connection between sexuality and military technology (or, perhaps more properly, military activity) has been documented. Chaim Shatan notes phenomena he terms "erotization of violence": "Helicopter door gunners with erections while firing . . . Rangers on ambush ejaculating at the sight of an enemy 'exploding' " (131).

This "erotization" can hardly be called sexual, in the same sense that rape is not driven by sex but rather power. Baker's glossary in *Nam* records the especially disturbing term "double veteran—having sex with a woman and then killing her" (321). The point is that, highly romanticized as the connection between sex and aircraft may be, the basis of such "erotization" is a disturbing conjunction of rape and violence.

14. Fred Kiley's and Tony Dater's anthology, *Listen, The War: A Collection of Poetry about the Viet-Nam War,* contains several poems on the air war in Indochina. There is no indication which of the poets are Vietnam veterans, except for W. D. Ehrhart, John Clark Pratt, Fred Kiley, and Tony Dater (from external evidence). Many of the poems are quite weak or amateurish, and the editors include a disclaimer: "We think it is important to mention that contributors would frequently tell us they had no intention of writing poetry for publication, but that they simply wanted to express a feeling in that medium."

15. Frances FitzGerald, in *Fire in the Lake,* alludes to *The Tempest,* applying the work of French ethnologist Otare Mannoni to the situation of Vietnam, by comparing the relationship of colonial and native (i.e., French and Vietnamese) to the relationship of Prospero and Caliban. If McDonald is using this analogy, then his Caliban could be either Vietnamese or a Vietnamese sympathizer (North or South).

16. Philip Beidler has a different reading of "Caliban in Blue." He images the pilot as a "worshiper and minion of a new Setobos, the old anthropomorphic god of the Browning poem now become something more like the name for an inertial guidance system," and this pilot "has transferred his fealty and employeeship from Setobos to Uncle Sam." Beidler, however, ends up in essentially the same place as my reading: a "sense of fundamental wrench and solitary displacement from earth" that is at bottom a comment on the war (*Re-Writing* 183–84).

Chapter Three. A New Babel

1. Loren Baritz's *Backfire,* which I have cited as a helpful source on technology and the Vietnam war, is a thorough investigation of how myths, particularly the "city on a hill," inescapably affect American national character and governmental policy. This quotation is cited by Baritz from Reagan biographer Peter Hannaford (350).

2. See Jacqueline E. Lawson, "She's a Pretty Woman . . . for a Gook" (Jason 15–37). See also Lorrie Smith, "Back Against the Wall: Anti-Feminist Backlash in Vietnam War Literature" (Lawson, *Gender and the War* 115–27); Smith asserts, "The very argot of war . . . suggests that military atrocity is simply an egregious expression of the misogyny and violence which define patriarchal culture" (121). We are reminded of the grunt slang "double veteran—having sex with a woman and then killing her" (Baker 321).

Chapter Four. New Generation, No Generation

1. Susan Jeffords has investigated the phenomenon of regeneration in the post-Vietnam-war representation of the Vietnam veteran in the United States: "the display and regeneration of a victimized American masculinity . . . aim[s] both to respond to recent feminist challenges to patriarchal structures, and, at the same time, to reinforce these structures through a reassertion of the values, definitions, and relations upon which patriarchy depends" ("Debriding" 525). My principal point in this chapter, that regeneration through violence fails as an antidote to guilt arising for war experience, is not at odds with Jeffords's assertion (with which I wholeheartedly agree); her argument is systemic in general, whereas mine has to do with individual psychic regeneration or rather its impossibility. See also Jeffords's landmark study, *The Remasculinization of America: Gender and the Vietnam War,* in which she fully develops her ideas on the regeneration of masculinity and patriarchy in post-Vietnam-war America. In her article "Tattoos, Scars, Diaries, and Writing Masculinity," Jeffords discusses the "unseen sexualized inscriptions of masculinity" on women in Vietnam and America (223). A related topic is addressed by Jeffords's article, "Point Blank: Shooting Vietnamese Women," which focuses on how American masculinity is threatened "by women—particularly women of color" (165).

2. Many personal narratives record this sort of experience. For example, Philip Caputo recalls how such movie-based fantasies led him into joining the Marines: "the heroic experience I sought was war; war, the ultimate adventure; war, the ordinary man's most convenient means of escaping from the ordinary. . . . Already I saw myself charging up some distant beachhead, like John Wayne in *Sands of Iwo Jima,* and then coming home a suntanned warrior with medals on my chest." Caputo's second incentive was a less tangible motivation that was directly related to the "regeneration" myth. "I had another motive for volunteering, one that has pushed young men into armies ever since armies were invented: I needed to prove something—my courage, my toughness, my manhood, call it whatever you like" (6). This need to "prove something" is a signpost into Slotkin territory.

3. See Margaret Stewart, *Ambiguous Violence.* "[G]overnment propagandists for the war eschewed the complexities of the issues in dispute in favor of a portrayal of the conflict that drew heavily on the frontier myth," claims Stewart. "South Vietnam played a role of nascent, helpless civilization, while the NLF and North Vietnam, and behind them China and international communism, played the role of the inherently barbarous assailant. The United States was to be hero-to-the-rescue" (4).

4. In the context of the Vietnam war as a "hunt for Asians" (to paraphrase Katsuichi Honda), one cannot help but remember that in WWII, within American national boundaries, only Japanese Americans were rounded up and shuffled off to internment camps; German Americans and Italian Americans were placed under curfew but not interned, despite the fact that the Army's relocation plan stipulated the contingency of interning all Americans who had ancestral ties to the Axis nations.

5. One extreme way that the "running" rule could be twisted was reported by a chopper pilot: "My unit, the gunships in my unit had installed MP sirens, police sirens on the helicopter and we used these for psychological effect, to intimidate people. There is one incident I recall where we flew over a large rice paddy, and there were some people working in the rice paddy, maybe a dozen or fifteen individuals, and we passed over their heads and they didn't take any action, they were obviously nervous, but they didn't try to hide or anything. So we then hovered a few feet off the ground among them with the two helicopters, turned on the police sirens and when they heard the police sirens, they started to disperse and we opened up on them and just shot them all down" (Gibson 138).

6. See also David J. DeRose, "*Soldados Razos:* Issues of Race in Vietnam War Drama," and Lea Ybarra, "Perceptions of Race and Class Among Chicano Vietnam Veterans." According to Ybarra, "More Hispanic veterans (38%) served during the Vietnam era than during any single period" (73); this percentage would equal roughly 337,500 veterans. Ybarra's article also contains a substantial collection of oral histories which nicely complement those in Trujillo's *Soldados.*

7. The case of Montagnard Man is an extreme example of a feeling widespread among black grunts of identification with the Montagnards. One Lurp remarked: "take the Montagnards, the brothers considered them brothers because they were dark. . . . The people in Saigon didn't have anything to do with Montagnards. It was almost like white people in the States didn't have anything to do with blacks in the ghetto. So we would compare them with us" (Terry 42).

8. Radical politicization was not limited only to blacks in Vietnam, but extended to blacks in American armed services all over the world. An Army machine gunner remembers shipping out of Vietnam, to be eventually transferred to Frankfurt: "In Germany I learned black people can live together in harmony and that we had to band together in order to make it back to the United States without going to jail. I got involved in a black study group, and I started reading black history" (Terry 61). Such radicalization also occurred in the United States. After one tour in Vietnam, a Marine rifleman was sent to NCO training: "When I went to Quantico, my being black, they gave me the black squad, the squad with most of the blacks, especially the militant blacks. And they started hippin' me. I mean I was against racism. I didn't even call it racism. I called it prejudice. They hipped me to terms like 'exploitation' and 'oppression.' . . . I would read black history where the white guys were going off on novels or playing rock music" (Terry 13).

9. During Kirk's interview of African Americans in Soul Alley, "one of them pulls out a plastic card printed on one side in red, black, and green stripes. 'That's the flag of the Black Liberation Front of the armed forces'" (Pratt, *Vietnam Voices* 485). The term *Black Liberation Front* is an interesting nexus of three leftist national/cultural strands: African Americans in Vietnam, African American radicals in the United States, and (in significant irony) Vietnam's National Liberation Front—the official name of the Vietcong.

10. According to my count, the number of sections is 229. This quantity, however, is difficult to determine because Layne's pages are not numbered, and one must resort to counting the leaves or paginating by hand.

11. See, for example, Tobey C. Herzog's articles, "Writing About Vietnam: A Heavy Heart-of-Darkness Trip" and "John Wayne in a Modern Heart of Darkness: The American Soldier in Vietnam," as well as James Aubrey's "Conradian Darkness in John Clark Pratt's *The Laotian Fragments.*" John Hellmann, in *American Myth and the Legacy of Vietnam,* treats at length Francis Ford Coppola's significant use of elements of *Heart of Darkness* in his movie *Apocalypse Now* (188–202).

Chapter Five. When Adam Comes Marching Home—What About Eve?

1. The version of "The Invasion of Grenada" in *To Those Who Have Gone Home Tired* differs slightly from what I have quoted; in my copy of the book, the author has corrected the text in ink and initialed the changes. The poem appears as corrected in the later *Carrying the Darkness* (103).

2. It is only relatively recently that collections of women's war poetry and critical studies of that poetry and other women's writing on war have appeared. *Scars Upon My Heart: Women's Poetry and Verse of the First World War* and *Chaos of the Night: Women's Poetry and Verse of the Second World War,* both edited by Catherine W. Reilly, appeared in 1981 and 1984, respectively. Nosheen Khan's study, *Women's Poetry of the First World War,* a collection of essays entitled *Arms and the Woman: War, Gender, and Literary Representation,* edited by Helen M. Cooper, Adrienne Auslander Munich, and Susan Merrill Squier, and Clair Tylee's *The Great War and Women's Consciousness* were published in quick succession—in 1988, 1989, and 1990. More recently, Susan Schweik's landmark critical study, *A Gulf So Deeply Cut: American Women Poets and the Second World War,* appeared in 1991, as did Lynne Hanley's *Writing War: Fiction, Gender, and Memory,* a fascinating mixture of thematically and chronologically related critical essays and short stories on women and war in the twentieth century. Apropos of women's narratives on the Vietnam war, the definitive commentary is Renny Christopher's " 'I Never Really Became a Woman Veteran Until . . . I Saw the Wall': A Review of Oral Histories and Personal Narratives by Women Veterans of the Vietnam War" (1989). Two articles that directly address women's poetry and the Vietnam war are "Women Poets of the Viet Nam War" by Sharman Murphy (1991), and "Women in the Light of Fire" by Daniela Gioseffi (1992).

In the larger sociocultural/historical arena, Jean Bethke Elshtain's work has been exemplary: *Women and War* (1987) and *Women, Militarism, and War,* coedited with Sheila Tobias (1990). Also of note from Europe are *Images of Women in Peace and War,* edited by Sharon Macdonald, Pat Holden, and Shirley Ardener (sponsored by the Oxford University Women's Studies Committee, 1987); *Women and War,* edited by Maria Diedrich and Dorothea Fischer-Hornung (sponsored by the European Association of American Studies, 1990); and the 1987 reprint of *Militarism versus Feminism,* a collection of essays by Catherine E. Marshall, C. K. Ogden, and Mary Sargant Florence, originally published in 1915. A wide-ranging collection of viewpoints may be found in *Women on War,* edited by Daniela Gioseffi (1988).

Of particular interest to feminist Vietnam-war scholars are Elizabeth M. Norman's *Women at War* (1990), an analysis of oral histories by military women nurses who served in the Vietnam war; *American Women Writers on Vietnam* (1990), an annotated bibliography by Deborah A. Butler sampling a variety of genres and types, particularly writing by non-Americans; and *Gender and the War: Men, Women and Vietnam,* a special issue of the journal *Vietnam Generation,* edited by Jacqueline Lawson in 1989.

3. Parenthetical citation of poets and poems from *Visions of War, Dreams of Peace* in this paragraph would have been intrusive; here instead is a list: Marilyn McMahon, from "The Kid" (33); Bobbie Trotter, from "Dear Mom" (40); Joan Arrington Craigwell, from "Dark Angel" (76); Sharon Grant, from "The Best Act in Pleiku, No One Under 18 Admitted" (14); Mary Lu Ostergren Brunner, from "Cheated" (45); Norma J. Griffiths, from "Under the Covers" (112); and Dana Shuster, from "Mellow on Morphine" (30).

Chapter Six. Warriors Against War

1. This poetry movement has been studied by James Mersmann in *Out of the Vietnam Vortex: A Study of Poets and Poetry Against the War* and also by Cary Nelson in "Whitman and Vietnam," the opening chapter of *Our Last First Poets*.

2. I am using the version of Kinnell's poem found in Bly's and Ray's *A Poetry Reading Against the Vietnam War* (1966) rather than the (presumably) final version in Kinnell's *Selected Poems* (1982) because the earlier version is the one with which Vietnam veterans would have been most familiar while the war was going on. They may also have seen the version printed in Walter Lowenfels's *Where Is Vietnam?* (1967)—but that version inexplicably leaves out the last four lines (which, by the evidence of the 1982 version, Kinnell wanted to leave in). The version in the *Selected Poems* is somewhat different from the 1966 version in lineation and some diction, but it has not been radically altered. One interesting deviation occurs in the phrase "the rack of deputies' rifles"—Lowenfels's anthology has "crack," as does the *Selected Poems* version.

3. Besides this excerpt found in *The New Soldier,* John Kerry's statement is also excerpted in William Appleman Williams et al., *America in Vietnam* (292–96). These two excerpts vary somewhat in what has been included; the full statement can be found in the proceedings of the Committee on Foreign Relations, *Legislative Proposals Relating to the War in Southeast Asia, Hearings . . . April 20, 21, 22, and 28 . . .* (Washington, D.C.: U.S. Senate, 1971), pp. 180–210, 251–62 (according to Williams et al. [292]).

Chapter Seven. Bruce Weigl: "Useful to the Wind"

1. The mean percentage is 23. The ratio of Vietnam-war-related to unrelated poems is 7:12 in *Executioner;* 3:23 in *A Sack Full of Old Quarrels;* 12:36 in *A Romance;* and 10:34 in *The Monkey Wars.*

Chapter Eight. Yusef Komunyakaa: "Depending on the Light"

1. Ngo Thi Trinh, the actual Hanoi Hannah, was interviewed in April 1992 on the C-SPAN retrospective documentary *Vietnam Revisited,* broadcast during the 1992 Memorial Day weekend. In this interview, Ngo Thi Trinh represented herself as providing a service—information—for Americans; for example, in response to a question about the day Saigon fell, she recalled that her broadcast that day had emphasized to Americans still in the city that now they could go home and no longer be afraid of being killed.

Conclusion: Radical Visions Extended

1. The biographical information on Lady Borton has been gleaned from her memoir, *Sensing the Enemy* (especially 4, 12), and from *Visions of War, Dreams of Peace,* ed. Van Devanter and Furey (210).

WORKS CITED

Adcock, A. St. John. *For Remembrance: Soldier Poets Who Have Fallen in the War*. London: Hodder and Stoughton, 1918.

America Takes Charge (1965–1967). Boston: WGBH Transcripts, 1983. Vol. 5 of *Vietnam: A Television History*. 13 vols.

America's Enemy (1954–1967). Boston: WGBH Transcripts, 1983. Vol. 6 of *Vietnam: A Television History*. 13 vols.

Anderson, Charles R. *The Grunts*. Novato, Calif.: Presidio Press, 1976.

Andrews, Bruce. "Text and Context." *The L=A=N=G=U=A=G=E Book*. Ed. Bruce Andrews and Charles Bernstein. Carbondale: Southern Illinois University Press, 1984. 31–38.

Anisfield, Nancy. *Vietnam Anthology: American War Literature*. Bowling Green, Ohio: Popular Press, 1987.

Aubrey, James R. "Conradian Darkness in John Clark Pratt's *The Laotian Fragments*." Jason 111–23.

Baker, Mark. *Nam: The Vietnam War in the Words of the Men and Women Who Fought There*. New York: Morrow, 1981.

Balaban, John. *After Our War*. Pittsburgh: University of Pittsburgh Press, 1974.

————. *Blue Mountain*. Greensboro, N.C.: Unicorn Press, 1974.

————. *Vietnam Poems*. Oxford, Eng.: Carcanet Press, 1970.

————. *Words for My Daughter*. Port Townsend, Wash.: Copper Canyon Press, 1991.

Baritz, Loren. *Backfire: A History of How American Culture Led Us into Vietnam and Made Us Fight the Way We Did*. New York: Morrow, 1985.

Barry, Jan, ed. *Peace Is Our Profession: Poems and Passages of War Protest*. Montclair, N.J.: East River Anthology, 1981.

————. *Veterans Day*. Samisdat 36.1, 141st release (1983).

————. *War Baby*. Samisdat 39.2, 154th release (1983).

Barry, Jan, and W. D. Ehrhart, eds. *Demilitarized Zones: Veterans After Vietnam*. Perkasie, Pa.: East River Anthology, 1976.

Barth, R. L. *Looking for Peace*. N.p.: n.d., 1981. Omaha: Abbatoir Editions, University of Nebraska, 1985.

————. *Forced-Marching to the Styx: Vietnam War Poems*. Perivale Poetry Chapbooks. Van Nuys, Calif.: Perivale Press, 1983.

———. *Simonides in Vietnam and Other Epigrams.* Santa Barbara, Calif.: John Daniel, 1990.

———. *A Soldier's Time: Vietnam War Poems.* Santa Barbara, Calif.: John Daniel, 1987.

Barthes, Roland. *Mythologies.* Selected and trans. Annette Lavers. 1957. London: Jonathan Cape, 1972.

Bauer, Bill. *The Eye of the Ghost: Vietnam Poems.* Kansas City: BkMk Press, University of Missouri, 1986.

Baum, L. Frank. *The Wizard of Oz.* Ed. Michael Patrick Hearn. Critical Heritage Series. 1900. New York: Schocken, 1983.

Behrendt, Stephen C. "Introduction: History, Mythmaking, and the Romantic Artist." *History and Myth: Essays on English Romantic Literature.* Ed. Stephen C. Behrendt. Detroit: Wayne State University Press, 1990. 13–32.

Beidler, Philip D. *American Literature and the Experience of Vietnam.* Athens: University of Georgia Press, 1982.

———. *Re-Writing America: Vietnam Authors in Their Generation.* Athens: University of Georgia Press, 1991.

Bergonzi, Bernard. *Heroes' Twilight: A Study of the Literature of the Great War.* London: Constable, 1965. Reprint. New York: Coward-McCann, 1966.

Bernstein, Charles. "Thought's Measure." *Content's Dream: Essays, 1975–1984.* Los Angeles: Sun and Moon Press, 1986. 61–86.

Berry, D. C. *saigon cemetery.* Foreword by George Garrett. Athens: University of Georgia Press, 1972.

"Bibliography of Literature on Asian Americans and the Vietnam War." King 158–59.

Bingaman, H. W. *Reckonings: Stories of the Air War over North Vietnam.* New York: Vantage, 1988.

Bly, Robert. *Iron John: A Book About Men.* Reading, Mass.: Addison-Wesley, 1990.

Bly, Robert, and David Ray, eds. *A Poetry Reading Against the Vietnam War.* Madison, Wis.: American Writers Against the Vietnam War, Sixties Press, 1966.

Borden, Robert. *True Tales and Tall.* [N.p.]: Robert Borden, 1992.

Borton, Lady. *Sensing the Enemy.* Garden City, N.Y.: Dial Press, 1984.

Bowman, Peter. *Beach Red.* New York: Random, 1945.

Bowra, Maurice. *Poetry and the First World War.* Taylorian Lecture, 1961. Oxford: Oxford University Press, 1961.

Brende, Joel Osler, and Erwin Randolph Parson. *Vietnam Veterans: The Road to Recovery.* New York: Plenum, 1985.

Brittain, Vera. *Poems of the War and After.* London: Gollancz; New York: Macmillan, 1934.

———. *Testament of Youth.* London: Gollancz; New York: Macmillan, 1933.

———. *Verses of a V.A.D.* Foreword by Marie Connor Leighton. London: Macdonald, 1918.

Brown, D. F. "The Other Half of Everything." *Ironwood* 31–32 (1988): 171–80.

———. *Returning Fire.* San Francisco: San Francisco State University, 1985.

Brown, William R. "Machine and Man in American Poetry of the Second World War." *Markham Review* 13 (Spring–Summer 1984): 21–27.

Browne, Corinne. *Body Shop: Recuperating from Vietnam.* New York: Stein and Day, 1973.

Browne, Malcolm W. *The New Face of War.* Indianapolis: Bobbs-Merrill, 1965.

Broyles, William. *Brothers in Arms: A Journey from War to Peace.* New York: Knopf, 1986.

Burgess, Anthony. *A Clockwork Orange.* 1962. New York: Norton, 1987.

Butler, Deborah A. *American Women Writers on Vietnam: Unheard Voices: A Selected Annotated Bibliography.* New York: Garland, 1990.

Byrd, Barthy. *Home Front: Women and Vietnam.* Berkeley, Calif.: Shameless Hussy Press, 1986.

Campbell, Joseph. *The Hero of a Thousand Faces.* Bollingen Series 17. Princeton, N.J.: Princeton University Press, 1968.

Caputo, Philip. *A Rumor of War.* New York: Holt, Rinehart and Winston, 1977.

Card, Josefina J. *Lives After Vietnam: The Personal Impact of Military Service.* Lexington, Mass.: Heath-Lexington, 1983.

Casey, Michael. *Obscenities.* Intro. Stanley Kunitz. Yale Series of Younger Poets, vol. 67. New Haven, Conn.: Yale University Press, 1972.

Chinnery, Philip D. *Life on the Line: Stories of Vietnam Air Combat.* New York: St. Martin's Press, 1988.

Chiron Review. Special issue on poetry by Vietnam veterans. 10.1 (Spring 1991).

Christopher, Renny. " 'I Never Really Became a Woman Veteran Until . . . I Saw the Wall': A Review of Oral Histories and Personal Narratives by Women Veterans of the Vietnam War." Lawson, *Gender and the War* 33–45.

Ciardi, John. *Selected Poems.* Fayetteville: University of Arkansas Press, 1984.

Cincinnatus. *Self-Destruction: The Disintegration and Decay of the United States Army During the Vietnam Era.* New York: Norton, 1981.

Clifton, Merritt, ed. *Those Who Were There: Eyewitness Accounts of the War in Southeast Asia, 1956–1975 and Aftermath.* Paradise, Calif.: Dustbooks, 1984.

Clover, Timothy. *The Leaves of My Trees, Still Green.* Chicago: Adams Press, 1970.

Coleman, Horace. *Between a Rock and a Hard Place.* In *Four Black Poets.* Kansas City: BkMk Press, University of Missouri, 1977.

Cooper, Helen M., Adrienne Auslander Munich, and Susan Merrill Squier. *Arms and the Woman: War, Gender, and Literary Representation.* Chapel Hill: University of North Carolina Press, 1989.

Cooper, James Fenimore. *The Last of the Mohicans.* 1826. Vol. 1 of *The Leatherstocking Tales.* 467–878.

———. *The Leatherstocking Tales.* Library of America. 2 vols. 1826–41. New York: Literary Classics of the United States, 1985.

Cramer, Steven. "Facts and Figures." Review of *Night Landings,* by Walter McDonald; *Dien Cai Dau,* by Yusef Komunyakaa; *The Night Parade,* by Edward Hirsch; *Black*

Wings, by Len Roberts; *Burden Lifters,* by Michael Waters; and *Once Out of Nature,* by Jim Simmerman. *Poetry* 156.2 (May 1990): 100–115.

Crawford, Fred D. *British Poets of the Great War.* Selinsgrove, Pa.: Susquehanna University Press; London: Associated University Press, 1988.

Cromie, Robert, ed. *Where Steel Winds Blow.* New York: David McKay, 1968.

Cronin, Cornelius A. "From the DMZ to No Man's Land: Philip Caputo's *A Rumor of War* and Its Antecedents." Searle 74–86.

Cross, Frank A., Jr. *Reminders.* Big Timber, Mont.: Seven Buffaloes Press, 1986.

cummings, e. e. *Complete Poems, 1913–1962.* New York: Harvest-Harcourt Brace Jovanovich, 1980.

Currey, Richard. *Crossing Over: A Vietnam Journal.* Cambridge, Mass.: Apple-wood Press, 1980.

DEROS. A poetry journal devoted to Vietnam veterans. Ed. Lee-Lee Schlegel and Ken Rose. 1981–87.

DeRose, David J. "*Soldados Razos:* Issues of Race in Vietnam War Drama." King 38–55.

Dickson, Paul. *The Electronic Battlefield.* Bloomington: Indiana University Press, 1976.

Diedrich, Maria, and Dorothea Fischer-Hornung, eds. *Women and War: The Changing Status of American Women from the 1930s to the 1950s.* New York: Berg, 1990.

Di Prima, Diane. *War Poems.* New York: Poets Press, 1968.

Doleman, Edgar C. *Tools of War.* The Vietnam Experience. Boston: Boston Publishing, 1984.

Donovan, David. *Once a Warrior King: Memories of an Officer in Vietnam.* New York: McGraw-Hill, 1985.

Douglas, Keith. *Complete Poems.* Ed. Desmond Graham. Oxford: Oxford University Press, 1978.

Dragonsun, Jabiya [Williams, Julius Nathaniel, Jr.]. *Hit Parade.* Ed. Zulma Gonzalez-Parker. Philadelphia: In the Tradition Press, 1989.

Eberhart, Richard. *Collected Poems: 1930–1986.* New York: Oxford University Press, 1988.

Eberhart, Richard, and Selden Rodman, eds. *War and the Poet: An Anthology of Poetry Expressing Man's Attitudes to War from Ancient Times to the Present.* New York: Devin-Adair, 1945.

Edelman, Bernard, ed. *Dear America: Letters Home from Vietnam.* New York: Norton, 1985.

Ehrhart, W. D. *The Awkward Silence.* South Thomaston, Me.: Northwoods, 1980.

——, ed. *Carrying the Darkness: American Indochina—The Poetry of the Vietnam War.* New York: Avon, 1985. Reprinted as *Carrying the Darkness: The Poetry of the Vietnam War.* Lubbock: Texas Tech University Press, 1988.

——. *Channel Fever.* Port Jefferson, N.Y.: Backstreet Editions, 1982.

——. *Empire. Samisdat* 17.3, 66th release (1978).

——. *A Generation of Peace.* New York: New Voices, 1975.

————. *A Generation of Peace*. Rev. ed. *Samisdat* 14.3, 54th release (1977).

————. *Going Back: An Ex-Marine Returns to Vietnam*. Jefferson, N.C.: McFarland, 1987.

————. *In the Shadow of Vietnam: Essays, 1977–1991*. Jefferson, N.C.: McFarland, 1991.

————. *Just for Laughs*. Special issue of *Vietnam Generation* 2.4. Silver Spring, Md.: Vietnam Generation and Burning Cities Press, 1990.

————. *Marking Time*. New York: Avon, 1986. Reprinted as *Passing Time: Memoir of a Vietnam Veteran Against the War*. Jefferson, N.C.: McFarland, 1987.

————. *Matters of the Heart*. Easthampton, Mass.: Adastra, 1981.

————. *The Outer Banks and Other Poems*. Easthampton, Mass.: Adastra, 1984.

————. *Rootless*. *Samisdat* 14.2, 53rd release (1977).

————. *The Samisdat Poems of W. D. Ehrhart*. *Samisdat* 24.1, 93rd release (1980).

————. "Soldier-Poets of the Vietnam War." *Virginia Quarterly Review* 63.2 (Spring 1987): 246–65. Reprinted in *Tell Me Lies About Vietnam: Cultural Battles for the Meaning of the War*. Ed. Alf Louvre and Jeffrey Walsh. Milton Keynes, Eng.: Open University Press, 1988. 149–63. Also reprinted in Gilman and Smith 313–31.

————. *To Those Who Have Gone Home Tired: New and Selected Poems*. New York: Thunder's Mouth Press, 1984.

————, ed. *Unaccustomed Mercy: Soldier-Poets of the Vietnam War*. Preface by John Clark Pratt. Lubbock: Texas Tech University Press, 1989.

————. *Vietnam-Perkasie: A Combat Marine Memoir*. Jefferson, N.C.: McFarland, 1983.

————. *Winter Bells*. Easthampton, Mass.: Adastra, 1988.

Eliade, Mircea. *Myth and Reality*. Trans. Willard R. Trask. World Perspectives 31. New York: Harper and Row, 1963.

Eliot, T. S. *The Complete Poems and Plays, 1909–1950*. New York: Harcourt, Brace and World, 1971.

Elshtain, Jean Bethke. *Women and War*. New York: Basic Books, 1987.

Elshtain, Jean Bethke, and Sheila Tobias, eds. *Women, Militarism, and War: Essays in History, Politics, and Social Theory*. New Feminist Perspectives Series. Savage, Md.: Rowman and Littlefield, 1990.

Emerson, Gloria. *Winners and Losers: Battles, Retreats, Gains, Losses and Ruins from a Long War*. New York: Random, 1976.

Falck, Colin. *Myth, Truth, and Literature: Towards a True Post-Modernism*. Cambridge: Cambridge University Press, 1989.

Fallaci, Oriana. *Nothing, and So Be It*. Trans. Isabel Quigly. 1969. Garden City, N.Y.: Doubleday, 1972.

Felstiner, John. "American Poetry and the War in Vietnam." *Stand* 19.2 (1978): 4–11.

————. "Bearing the War in Mind." *Parnassus: Poetry in Review* 6.2 (Spring/Summer 1978): 30–37.

Fiedler, Leslie A. *Love and Death in the American Novel.* Rev. ed. New York: Delta-Dell, 1966.

FitzGerald, Frances. *Fire in the Lake: The Vietnamese and the Americans in Vietnam.* Boston: Atlantic Monthly Press-Little, Brown, 1972.

Flamm, Matthew. "Facing Up to the Deadly Ordinary." Review of *Skating with Heather Grace,* by Tom Lynch; *I Apologize for the Eyes in my Head,* by Yusef Komunyakaa; and *Rose,* by Li-Young Lee. *New York Times Book Review* 137 (October 4, 1987): 24.

Fletcher, Harvey D. *Visions of Nam.* 2 vols. Raleigh, N.C.: Jo-Ely, 1987.

Floyd, Bryan Alec. *The Long War Dead: An Epiphany.* New York: Bard-Avon, 1976.

Force, Peter. *Tracts and Other Papers, Relating Principally to the Origin, Settlement, and Progress of the Colonies in North America, From the Discovery of the Country to the Year 1776.* 3 vols. Washington, D.C., 1836–38.

Forché, Carolyn. "El Salvador: An Aide Memoir." *American Poetry Review* 10.4 (July/August 1981): 3–7.

Forshaw, Charles Frederick, ed. *One Hundred of the Best Poems on the European War by Women Poets of the Empire.* Vol. 2 of *One Hundred of the Best Poems on the European War.* London: E. Stock, 1916. 2 vols.

Francillon, René J. *Vietnam: The War in the Air.* New York: Arch Cape Press, 1987.

Freeman, James M., ed. *Hearts of Sorrow: Vietnamese-American Lives.* Stanford, Calif.: Stanford University Press, 1989.

Frost, Robert. *The Poetry of Robert Frost.* Ed. Edward Connery Lathem. New York: Holt, Rinehart and Winston, 1969.

Frye, Northrop. *Anatomy of Criticism.* New York: Atheneum, 1966.

———. *Fearful Symmetry: A Study of William Blake.* 1947. Princeton, N.J.: Princeton University Press, 1969.

———. *Myth and Metaphor: Selected Essays, 1974–1988.* Ed. Robert D. Denham. Charlottesville: University Press of Virginia, 1990.

Fryer, Judith. *The Faces of Eve.* Oxford: Oxford University Press, 1976.

Fussell, Paul. *The Great War and Modern Memory.* New York: Oxford University Press, 1975.

Gadd, Charles. *Line Doggie: Foot Soldier in Vietnam.* Novato, Calif.: Presidio Press, 1987.

Gaffney, Zook. *Eating Little Dogs During the Revolution.* Morristown, N.J.: Suitcase Bookstore, 1978.

Gardner, Brian, ed. *Up the Line to Death: The War Poets, 1914–1918.* London: Methuen, 1964.

Gershman, Herbert S. *The Surrealist Revolution in France.* Ann Arbor: University of Michigan Press, 1969.

Gettler, Andrew. *Footsteps of a Ghost: Poems from Viet Nam.* New Brunswick, N.J.: Iniquity Press, 1991.

———. "Johnny's Song: Poetry of a Vietnam Veteran." Review of *Johnny's Song* by Steve Mason. *Chiron Review* 10.1 (Spring 1991): 14.

————. *lurid dreams . . . because we all have them.* Tucson: Experimental Press, 1991.

————. *Only the Mountains Are Forever.* Croydon, Pa.: Black Bear Publications, 1987.

————. *Zen and the Art of Perfect Desire.* Portlandville, N.Y.: M.A.F. Press, 1990.

Gibson, James W. *The Perfect War: Technowar in Vietnam.* Boston: Atlantic Monthly Press, 1986. Reprinted as *The Perfect War: The War We Couldn't Lose and How We Did.* New York: Vintage, 1988.

Gilman, Owen W., Jr., and Lorrie Smith, eds. *America Rediscovered: Critical Essays on Literature and Film of the Vietnam War.* New York: Garland, 1990.

Gioseffi, Daniela. "Women in the Light of Fire." Review of *Visions of War, Dreams of Peace,* ed. Lynda Van Devanter and Joan A. Furey. *American Book Review* 13.6 (February–March 1992).

————, ed. *Women on War: Essential Voices for the Nuclear Age.* New York: Touchstone, 1988.

Glade, Jon Forrest. *Photographs of the Jungle.* St. John, Kans.: Chiron Review Press, 1990.

Glasser, Ronald J. *365 Days.* New York: George Braziller, 1971.

Goff, Stanley, and Robert Sanders, with Clark Smith. *Brothers: Black Soldiers in the Nam.* Novato, Calif.: Presidio Press, 1982.

Gotera, Vicente F. "Bringing Vietnam Home: Bruce Weigl's *The Monkey Wars.*" Searle 160–69.

————. " 'Depending on the Light': Yusef Komunyakaa's *Dien Cai Dau.* " Gilman and Smith 282–300.

————. "The Fragging of Language: D. F. Brown's Vietnam-War Poetry." Special issue on poetry and the Vietnam War. Ed. Vince Gotera and Theresa L. Brown. *Journal of American Culture* 16.3 (Fall 1993): 39–45.

————. "Killer Imagination." Review of *Dien Cai Dau,* by Yusef Komunyakaa. *Callaloo* 13.2 (1990): 364–71.

————. " 'Lines of Tempered Steel': An Interview with Yusef Komunyakaa." *Callaloo* 13.2 (1990): 215–29.

————. "Peter Bowman's *Beach Red* and Viet Nam War Poetry." *Viet Nam Generation.* Forthcoming.

————. "Vietnam Souvenirs: Poetry by Veterans." *North Coast Journal* 1.11 (November 1990): 22–23.

Gray, Jim. *War Poems: A Collaboration.* Art by Richard J. Olsen. [Athens, Ga.]: Richard J. Olsen, Jim Gray, 1986.

Guillory, Daniel L. Review of *The Monkey Wars,* by Bruce Weigl. *Library Journal* 110.11 (June 15, 1985): 64.

Hackworth, David H., and Julie Sherman. *About Face.* New York: Simon and Schuster, 1989.

Haines, Harry W., ed. *GI Resistance: Soldiers and Veterans Against the War.* Special issue of *Viet Nam Generation* 2.1 (Winter 1990).

Halberstam, David. *The Making of a Quagmire: America and Vietnam during the Kennedy Era*. Ed. and intro. Daniel J. Sangel. Rev. ed. New York: Knopf, 1988.

Hall, David. *Werewolf and Other Poems*. Fort Collins, Colo.: Bald Mountain, 1981.

Halstead, Fred. *GIs Speak Out Against the War*. New York: Merit-Pathfinder, 1970.

Hanley, Lynne. *Writing War: Fiction, Gender, and Memory*. Amherst: University of Massachusetts Press, 1991.

Hansen, J. Vincent. *Blessed Are the Peacemakers*. Saint Cloud, Minn.: North Star Press, 1989.

Hawthorne, Lesleyanne, ed. *Refugee: The Vietnamese Experience*. Melbourne: Oxford University Press, 1982.

Hayslip, Le Ly, and Jay Wurts. *When Heaven and Earth Changed Places: A Vietnamese Woman's Journey from War to Peace*. New York: Doubleday, 1989.

Hellmann, John. *American Myth and the Legacy of Vietnam*. New York: Columbia University Press, 1986.

Helmer, John. *Bringing the War Home: The American Soldier in Vietnam and After*. New York: Free Press, 1974.

Herr, Michael. *Dispatches*. New York: Knopf, 1977; New York: Avon, 1978.

Hertzler, Terry. *The Way of the Snake and Other Poems: Writings from the War in Vietnam*. San Diego: Caernarvon Press, 1985.

Herzog, Tobey C. "John Wayne in a Modern Heart of Darkness: The American Soldier in Vietnam." Searle 16–25.

———. "Writing About Vietnam: A Heavy Heart-of-Darkness Trip." *College English* 41.6 (February 1980): 680–95.

Higgins, Hugh. *Vietnam*. 2d ed. Studies in Modern History. London: Heinemann, 1982.

Holdstein, Deborah H. "Vietnam War Veteran-Poets: The Ideology of Horror." *USA Today* (Periodical) 112 (September 1983): 59–61.

Hollis, Jocelyn, ed. *Vietnam Poems: The War Poems of Today*. Philadelphia: American Poetry Press, 1983.

———, ed. *Vietnam Poems II: A New Collection*. Philadelphia: American Poetry Press, 1983.

Holm, Tom. "Forgotten Warriors: American Indian Servicemen in Vietnam." King 56–68.

Hope, Warren. *An Unsuccessful Mission*. Florence, Ky.: R. L. Barth, 1983.

Horne, A. D., ed. *The Wounded Generation: America After Vietnam*. Englewood Cliffs, N.J.: Prentice-Hall, 1981.

Huddle, David. *Stopping by Home*. Peregrine Smith Poetry Series 2. Salt Lake City: Peregrine-Gibbs Smith, 1988.

James, Allston. *The Mile Away Contessa*. N.p.: Angel, 1977.

Jameson, Fredric. "Postmodernism, or The Cultural Logic of Late Capitalism." *New Left Review* 146 (1984): 53–92.

Jarrell, Randall. *The Complete Poems*. New York: Farrar, Straus and Giroux, 1969.

Jason, Philip K., ed. *Fourteen Landing Zones: Approaches to Vietnam War Literature*. Iowa City: University of Iowa Press, 1991.

Jeffords, Susan. "Debriding Vietnam: The Resurrection of the White American Male." *Feminist Studies* 14.3 (Fall 1988): 525–43.

———. "Point Blank: Shooting Vietnamese Women." Lawson, *Gender and the War* 152–67.

———. *The Remasculinization of America: Gender and the Vietnam War*. Bloomington: Indiana University Press, 1989.

———. "Tattoos, Scars, Diaries, and Writing Masculinity." *The Vietnam War and American Culture*. Ed. John Carlos Rowe and Rick Berg. New York: Columbia University Press, 1991.

Johnson, G. P. *I Was Fighting for Peace, But Lord, There Was Much More*. Hicksville, N.Y.: Exposition Press, 1979.

Johnston, John H. *English Poetry of the First World War: A Study in Evolution of Lyric and Narrative Form*. Princeton, N.J.: Princeton University Press, 1964.

Jones, Ann Rosalind. "Writing the Body: Toward an Understanding of *l'Écriture féminine*." Showalter 361–77.

Jones, Howard Mumford. *O Strange New World: American Culture: The Formative Years*. 1952. London: Chatto and Windus, 1965.

Jones, James. *Viet Journal*. New York: Delacorte, 1974.

Karlin, Wayne, Basil T. Paquet, and Larry Rottmann, eds. *Free Fire Zone: Short Stories by Vietnam Veterans*. Coventry, Conn.: 1st Casualty Press, 1973.

Kearns, Doris. *Lyndon Johnson and the American Dream*. New York: Harper and Row, 1976.

Kerry, John, and Vietnam Veterans Against the War. *The New Soldier*. Ed. David Thorne and George Butler. New York: Macmillan, 1971.

Ketwig, John. *And a Hard Rain Fell: A GI's True Story of the War in Vietnam*. New York: Macmillan, 1985.

Khan, Nosheen. *Women's Poetry of the First World War*. Lexington: University Press of Kentucky, 1988.

Khiev, Virak. "Breaking the Bonds of Hate." *Newsweek,* April 27, 1992: 8.

Kiang, Peter Nien-Chu. "About Face: Recognizing Asian and Pacific American Vietnam Veterans in Asian American Studies." *Amerasia* 17.3 (1991): 22–40.

Kiley, Fred, and Tony Dater, eds. *Listen, The War: A Collection of Poetry About the Vietnam War*. [Colorado Springs, Colo.]: U.S. Air Force Association of Graduates, 1973.

King, William, ed. *A White Man's War: Race Issues and Vietnam*. Special issue of *Viet Nam Generation* 1.2 (Spring 1989).

Kinnell, Galway. *Selected Poems*. Boston: Houghton Mifflin, 1982.

Kissam, Edward. *Vietnamese Lessons*. London: Anvil Press, 1970.

Klein, Robert. *Wounded Men, Broken Promises*. New York: Macmillan; London: Collier Macmillan, 1981.

Knight, Cranston Sedrick, ed. *Tour of Duty*. Samisdat 46.2, 182nd release (1986).

Koestenbaum, Wayne. "Distortions in the Glass." Review of *Applause* by Carol Muske and *Dien Cai Dau* by Yusef Komunyakaa. *New York Times Book Review* 139 (September 24, 1989): 50–51.

Kolko, Gabriel. *Anatomy of a War: Vietnam, the United States, and the Modern Historical Experience.* New York: Pantheon, 1985. Reprinted as *Vietnam: Anatomy of a War, 1940–1975.* London: Unwin Hyman, 1986.

Kolodny, Annette. *The Land Before Her: Fantasy and Experience of the American Frontiers, 1630–1860.* Chapel Hill: University of North Carolina Press, 1984.

———. *The Lay of the Land: Metaphor as Experience and History in American Life and Letters.* Chapel Hill: University of North Carolina Press, 1975.

Komunyakaa, Yusef. *Copacetic.* Middletown, Conn.: Wesleyan University Press, 1984.

———. *Dedications and Other Darkhorses.* Laramie, Wyo.: *Rocky Mountain Creative Arts Journal* Books, 1977.

———. *Dien Cai Dau.* Middletown, Conn.: Wesleyan University Press, 1988.

———. *February in Sydney.* Unionville, Ind.: Matchbooks, 1989.

———. "Ia Drang Valley." *The Made Thing: An Anthology of Contemporary Southern Poetry.* Ed. Leon Stokesbury. Fayetteville: University of Arkansas Press, 1987. 145.

———. *I Apologize for the Eyes in my Head.* Middletown, Conn.: Wesleyan University Press, 1986.

———. "Losses." *Indiana Review* 10.1–2 (1987): 154–55.

———. *Lost in the Bonewheel Factory.* [Amherst, Mass.]: Lynx House Press, 1979.

———. *Magic City.* Hanover, N.H.: University Press of New England, 1992.

———. *Premonitions of the Bread Line.* Master's thesis. University of California at Irvine, 1980.

———. *Toys in a Field.* New Orleans: Black River Press, 1987.

Kovic, Ron. *Born on the Fourth of July.* New York: McGraw-Hill, 1976.

Kunen, James Simon. *Standard Operating Procedure: Notes of a Draft Age American.* New York: Avon, 1971.

Kunitz, Stanley. Foreword. Casey, *Obscenities* vii–xii.

Lane, Mark. *Conversations with Americans.* New York: Simon and Schuster, 1970.

Lanquist, Norman. *Angels.* Thatcher, Ariz.: Third Wheel Press, 1987.

Larsen, Wendy Wilder, and Tran Thi Nga. *Shallow Graves: Two Women in Vietnam.* New York: Harper and Row, 1986.

Lawrence, D. H. *Studies in Classic American Literature.* 1923. New York: Viking, 1964.

Lawson, Jacqueline, ed. *Gender and the War: Men, Women and Vietnam.* Special issue of *Viet Nam Generation* 1.3–4 (Summer–Fall 1989).

———. "She's a Pretty Woman . . . for a Gook." Jason 15–37.

Layne, McAvoy. *How Audie Murphy Died in Vietnam.* Garden City, N.Y.: Anchor-Doubleday, 1973.

Lecomte, Serge. *Crimson Rice.* Reston, Va.: Librado Press, 1990.

Lederer, William, and Eugene Burdick. *The Ugly American.* New York: Norton, 1958; New York: Fawcett, 1961.

Lewis, R. W. B. *The American Adam: Innocence, Tragedy and Tradition in the Nineteenth Century.* Chicago: University of Chicago Press, 1955.

Lifton, Robert Jay. *Home from the War: Vietnam Veterans: Neither Victims Nor Executioners*. New York: Simon and Schuster, 1973.

Lomperis, Timothy J. *"Reading the Wind": The Literature of the Vietnam War*. Durham, N.C.: Duke University Press, 1987.

Lowenfels, Walter, ed. *Where Is Vietnam?* Garden City, N.Y.: Anchor-Doubleday, 1967.

McCarthy, Gerald. *War Story: Vietnam War Poems*. Trumansburg, N.Y.: Crossing Press, 1977.

———. *Shoetown*. Bristol, Ind.: Cloverdale Library, 1992.

Macdonald, Sharon, Pat Holden, and Shirley Ardener, eds. *Images of Women in Peace and War: Cross-Cultural and Historical Perspectives*. London: Macmillan, 1987; Madison: University of Wisconsin Press, 1988.

McDonald, Walter. *After the Noise of Saigon*. Amherst: University of Massachusetts Press, 1988.

———. *Anything Anything*. Seattle: L'Epervier, 1980.

———. *Burning the Fence*. Lubbock: Texas Tech University Press, 1981.

———. *Caliban in Blue and Other Poems*. Lubbock: Texas Tech University Press, 1976.

———. *The Flying Dutchman*. Columbus: Ohio State University Press, 1987.

———. *Night Landings*. New York: Harper, 1989.

———. *One Thing Leads to Another*. New Braunfels, Tex.: Cedar Rock, 1978.

———. *Rafting the Brazos*. Denton: University of North Texas Press, 1988.

———. *Splitting Wood for Winter*. Denton: University of North Texas Press, 1988.

———. *Witching on Hardscrabble*. Peoria, Ill.: Spoon River Poetry, 1985.

———. *Working Against Time*. Walnut Creek, Calif.: Calliope, 1981.

McFarland, Keith D. *The Korean War: An Annotated Bibliography*. New York: Garland, 1986.

McGann, Jerome J. "Contemporary Poetry, Alternate Routes." *Politics and Poetic Value*. Ed. Robert von Hallberg. Chicago: University of Chicago Press, 1987. 253–76.

McHale, Brian. *Postmodernist Fiction*. London: Methuen, 1987.

McMahon, Marilyn. *Works in Progress*. Seattle: Marilyn M. McMahon, 1988.

———. *Works in Progress II*. Seattle: Marilyn M. McMahon, 1990.

MacPherson, Myra. *Long Time Passing: Vietnam and the Haunted Generation*. Garden City, N.Y.: Doubleday, 1984.

Magdaleno, Richard P. *Vietnam Rose*. Meriden, Conn.: Rianta, 1971.

Mangold, Tom, and John Penycate. *The Tunnels of Cu Chi*. New York: Random, 1985.

Marcus, Jane. "Corpus/Corps/Corpse: Writing the Body in/at War." Cooper, Munich, and Squier 124–67.

Marshall, Catherine, C. K. Ogden, and Mary Sargant Florence. *Militarism versus Feminism: Writings on Women and War*. Ed. Margaret Kamester and Jo Vellacott. 1915. London: Virago Press, 1987.

Marshall, Kathryn. *In the Combat Zone: An Oral History of American Women in Vietnam, 1966–1975*. Boston: Little, Brown, 1987.

Martin, Earl E. *A Poet Goes to War*. Bozeman: Big Sky Books, Montana State University, 1970.

Marx, Leo. *The Machine in the Garden: Technology and the Pastoral Ideal in America*. New York: Oxford University Press, 1967.

Mason, Robert. *Chickenhawk*. New York: Viking, 1983. Harmondsworth, Eng.: Penguin, 1984.

Mason, Steve. *The Human Being: A Warrior's Journey Toward Peace and Mutual Healing*. New York: Touchstone-Simon and Schuster, 1990.

———. *Johnny's Song*. New York: Bantam, 1986.

———. *Warrior for Peace*. Intro. Oliver Stone. New York: Touchstone-Simon and Schuster, 1988.

Maurer, Harry, ed. *Strange Ground: Americans in Vietnam, 1945–1975, An Oral History*. New York: Henry Holt, 1989.

May, Rollo. *The Cry for Myth*. New York: Norton, 1991.

Melville, Herman. *Moby-Dick; or, The Whale*. Ed. Harrison Hayford et al. 1851. Evanston, Ill.: Northwestern University Press; Chicago: Newberry Library, 1988.

Merritt, William E. *Where the Rivers Ran Backward*. Athens: University of Georgia Press, 1989.

Mersmann, James F. *Out of the Vietnam Vortex: A Study of Poets and Poetry Against the War*. Lawrence: University Press of Kansas, 1974.

Merton, Thomas. "War and the Crisis of Language." *The Critique of War*. Ed. Robert Ginsberg. Chicago: Henry Regnery, 1969. 99–119.

Miller, Nancy K., ed. *The Poetics of Gender*. New York: Columbia University Press, 1986.

Miller, Stephen P. *An Act of God*. [Rev. ed.] 1982. Eureka, Calif.: Northcoast View Press, 1987.

Murphy, Sharman. "I Thought My War Was Over: Women Poets of the Viet Nam War." *Poetry Flash* 216 (March 1991): 1+.

Musgrave, John. *On Snipers, Laughter and Death: Vietnam Poems*. *Coal City Review* 6 (March 1993).

Myers, Thomas. *Walking Point: American Narratives of Vietnam*. New York: Oxford University Press, 1988.

Nelson, Cary. *Our Last First Poets: Vision and History in Contemporary America*. Urbana: University of Illinois Press, 1981.

Newman, John, with Ann Hilfinger. *Vietnam War Literature: An Annotated Bibliography of Imaginative Works about Americans Fighting in Vietnam*. 2d ed. Metuchen, N.J.: Scarecrow, 1988.

Nixon, Richard. *No More Vietnams*. New York: Arbor House, 1985.

Norman, Elizabeth M. *Women at War: The Story of Fifty Military Nurses Who Served in Vietnam*. Philadelphia: University of Pennsylvania Press, 1990.

O'Brien, Tim. *Going After Cacciato.* New York: Delacorte-Seymour Lawrence, 1978; New York: Laurel-Dell, 1987.

———. *If I Die in a Combat Zone.* New York: Delacorte-Seymour Lawrence, 1973.

Oldham, Perry. *Vinh Long.* Meadows of Dan, Va.: Northwoods, 1976.

Orwell, George. *1984.* 1949. New York: Harcourt Brace Jovanovich, 1984.

———. "Politics and the English Language." 1946. *In Front of Your Nose, 1945–1950.* Vol. 3 of *The Collected Essays, Journalism and Letters of George Orwell.* Ed. Sonia Orwell and Ian Angus. London: Secker and Warburg, 1968. 127–40. 4 vols.

Owen, Wilfred. *The Poems of Wilfred Owen.* Ed. Edmund Blunden. 1931. London: Chatto and Windus, 1963.

Page, Tim. *Page After Page.* London: Sidgwick and Jackson, 1988.

Palmer, Laura, ed. *Shrapnel in the Heart: Letters and Remembrances from the Vietnam Veterans Memorial.* New York: Random, 1987.

Parks, David. *GI Diary.* 1968. Washington, D.C.: Howard University Press, 1984.

Parrish, John A. *12, 20 and 5: A Doctor's Year in Vietnam.* New York: Dutton, 1972; New York: Bantam, 1986.

Pentagon Papers: The Senator Gravel Edition, The. Boston: Beacon Press, 1972.

Perloff, Marjorie. "William Carlos Williams." *Voices and Visions: The Poet in America.* Ed. Helen Vendler. New York: Random, 1987. 157–203.

Peters, Robert. "Vietnam Poems." *Hunting the Snark: A Compendium of New Poetic Terminology.* New York: Paragon House, 1989. 339–42.

Pick, Michael Robert. *Childhood/Namhood/Manhood: The Writings of Michael Robert Pick, A Vietnam Veteran.* San Gabriel, Calif.: Blacksmith Books, 1982.

Pierce, Peter. " 'The Funny Place': Australian Literature and the War in Vietnam." *Australia R&R: Representations and Reinterpretations of Australia's War in Vietnam.* Ed. Jeff Doyle and Jeffrey Grey. *Viet Nam Generation* 3.2 (1991): 98–108.

Platke, Stan. *Antietam to Vietnam.* St. Louis: Theatre in Translation, 1974.

Poetry East. Special issue on political poetry. 9/10 (Winter 1982/Spring 1983).

Pratt, John Clark. *The Laotian Fragments.* New York: Viking, 1974.

———. Preface. Ehrhart, *Unaccustomed Mercy* vii–xvi.

———, ed. *Vietnam Voices: Perspectives on the War Years, 1941–1982.* New York: Penguin, 1984.

Primm, Sandy. Review of *Visions of War, Dreams of Peace,* ed. Lynda Van Devanter and Joan A. Furey. *Viet Nam Generation Newsletter* 3.3 (November 1991): 78.

———. *Short Time.* St. Louis: Cauldron, 1977.

Quintana, Leroy V. *Interrogations.* Chevy Chase, Md.: Viet Nam Generation and Burning Cities Press [1992].

———. *Sangre.* Las Cruces, N.M.: Prima Agua Press, 1981.

Ratner, Rochelle. Review of *Copacetic,* by Yusef Komunyakaa. *Library Journal* 109.4 (June 15, 1985): 494.

Rawlings, Doug. *Survivor's Manual. Samisdat* 30.4, 120th release (1982).

"The Red Pen: Poetry, Politics and Publishing." *Poetry East* 9/10 (Winter 1982/Spring 1983): 47–74.

Reilly, Catherine W., ed. *Chaos of the Night: Women's Poetry and Verse of the Second World War*. London: Virago, 1984.

———, ed. *Scars Upon My Heart: Women's Poetry and Verse of the First World War*. London: Virago, 1981.

Richman, Elliot. *Blastin' Out of Abilene*. Fort Wayne, Ind.: Windless Orchard, 1988.

———. *A Bucket of Nails: Poems from the Second Indochina War*. Samisdat 55.4, 220th release (1990).

———. *Fucking in Stupid Hope: Love Poems for the Death of the 80s*. Niagara Falls, N.Y.: Slipstream, 1989.

Rosenberg, Isaac. *The Collected Poems of Isaac Rosenberg*. Ed. Gordon Bottomley and Denys Harding. Intro. Siegfried Sassoon. London: Chatto and Windus, 1962.

Rottmann, Larry. "A Porter on the Trail." *Christian Science Monitor,* November 9, 1990: 16.

Rottmann, Larry, Jan Barry, and Basil T. Paquet, eds. *Winning Hearts and Minds: War Poems by Vietnam Veterans*. Brooklyn: 1st Casualty Press; New York: McGraw-Hill, 1972.

Rubin, William S. *Dada, Surrealism, and Their Heritage*. New York: Museum of Modern Art [1968].

Santoli, Al, ed. *Everything We Had: An Oral History of the Vietnam War by Thirty-Three American Soldiers Who Fought It*. New York: Random, 1981.

———. *To Bear Any Burden: The Vietnam War and Its Aftermath in the Words of Americans and Southeast Asians*. New York: Dutton, 1985.

Sassoon, Siegfried. *The War Poems of Siegfried Sassoon*. Ed. Rupert Hart-Davis. London: Faber and Faber, 1983.

Scannell, Vernon. *Not Without Glory: Poets of the Second World War*. London: Woburn, 1976.

Schlosser, Robert. *The Humidity Readings*. Samisdat 29.1, 113th release (1981).

Schulze, Richard C. *Leatherneck Square: A Professional Marine's Personal Perspective of the Vietnam War*. [Incline Village, Nev.]: Huckleberry Press, 1989.

Schweik, Susan. *A Gulf So Deeply Cut: American Women Poets and the Second World War*. Madison: University of Wisconsin Press, 1991.

———. "A Needle with Mama's Voice: Mitsuye Yamada's *Camp Notes* and the American Canon of War Poetry." Cooper, Munich, and Squier 225–43.

Scott, Joanna C., ed. *Indochina's Refugees: Oral Histories from Laos, Cambodia and Vietnam*. Jefferson, N.C.: McFarland, 1989.

Scruggs, Jan C., and Joel L. Swerdlow. *To Heal a Nation: The Vietnam Veterans Memorial*. New York: Harper and Row, 1985.

Scully, James. *Line Break: Poetry as Social Practice*. Seattle: Bay Press, 1988.

Searle, William J., ed. *Search and Clear: Critical Responses to Selected Literature and Films of the Vietnam War*. Bowling Green, Ohio: Popular Press, 1988.

Selden, Raman. *A Reader's Guide to Contemporary Literary Theory.* 2d ed. Lexington: University Press of Kentucky, 1989.

Shakespeare, William. *The Tempest. The Complete Works.* New York: Viking, 1969. 1369–95.

Shaplen, Robert. *Bitter Victory.* New York: Harper and Row, 1986.

Shatan, Chaim F. "Happiness Is a Warm Gun: Militarized Mourning and Ceremonial Vengeance." Lawson, *Gender and the War* 127–51.

Shea, Dick. *vietnam simply.* Coronado, Calif.: Pro Tem, 1967.

Shepard, Elaine. *The Doom Pussy.* New York: Trident; New York: Pocket, 1967.

Shields, Bill. *Drinking Gasoline in Hell.* Wichita, Kans.: Mumbles Publications, 1989.

———. "how the hell can." *New York Quarterly* 46 (1991): 73.

———. *Human Shrapnel.* Los Angeles: 2.13.61, 1992.

———. "jingoism." *Viet Nam Generation Newsletter* 3.3 (November 1991): 66.

———. "miles of bones." *Viet Nam Generation Newsletter* 3.3 (November 1991): 65–66.

———. *Nam Poems.* N.p.: Mad Dog, 1987.

———. *The Nam Poems.* Bantry [Eng.]: Publishers Group South West, 1987.

———. *Nam: Selected Poems.* Long Beach, Calif.: P.O. Press, 1989.

———. *Post Vietnam Stress Syndrome. Samisdat* 52.4, 205th release, 1988.

———. *Post Vietnam Stress Syndrome II. Art Mag* 9 (1988).

———. *Post Vietnam Stress Syndrome [III]. Second Coming* 17.3 (1989).

———. *Sparks of Hell.* Vandergrift, Pa.: Zelot Press, 1987.

———. *We Killed Like Champions.* Vandergrift, Pa.: Zelot Press, [1986].

———. *Where I Live.* [Minneapolis]: Zelot Press, 1986.

———. *Winners and Other Losers.* Emsworth, Pa.: Burnt Orphan Press, [1989].

Shiplett, Paul D. *Dog Ears.* Chicago: Broken Whisper Studio, 1979.

Showalter, Elaine. "Feminist Criticism in the Wilderness." Showalter, *New Feminist Criticism* 243–70.

———, ed. *The New Feminist Criticism: Essays on Women, Literature, and Theory.* New York: Pantheon, 1985.

———. "Piecing and Writing." Miller 222–47.

Silkin, Jon. *Out of Battle: The Poetry of the Great War.* London: Oxford University Press, 1972.

———, ed. *The Penguin Book of First World War Poetry.* 2d ed. Harmondsworth, Eng.: Penguin, 1981.

Slolock, Caroline. "Winning Hearts and Minds: The 1st Casualty Press." *Journal of American Studies* 16.1 (April 16, 1982): 107–17.

Slotkin, Richard. "Dreams and Genocide: The American Myth of Regeneration Through Violence." *Journal of Popular Culture* 5 (Summer 1971): 38–59.

———. *The Fatal Environment: The Myth of the Frontier in the Age of Industrialization, 1800–1890.* New York: Atheneum, 1985.

————. *Regeneration Through Violence: The Mythology of the American Frontier,*
1600–1860. Middletown, Conn.: Wesleyan University Press, 1973.

Smith, Henry Nash. *Virgin Land: The American West as Symbol and Myth.* 1950.
Cambridge, Mass.: Harvard University Press, 1970.

Smith, Lorrie. "Back Against the Wall: Anti-Feminist Backlash in Vietnam War Literature." Lawson, *Gender and the War* 115–27.

————. "Disarming the War Story." Gilman and Smith 87–99.

————. "Resistance and Revision in Poetry by Vietnam War Veterans." Jason 49–66.

————. "A Sense-Making Perspective in Recent Poetry by Vietnam Veterans." *American Poetry Review* 15.6 (November/December 1986): 13–18.

Smith, Ralph. *Viet-Nam and the West.* New York: Cornell University Press, 1971.

Sossaman, Stephen. *A Veteran Attends a July Fourth Barbecue.* Huntington, Mass.:
New Traditions, 1982.

Spencer, Duncan. *Facing the Wall: Americans at the Vietnam Veterans Memorial.* New
York: Macmillan, 1986.

Spencer, Ernest. *Welcome to Vietnam, Macho Man: Reflections of a Khe Sanh Vet.* N.p.:
Corps Press, 1987; New York: Bantam, 1989.

Spender, Stephen. "Poetry of the Unspeakable." Review of *Winning Hearts and Minds,*
ed. Larry Rottmann, Jan Barry, and Basil T. Paquet, and *Obscenities,* by Michael
Casey. *New York Review of Books* 20.1 (February 8, 1973): 3.

Stallworthy, Jon, ed. *The Oxford Book of War Poetry.* New York: Oxford University
Press, 1984.

Stamm, Geoffrey. *Atrocities: Vietnam Poetry. Hiram Poetry Review,* Supplement No. 10
(1989).

Starhawk. *The Spiral Dance: A Rebirth of the Ancient Religion of the Great Goddess.*
San Francisco: Harper and Row, 1979. Reprinted with a new introduction and commentary. San Francisco: Harper and Row, 1989.

Stephens, Michael. "Combat Zones." Review of *The Monkey Wars,* by Bruce Weigl.
Nation 242.5 (February 8, 1986): 149–50.

————. *The Dramaturgy of Style: Voice in Short Fiction.* Crosscurrents/Modern Cri-
tiques, Third Series. Carbondale: Southern Illinois University Press, 1986.

Steptoe, Lamont B. *Crimson River.* Philadelphia: Slash and Burn, 1984.

————. *Crimson River.* Rev. ed. Camden, N.J.: Whirlwind Press, 1989.

————. *Mad Minute.* Camden, N.J.: Whirlwind Press, 1990.

Stewart, Margaret E. *Ambiguous Violence: Myths of Regeneration and Proficiency in
U. S. Novels of the Vietnam War.* Wisconsin Papers on Southeast Asia 10. Madison:
Center for Southeast Asian Studies, University of Wisconsin, 1986.

————. "Death and Growth: Vietnam-War Novels, Cultural Attitudes, and Literary
Traditions." Ph.D. diss. University of Wisconsin at Madison, 1981.

Stone, Oliver. Introduction. Mason, *Warrior for Peace* 9–13.

Tal, Kalí. "Speaking the Language of Pain: Vietnam War Literature in the Context of a
Literature of Trauma." Jason 217–50.

Taylor, Clyde, ed. *Vietnam and Black America: An Anthology of Protest and Resistance.* Garden City, N.Y.: Anchor-Doubleday, 1973.

Terry, Wallace, ed. *Bloods: An Oral History of the Vietnam War by Black Veterans.* New York: Random, 1984.

Terry, Wallace, and Janice Terry. "The War and Race." Horne 167–82.

Thomas, Evan. "The Reluctant Warrior." Review of *The Commanders,* by Bob Woodward. *Newsweek,* May 13, 1991: 18–22.

Topham, J., ed. *Vietnam Heroes: A Tribute.* Claymont, Del.: American Poetry Press, 1982.

———, ed. *Vietnam Heroes II: The Tears of a Generation.* Philadelphia: American Poetry Press, 1983.

———, ed. *Vietnam Heroes III: That We Have Peace.* Philadelphia: American Poetry Press, 1985.

———, ed. *Vietnam Heroes IV: The Long Ascending Cry: Memories and Recollections in Story and Poem.* Philadelphia: American Poetry and Literature Press, 1985.

———, ed. *Vietnam Literature Anthology: A Balanced Perspective.* Philadelphia: American Poetry and Literature Press, 1984.

Trail, B. D. *Flesh Wounds. Samisdat* 54.4, 216th release, [1989].

Tran Van Don. *Our Endless War: Inside Vietnam.* San Rafael, Calif.: Presidio Press, 1978.

Trotti, John. *Phantom Over Vietnam: Fighter Pilot, USMC.* Novato, Calif.: Presidio Press, 1984.

Trujillo, Charley, ed. *Soldados: Chicanos in Viet Nam.* San Jose, Calif.: Chusma House, 1990.

Truong Nhu Tang. *A Vietcong Memoir.* New York: Harcourt, 1985. Also published as *Journal of a Vietcong.* London: Cape, 1985.

Tylee, Claire M. *The Great War and Women's Consciousness: Images of Militarism and Womanhood in Women's Writings, 1914–1964.* Iowa City: University of Iowa Press, 1990.

Van Devanter, Lynda, and Christopher Norman. *Home Before Morning: The Story of an Army Nurse in Vietnam.* New York: Beaufort, 1983.

Van Devanter, Lynda, and Joan A. Furey, eds. *Visions of War, Dreams of Peace: Writings of Women in the Vietnam War.* New York: Warner, 1991.

Vance, Samuel. *The Courageous and the Proud.* New York: Norton, 1970.

Vietnam Veterans Against the War. *The Winter Soldier Investigation: An Inquiry into American War Crimes.* Boston: Beacon, 1972.

"Vietnam Veterans Memorial: America Remembers." *National Geographic* 167 (May 1985): 552–73.

Villani, Jim, et al., eds. *Viet Nam Flashbacks: Pig Iron, No. 12.* Youngstown, Ohio: Pig Iron Press, 1984.

Walker, Keith. *A Piece of My Heart: The Stories of 26 American Women Who Served in Vietnam.* Novato, Calif.: Presidio Press, 1985.

Walsh, Jeffrey. *American War Literature: 1914 to Vietnam*. New York: St. Martin's Press, 1982.

Weigl, Bruce. *Executioner*. Tucson, Ariz.: Ironwood Press, 1976.

———. *The Monkey Wars*. Athens: University of Georgia Press, 1985.

———. *A Romance*. Pittsburgh: University of Pittsburgh Press, 1979.

———. *A Sack Full of Old Quarrels*. Cleveland: Cleveland State University Poetry Center, 1976.

———. *Song of Napalm*. New York: Atlantic Monthly Press, 1988.

Westmoreland, William C. *A Soldier Reports*. Garden City, N.Y.: Doubleday, 1976.

Wilbur, Richard. *New and Collected Poems*. San Diego: Harcourt Brace Jovanovich, 1988.

Wilcox, Fred A. *Waiting for an Army to Die: The Tragedy of Agent Orange*. New York: Vintage, 1983.

Willenson, Kim, with the correspondents of *Newsweek*. *The Bad War: An Oral History of the Vietnam War*. New York: New American Library, 1987.

Williams, Oscar, ed. *The War Poets: An Anthology of the War Poetry of the Twentieth Century*. New York: John Day, 1945.

Williams, William Appleman, et al., eds. *America in Vietnam: A Documentary History*. Garden City, N.Y.: Anchor-Doubleday, 1985.

Willson, David A. "Mad Minute." Review of *Mad Minute*, by Lamont B. Steptoe. *Chiron Review* 10.1 (Spring 1991): 15.

Wilson, James. *Vietnam in Prose and Film*. Jefferson, N.C.: McFarland, 1982.

Winthrop, John. "A Modell of Christian Charity." 1630. *The Winthrop Papers, 1498–1649*. [Boston]: Massachusetts Historical Society, 1929–47. 5 vols. Excerpt reprinted in Paul Lauter et al., eds. *The Heath Anthology of American Literature*. Vol. 1. Lexington, Mass.: Heath, 1990. 191–99.

Wittman, Sandra M. *Writing About Vietnam: A Bibliography of the Literature of the Vietnam Conflict*. Boston: G. K. Hall, 1989.

Woodward, Bob. *The Commanders*. New York: Simon and Schuster, 1991.

Yamada, Mitsuye. *Camp Notes and Other Poems*. 1976. Berkeley, Calif.: Shameless Hussy Press, 1986.

Ybarra, Lea. "Perceptions of Race and Class Among Chicano Vietnam Veterans." King 69–93.

Young, Perry Deane. *Two of the Missing: A Reminiscence of Some Friends in the War*. New York: Coward, McCann and Geoghegan, 1975.

INDEX

Adams, Lily Lee, 155; "Being a Vet Is Like Losing a Baby," 231–32, 234
Adcock, A. St. John, 10
Aesthetic poetry, xiii, 4, 25, 27–28, 29, 46, 52, 58, 80, 90, 111, 112, 169, 175, 182, 189, 217, 218, 219, 260, 264, 275, 279, 284, 297, 302, 317, 320
African Americans, 152, 153, 154, 160, 163–67, 210, 214–15, 258–60, 313–14, 323–24 (n. 3), 332 (nn. 8, 9)
Agent Orange, 71–73, 216, 243–44
Allen, Bert: "[at the airport]," 197
Alurista, 154
American Adam, xii, 195–245
American Eve, 236, 245
Anderson, Charles, 133–34, 140–41, 147, 148, 164, 196, 205
Andrews, Bruce, 119
Antipoetic poetry, xiii, 4, 25, 26–27, 29, 46, 80, 90, 106, 111, 169, 175, 189, 217, 219, 260, 263, 280, 284, 297, 317, 319
Antiwar movement, 249–54; activism by Vietnam veterans, 251–53, 273; poetry and, 12, 22, 45, 181, 249, 334 (n. 1)
Armstrong, Neil, 241
Arnold, Matthew, 9
Asian Americans, 154–56, 324 (n. 3)

Baker, Mark, 31, 33, 35, 67, 77, 99, 134, 141, 142, 148, 149, 150, 193, 196, 205, 249, 330 (nn. 2, 13)
Balaban, John, 265, 275; "After Our War," 319–20
Baritz, Loren, 33, 75, 76–77, 136, 143, 196, 326 (n. 1), 327 (n. 5), 330 (n. 1)
Barry, Jan, 29, 42, 190–91, 192, 254, 257, 261–64, 280, 288; "Christmas in Hanoi," 75–76; "Floating Petals," 262–63; "Green Hell, Green Death," 35–36; "Harvest Moon," 263; "In the Footsteps of Genghis Khan," 261–62; "A Nun in Ninh Hoa," 37; *Veterans Day*, 262, 263, 264; "Veterans Day," 264; "Viet Nam," 263; *War Baby*, 37, 263, 264. See also *Demilitarized Zones; Peace Is Our Profession; Winning Hearts and Minds*
Barth, R. L., 27, 28, 175–82; "Dead Heroes," 179; "Fieldcraft," 180–81; *Forced-Marching to the Styx*, 74; "From the Forest of Suicides," 139–40; "The Last Patrol," 71; "Lessons of Indochine," 179; "Letter from the Bush," 36–37; "Letter to My Infant Son," 179–80; "Letter to the Dead," 176–77; *Looking for Peace*, 74; "March 1954," 177–78; "Nightpiece," 74; "Office of the Dead," 180; "Reading the *Iliad*," 175–76; *Soldier's Time*, 37, 71, 74, 140, 175–82; "Two for Any Memorial Day," 181
Barthes, Roland, xi, 7, 8
Baum, L. Frank: *Wizard of Oz*, 299
Behrendt, Stephen, 8
Beidler, Philip, 4, 5, 52, 58, 118–19, 250, 265, 281, 287, 290, 316, 330 (n. 16)
Bergonzi, Bernard, 7
Bernstein, Charles, 119
Berry, D. C., 28, 52–58; "[An airplane jets]," 56–57; "[The dark mountains rise]," 54–55; "[Lightning reaching out with electric]," 77–78; "[A poem ought to be a salt lick]," 58; *saigon cemetery*, 52–58, 302; "[The sun goes]," 52–53; "[The way popcorn pops is]," 100–101
Blunden, Edmund, 9, 10, 27, 175, 268
Bly, Robert, 9, 249, 250
Borden, Robert: "Meat Dreams," 133, 136–38
Borton, Lady: "A Boom, A Billow," 318–19
Bowman, Peter: *Beach Red*, 22–25, 45–46, 52, 103, 171
Bowra, Maurice, 3
Brecht, Bertolt, 27

Brende, Joel Osler, 198, 206–7

Brittain, Vera: "To Them," 11–12; "We Shall Come No More," 11–12

Brobowsky, Igor [pseud. Serigo]: "Free Fire Zone," 145–46

Brown, D. F., 28, 101, 102, 118–29, 213; "Bluto Addresses the Real," 119–21; "First Person—1981," 123–24; "Illumination," 121–22; "Little Fire in Burgerland," 128; "Napalm Elegy," 128; "Other Half of Everything," 126–28; *Returning Fire*, 119–26; "Still Later There Are Memories," 125–26; "When I Am 19 I Was a Medic," 122–23

Brown, Steven Ford: "After the Vietnam War," 50

Brown, William R., 19–20

Browne, Malcolm W., 68

Brownstein, Stanley: "Sounds of War," 62

Broyles, William, 274

Brunner, Mary Lu Ostergren: "Cheated," 230, 334 (n. 3)

Buckley, Lynda Van Devanter. *See* Van Devanter, Lynda

Burgess, Anthony: *Clockwork Orange*, 291

Burke, Edmund, 311

Bush, George, xiii, 6, 8, 217, 232

Campbell, Joseph, xii, 247, 248

Caputo, Philip, 4, 33–34, 35, 36, 37, 59, 94–95, 114, 139, 141–42, 148, 254, 265, 331 (n. 2)

Carrying the Darkness (ed. Ehrhart), 112, 253, 254, 257, 276

Casey, Michael, 27, 101, 107–8, 112, 115, 129, 177, 182, 284, 288, 297; "A Bummer," 105; "Hoa Binh," 39–40; "LZ Gator Body Collector," 102–3, 180; "National Guardsman," 103–4; *Obscenities*, 26, 102–6, 111, 153, 312; "On Death," 106; "Paco," 104

Cathartic poetry, xiii, 4, 25, 28–29, 49–50, 52, 80, 90, 182, 189, 284, 288, 317, 318

Césaire, Aimé, 308

Chandler, Robert, 71

Charles, Ray, 313

Chee, Yoshia, 155–56

Chicanos, 153–54, 160, 324 (n. 3), 332 (n. 6). *See also* Latinos

China Beach, 65

Churchill, Sarah, 17; "The Bombers," 16

Churchill, Winston, 16

Ciardi, John, 19; "Elegy Just in Case," 17; "V-J Day," 18

Cincinnatus, 327–28 (n. 8)

Citizens' Commission of Inquiry on U.S. War Crimes in Vietnam (CCI), 251

City on the hill: as new Babel, xii, 93–94

Cixous, Hélène, 231

Clifford, Clark, 143

Clifton, Merritt, 265

Clockwork Orange (Burgess), 291

Coleman, Horace, 28, 165–69, 276; *Between a Rock & A Hard Place*, 165; "Black Soldier Remembers," 209–10; "Downed Black Pilot Learns How to Fly," 166–67; "I Drive the Valiant," 254–56; "In Ca Mau," 168; "Night Flare Drop, Tan Son Nhut," 167–68; "OK Corral East/Brothers in the Nam," 165–66; "Remembrance of Things Past," 168–69

Coleman, Wanda, 259

Coleridge, Samuel Taylor: "Rime of the Ancient Mariner," 243

Conrad, Joseph, 20

Cooper, Gary, 132

Cooper, James Fenimore: *Last of the Mohicans*, 156–57; *Leatherstocking Tales*, 130, 131,

Costilow, Jim, 157

Craigwell, Joan Arrington: "Dark Angel," 154–55, 230, 334 (n. 3)

Crawford, Fred D., 11, 28

Cronin, Cornelius, 246, 249

Cross, Frank A., Jr., 101; "B-52s Over Home," 76–77, 86; "Gliding Baskets," 97–98; "Rice Will Grow Again," 200–201, 203

cummings, e. e., 10; "[in Just-/spring]," 53; "['next to of course god america i]," 14–15, 181

Currey, Richard, 49–52, 58; *Crossing Over*, 50–52

Dater, Tony, 330 (n. 14); "Thunderbirds," 79–80

Demilitarized Zones (eds. Barry and Ehrhart), 50, 76, 132, 197, 198, 199, 201, 202, 204, 207, 208, 209, 210, 253, 254, 263

Denham, Robert, 8

Derrida, Jacques, 8
Dickinson, Emily, 14, 17, 22, 237–38, 276
Dickson, Paul, 62, 326 (n. 2), 326–27 (n. 3)
Diem, Ngo Dinh. *See* Ngô Dinh Diêm
Dioxin. *See* Agent Orange
Di Prima, Diane, 249
Documentary impulse, 3, 4; and docupoetry, 25, 104. *See also* Memoir
Doleman, Edgar C., 63, 327 (n. 5)
Douglas, Keith, 17, 18, 102; "Desert Flowers," 14, 15; "Landscape with Figures 1," 15–16
Drug use, 105, 203–5
Ducasse, Isidore (comte de Lautréamont), 308
Dusty: "Hello David," 233

Eberhart, Richard: "Aesthetic after War," 19–20
Ehrhart, W. D., 29, 57, 103, 112, 165, 169–70, 182, 228, 254, 257, 261, 264–80, 283, 285, 288, 316, 330 (n. 14); "Children of Hanoi," 277, 278; "Christ," 268; "Coming Home," 197; "Confirmation," 272–73, 275; "Ducks on Wissahickon Creek," 277; "Facts of Life," 278; "For Anne, Approaching Thirty-Five," 277; "For Mrs. Na," 274–75; *Generation of Peace*, 264; "Guerrilla War," 141; "Hawk and Two Suns," 78–79, 87; "Heart of the Poem," 279; "How I Live," 277; "Hunting," 149; "Imagine," 205–6, 268; "In the Valley of the Shadow," 275–76, 278; "Invasion of Grenada," 211–12; *Just for Laughs*, 264, 274–79; "Last Flight Out From the War Zone," 275; "Letter," 270–72; "Love in an Evil Time," 277; "Making the Children Behave," 269–70; "Next Step," 267–68; "Next World War," 277; "One Night on Guard Duty," 62; "Parade," 278; "Poet as Athlete," 279; "Relative Thing," 269; "Scientific Treatise for My Wife," 276, 278; "Second Thoughts," 277; "Small Romance," 276, 278; "Small Song for Daddy," 276; "Sniper's Mark," 266–67; "Souvenirs," 266, 267; "Starting Over," 277; "Time on Target," 149–50; "To the Asian Victors," 270; *To Those Who Have Gone Home Tired*, 78, 141, 149, 150, 197, 266–73; "To Those Who Have Gone Home Tired," 273; "Unaccustomed Mercies,"

276; "Viet Nam—February 1967," 265–66; "The Way Light Bends," 277–78; "What Keeps Me Going," 277, 278; "What We're Buying," 277; "Who Did What to Whom," 278; "Winter Bells," 278. See also *Carrying the Darkness; Demilitarized Zones; Unaccustomed Mercy*
Eliade, Mircea, 7
Eliot, T. S.: "Love Song of J. Alfred Prufrock," 186; *Waste Land*, 13–14, 303
Ellis, R. Joseph: "Memory Bomb," 202–3

Falck, Colin, 9
Felstiner, John, xii, 97, 103, 115, 142, 188, 202, 207, 250–51, 291
Feminism, 34, 195–96, 227, 228–45 passim, 330 (n. 2), 331 (n. 1)
Fiedler, Leslie, 156–57
1st Casualty Press, 190
FitzGerald, Frances, 38–39, 203, 330 (n. 15)
FitzRoy, Olivia: "Toast," 16–17
Flamm, Matthew, 305
Floyd, Bryan Alec: *Long War Dead*, 317; "Private First Class Brooks Morgenstein, U.S.M.C.," 317–18
Fonda, Jane, 251
Forché, Carolyn, 189, 190, 191
Forster, E. M., 312
"Fort Jackson 8," 252, 253
Frost, Robert, 18, 86
Frye, Northrop, xi, 8
Fryer, Judith, 195
Furey, Joan A., 215, 229, 234, 239, 254. See also *Visions of War, Dreams of Peace*
Fussell, Paul, 13, 14, 65, 246–47, 249, 255, 268

Gardner, Brian, 9
Garrett, George, 302
Geffert, Paul, 251–52
Gender, 34–35; and poetry, 20, 228–39, 325 (n. 6), 325–26 (n. 7); and warfare, 77, 81, 82, 105, 298, 327 (n. 6), 329–30 (n. 13), 333–34 (n. 2). *See also* Feminism
Gettler, Andrew, 224, 227, 228
Giap, Vo Nguyen. See Vo Nguyen Giap
Gibson, James W., 71, 75, 90, 142, 144, 146, 215, 326 (n. 1), 328 (n. 8), 328 (n. 9), 329 (n. 12), 332 (n. 5)
GIs United Against the War, 252–53

Glade, Jon Forrest, 27; "Blood Trail," 140; "Business as Usual," 144; "City Kid," 38; "Weight of the Sheets," 201–2, 203
Glasser, Ronald J., 328 (n. 10)
Goff, Stanley, 75, 152, 162, 164
Gotera, Vicente F., 311
Grant, Sharon: "Best Act in Pleiku, No One Under 18 Admitted," 230, 334 (n. 3); "Dreams That Blister Sleep," 237
Grauwin, Paul, 177, 178
Graves, Robert, 10
Great War. *See* World War I
Greville, Fulke, 74
Griffiths, Norma J., 236; "Keep Mum," 281–82; "The Statue," 28–29; "Under the Covers," 230, 334 (n. 3)
Guillory, Daniel L., 291, 292
Gulf war, xiii, 6, 8, 92, 217, 232, 316

Håkansson, Björn, 302, 310
Halberstam, David, 90, 91
Hall, David: "Ambush of the Fourth Platoon," 134–35
Halstead, Fred, 253
Hanley, Lynne, 12
Hanoi Hannah. *See* Ngo Thi Trinh
Hanoi Helen, 161
Hardy, Thomas, 22
Hathaway, Dev, 190
Hellmann, John, 5, 59, 139, 156, 158
Helmer, John, 34
Herr, Michael, 4, 28, 48, 54, 66, 68–69, 70, 73–74, 77, 95, 132, 135–36, 150, 192, 257
Herzog, Tobey, 192
Hispanic Americans. *See* Latinos
Hitchcock, Alfred, 48
Hitler, Adolf, 96
Ho Chi Minh, 82, 225–26, 271, 329 (n. 12)
Ho Chi Minh trail, 75, 150, 327 (n. 3), 329 (n. 12)
Holdstein, Deborah, 25, 104
Hollis, Jocelyn: "Defoliation—Agent Orange," 73
Holm, Tom, 154
Homer, 3, 176; *Iliad*, 46, 175
Honda, Katsuichi, 141, 331 (n. 4)
Hope, Bob, 302, 308
Horne, A. D., 77, 152
Huddle, David, 28, 101, 102, 129, 177; "Cousin," 111–12; "Nerves," 107; "New

York Laundry," 109; *Stopping by Home*, 107–12; "Them," 157–58; "Vermont," 109–10; "Words," 110–11; "Work," 108–9
Hughes, Langston, 259
Hussein, Saddam, 6–7, 129

Indians. *See* Native Americans
Irigaray, Luce, 231
"I Wanna Go to Vietnam," 64

Jameson, Fredric, 282, 320
Jargon stream, 94, 95, 100, 117, 129, 291
Jarrell, Randall, 102; "Death of the Ball Turret Gunner," 21–22, 117
Jason, Philip K., 5
Jeffords, Susan, 228, 230, 235, 245, 247, 331 (n. 1)
Johnson, Lyndon B., 6, 8, 34–35, 59, 75, 82, 131, 329 (n. 12)
Johnston, John H., 10, 11
Jones, Ann Rosalind, 231
Jones, David, 10
Jones, John Paul, 195

Karlin, Wayne, 98
Karnow, Stanley, 265
Kearns, Doris, 35
Keats, John, 26, 28
Kelly, Thomas, 129
Kennedy, John F., 59, 283, 316
Kennedy, X. J., 175
Kerry, John, 251–52, 281
Khan, Nosheen, 11
Khiev, Virak, 325 (n. 4)
Kiang, Peter Nien-Chu, 155
Kiley, Fred, 79, 80, 330 (n. 14)
Kilmer, Joyce, 10
King, Martin Luther, Jr., 161, 313
King, Rodney, 260
Kinnell, Galway: "Vapor Trail Reflected in the Frog Pond," 249–50, 251, 334 (n. 2)
Kirk, Donald, 163, 164, 332 (n. 9)
Knight, Etheridge, 259
Koestenbaum, Wayne, 316
Kolko, Gabriel, 69
Kolodny, Annette, 34, 196, 236
Komunyakaa, Yusef, xiii, 29, 282, 302–16; "Camouflaging the Chimera," 309–10; "Combat Pay for Jody," 314; *Copacetic*, 303, 305; Death Threat Note," 304–5;

Dedications and Other Darkhorses, 303;
Dien Cai Dau, 302, 303, 305–7, 308–16;
"Facing It," 307, 314–15; "Greenness
Taller Than Gods," 307; "Hanoi Hannah,"
313; "Ia Drang Valley," 306–7; *I Apologize
for the Eyes in My Head*, 303, 305; "Le
Xuan, Beautiful Spring," 307; "Like
Something from Fellini," 306; "Losses,"
305–6; *Lost in the Bonewheel Factory*, 304;
"1984," 303; "Nude Pictures," 306,
311–12; *Toys in a Field*, 307; "2527th
Birthday of the Buddha," 308–9, 312;
"Villon/Leadbelly," 303; "Water Buffalo,"
307; " 'You and I Are Disappearing,' " 307,
310–11
Korean war, 139, 323 (n. 2)
Kovic, Ron, 4, 59, 70, 130–31, 174, 252
Kristeva, Julia, 231
Kunen, James Simon, 145, 146, 148, 149, 251
Kunitz, Stanley, 26, 102, 103, 104, 105, 111,
177, 182

Lane, Mark, 158, 159, 251
Language, 93–129; myth and, 93–94;
tautology and distortion in, xii, 94–97, 129,
248, 285, 320; war and, 65, 146–47. *See
also* Jargon stream
Language Poetry, xiv, 102, 118–19, 122, 126
Larsen, Wendy Wilder: *Shallow Graves*, 235
Last of the Mohicans (Cooper), 156–57
Latinos, 152–54; Chicanos, 153–54, 160, 324
(n. 3), 332 (n. 6); Puerto Ricans, 153
Lawrence, D. H., 60, 62, 90
Layne, McAvoy, 27, 165, 169–75; *How Audie
Murphy Died in Vietnam*, 169–75
Leatherstocking Tales (Cooper), 130, 131
Lewis, R. W. B., 195, 196, 227, 245
Lifton, Robert Jay, 143, 206, 247, 248
Lin, Maya, 211
Lomperis, Timothy J., 264, 275
Lowenfels, Walter, 249
Lucretius, 27, 175
Lupack, Alan C.: "Army Experience,"
214–15

McAfee, John P.: "War Story," 72–73
McCarthy, Gerald, 29, 165; "Ambuscade,"
186; "Hooded Legion," 212; "I'll Bring
You a Frozen Chocolate Pie," 186–88;
"Marking Time," 256; *Shoetown*, 212;

"Sound of Guns," 188; "War Story,"
182–86; *War Story*, 182–89
McDonald, Walter, 28, 80–90, 330 (n. 15);
"After a Year in Korea," 89; *After the Noise
of Saigon*, 80, 85–88; "After the Noise of
Saigon," 88; "After the Rains of Saigon,"
89; "Bluejays in Summer," 88, 89; *Burning
the Fence*, 80, 83–84, 214; "Caliban in
Blue," 81–82; *Caliban in Blue and Other
Poems*, 80, 81–83, 184; "Children of
Saigon," 89; "Crosswind Landings," 87;
"Ejecting from Jets," 88; "First Solo in
Thunderstorms," 88; "Flying a Perfect
Loop," 88; *Flying Dutchman*, 80, 84–85;
"Food-Pickers of Saigon," 85; "Getting It
Done," 84–85; "How the World Ends,"
86–87; "Interview with a Guy Named
Fawkes, U.S. Army," 184; "Last Still Days
in a Bunker," 89; "Learning to Live with
Nightmares," 89; "New Guy," 86; *Night
Landings*, 80, 88–89; "Night Landings,"
88; "Praying a Stall Won't Spin Us," 84;
"Rocket Attack," 82–83, 85; "Taking
Aim," 83–84; "Veteran," 213–14; "We
Called It Entering Heaven," 87; "Wild
Swans of Da Lat," 88
McGann, Jerome, 122
McHale, Brian, 118
Machine in the Garden, 60
McKuen, Rod, 227
McMahon, Marilyn, 29, 215, 239–45;
"Confession," 242; "Crone," 243; "Dying
with Grace," 242; "In the War Zone," 241;
"In This Land," 240–41, 243; "July 20,
1969," 241–43; "The Kid," 230, 334
(n. 3); "Knowing," 234, 243–45; *Works in
Progress*, 239–41, 244; *Works in
Progress II*, 239; 241–43; "Wounds of
War," 239–40
McNamara, Robert, 6, 327 (n. 5)
MacPherson, Myra, 135, 139, 164, 204–5,
249, 251, 254
McVicker, Sara J.: "Saigon?," 234
Mahoney, Peter P.: "The Airport," 199
Mangold, Tom, 91–92, 181
Mannoni, Otare, 330 (n. 15)
Marcus, Jane, 230, 231
Marshall, Jack, 119
Marshall, Kathryn, 155
Martial, 27, 175

Martin, Earl E., 159; "The trouble with me is I used to believe," 132
Marx, Leo, 60, 62
Mason, Robert, 64, 65, 327 (n. 7)
Mason, Steve, 29, 215, 218–28; "Angry Little Poem of Spring," 222–23; "The Casualty," 72, 223; "Closure: A Much Needed War," 218; *Human Being*, 218, 225–26; *Johnny's Song*, 218–24, 227; "Last Patrol," 219–22; "Perfect Pink Belly," 225; "Sonnet for a Dead Brother," 224–25; "Uncle Ho," 225–26; "Wall Within," 218, 222; *Warrior for Peace*, 218, 224–25, 226, 227
Masters, Edgar Lee: *Spoon River Anthology*, 317
Maurer, Harry, 156
May, Rollo, 9
Media: cinema, 33, 66, 105, 131–32, 156, 158, 161, 173, 184–85, 195, 229–30, 231, 331 (n. 2); television, 33, 65–66, 105, 133, 138, 156, 231, 270, 294, 329 (n. 12)
Meleson, Matthew, 71
Melville, Herman, 110; *Moby-Dick*, 5, 130
Memoir, 109, 179, 246. *See also* Personal narrative
Merton, Thomas, 75, 92, 96–97, 129
Miller, Stephen P., 27; "Caesarian/Army Style," 147; "Catch a Falling Star," 159
Moby-Dick (Melville), 5, 130
Modernism, 13–14, 56
"Montagnard Man," 160–61, 162, 199, 221, 222, 332 (n. 7)
Mowlana, Hamid, 251–52
Murphy, Audie, 131, 132, 173, 195
Murphy, Sharman, 228, 235
Myers, Thomas, 5
Myth: as "lens," xi, 5–8; (de)naturalized, 7–8, 59, 111, 245; monomyth ("hero of a thousand faces"), xii, 247–48; popular culture and, 9, 55, 105, 132, 195
Myth criticism, xiv, 8–9

"Napalm Sticks to Kids," 65
National Veterans' Inquiry, 149, 251
Native Americans, 154, 155, 158, 324 (n. 3)
Navarre, Henri, 179
Nelson, Cary, 320
New soldier, xii, 281
Ngô Dinh Diêm, 37, 60, 91

Ngo Thi Trinh ("Hanoi Hannah"), 308, 313, 334 (n. 3)
Nguyen Thanh Linh, 91–92, 181
Nixon, Richard M., 153, 174, 248, 285
Norris, Chuck, 227

O'Brien, Tim, 4, 50, 131, 265, 302
Oldham, Perry: "Evening Pastimes," 148; "Happy Warrior Returns Home," 207
Olson, Charles, 53
Orwell, George, 96, 146–47
Owen, Wilfred, 3, 26, 27, 28, 102, 111, 112–13, 114, 165, 175, 176, 181, 182, 191, 276; "Anthem for Doomed Youth," 10–11, 113; "At the Cavalry Near the Ancre," 268

Paine, Thomas, 281
Paquet, Basil T., 27–28, 101, 112–18, 129, 190–91, 192, 313; "Basket Case," 114; "Christmas '67," 27, 112–13; "Easter '68," 113–14; "Graves Registration," 116; "Morning—A Death," 115–17, 150; "Night Dust-Off," 69–70; "They Do Not Go Gentle," 117–18, 267. *See also Winning Hearts and Minds*
Parson, Erwin Randolph, 198, 206–7
Peabody, Richard, 189
Peace Is Our Profession (ed. Barry), 65, 76, 165, 215, 253, 254–57
Penycate, John, 91–92, 181
Perloff, Marjorie, 311
Personal narrative, 179, 323–25 (n. 3), 331 (n. 2). *See also* Memoir
Peters, Robert, xii
Pham Van Dong, 329 (n. 12)
Pierce, Peter, 6
Piroth, Charles, 177, 178
Platke, Stan: "And Then There Were None," 191–92; "Fathers Day, 1975," 210
Poetry: dissident poetry, 280, 282, 297, 301; language and, 10, 14, 24, 40, 53, 55, 63, 84, 97–98, 100–101, 103–4, 105, 110–11, 112, 113–14, 117, 118–19, 121–22, 137, 199, 215, 279–80, 286–87, 290–92; outpouring of Vietnam-related poems, xii, 321–23 (n. 1); politics and, 14, 25, 45, 86, 181, 189–91, 249–50, 253–54, 257–61, 263–64, 280–82, 310; prosodic techniques, 11, 17, 27, 47–49, 53, 56–57, 63, 101, 107,

108, 111–12, 128, 170, 176, 178, 181–82,
217, 219–20, 224–25, 276–78; sonnet, 15,
107–13, 224–25; verse novel, 22, 45, 171;
villanelle, 237, 277; war-poetry
anthologies, 321 (n. 1). *See also* Aesthetic
poetry; Antipoetic poetry; Cathartic poetry;
Documentary impulse: and docupoetry;
Gender: and poetry; Language Poetry
Postmodernism, xiv, 118, 129, 282, 320
Poststructuralism, xiv, 120
Posttraumatic stress disorder syndrome
(PTSD), 200, 206–7, 215
Pound, Ezra, 14
Powell, Colin, 6
Pratt, John Clark, xiii, 27, 80, 101, 163, 164,
330 (n. 14); "Words and *Thoughts*,"
99–100, 110; "Words for Don Morris," 79
Primm, Sandy, 218, 229
Puerto Ricans, 153. *See also* Latinos

Quang Duc, 37, 308
Quintana, Leroy V.: "Eight Years after Viet
Nam," 26–27; *Interrogations*, 153–54;
"Jump School—Detail," 153–54; "Twenty
Years after Viet Nam," 27

Race: Amerasian children in Vietnam,
209–10; literature and racism, 156–58; race
relations among Americans in Vietnam,
152–56, 161–63; racism, 131, 141–42, 150,
152, 331 (n. 4). *See also* African
Americans; Asian Americans; Latinos;
Native Americans
Radical vision, xi, 317–20
Ratner, Rochelle, 305
Rawlings, Doug: "Jen," 207–8; "Mainline
Quatrains," 203–4; "Medic," 198; "A
Soldier's Lament," 208–9
Ray, David, 249, 250
Read, Herbert, 10
Reagan, Ronald, 76, 94
Receveur, Don, 27; "Cobra Pilot," 31, 59,
66–67, 74, 327 (n. 7); "Doper's Dream,"
203; "night fear," 49
Regeneration, xii, 6–7, 90, 130–92;
regeneration through violence, 130–32, 138,
140, 141, 143, 150, 151, 157, 192, 247, 273
Reilly, Catherine W., 16, 17
Richman, Elliott: "Ballad of an Old

Vietnamese Woman," 151; "Ballad of a
V.C. Truck Driver," 151; "Jungle Ambush
in Monument Valley," 151–52
Romanticism, 13, 46, 79–80
Romero, Leo, 154
Rosenberg, Isaac, 10, 12, 16, 18; "Break of
Day in the Trenches," 13–14
Rottmann, Larry, 190–91, 192; "Frolicking in
the Autumn Mist," 74; "Porter on the
Trail," 150–51; "Rifle, 5.56MM,
XM16E1," 63; "S. O. P.," 142; "Weather
of Vietnam," 35. See also *Winning Hearts
and Minds*
Rowlandson, Mary, 6

Sanders, Robert, 75, 152, 162, 164
Santoli, Al, 75, 91, 135, 143, 144–45, 163,
164, 261
Sassoon, Siegfried, 10, 13, 14, 22, 27, 111,
175, 181, 191, 268, 282; "Glory of
Women," 11
Scannell, Vernon, 16, 21
Schweik, Susan, 20, 229, 326 (n. 8)
Scruggs, Jan, 211
Scully, James, 190, 191, 280, 297
Seeger, Alan, 10
Selden, Raman, 27
Serigo. *See* Brobowsky, Igor
Shakespeare, William, 113, 178; *Tempest*, 17,
81, 330 (n. 15)
Shange, Ntozake, 259
Shatan, Chaim, 329 (n. 13)
Shea, Dick, 27, 58; *vietnam simply* 40–49,
103, 171
Shea, Joseph M.: "After the Bomb," 256–57
Shields, Bill, 27, 215–18, 245, 297, 317;
"Better Living Thru Chemistry," 216;
"Day," 193; *Drinking Gasoline in Hell*, 73,
216–17; "drinking gasoline in hell," 217;
"8 Years Ago," 216; *Human Shrapnel*, 215;
"Inappropriate," 216; "In Country," 216;
"jingoism," 218; "miles of bones," 213;
"Minutes Become Years," 217; "My
Daughter," 73; "My Easter Poem," 216;
Nam, 73, 193, 215–16, 217; "phoenix,"
216; *Post Vietnam Stress Syndrome*, 215;
"Saving Grace," 217; "there is no metaphor
for the pain," 217; "Tour of Duty," 216;

Shields, Bill (*continued*)
  "When a Man Explodes," 215; "Wife,"
  216; "years," 217
Showalter, Elaine, 231
Shuster, Dana, 28; "Grandfathers Rocking,"
  238–39; "Like Emily Dickinson," 237–38;
  "Mellow on Morphine," 231, 334 (n. 3)
Silkin, Jon, 10, 13
Slolock, Caroline, 142, 190
Slotkin, Richard, 6, 7, 130, 131, 141, 247, 331
  (n. 2)
Smith, Henry Nash, 33
Smith, Lorrie, xii, 97, 120, 124, 125, 126, 127,
  128, 131, 227, 228, 264, 271, 273, 279–80,
  285, 286, 289–90, 294, 295, 296, 297,
  316, 330 (n. 2)
Smith, Michael, 253
Smith, Ralph, 37
Sorrin, Lou McCurdy: "Short 1968–1990,"
  232–33
Soto, Gary, 154
Spender, Stephen, 26, 105–6, 111, 112, 191,
  217–18
Spoon River Anthology (Masters), 317
Stamm, Geoffrey, 27; "Red Sash," 160
Starhawk, 9
Steele, Timothy, 175
Stephens, Michael, 275, 290, 295
Steptoe, Lamont B., 27, 280, 288; "Gulf of
  Tonkin," 259–60; "Mad Minute," 257;
  Mad Minute, 257–61; "On the March,"
  257–58; "Returnee," 258–59
Stevens, Wallace, 9
Stewart, Margaret E., 98, 131, 331 (n. 3)
Stone, Oliver, 224, 226, 227
Strahan, Jack: "God Is My Helicopter," 68
Surrealism, 5, 49–50, 54, 250, 284, 286, 302,
  305, 307, 309, 318, 320

Tal, Kalí, 325 (n. 5)
Technology, 60–92, 326 (n. 2), 326–27 (n. 3),
  327 (nn. 4, 5), 327–28 (n. 8), 328 (nn. 9,
  10), 329 (n. 12); and technowar, xii, 61, 78,
  86, 88, 92, 169, 326 (n. 1). *See also* Agent
  Orange
Terry, Janice, 152
Terry, Wallace, 152, 160, 161, 162, 163, 164,
  165, 199–200, 332 (n. 7), 332 (n. 8), 332
  (n. 9)
Thomas, Dylan, 118

Thomas, Evan, 6
Thompson, Robert, 90
Ton That Tung, 329 (n. 12)
Topham, J., 68, 73, 157
Tran Thi Nga: *Shallow Graves*, 235
Tran Van Don, 91
Trew, Kathleen: "Mamasan," 38
Trotter, Bobbie: "Dear Mom," 230, 334 (n. 3)
Trotti, John, 79, 327 (n. 6)
Troupe, Quincy, 259
Trujillo, Charley, 152–53, 160
Turner, Tina, 313

Unaccustomed Mercy (ed. Ehrhart), 112,
  165–69, 210, 253, 276

Van Devanter, Lynda, 29, 215, 229, 234, 239,
  254, 274; "For Molly," 235–36. See also
  Visions of War, Dreams of Peace
Vann, John Paul, 90, 91
Verrett, Jacqueline, 71
Vietnam Veterans Against the War (VVAW),
  25, 251, 252, 254, 281
Vietnam Veterans Memorial, 160, 210–13,
  222, 264, 314–15
Vietnam Veterans of America, 218
Villani, Jim, 107
Visions of War, Dreams of Peace (ed. Van
  Devanter and Furey), 29, 155, 213, 215,
  228–39, 253, 254, 319
Vo Nguyen Giap, 177

Wall, the. *See* Vietnam Veterans Memorial
Walsh, Jeffrey, xii, 3, 14, 17, 18, 21, 22, 28,
  49, 95, 101–2, 283–84, 291
Warriors against war, xii–xiii, 246–82
Wayne, John, 131, 132, 152, 195, 331 (n. 2)
Weigl, Bruce, xiii, 29, 275, 282, 283–301,
  316; "Amnesia," 289–90, 295; "Anna
  Grasa," 288; "Burning Shit at An Khe,"
  295, 297; "Elegy," 300–301; *Executioner*,
  283, 335 (n. 1); "Executioner on Holiday,"
  284, 285; "Flight," 292; "Fourth of July:
  Toledo, Ohio," 299; "Hand to Hand," 287;
  "Him, on the Bicycle," 285; "Homage to
  Elvis, Homage to the Fathers," 300;
  "Hope," 293; "Killing Chickens," 292–93;
  "The Kiss," 298–99, 300; "LZ Nowhere,"
  297–98; "Man Who Made Me Love Him,"
  287–88; "Monkey," 276, 284, 285–87;

Monkey Wars, 276, 283, 288–97, 298, 335
(n. 1); "Noise," 295; *A Romance*, 283,
284–88, 293, 298, 299, 300, 335 (n. 1); "A
Romance," 287; *Sack Full of Old Quarrels*,
283, 335 (n. 1); "Sailing to Bien Hoa," 284,
298; "The Sharing," 284; "Small Song for
Andrew," 292; "Snowy Egret," 293, 300;
"Song for a Lost First Cousin," 292; "Song
of Identities," 299–300; *Song of Napalm*,
283, 297–301, 316; "Song of Napalm,"
296; "Song of the Lost Private," 292;
"Temple Near Quang Tri, Not on the Map,"
294–95, 296
Westmoreland, William, 61–62, 71, 143, 146,
326 (n. 2)
Whitman, Walt, 14, 22, 151
Wilbur, Richard: "On the Eyes of an SS
Officer," 18–19
Wilcox, Fred A., 71–72
Wild West (or western) myth, 6, 33–59, 67,
71, 131, 138, 151, 157; as extension of
"virgin land" myth, xii, 33–35, 60, 90
Williams, William Carlos, xiii, 311

Willson, David, 260
Winning Hearts and Minds (eds. Rottmann,
Barry, and Paquet), 28, 35, 36, 49, 62, 63,
64, 67, 70, 74, 112, 113, 114, 115, 116, 117,
118, 146, 190, 197, 203, 239, 253, 254,
262, 265
Winter Soldier Investigation, 251
Winthrop, John, 93
Wizard of Oz (Baum), 299
Woodward, Bob, 6
World War I (WWI), 3, 4, 9–15, 65, 139, 176,
230, 231, 246, 268, 282, 292
World War II (WWII), 4, 7, 15–24, 111, 117,
131, 133, 135, 138, 139, 173, 237, 300
Wright, Richard, 215
Wyatt, Janet Krouse: "We Went, We Came,"
213

Yamada, Mitsuye: *Camp Notes* 20–21, 237,
326 (n. 8); "Cincinnati," 20–21;
"Minidoka, Idaho," 237
Yeats, William Butler, 191; "Second
Coming," 303